AF386500

Praise for *Mother of the Lamb*

"Matthew Milliner's *Mother of the Lamb: The Story of a Global Icon* is a book of remarkable scholarship combined with deep humanity. The story of the pervasive influence of a single, poignant icon of Mary and Christ—first painted in the hills of Cyprus in the last days of the Crusades and the sad twilight of Byzantium, then copied throughout the world—opens the mind and the heart to a long-neglected chapter in the history of the Christian imagination. It challenges the reader to give thought to what its serene, sad lines and gracious posture might yet have to say to our own times."

PETER BROWN, professor emeritus, department of history, Princeton University

"Byzantine icons, fruit of Byzantium's distinctive material theology, exert an unexpected claim on our attention now. Matthew Milliner explores the vast, evolving afterlife of one great icon, variously known as the Virgin of the Passion or Our Lady of Perpetual Help. Welding the events of a passionate and violent era to his own passionate response to the icon, Milliner roots the image in the circumstances of its earliest surviving rendition: a fresco of consummate artistry painted on the island of Cyprus in the immediate wake of its Crusader conquest. Wrenched forever from its parent culture of Byzantium, an empire triumphant for centuries under the aegis of a conquering Mary, Cyprus saw the birth of a new image of Mary. Here a half a millennium's ardent Marian veneration, expressed in Byzantium's radiant theology of liturgical worship and holy imagery, was distilled into a new image of Mary for a coming half-millennium of inexorable imperial decline. It is an image of sustained and compassionate sorrow. Milliner unfolds the image's many theological dimensions—Trinitarian, sacramental, ecclesiological, and emotional—and then traces the paths by which it traveled from a small Mediterranean island on the verge of an encroaching Islam to the heart first of Orthodoxy and then of Roman Catholicism, and from there into the hearts of people literally across the entire globe. The book's early chapters vivid with evocations of Byzantium's luminous and beautiful forms of worship give way by the end to earnest inquiries about this image's message for issues of contemporary faith: social justice, political violence, ecumenism, the role of women in a faith system that revolves around a figure like Mary. The book is written with energy and clear theological conviction, and it reveals how simple and yet how deeply complex a creation like the Virgin of the Passion is. Readers must not slight the endnotes. They are dense with interest."

ANNEMARIE WEYL CARR, university distinguished professor
of art history emerita, Southern Methodist University

"Abounding with vivid detail and told with unerring dramatic flair, Matt Milliner's new book traces the evolution of one of Christianity's central motifs—the Virgin and Child—as it evolved across the Eastern Mediterranean from the eleventh to the fifteenth century. We have a front-row seat as Milliner takes us through the many dramatic twists and turns in Byzantine icon theology and practice and its tangled political and ecclesial background. *Mother of the Lamb* is an absorbing and compelling story unfolded by an immensely gifted art-historian and storyteller."

THOMAS PFAU, professor of English and professor of German,
Duke Divinity School

"This captivating book invites readers on a spiritual adventure. Starting from his own first encounter as a young scholar, the author introduces us to a special icon: the Virgin of the Passion. This extraordinary image witnessed both the glory and the downfall of an empire, providing both protection and succor. As her story unfolds, we understand her unparalleled power to humble the proud, to encourage the meek, and to console the defeated."

ROBIN M. JENSEN, Patrick O'Brien Professor of Theology,
University of Notre Dame

"It is rare to find a scholar who is equally at home in history and theology. Matthew Milliner shows how the history of a devotional image in its many cultural contexts opens up new horizons of understanding about the complex relationships that connect politics, faith, and theology. Throughout Christian history, the sorrow of the Mother of God has been an expressive medium for those who find their lives overwhelmed by suffering and violence. I was deeply affected by this book and confirmed in my conviction that no understanding of history is possible without an understanding of the role played by religion in the shaping of the human story."

Tina Beattie, professor emerita of Catholic studies,
University of Roehampton

"*Mother of the Lamb* is an extraordinary book: a scholarly detective story, a historical travelogue, a tracing of an image's persistent crossing of cultural boundaries, a spiritual meditation—and above all, an endlessly stimulating delight."

Alan Jacobs, distinguished professor of humanities,
Baylor University

"In the beautifully produced and sumptuously illustrated *Mother of the Lamb*, Matthew Milliner shows the now global reach of the Virgin of the Passion whose icon, as he concisely puts it, 'contains the compressed theological wisdom of the Byzantine Empire.' For those who seek to understand more deeply the meanings of this Christian icon, here's your indispensable book."

Arthur Versluis, religious studies,
Michigan State University

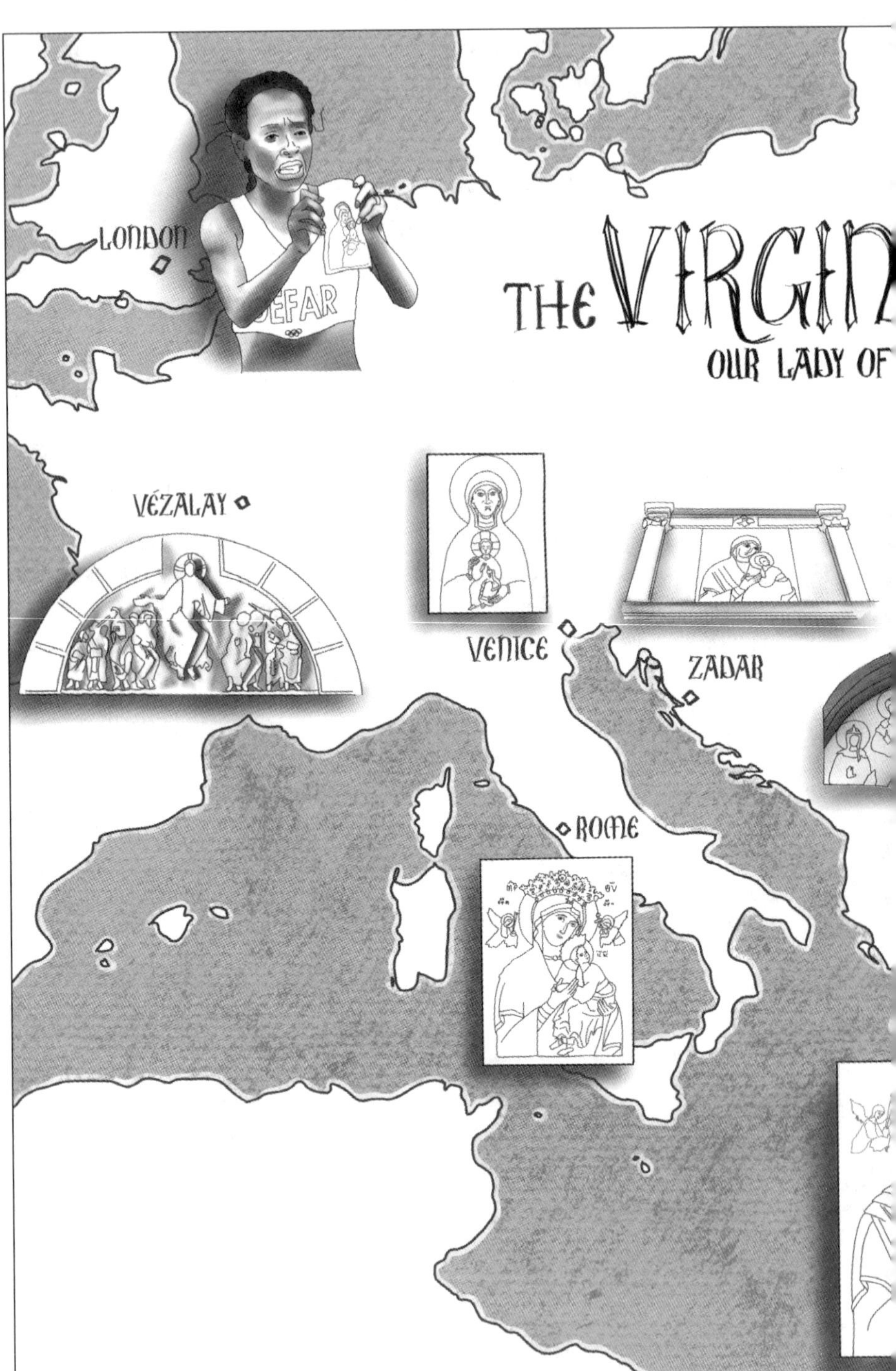

LONDON
DEFAR
THE VIRGIN
OUR LADY OF
VÉZALAY
VENICE
ZADAR
ROME

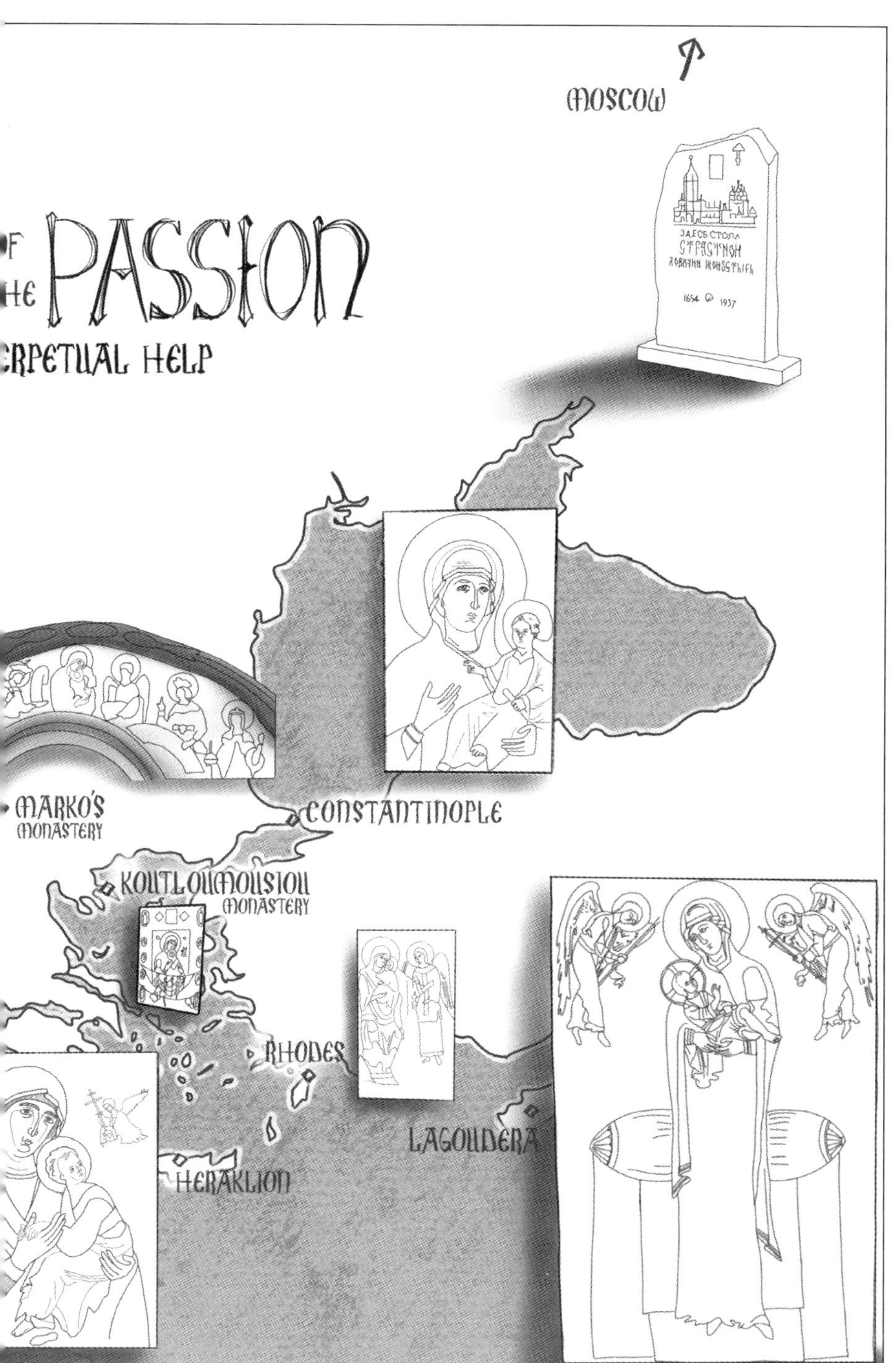
OF
THE PASSION
PERPETUAL HELP
MOSCOW
CONSTANTINOPLE
MARKO'S
MONASTERY
KOUTLOUMOUSIOU
MONASTERY
RHODES
HERAKLION
LAGOUDERA
1654   1937

Mother of the Lamb

Mother of the Lamb

The Story of a Global Icon

Matthew J. Milliner

Fortress Press
Minneapolis

MOTHER OF THE LAMB
The Story of a Global Icon

For Clement, Polly, and Peter

I preferred her to scepters and thrones.

—Wisdom of Solomon 7:8

He entered once for all into the holy places, not by means of the blood of goats and calves but by means of his own blood, thus securing an eternal redemption.

—Hebrews 9:12

For the way to the Love of God is Folly to the World, but is Wisdom to the Children of God. . . . Whosoever obtaineth it, is richer than any Monarch on Earth and [whosoever] getteth it, is nobler than any Emperor can be, and more potent and absolute than all Power and Authority.

—Jacob Boehme, *Dialogues on the Supersensual Life*

There is not a shadow of a doubt for anyone who takes the spiritual life of mankind seriously, even if he is short of authentic spiritual experience, that the Blessed Virgin is not an ideal only, nor a mental image only, nor an archetype of the unconscious (of depth psychology), nor, lastly, an occultist egregore (a collective astral creation of believers), but rather a concrete and living individuality—like you or I—who loves, suffers, and rejoices.

—Valentin Tomberg, *Meditations on the Tarot*

The curtain began to rise not through the efforts of theology, but through the development of sacred symbology . . . theologians had considered symbolism to belong to the domain of archeology, or they were hostile towards it, thinking that it signified a misunderstanding of dogma . . . but the time has come to decipher this sacred message (the Sophia icons and churches) and to reawaken the living tradition which has been interrupted.

—Sergius Bulgakov, *La Sagesse de Dieu*

The promised kingdom of God is manifest not in triumphalist crusades, but in the cruciform witness of the church.

—Fleming Rutledge, *The Crucifixion*

CONTENTS

INTRODUCTION

THE VIRGIN OF THE PASSION

I play not marches for accepted victors only, I play marches
for conquer'd and slain persons.
—Walt Whitman, *Song of Myself*

His Christmas day and his Good Friday, are but the evening
and morning of one and the same day.
—John Donne, *Sermon on Christmas Day* (1626)

Reversion to matriarchy only excludes the masculine;
fixation on patriarchy only cuts out the feminine. . . . We
must acknowledge the threat within us that we attribute to
the opposite sex and struggle to house it and realize that
struggle is also our struggle to relate to God.
—Ann Belford Ulanov, *The Wisdom of the Psyche*

The Mother of God . . . is so closely united to the sacrifice
of her divine Son that she has been called the Virgin Priest
by the Fathers of the Church.
—Pope Pius IX, preface to *Marie et le Sacerdoce* (1875)

IN THE EARLY years of this century, when America was renegotiating both
faith and *power*, an exhibition of that title came to Manhattan's Metropolitan Museum of Art. Still reeling from the September 11, 2001, attacks,
the city was now hosting icons from the Eastern Roman (a.k.a. Byzantine)
Empire, which had lasted approximately from 330 to 1453 CE.[1] The
Byzantines had endured similar calamities on an increasingly frequent
basis as they approached their demise, and the icons glowing in the darkened rooms of the Met were veterans of this civilizational collapse.

Unable to keep pace with the new methods of weaponry that would eventually destroy the empire, late Byzantines instead forged new methods of prayer, the kind of prayer that only arises when a world is coming to an end. This Christian yoga of sorts, including special breathing techniques and postures, was known as "hesychasm," from the Greek word *hesychia*, which simply means "silence."[2] Icons like the ones at the Met that year were the fruit of this late-blossoming tree of prayer. They were therefore nothing like the other art in the museum. They were bricks of golden light dense with the wisdom of another age, antidotes to American triumphalism, tutorials in grief.

I was then a seminary student, and the best theological ideas I was learning about were materialized in this exhibition. The incarnation was an idea in the classroom, but here it had a face. The figures I had become familiar with in church history class were here, literally: one tiny mosaic of the suffering Jesus was ensconced by a surrounding mosaic of his suffering saints. I do not mean the mosaic of Christ was surrounded by *pictures* of those saints; rather, he was surrounded by fragments of their actual bodies, wrapped in silk, neatly labeled and preserved in cubbyholes that created an enclosing chessboard around the Man of Sorrows. But whether the icons in this show contained body parts of saints departed, each icon was freighted with presence nonetheless. Which is to say, the *Faith and Power* exhibition introduced me to a power that my faith lacked. The icons overran my cerebral defenses just as the Ottomans had once overran the civilization from which these icons had emerged. In a world that was grieving a shattered architectural icon, these icons forged a footpath through the ruins that avoided resentment or revenge. I might have fled to the Met's contemporary art collection for a break from what these icons demanded, but it was too late. Shortly after my visit to that Manhattan exhibition, I switched my field of study from theology to Byzantine art.

Soon I felt enough in command of the material to offer a talk on the subject as a graduate student at the Princeton University Art Museum. In the Q and A session afterward, I was asked about a large Cretan icon hovering behind me during my talk, a marvelous example of the type known as the Virgin of the Passion (fig. 0.1). But before I could conjure an answer to the question, an anonymous woman offered one for me instead. "That's Our Lady of Perpetual Help," she blurted out, and then—embarrassed by her interruption—she scurried away. This, it turns out, is the icon's second name, though I had heard neither of its names before.

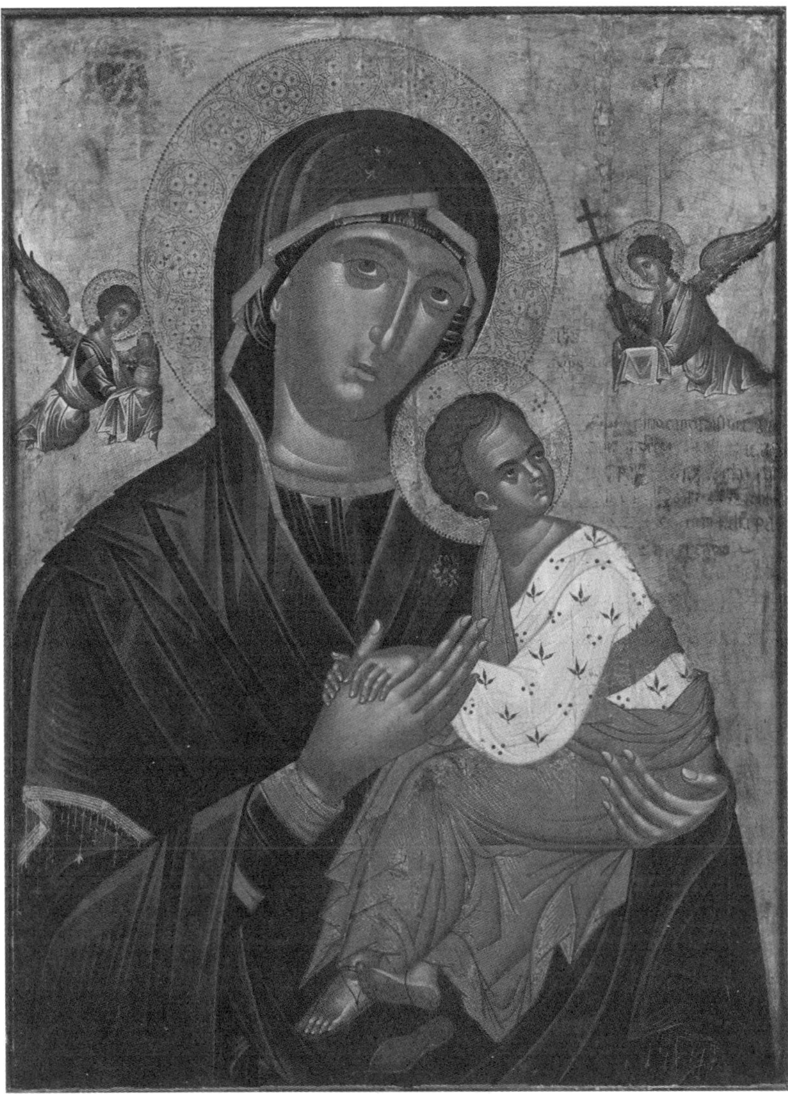

Figure 0.1. The Virgin of the Passion (Our Lady of Perpetual Help) at the Princeton University Art Museum.

That woman's preemptive declaration in the museum was the beginning of this icon's hold on me, a hold that has always been as gentle as the way that Mary holds Jesus in the image itself. If I occasionally use the words *she* or *her* to refer to the icon, it is on account of the relationship I have developed with the image over time, not because of any fetishizing psychological projection I am conscious of, still less because I believe wood or pigment to be actually alive.[3] In the course of my research, when my wife and I lost a child in a late miscarriage, there was something in the traditional icons of Virgin and Child that seemed discordant. Mary's fecundity almost mocked our barrenness. But in the Virgin of the Passion, the angels above do not bear glad tidings of a birth announcement. Instead, they bear the cross, spear, and sponge, testifying that Mary would lose a child as well. The icon's ability to address pain seems to be its secret, partly explaining why it has proliferated so dramatically throughout the globe. The image, I slowly learned, was saturated not with tidy answers to suffering but with *hesychia*, a silent presence that was answer enough.

To study this icon is to study not just one particular object but a much broader category of an icon "type."[4] So long as the image contains the Virgin and Child with the angels hovering above with the instruments of the passion, a given image qualifies—for my purposes—as a Virgin of the Passion. I visited her original haunts in Cyprus, Crete, Constantinople (now Istanbul), and especially Saint Catherine's monastery at the foot of Mount Sinai in Egypt, where so many such icons are kept. But I was surprised to discover the Virgin of the Passion everywhere else as well. In fact, I encountered the image in so many unexpected places, from convenience stores to contemporary art exhibitions, that soon I stopped being surprised when I encountered the image and settled into expecting her instead. After all, her major shrines are scattered throughout the globe: Brooklyn, Boston, Curitiba, Manila, Cairo, Chicago, Singapore, and Mexico City (to name just a few). Lesser churches and schools devoted to this particular image are frankly innumerable, such that it has been called "perhaps the most popular religious icon of the twentieth century" and possibly of the present century as well.[5]

Beyond "Power"

THE PROLIFERATION OF the Virgin of the Passion is certainly impressive, but the upshot of such ubiquity need not be a triumphalist appeal to the all-powerful Virgin Mary. On the contrary, the reason the icon has such prominence is because it testifies to something far more than mere "power."[6] A focus on mere power in academic study, I believe, has led to a misunderstanding of this particular icon. It is true enough that devotion to the Virgin "supported the idea of empire in Byzantium."[7] Mary surely functioned as a protector in the Byzantine world and even could go on the offensive against enemies, especially in the empire's earliest years. Mary has been called "a divine entity like the mother of the gods. . . . The goddess' duties of protection, defense, nurturance, and well-being were foisted upon the Theotokos."[8] The Mother of God "rose to become the protector of city and state, whose undefeatable power stemmed from her paradoxical virginal motherhood."[9] She "appeared as an actual sovereign, in whose name even the emperor acted."[10] She was "enlivened by the human features of Greek religion and endowed with unlimited power."[11]

But it is less frequently noticed that Mary was a chief source of support during the empire's collapse as well. The long view of the empire's history also shows not only that the Mother of God was the bearer of "undefeatable power" but that she was eminently defeatable as well, at least on the political plane.[12] Unlike the pagan goddesses that preceded her, Mary could also navigate military disaster.[13] It took centuries for these features of the Marian tradition to finally surface in Byzantine culture, but surface they did. When the empire's winning streak was broken, the Virgin of the Passion often appeared, testifying not to mere power but to the suffering love that power's theatrics left in its wake. Conveniently enough, the first surviving Virgin of the Passion in all of art history emerged as a Christian response to the Christian violence of the Crusades.[14] She might even be understood, for that reason, as the conscience of the Crusades.[15] Remarkably, we even know the name of the artist who gave us the first surviving example of the type, which was painted in response to Richard the Lionheart's conquering of Cyprus in 1191. It was, in all likelihood, Theodore Apsevdis (pronounced *ApsevDEES* in modern Greek).[16] Apsevdis, which may be a monastic epithet, simply means "who does not lie." It is a fitting title for what may be the first surviving name of a monumental painter of the Byzantine world.[17]

After surfacing in Cyprus and repeatedly in the Balkans, often at flash points of military failure, the Virgin of the Passion type was popularized as a portable icon in fifteenth-century Crete to meet a growing demand for icons—tokens of an empire that had finally collapsed in 1453. On Crete, it was an artist named Andreas Ritzos who gave us the image's most enduring formulation. It is certainly an irony that the postmodern goddess movement, which so often appeals to Crete as its contested starting point, is in fact the uncontested origin for the modern Virgin of the Passion instead.[18] The goddess movement's connections to Crete are tenuous, but the Virgin of the Passion's connection to the island is as solid as the rocky coastline itself.[19]

Partly in response to Napoleon's destructive romp through the city of Rome, Ritzos's version of the icon was further popularized under the aegis of the Redemptorist order of priests. They were personally directed by Pope Pius IX (d. 1878) to spread the icon around the world. The Redemptorists were extraordinarily successful in doing so, which largely accounts for the image's popularity today.

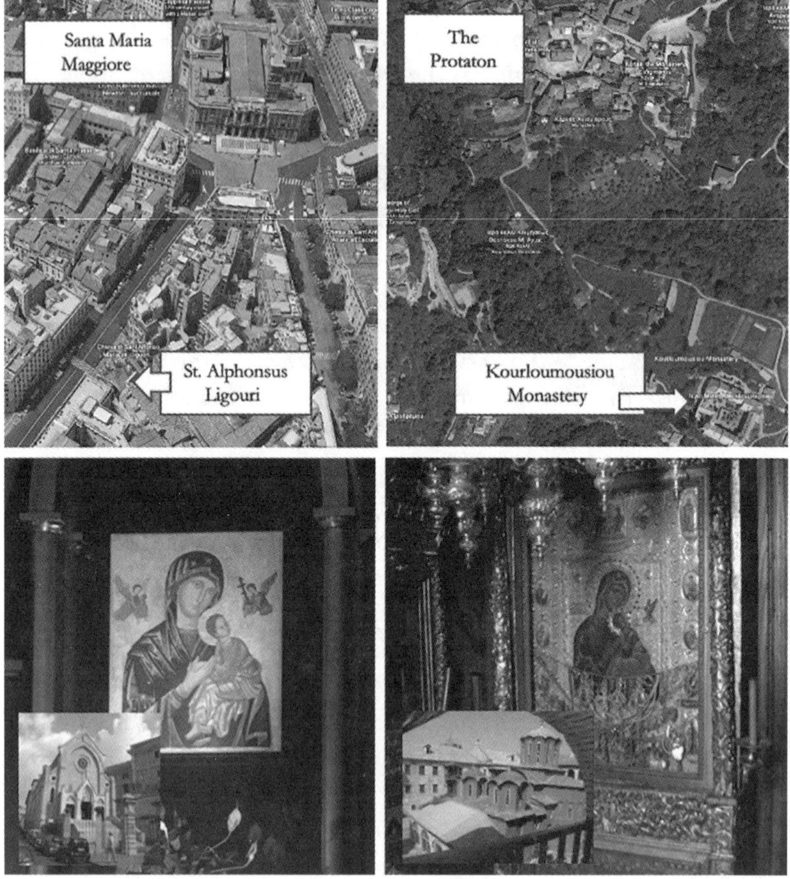

Figure 0.2. Our Lady of Perpetual Help at the Church of Saint Alphonsus Liguori in Rome and the Virgin of the Passion at Koutloumousiou Monastery. Both are just beyond the main Marian centers of Santa Maria Maggiore in Rome and the Protaton on Mount Athos, respectively.

Understanding the icon's original connection to military failure lends an unexpected inflection to the image's global presence today (fig. 0.2). For example, the Virgin of the Passion seems to shadow two of the most famous Marian icons in Catholic and Orthodox Christianity, respectively. The Church of Saint Alphonsus Liguori in Rome, which houses the most famous Virgin of the Passion, is just several blocks from the *Salus Populi Romani* icon at the Santa Maria Maggiore (Saint Mary Major) basilica, the greatest Marian shrine of Rome.[20] Hence just across the street from a church with its ceiling said to be gilded with gold recently plundered from the Americas is a shrine to the Virgin of the Passion, who became an emblem not of conquest but of loss.[21] Likewise, an equal distance from the famous *Axion Estin* icon of Mary in the Protaton, the chief church of the monastic enclave of Mount Athos, lies a chapel dedicated to the Virgin of the Passion attached to the Koutloumousiou Monastery.[22] Accordingly, right next to an icon (the *Axion Estin*) that is still carried in procession on a military jeep lined with gun-bearing soldiers is a shrine to an icon (the Virgin of the Passion) that first emerged when Latin Christians conquered the Byzantine Empire.[23] The cross that hovers above the Virgin of the Passion, one might even be tempted to say, proclaims not "In this sign, conquer" (to recall Emperor Constantine's famous vision) but "This sign gives hope to the conquered" instead.[24] She is the mother, in other words, not just of the lion but of the lamb.

In short, measuring Mary's success using only the gauge of political power is like measuring an earthquake with a thermometer: an entirely useful tool, but an inadequate one for the job. Devotion to the Virgin Mary in the Byzantine Empire predated imperial sponsorship, endured such sponsorship, and flourished all the more after that sponsorship's expiration. The Virgin of the Passion is not the whole story of Mary in Byzantium, but she is an undertold part of it.[25] The empire is best summarized not by Nietzsche ("What doesn't kill me makes me stronger") but by Rilke, for whom growth comes from "being defeated, decisively, by constantly greater beings."[26] The Byzantine Empire, after all, was not just a political project; it was an incubator for a faith that transcended it.

Even so, this icon's connection to military defeat does not make Mary a passive plaything. This Virgin is not hopelessly supine. Mary has not been a quiet noncombatant in the liturgical and theological affairs of men. Her humility is not to be confused with obsequiousness. When the original fresco series in Cyprus from which the image emerged is understood, Mary is an illustration of Wisdom herself, the female figure that emerges in the book of Proverbs. Wisdom's eternal quality makes the Mary in this icon also the mother of the "lamb slain from the foundation of the world" (Rev 13:8 KJV). The icon reaffirms the traditional heart of Christian theology, encapsulated in the Nicene Creed, and awakens a frequently dormant biblical motif that offers the answer to the questions that so many today legitimately ask: Is there adequate space for women in the traditional Christian understanding of God?[27] Mary's Wisdom dimension suggests that there is room not only for women in the bliss of the Godhead but for all of humanity, past, present, and future. For Mary also functions as the collective symbol of redeemed humanity: the church.

Mary is mother of the lamb in another sense as well. Which is to say, she is not just Mother of God (her most famous title) but mother of the eucharistic lamb. It was the same pope who did so much to spread this image throughout the globe, Pius IX—defender of tradition par excellence—who hailed Mary as a "Virgin Priest."[28] Evidence for this overlooked role of Mary abounds in mainstream (i.e., not heretical) sources, and the Virgin of the Passion may be the most pervasive example of Mary in her ministerial role.[29] Moreover, Mary takes on this priestly role not while pretending to be male but as a woman.[30]

Her status as Wisdom and as priest effectively undermines the presumed passivity that has caused many to prematurely dismiss her. "Mary's chief traits," describe observers of this icon type, "are the passive abilities to console and nurture."[31] But while consolation and nurture are laudable qualities, Mary in this image *also* deposes emperors, contests crusaders, lifts her son to his death at the altar, and proclaims the message of salvation extended to all—not activities ideally described as "passive." Abraham was spared the sacrifice of his son Isaac, but Mary, the new Abraham, was not.[32]

The Marian Catch-22

TAKEN TOGETHER, THE dynamics at work in the Virgin of the Passion—Mary's connection to military defeat and her sophianic and priestly dimensions—respond to two important issues that have surfaced in the recent and welcome waves of Marian literature.[33] On the one hand are studies that point out that Mary is aggressive and warlike.[34] On the other hand are books that criticize Marian culture for perpetuating female subordination.[35] These volumes are important contributions in their own right and reflect realities about how the Virgin Mary has been and is received. The data in such volumes are not invented, and the Marian features they uncover are real. But they put those who wish to understand Mary for the present in a catch-22.[36] For to offer evidence for Mary's assertiveness contributes to critiques of her aggression, and to proffer proof of Mary's humility fuels critics of her passivity.[37] To show her exalted means she leaves regular women behind, and to show her compassion means she lacks power.[38]

To modify the words of G. K. Chesterton, Mary is at once "quakerish and bloodthirsty, too gorgeous and too thread-bare, austere, yet pandering preposterously to the lust of the eye, the enemy of women and their foolish refuge, a solemn pessimist and a silly optimist." One conclusion to be drawn from these criticisms is that Mary is especially horrible, containing within herself a legion of contradictory evils rightfully discerned by her diverse critics. On the other hand, there is the possibility that Mary, "abused for being too plain and for being too coloured," contains remarkable plenitude, "not an amalgam or compromise, but both things at the top of their energy."[39] Indeed, the tradition of the Virgin Mary is so ample that any perceived logical impasse can be overcome.[40] One need not choose between "high" and "low" views of Mary, for she is truly "both ordinary woman and the Mother of God."[41] I know of no better illustration of these twin dynamics than the Virgin of the Passion. The icon shows her to be both pacific and priestly at once, both acquiescent and audacious, the mother of the lamb in both the political and liturgical senses.[42]

In short, the icon contains no concealed cryptic messages, gnostic secrets, or hidden hieroglyphs reserved for initiates. The truth the icon contains is much more interesting than that, and the news it bears is too good to be reserved for the few. The icon announces a community of divine persons in unified resolve to rescue marooned humanity. It showcases infinite power's cheerful condescension, a mission set in motion even before the universe began. In short, the Virgin of the Passion, when the controversy that helped generate it is fully understood, contains the compressed theological wisdom of the Byzantine Empire, all of which is preserved in the image's more recent manifestation as Our Lady of Perpetual Help.

If this icon helped Byzantium navigate its decline with grace, the icon may be relevant to contemporary democracies, some of which also appear to be in precipitous decline or at least in a state of decadence.[43]

This is not to invoke doom but to suggest that the compassion and grace that this icon represents may help some to navigate this descent more effectively or perhaps even to delay it. The great Byzantine Empire has afforded the world many stories, but the story of this global icon that emerged from that empire may be the one that modern civilizations most need to hear. If beauty and affliction are "the two things piercing enough to penetrate our souls," the Virgin of the Passion offers both.[44] The icon echoes the words of Mary herself: "He hath scattered the proud in the imagination of their hearts"—that is, any imagining that empires are forever. He "hath exalted the humble and meek"—that is, he has brought forth Wisdom from the shadows.[45] He has elevated Mary to her overlooked ministerial role.[46]

The story of this image starts with an Orthodox icon painter in Constantinople, Theodore Apsevdis, about to embark on a journey to Cyprus, and so, therefore, must this journey as well.

PART I

THE ARTIST

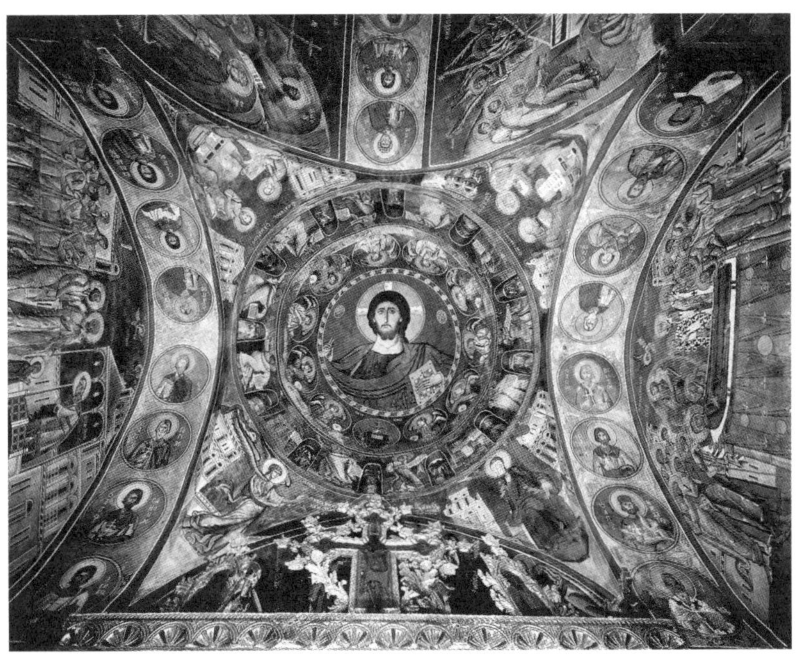

❦ **1** ❦

A PORTABLE CONSTANTINOPLE

Constantinople was Paris, London, New York, all of them in one—and more.

—Richard Temple, Temenos Academy lecture (2021)

Hagia Sophia is explicitly not a "cave of cognition" in the Platonic sense, but a "sanctuary of wisdom" with a distinctive Christian connotation.

—Nadine Schibille, *Hagia Sophia and the Byzantine Aesthetic Experience*

[Beauty] would shake the soul to its depths, but gently now, much as the impalpable sweetness of the liturgy now swayed the heart of the monk.

—Peter Brown, *The Body and Society*

Instead of thinking of "God" language as really being about sex (Freud's reductive ploy), we need to understand sex as really about God, and about the deep desire that we feel for God—the precious clue that is woven into our existence about the final and ultimate union that we seek.

—Sarah Coakley, *The New Asceticism*

The Great Church

ONE THING WE know for certain about the elusive artist who gave us the first known Virgin of the Passion is that he was highly skilled. Following the late twelfth-century accomplishments of the painter who was likely named Theodore Apsevdis in Cyprus, the quality of art on the island, at least by classical standards, plummets. Paintings made after Theodore's career become awkward, disproportionate, imitative.[1] It is exceedingly likely that an artist of such refinement would have been trained in

13

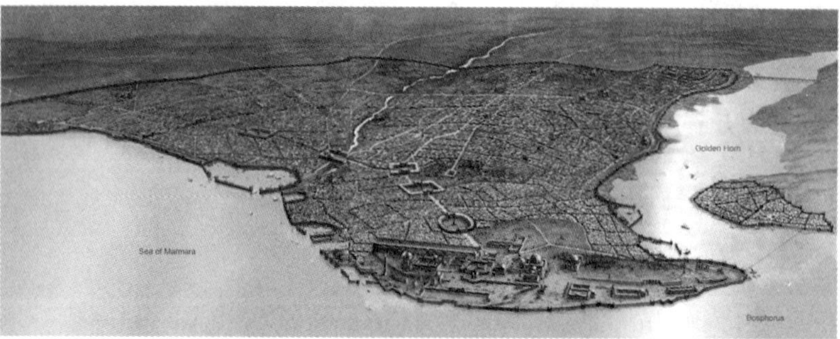

Figure 1.1. Constantinople.

the empire's queen city, Constantinople, whose opulence and splendor made her the envy of every European king.[2] Which is to say, Theodore would have enjoyed the City of Gold in its magnificent sunset, on the eve of its defeat by the Latin Crusaders in 1204, after which it would be but a shattered reflection of the city Theodore once knew.[3]

We might therefore compare Theodore to an Israelite artisan in 600 BCE perfecting the interior of Solomon's Temple, unaware that Babylonian armies gathered in the east with destruction in their hearts. Or perhaps he was like a young modernist architect in the freewheeling Weimar Republic enjoying the last days of the Bauhaus before the troubles of Germany forced it to close. Though conflict loomed, Theodore could probably not have anticipated the disasters that were to come in his lifetime any more than an employee at the World Trade Center could in early September of 2001. Constantinople must still have felt somewhat secure.[4]

Before he ventured to Cyprus, more than once Theodore would likely have taken refuge from Constantinople's bustling streetscape in the precincts of the city's cathedral, Hagia Sophia—that is, Holy Wisdom. She was envisioned by an emperor for an empire that, with every passing year, seemed less worthy of the name. But to Theodore, Hagia Sophia's hulking exterior was indifferent to reports of territory surrendered or battles lost. Her confident dome was uncluttered by the minarets that fence the building today. But the evening sun would still have reddened the brick exterior; the same light we see today piercing Hagia Sophia's innumerable windows Theodore would have seen as well. Still, the mosaics that welcomed and refracted that light were not, as they mostly are today, concealed.

The aesthetic tradition Theodore absorbed within the walls of this imperial chapel was far older than Christianity itself. The beauty of the Lord manifested in art, Theodore must have known, was as ancient as the Hebrew tabernacle, as venerable as the chanted Psalms that still echoed off Constantinople's many monastery walls. Theodore would certainly have heard the Psalms sung in the Greek translation we know as the Septuagint. Likely, he chanted the words himself, perhaps even from memory:

One thing I have asked from the Lord, that I shall seek:
That I may dwell in the house of the Lord all the days of my life,
To behold the beauty of the Lord
And to meditate in His temple.[5]

In time, the Hebrew temple tradition faced the challenge of Hellenic temples, columned wonders from the Parthenon in Athens to the Temple of Jupiter in Rome. These temples had inherited and refined millennia of Egyptian architecture that grew like permanent papyrus stalks up and down the banks of the Nile. But rather than oppose, defy, or be seduced by what we have come to know as the classical tradition, Hagia Sophia absorbed it, channeling it toward the worship of a mysterious threefold yet unified God.[6]

Which is to say, for Theodore, the classical tradition of Greece and Rome was not a buried reality. On the contrary, Theodore's Constantinople was bedecked with sumptuous pagan statuary. The first Christian emperor, Constantine, had brought them to his newly founded city as badges of honor, reminders that the old Rome had been surpassed. Naked sculptures of the Labors of Hercules, Prometheus the fire thief, and the sleeping Endymion enhanced the city's walls, while a bronze statue of Athena stood in the hippodrome.[7]

These statues were not just feared as the empire became increasingly Christian but admired.[8] Some early Christians may have carved crosses into statues of Aphrodite, and perhaps for good reason.[9] If the famously nude Aphrodite gave form to "the continued and incessant idealization of female humiliation in the Western tradition from ca. 340 BCE to the present," the image might require some amendment.[10] Even so, the Christian eunuch Lausos was pleased to display a statue of Aphrodite in Constantinople. It was ultimately destroyed by fire, not puritanical fury.[11] In addition, a bronze Aphrodite stood outside the

Senate house of Constantinople, and other Aphrodite statues enhanced baths throughout the Byzantine Empire.[12] We might see in such secret sentinels evidence for the cautious Christian transformation of eros, a distilled and purified beauty that would be reflected in all of the paintings that issued from Theodore's hand.[13]

But there were no statues of Aphrodite inside Hagia Sophia. The dynamics at play within the cathedral surpassed anything a three-dimensional statue could offer or any skin-deep desires such statues might evoke.[14] The longings that unfolded in this sanctuary were of a much higher grade.[15] The play of light in Christian mosaics, Theodore well knew, outdid the sensuous statues that decorated the city streets. The depictions of Athanasius, John Chrysostom, Mary, and Christ himself were not "two-dimensional," as some uncharitable critics of Byzantine art today still suggest, but four- or even five-dimensional, as so many modern artists inspired by Byzantium intuitively understood. The art was restrained because the subject matter exceeded what mere portraiture could accomplish. The state of a divinized human, let alone that of Christ himself, could be evoked but never captured. "[By God's] youthful beauty I was wounded," wrote the Constantinopolitan mystic Symeon the New Theologian. "I was enflamed and burning, all of me set on fire."[16]

Forgetting Solomon's maxim, "Pride goes before destruction" (Prov 16:18 NRSV), it was said that the emperor Justinian (r. 527–65) uttered upon Hagia Sophia's completion, "O Solomon, I have surpassed you," boasting that he had bested the Jewish temple.[17] Theodore might have known that story. But he also knew that his city had bested not only Solomon but Alexander the Great and the Caesars as well. Even the Pantheon, that great domed Roman temple to all the gods, was outflanked by the soaring dome and muscular columns of Hagia Sophia, sometimes simply called the Great Church. In addition—Theodore could only assume from the disheveled appearance of visiting Crusaders—no churches that the Latin Christians worshipped in could equal the Church of Holy Wisdom.[18] These uncouth Christians from the West didn't even speak Greek.[19]

From the right distance, Theodore might well have felt that Hagia Sophia's dome seemed to arc not only over the building but over the entire city, even over all of known history, as if it were the protective mantle of the Virgin herself. That Theodore was destined to enhance his own miniature Hagia Sophia on Cyprus, equal in mystical intensity to the original but absent its triumphalist streak, he surely could not have grasped.

The Liturgy

THE MATERIAL MYSTICISM of Byzantium that scholars attempt to reconstruct through study in the present was, for Theodore, an effortless birthright. The artist would not have passed Hagia Sophia's threshold without crossing himself, as Orthodox Christians still do when they enter their more modest sanctuaries today. Intuitively, Theodore understood that Hagia Sophia transcended the brick, stone, and glass of her construction; she represented the totality of the cosmos and that which is beyond the cosmos as well.[20]

He would not have craned his neck and gawked like a tourist.[21] Instead, he was humbled, his head instinctively lowered by the soaring structure until he lost himself in her swirling marble floors. The sensuous pavement upon which he walked reflected the primordial chaos of the ocean but also the chaos within himself. The churning gray, red, green, and white of the marble evoked what Dante would call, more than a century later in the less civilized land of Italy, the "sea of twisted love."[22] This ocean threatened to engulf Theodore and the covey of worshippers who accompanied him in the nave, each of them an expugnable mortal like himself. He would have known, as did all these supplicants, that desire could be his undoing. But Theodore entered Hagia Sophia not to drown in, suppress, or extinguish his passions but to overwhelm them.[23]

Even before the incense in the thuribles was lit and the chanters began their intonations, he would have perceived an undetectable but still definite sense of lift—an interior ascent triggered by the space. His eyes were steadied by hundreds of marble pillars sprouting with wild leaves, as if the tree of life had here seeded to become a forest. His eyes extended to the galleries, where shimmering saints fired back their glances, seducing him upward. The waves of the marble floor then climbed the walls, clothing the building with a callithump of patterns evoking Persian silks. Primordial passion would be refined, not abandoned, in the building's ascent.

Still, as Theodore's eyes extended upward, the gold, which clothed the building like the scales of a celestial dragon, communicated an unearthly peace. The building's square base, representing the terrestrial plane, gave way to the circular dome representing heaven's intensity, mediated by massive seraphim in each of the four pendentives.[24]

Whether they were mere mosaics of seraphim or actual angels ceased to matter, because material symbols participate in the spiritual realities they evoke. The angels beckoned Theodore farther upward, each with six muscular wings that seemed large enough to bear the building aloft. Finally, the artist allowed the ray of his eyes to penetrate the dome—his neck stretched back to its limit and his mouth involuntarily agape.

But within the dreamy, imponderable light of the dome came an unexpected point of focus. At its apex was a glistening mosaic, not of an abstract deity, but of the gentle God-man. The book of the law was cradled by his left hand, while his right hand, signifying grace, reached out almost importunately to bless. That the summit of cosmic being could be crowned with human form, and gracious form at that, was more than even the greatest Platonist mystic would dare conceive. The eyes of the Lord, barely visible even when Theodore squinted his own, suggested he was both unimpressed with his admirers and affectionate toward them at once. The Pantocrator—that is, the ruler of all—contemplated his costly errand downward, the incarnation, just as his worshippers completed their upward ascent. Indeed, for all the sense of lift, the pendentives, like the tips of four immense fountain pens, seemed to push the building earthward as well, as if to announce the Word's eternal desire to take on flesh.

And the liturgy hadn't even begun.

When it did, robed deacons equipped with poles emerged from the structure's darkened corners. They spun the elaborate candelabras, each spangled with constellations of wax-fueled light, in a circling motion until they churned like the golden gears of some kind of saint-making machine. The sweet exhaust from hundreds of candles merged with the more pungent smoke that wafted from expertly wielded thuribles. This cumulative cloud, the original icon of the undepictable God, rose with the throng and thrum of the choir's comingled voices.[25] Somehow the hymns uncoiled forgotten corners of Theodore's congested soul. His eyes were drawn upward again just as the smoke exposed the shafts of sun that beamed through the dome's forty windows, expertly engineered to smuggle light within. The light had long been there, of course, unobtrusively present; but it was only the smoke that revealed it (fig. 1.2). In the same way, Theodore might have then conjectured, the divine regard is ever present but only revealed through the acknowledgment of failures, shortcomings, shadows, and sins.

Of these, Theodore had plenty. He nearly permitted himself to be looked at by the eyes of Christ above him. Until, that is, the marbled chaos beneath his feet and within him drew the artist back to the floor long before the gentle gaze could penetrate more than the surface of his interior life. He would soon replicate the eyes of Christ that he contended with at Hagia Sophia on Cyprus, in the very church in which the first surviving Virgin of the Passion was to appear.

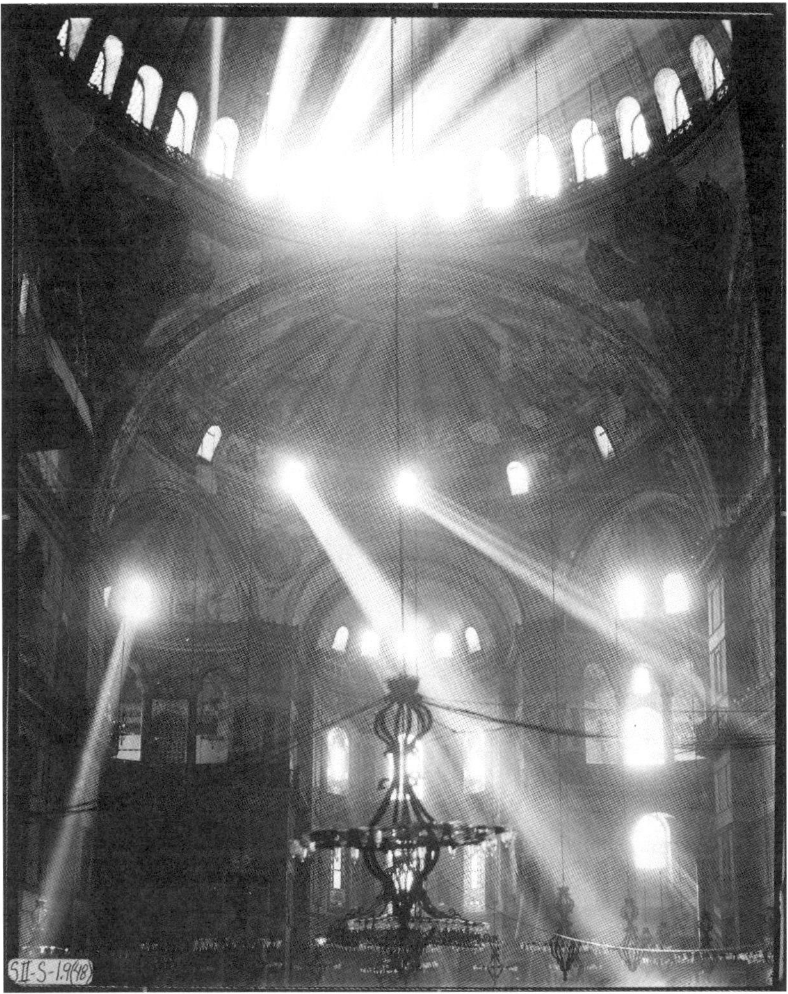

Figure 1.2. Study of light in the apse of Hagia Sophia, 1948.

Into a Threatened City

THEODORE, I EXPECT, was grateful to have work to distract him. Exiting the great church, I doubt he would have been overcome with envy at the accomplishments of his artistic predecessors in the Byzantine world, a world he would simply have known as Roman. He would have harbored no ambition to equal the work of Theodore of Miletus and Isidorus of Tralles, the heroic sixth-century mathematicians who had constructed the imperial church. They, after all, enjoyed the funding of Byzantium at its zenith, when Anatolia, Rome, Jerusalem, and even Egypt and parts of Spain were imperial possessions of Emperor Justinian. Theodore must have known that Hagia Sophia was a one-off. The empire was weaker now, and new threats engulfed it.

The Komnenian family, whose representatives now held the imperial throne, had attempted to equal Justinian's military accomplishments—and had failed. Emperor Justinian might once have fantasized that the exotic marble of Hagia Sophia—from Greece, Egypt, and Libya, even from the milky crags of the Celts—represented the total claims of the Eastern Christian Empire.[26] But now a more humbled emperor had to acknowledge such lands belonged only to God. The hundreds of priests, deacons, lectors, and doorkeepers that managed Hagia Sophia in her prime had been whittled down to several dozen overworked liturgists. Parts of the building, Theodore likely noticed on his way out, were even in disrepair. The Komnenians, after all, had to contend with threats that Justinian never knew: increasingly assertive Latin Christian neighbors and, of course, the great monotheistic military rival of Islam.

Theodore knew only too well that the Seljuk Turks had taken a massive chunk of the Byzantine Empire's Anatolian heartland (modern Turkey). Refugees from this conflict were pouring into the walled city of Constantinople, swelling its population to nearly half a million souls.[27] But these souls needed icons, icons that would have enhanced homes and filled the city's countless churches. Fresh monasteries and neighborhood shrines were being constructed throughout the city, and nearby residents would have been impatient with their white, figureless walls.

Centuries beforehand, the empire had undergone a civil war, prompted in part by Islam, over whether icons were permissible in Christian worship. After first refusing the possibility of images of Christ, the emperors had at last issued a resounding yes, overcorrecting for any temporary reticence, doubling down on the aesthetic ramifications of having a fully embodied God.[28] This bold pronouncement in favor of images was still fully in effect in Theodore's day. It was paramount, therefore, that these new, more modest churches be inhabited by colorful saints. There was a demand for art that conveyed the Christian tradition's visible splendor, and Theodore was among those who could perpetuate that heritage with his well-trained hands.

As he walked the city, observing the newer and more modest monuments, he would have seen examples of the kind of art that could be propagated throughout the empire's still-impressive domain, which included all of what is now mainland Greece alongside Mediterranean islands such as Rhodes, Crete, and Cyprus. And not only did Theodore know these paintings well; he might have created some of them himself. Working as an apprentice and eventually as a master in these smaller churches, he might even have experimented in the art of mosaic that gave Hagia Sophia her glittering effect.

But just as the Komnenians had to be content with more minor military victories, Theodore had to be content to clothe churches not in golden mosaics but in paint. Fresco was the modest, more affordable medium that could enhance what was left of the empire.[29] The well-funded architects of yesteryear might have created a dome that surpassed the Pantheon of Rome, but there was no use in pining for the past. Theodore could evoke the same sense of mystery with a more modest screen of painted icons at a fraction of a fraction of Hagia Sophia's original cost.

To the Provinces

FOR REASONS THAT remain a mystery, Theodore would soon find himself in the distant Byzantine outpost of Cyprus. It was then a proudly Orthodox island. Its residents boasted that when the rest of the empire had forbidden images, Cyprus remained true to the possibility of painting God.[30] Which is to say, Cyprus's tradition of Christian art was unbroken. Theodore's mission would have been to enhance the island with the icons and wall paintings that he had been trained to produce (fig. 1.3).

An artist with more secure connections might have been able to establish himself permanently in the empire's central city. It is not impossible that the voyage to Cyprus was some kind of punishment for an infraction. Perhaps Theodore had offended certain personages and was being penalized with a career in an impressive outpost of the empire, but an outpost nonetheless.[31] Or possibly, he was simply under obedience to an ecclesial superior who commanded him to go. On the other hand, maybe the prospect of setting sail from Constantinople was desirable, a result of Theodore's free choice. There would be less competition and, accordingly, more opportunity. Perhaps we could compare him to a young person today who forgoes a career in London or Los Angeles in pursuit of the affordability and opportunity that a lesser-known city provides. Whatever the reason for his departure, this highly skilled, sensitive Byzantine painter boarded a boat for the faraway Mediterranean island. He could not have known it, but the journey could be compared to an American's choice to take a vacation in Hawaii in early December 1941.

Departing the city he knew so well, Theodore would have turned and seen the imperial church, not yet topped by the flags of Western Christian kingdoms. As Hagia Sophia receded from Theodore's vision, glowing with the radiance not only of wealth but of faith, he carried her within him. The pure forms of the Orthodox liturgy resonated not only in her hallowed interior but in the interior of Theodore himself. As his ship sailed down the city's southern seawall, Theodore would have seen the Stoudios monastery—home to the monk whose name he shared, Theodore the Studite, who had so ably argued the case for icons when the empire was considering eliminating them altogether.[32] Whatever the reason for his departure, Theodore might have been filled

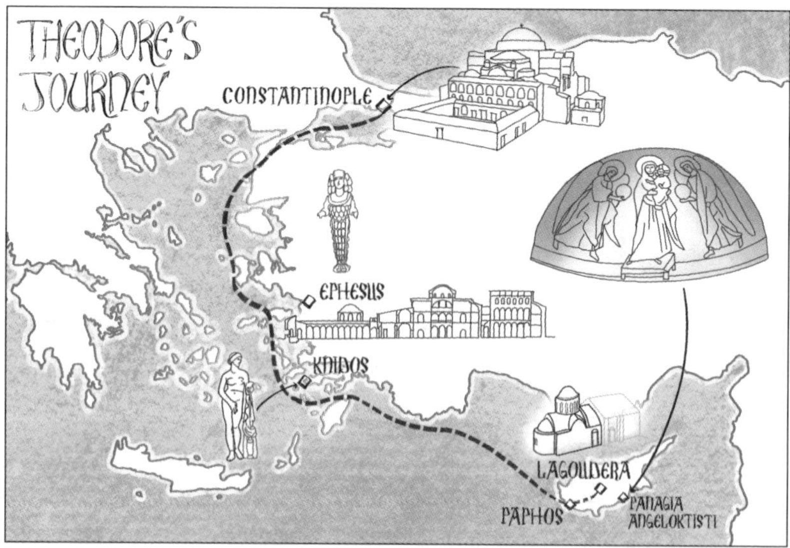

Figure 1.3. Journey of Theodore from Constantinople to Cyprus.

with confidence. He was, after all—thanks to his talent and training—a portable Constantinople himself.

Exiting the Sea of Marmara through the funnel of the Dardanelles, Theodore's ship would have entered the Aegean, legends about which he might well have been aware. Those trained in Constantinople would have been familiar with the tales of Homer, and this journey was Theodore's odyssey of sorts. But he knew of truths higher than Homer's. As his ship hugged the island-crowded coast of Anatolia, he would have sailed not far from the ancient remains of the Temple of Artemis at Ephesus. Artemis was a fair-weather goddess, powerless to reply to famine, plague, climatic change, the earthquake that rocked her sanctuary, or the plundering of her temple by the Goths in 262 CE.[33] Human sacrifice is a steady reference in Greek literature regarding Artemis, a tradition substituted later with animals and nicks on the throat.[34] Records survive of human blood and gore associated with the cult turning some initiates away.[35]

Whether Theodore knew any of this, he would certainly have known that Mary had emerged victorious in her contest with Artemis. As his ship moved southward, he might have pondered the truths of the Council of Ephesus (431 CE), where Mary was at last proclaimed Theotokos (Mother of God). "What we celebrate is the pride of women and the glory of the female," announced Mary's preachers, "thanks to the one who was at once both mother and virgin. . . . Let nature leap for joy, and let women be honoured!"[36] It was a dance that had been welling up for centuries, and not just the Christian centuries: a dance continued by Theodore's colorful portraits of the Mother of God.[37] Even so, the churches that had been constructed from the remains of the Temple of Artemis were now in a precarious position, faced with the looming threat of the Turks.

Farther south, Theodore's ship would have passed the site of the ancient Temple of Knidos, which had commissioned the sculptor Praxiteles to create the Knidian Aphrodite in the fourth century BCE.[38] Praxiteles dared to depict her nude, with a draped version as a backup plan lest the residents become offended, or fearful, of the goddess exposed. Knidos welcomed the nude figure, and its temple grew famous as a result. Kos, home of the ancient healing shrine of Asclepius, through which Theodore's ship might have threaded, chose a draped image of the statue instead, one that I suspect Theodore would have preferred.

Had he known these stories, Theodore might have been troubled to pass such sites. It was one thing to encounter Aphrodite safely in the confines of Constantinople, but now he was nearing the goddess's home terrain. He was, after all, heading to Cyprus, where the nubile Aphrodite was said to have first emerged from Uranus's testicular foam. That said, Theodore's was a world where the breast-blanketed Artemis had been replaced with the nursing Virgin, the uncovered Aphrodite draped with Mary's miraculous mantle, and the healing power of Asclepius supplanted by the Great Physician himself. But whether Mary and Jesus could save the Christian empire from its new threats of destruction remained to be seen.

Theodore's ship would have passed the island of Rhodes, which had been recaptured by Byzantine forces and was still one of the empire's Mediterranean gems. Had his ship docked on the island for resupply, Theodore would have encountered a still-Orthodox, Greek-speaking land that felt familiar. The Colossus of Rhodes, one of the wonders of the ancient world, had long since been destroyed by an earthquake, but no matter. The humble shrine of Saint Phanourios, an early Christian saint martyred by the Romans, was a more fitting stop for a Christian traveler. Theodore might have examined the wall paintings in the island's chapels, comparing them to the city he knew so well and no doubt judging them inferior.

On the last leg of this Mediterranean journey, the sight of Cyprus's forest-topped Troodos Mountains would have appeared as the traveler's long-desired reward. Theodore might have heard of the pagan tradition, recounted by Herodotus, that at least once in their lifetime, Cypriot women were to give themselves to male pilgrims at the Temple of Aphrodite to show their piety to the goddess.[39] But Theodore was no pagan pilgrim, and this was Aphrodite's island no more. This was the island where the apostles Paul and Barnabas had journeyed (Acts 13:6–12) and even where Lazarus, who had been raised from the dead by Jesus, was supposed to have traveled as well. The apostles were how the island now chose to remember itself, as evidenced by the churches, named after these saints and bearing objects associated with them. Theodore—we can safely surmise—was soon to visit these churches and venerate these relics himself.

Theodore's hosts might have welcomed their new prize artist with some degree of fanfare. Or perhaps he was simply viewed as a visiting craftsman, their attention drawn instead to fortifying soldiers and supplies.[40] But whatever they thought of him, Theodore was called to press the seal of the Virgin on Aphrodite's Cyprus even more firmly than had the many Christian artists who preceded him. As he set to work, Theodore could scarcely have imagined that *his* name would be recalled centuries later as a painter of Byzantium rather than the names of the mosaicists in the City of Gold.

But knowing this would certainly have cheered him.

DEPICTING DIVINIZATION

And since, then, God is made human, so humanity is perfected as God, and that is my glory.

—Gregory of Nazianzus, *De Incarnatione*

There are as many unions with God as there are human persons, each person having an absolutely unique relation with the Divinity . . . as many possible sainthoods exist in heaven as there are personal destinies on earth.

—Vladimir Lossky, *In the Image and Likeness of God*

Christ's death is your death, his resurrection from the grave is your resurrection, his ascension is your ascension, and his eternal kingdom is your kingdom.

—Jacob Boehme, *On the Human Genesis of Christ*

Humility is a transcendent form of self-confidence.

—Robert C. Roberts, *Spiritual Emotions*

Encountering the Recluse

WHEN THEODORE APSEVDIS, painter of history's first surviving Virgin of the Passion, arrived on the island of Cyprus, a unique task was laid before him. Sometime before or during the year 1183, he would have encountered Neophytos (1134–1214), an island personality beloved to this day, who Theodore would memorialize in paint. Understanding the Virgin of the Passion requires understanding these paintings first, which are crammed into the curves and nooks of Neophytos's mountain Hideaway (from *Enkleistra*, meaning "place of seclusion"). Which is to say, the cavernous interior of Hagia Sophia once enjoyed by Theodore would be replaced on Cyprus with the warped and winding walls of an actual cave.

It is for these paintings that Theodore Apsevdis appears to have been brought to the island. So far as we know, perhaps enhancing the personal abode of Neophytos was the entirety of the reason Theodore had arrived on Cyprus. Theodore, in other words, the well-trained painter of Constantinople, was a gift. The century beforehand, Cypriot monks had managed to secure one of the capital's finest icons for the island, presumably painted by Saint Luke, the Virgin of Kykkos.[1] More such tokens were of course desirable, but gaining a gift of that prestige from the capital once more would be difficult. What could be attained, however, was a painter with Theodore's level of skill. If another icon painted by Saint Luke could not be obtained, at least the Cypriots could import an icon painter good enough to replicate them.

Neophytos had a refined taste for painting, advising his fellow monks that imperial sponsorship was necessary in church decoration: "Holy works of such magnitude have need of very great expenditure."[2] And Neophytos had precisely the connections, and donations, necessary to secure what he desired. The bishop of Paphos, Basil Kinnamos, was connected to a prominent family in Constantinople, a family that included the secretary to the emperor, and the bishop of Paphos was a fan of Neophytos.[3] So it was determined that local talent was inadequate for the series of interior frescoes Neophytos desired: a program of paintings especially designed for him.

Braggart or Beloved

BORN IN CYPRUS, Neophytos resisted the betrothal arranged by his parents, fleeing to a monastery instead. His parents dragged him back but, seeing the young man's resolve, finally permitted him to stay. But even a monastery was not enough for Neophytos. On pilgrimage to the Holy Land occupied by the Crusaders, he wandered through Palestine seeking to apprentice himself to a hermit but could not find one willing to take him on.[4] Therefore, Neophytos returned to his Cypriot homeland, eventually to literally carve out a cliffside monastic dwelling in 1159, at the age of twenty-five. A large monastery eventually emerged around this Hideaway, but Neophytos stayed in his cramped quarters, reluctantly attending to visitors and producing a vast body of writing (sixteen volumes).[5] When Neophytos was offered the gift of a painter from Constantinople to enhance his self-appointed cell, he was fifty.

Neophytos's writings and his commissions survive to the point that we know a great deal about the recluse, information that has caused some to dismiss him as an insufferable braggart.[6] Following the custom in Byzantine society, Neophytos was violently opposed to any perspective opposing his own Orthodoxy, especially those of Muslims, Jews, and Latin Christians.[7] He fawned over his favorite emperors, exonerating them of all wrongdoing.[8] Moreover, we know so much of Neophytos's life not because someone else praised him in a posthumous biography, as would normally be the case in Byzantium, but because of Neophytos's own forceful campaign to canonize himself (even to the point of securing his own feast day).[9] He applied the template of the lives of miracle-working saints to his own life to almost comic effect. An accident he survived while digging a toilet not only became an occasion for a sermon but was an event solemn enough that it should be commemorated annually.[10]

But above all, it is the paintings that appear to give critics of Neophytos the upper hand, betraying his egotism over his self-appointed sainthood.[11] Multiple self-portraits in one's own monastic retreat painted by the best artists available seem to be sufficient proof of a lack of humility, even if Neophytos's writings protest otherwise. It is tempting to compare Neophytos to today's social media personalities who exhibit even minor details of life for the public's notice and commendation and use all their power to perpetuate images of themselves. Theodore, it appears, had been whisked away from Constantinople to polish the mirror of a narcissist.[12]

But there is also reason to dispute this dismissive approach. Neophytos was able to attract a large following in his lifetime precisely because he was in touch with the concerns of peasants (he was once a peasant himself) and forcefully criticized the elite, including the emperor.[13] His surviving sermons are not without penetrating and insightful reflections. The Neophytos-as-narcissist critique neglects to realize the entire aim of the hermit's life was to flee the world, not to welcome it. If he was seeking acclaim and attention, it hardly seems to follow that he would celebrate any moment he gained relief from persistent intruders.[14] His theologizing of his own injuries might be understood as the application of Christ's counsel that "even the hairs of your head are all numbered" (Matt 10:30). One scholar analyzes Neophytos's dreams using Freudian psychology to diagnose his arrogance.[15] But such dreams could just as easily be seen as proper confidence, a healthy understanding that he too could make a contribution to the church.[16] If a given figure does not match stereotypes of Byzantine self-debasement, it may be a sign less of arrogance than of a considerable measure of self-respect.[17] New research, moreover, shows that there were multiple local hermits on Cyprus whose careers followed a similar trajectory.[18] Neophytos, in other words, is not as peculiar as he may have previously appeared. His pursuit of holiness was part of a collective mission to sanctify the land.

In short, the Hideaway needs no longer be viewed as a theater of vainglory—that sin that Byzantine monks were especially watchful to avoid.[19] Neophytos's claim that all he wrote and created was "not for the sake of vainglory, but for the praise of God and the benefit of the audience" might be genuine.[20] After all, the same Sermon on the Mount where Christ warns not to be "like the hypocrites . . . [who] love to stand and pray . . . that they may be seen by others" (Matt 6:5) also advises to "let your light shine before others" (Matt 5:16).[21] The saints of Byzantium were wary of pride in all its forms, but they also counseled that there is "glory proper to human dignity" as well.[22] The same ascetic manuals that promulgated "extreme humility" also reminded their readers that "those who honor me I will honor" (1 Sam 2:30).[23]

Deluded or Divinized

TO ENTER NEOPHYTOS's cave chapel today (fig. 2.1) is to encounter a confusing array of warped walls wrapped with painting. Wading through the fog of later, lesser art, one moves toward the end of a jumbled program where a marked refinement can be recognized. This is the work of Theodore Apsevdis, who depicted his patron in a dramatically exalted way.[24] Above the image (fig. 2.2), Neophytos's prayer that he be received into the company of angels is brilliantly illustrated by two angels whose wings—while remaining the wings of the angels—appear to belong to Neophytos as well. Theodore thereby managed to glorify the living Neophytos while still being able to claim, with a wink, that the angelic resemblance was just a coincidence.[25]

Rather than dismiss these images as pompous, it is possible to see them as an illustration of the well-known Orthodox understanding of divinization, when humans—by grace and not by nature—participate in the divine life.[26] Commenting on the puzzling verse where God appears to send an angel to kill Moses (Exod 4:24), Maximus the Confessor (d. 662) interprets the passage as the death and resurrection of the ego, pleading God to send him the "'angel' of his illumining word within our conscience" to purify him.[27] Read in this way, Michael and Gabriel in the portrait might be seen as angels who have put to death the old Neophytos and helped bring the new Neophytos to life.[28] Which is to

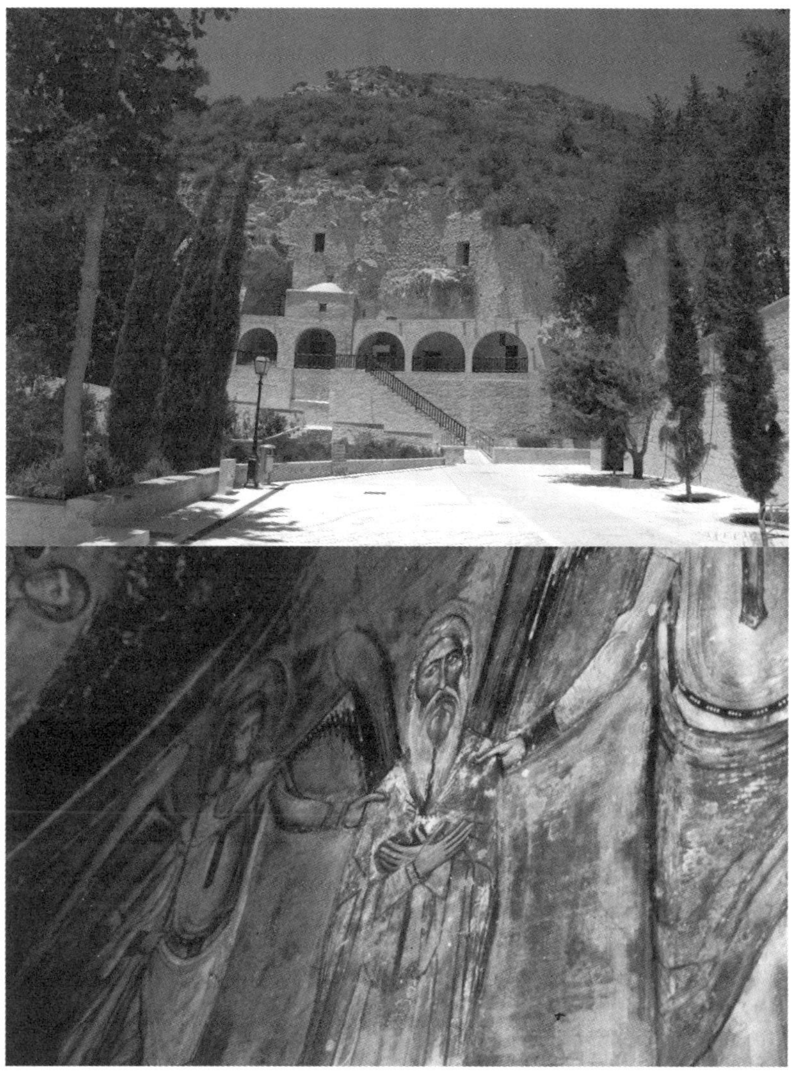

Figure 2.1. Neophytos's mountain monastery escape, known as the Hideaway (*Enkleistra*, "place of seclusion") and his portrait within.

say, such a self-exalting portrait might be seen as a daring illustration of the words Symeon the New Theologian (d. 1022):

> *Purified by repentance*
> *And by floods of tears,*

Partaking of the divinized body,
As of God Himself,
I myself become a god.
By this unspeakable union.[29]

Looking at the portrait in context (fig. 2.3), Neophytos even appears to be imitating the image of the ascended Christ above him, who is also borne by angels. The two juxtaposed images recall the words of Maximus the Confessor again: "Love, the divine gift, perfects human nature until it makes it appear in unity and identity by grace with the divine nature."[30] Or as Symeon puts a similar idea, "The one Whom I see sees me. . . . I saw Him within my house . . . and I became that which I had seen."[31] Even so, limits are nonetheless imposed on this depiction of deification. Neophytos has no halo as the angels do. The angels that bear Neophytos, it should also be noted, have their feet firmly planted on the ground.[32]

Neophytos's radical portrait was further offset with an image of humility (fig. 2.4). After all, the same Psalm that proclaims "You are 'gods'"

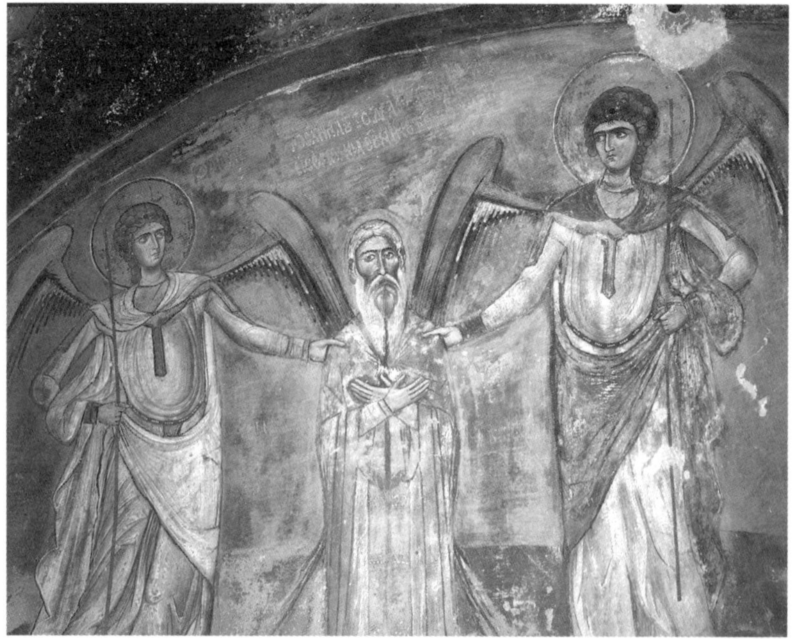

Figure 2.2. Theodore's portrait of Neophytos with the accompanying angels lending him their wings.

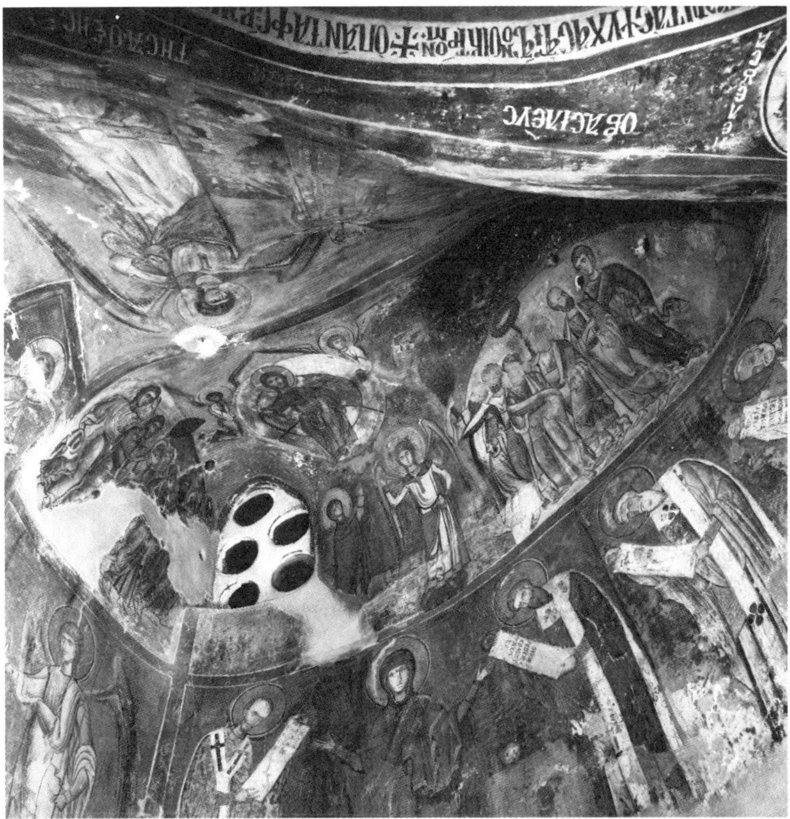

Figure 2.3. Christ's ascension paired with Neophytos's portrait on the other side of the ceiling.

(Ps 82:6; John 10:34) says "You shall die" as well (Ps 82:7). Neophytos therefore asked Theodore to visualize Neophytos's own description of himself as a wretched, unlearned, and uncultured hermit.[33] Comparing this downcast portrait to the exalted one, we might see here not carefully managed self-effacement meant to conceal pride but a complex psychological self-understanding of being both sinful and beloved at once. As a mystic of another Christian tradition put it, "I died within for you, and for you I revived."[34]

Next to Neophytos's planned tomb, Theodore painted a Virgin and Child. Mary holds a scroll that reads, "Grant, O my Son, remission to him that lies here." Christ's answer is also written: "I grant it, moved as I am by thy prayers."[35] Perhaps images such as this were born from

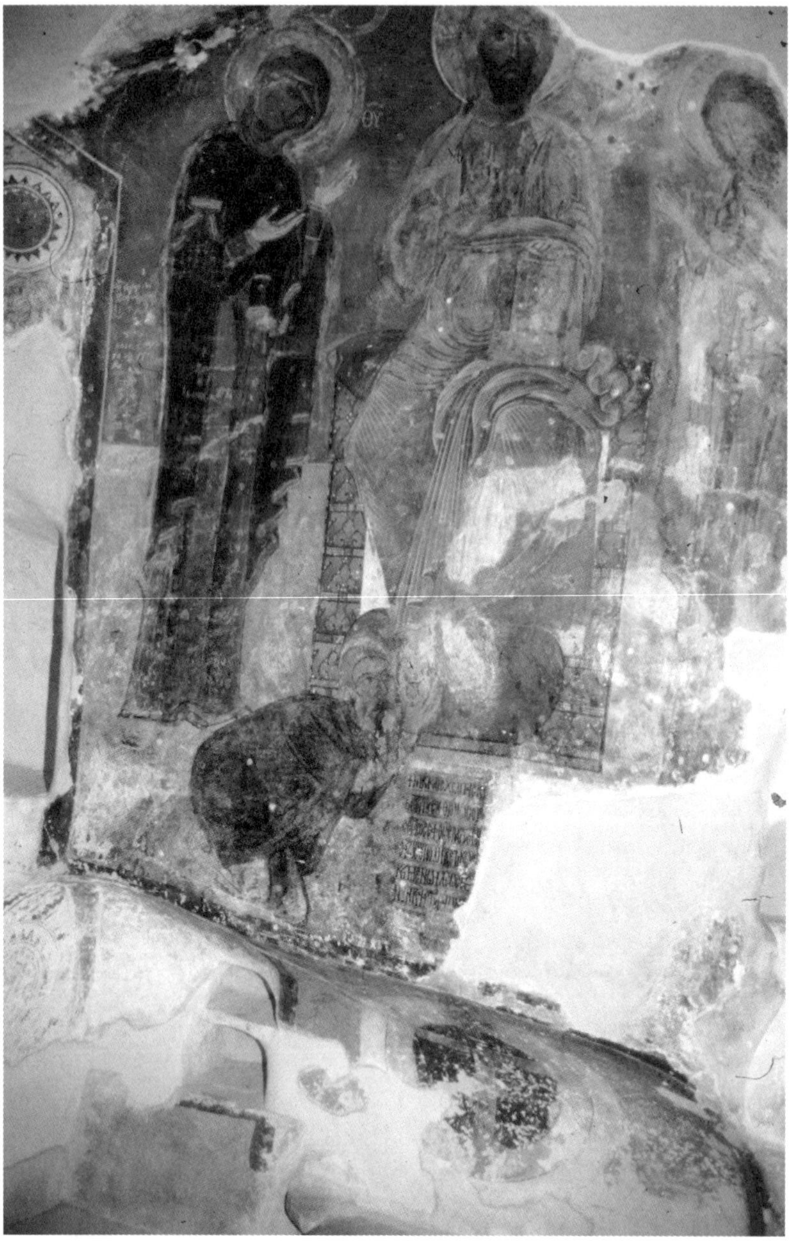

Figure 2.4. Neophytos kneeling beneath the Deësis (Jesus flanked by Mary and John the Baptist) at the Hideaway.

Neophytos's richly imaginative prayer life. Which is to say, long before contemporary psychologists refined the practice of active imagination, and well before Ignatius of Loyola systemized the long-standing meditation strategy of imagining oneself in biblical scenes, Neophytos pioneered this technique himself.[36] He dared to imagine himself interacting with key biblical figures, using a "kinetic and participatory contemplation."[37] He then had Theodore enshrine such meditations in paint. In addition, Neophytos was profoundly aware of, and made his own contributions to, sophisticated theological debates taking place in Constantinople.[38] Both of these traits—Neophytos's imaginative recasting of biblical scenes and his creative intervention in theological controversy—would mark the later work of Theodore Apsevdis as well.

Day in and day out, Theodore Apsevdis labored on these frescoes— and he lets us know it. An artist's signature survives at the bottom of one composition, painted just above Neophytos's writing desk. Which is to say, the artist too asserted himself. Only 15 percent of late Byzantine churches that survive contain the names of artists.[39] And when they do, artists go out of their way to avoid self-exaltation.[40] But there is no such debasement here. Instead, the signature shows evidence of an entirely appropriate level of self-regard.[41] It is one of the earliest signatures on record in Byzantine monuments, reading, "The Enkleistra . . . was painted by the hand of Theodore Apseudes [Apsevdis] in the year 6691 [1183 CE]."[42] Moreover, the fact that the signature would be so conspicuous at a place where Neophytos spent countless hours suggests a sign of friendship between the patron and the painter. It may have been Neophytos who offered Theodore the confidence to so sign his work and who taught him the techniques of imaginative contemplation that would make their way into the next monument the artist would paint.

But all of Theodore's work completed at the Hideaway in 1183 was before the troubles of Cyprus. Soon Neophytos—surrounded by custom-painted splendor—would be chronicling an Orthodox Christian crisis of refugees: "Rich men have forgotten their wealth, their fine dwellings, families, servants, slaves, their many flocks . . . and with great care and secrecy have sailed away to foreign lands and to the queen of the cities. And those who could not fly, who is fit to set forth the tragedy of their sufferings?"[43] The answer to Neophytos's question came from the same artist who had painted Neophytos's enclosure: Theodore

Apsevdis. His future frescos would chronicle not just the prayers of an ascetic but the pathos of an entire island. Still, before the mountain church painted by Theodore that gave us the first Virgin of the Passion can be examined, it is necessary to grapple with the event that made this church, Theodore's masterpiece, possible—the Third Crusade.

❧ 3 ❧

THE CRUSADER CAPTURE OF CYPRUS

It used to be thought preferable, even in [the case of the Turks], to win them over to the religion of Christ by teaching and by the example of good deeds and a blameless life rather than mounting an armed attack. However, if war . . . were not wholly avoidable, that kind would be a lesser evil than the present unholy conflicts and clashes between Christians.

—Erasmus of Rotterdam, *A Complaint of Peace*

[When] we get a glimpse of how broken, how poor we are . . . the heroic male response is to attack it, fix it, deny it, or dramatically share it. The saint merely weeps over it, until its lesson is learned.

—Richard Rohr, *Quest for the Grail*

This Aryan, domineering thing in our culture springs from our failure at the Grail Castle.

—Robert Johnson, *He*

FOLLOWING THEODORE'S DARING portraits of Neophytos, the prized Mediterranean gem of the Byzantine Empire, the island of Cyprus, would not stay Byzantine for long. It was about to be pocketed by a king to fund his quest for Jerusalem. Art history's first surviving Virgin of the Passion, painted by Theodore Apsevdis, was a response to that event. As a result, the original painting, and the icon that came after it, cannot be understood without a full examination of what made the Christian conquering of a Christian island possible in the first place. The Crusaders may have set out to recapture the Holy Land, but the third of these missions precipitated the birth of a global icon instead.

Jerusalem Lost

THOUGH ABLE TO capture Jerusalem at the end of the First Crusade in 1099, the Crusaders were not able to keep it. The city slipped through the fingers of a French knight named Guy de Lusignan (ca. 1150–94). This ambitious adventurer from the Lusignan region of western France arrived in Palestine hoping to make a name for himself, and his gamble was rewarded. Guy soon gained the title "king of Jerusalem" through both his charm and dumb luck. Charm won him the heart of Sibylla, the sister of Jerusalem's famous leper king, Baldwin IV (r. 1174–85). Guy and Sibylla were wed, and as Guy's luck would have it, both Baldwin IV and his child successor died, making Sibylla queen and Guy king by default.

However, so few in the Crusader court of Jerusalem trusted this Lusignan upstart that Sibylla was forced to agree to a divorce. She consented but shrewdly secured the condition that thereafter, she could marry whomsoever she desired. Her request was granted, and to the frustration of her handlers, Sibylla chose for her next husband the man from whom she had just been divorced, citing the unrestrained condition.[1] Having outwitted her managers, Sibylla proudly placed the crown on Guy herself.

It was a terrible second wedding gift. As one contemporary chronicler put it, Guy "did not carefully appraise his own strength in comparison to the obligation that he assumed. His strength and his prudence were not equal to the intolerable burden . . . placed upon his shoulders."[2] The powerful barons of Jerusalem, moreover, described him as *simplex et insufficiens* (softheaded and inadequate).[3]

At the outset of his reign, Guy showed wisdom in refusing to directly challenge Saladin (ca. 1137–93), the formidable sultan of Egypt and Syria. What was wise in practice, however, compromised his reputation, and Guy was accused of cowardice.[4] Accordingly, when another opportunity to challenge Saladin emerged, the Lusignan, yielding to a bellicose midnight advisor from the Knights Templar, took the bait.[5]

Responding to Saladin's capture of Tiberias, a Crusader town perched on the Sea of Galilee, Guy foolishly mobilized the Crusader army. After a grueling summer march, his exhausted forces hunkered down on an extinct volcano for a miserable night. Its twin peaks gave it the name the Horns of Hattin, the theater of Guy's defeat. Saladin shrewdly stopped up the wells, controlled access to the shoreline, and lit brushfires to further increase the thirst of his victims the next morning.

Waiting until the day's maximum heat to attack, Saladin routed the Crusader army on July 4, 1187, in view of the Sea of Galilee, beside which the beatitudes had been preached.

In the closing ceremonies of the Battle of Hattin, Sufis and scholars in Saladin's entourage were each granted the privilege to personally behead the most respected warriors—the Knights Templar and Hospitallers—themselves. "I saw how [they] killed unbelief to give life to Islam and destroyed polytheism to build monotheism," wrote the Muslim witness Imad al-Din.[6] A Christian chronicler was just as severe, claiming Saladin to be an instrument of Christ for the punishment of Crusader sin.[7]

Those among the captured who could not gain a ransom were put up for sale in the Damascus market, where oversupply caused the price of slaves to plummet.[8] Fortunately for Guy, Saladin's policy with defeated kings was to catch and release. Saladin even offered his delirious royal victim some iced julep to quench his thirst. When Guy in turn offered some to his companion, Raynald of Châtillon—who had slain pilgrims headed for Mecca—Saladin decapitated Raynald before he could drink it. The cup of mercy, Guy learned, was not to be shared.[9]

The Third Crusade

IN THE WAKE of the disaster at Hattin, Crusader fortresses fell one by one, inevitably including the stronghold of Jerusalem itself. As news of the city's fall rippled through Europe, it led to a frail Pope Urban III's early death. Within weeks, his successor, Pope Gregory VIII, called a for a new Crusade. The papal bull, *Audita Tremendi*, struck a penitential note and promised "full remission of their sins and eternal life to those who take up the labor of this journey with a contrite heart and a humble spirit and depart in penitence of their sins and with true faith."[10]

Pope Gregory VIII's call was heeded. It was even enough to cause the kings of England and France to put aside their differences, or so it appeared, and launch what became known as the Third Crusade. And so, on July 4, 1190—three years to the day from Saladin's triumph at Hattin—King Richard the Lionheart of England (1157–99) and King Philip Augustus of France (1165–1223) met together at Vézelay Abbey in central France. After all, a dual mission conveniently ensured that neither could confiscate the other absentee's land.

Vézelay Abbey was a fitting point of departure. The famous Cistercian monk Bernard of Clairvaux (1090–153) had preached a call for the previous Crusade from this town in 1147. So many had responded to his appeal that he ran out of fabric for the cloth crosses made on the spot to mark new recruits. Ever the showman, Bernard supplemented the lack by tearing his own habit into strips to make more.[11] But there was an embarrassing breach between the dazzling success of Bernard's rhetoric on that occasion and the failure of the mission he inspired. The Second Crusade was an unmitigated disaster, and now even Jerusalem had been lost. The royal meeting at Vézelay, therefore, was a chance to vindicate the recently canonized Cistercian by launching a mission that this time, all who were present must have prayed, would succeed. Bernard himself complained that "you will find very few men in the vast multitude of throngs to the Holy Land who have not been unbelieving scoundrels, sacrilegious plunderers, homicides, perjurers, adulterers, whose departure from Europe is certainly a double benefit, seeing that people in Europe are glad to see the back of them."[12] That accusation, however, could not be leveled at a Crusade led this time by kings themselves.

Richard, tall with reddish-blond hair, was thirty-three years old. His good looks were spiked with vanity but mellowed with a healthy sense of humor, and he exhibited justified confidence. He would show himself one of the most, if not the most, capable military commanders of the entire crusading enterprise. Philip was shorter, blind in one eye, a decade younger, and would be cast in Richard's shadow both during his lifetime and in historical memory. Still, the French king might already have been planning an early return to capitalize on his able competitor's Levantine delay.

Before their departure, Kings Richard and Philip may very well have admired Vézelay Abbey's sumptuously carved tympanum, completed in 1130 (fig. 3.1). It was carved after the First Crusade in time to help launch the Second, and now it would do the same for the Third. Christ's massive hands emit pneumatic fire, and his robes billow in a Pentecostal wind.[13] He presides over handsomely invigorated, book-bearing disciples. Their knees, bent as their Master's, are poised to spring to the farthest reaches of the earth. The depictions of those who populated such distant lands, however, are not so flattering. Embellishing the archivolts are dwarves who mount horses by ladder; Siamese twins; and the pig-nosed, dog-headed, and elephant-eared.[14] In their discomfort with such exoticizing imagery, contemporary art historians echo Bernard's moralizing critique of the contortions of Romanesque art, and with good reason.[15] Playful as such imagery may have been, monstrous

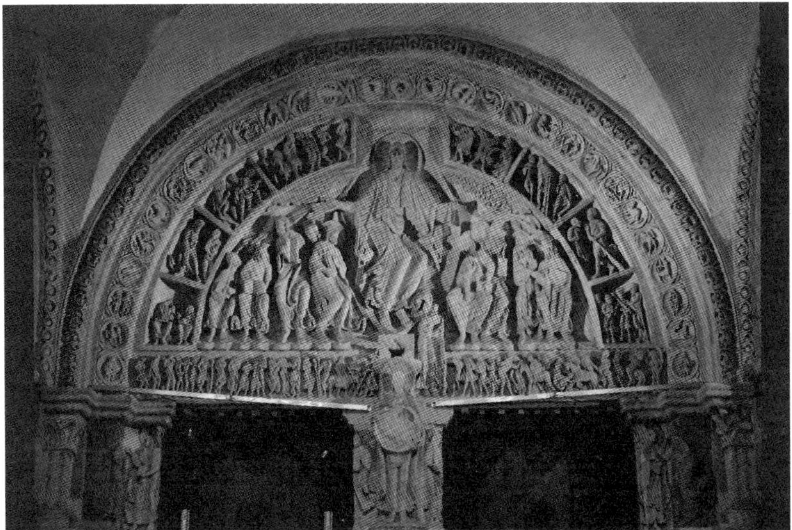

Figure 3.1. The tympanum at Vézelay Abbey in northern France, where the kings of England and France together launched the Third Crusade.

depictions of the subhuman have been correlated with a license to kill.[16] Bernard had even issued just such a license in his defense of the newly created military orders of knights.[17]

Indeed, so much unlike the apostolic mission depicted in the tympanum, the Crusades launched from Vézelay would bring not just a message but a sword. Galvanized by such depictions, the two kings set off, blades freshly sharpened. Following the legendary King Arthur, Richard had even gone so far as to name his Excalibur.[18]

Still, it would be unfair to suggest that there were no internal critiques of such ventures being surreptitiously crafted as well. Five years before the completion of the tympanum at Vézelay, Hugh of Saint Victor, just outside the wall of Paris, wrote of a more important interior construction: "You shall build a house for the Lord out of your own self. He himself will be the builder; your heart will be the place; your thoughts will supply the material."[19] And before the Third Crusade departed, literary critiques were aimed at the gallantry of the knights as well. One of the earliest forms of the Grail legend itself, composed by Chrétien de Troyes for the French court, was penned at this time. It described an able but foolish young knight named Perceval, who refused to ask the proper questions about life's ultimate purpose represented by the Grail. The account may have had Philip Augustus particularly in mind.[20] Perceval painfully learned humility and charity, at least in the realm of literature. Similarly, in 1191, the same year of Richard's conquest of Cyprus, the monks of Glastonbury Abbey claimed to have discovered King Arthur's body, inaugurating a great literary tradition of

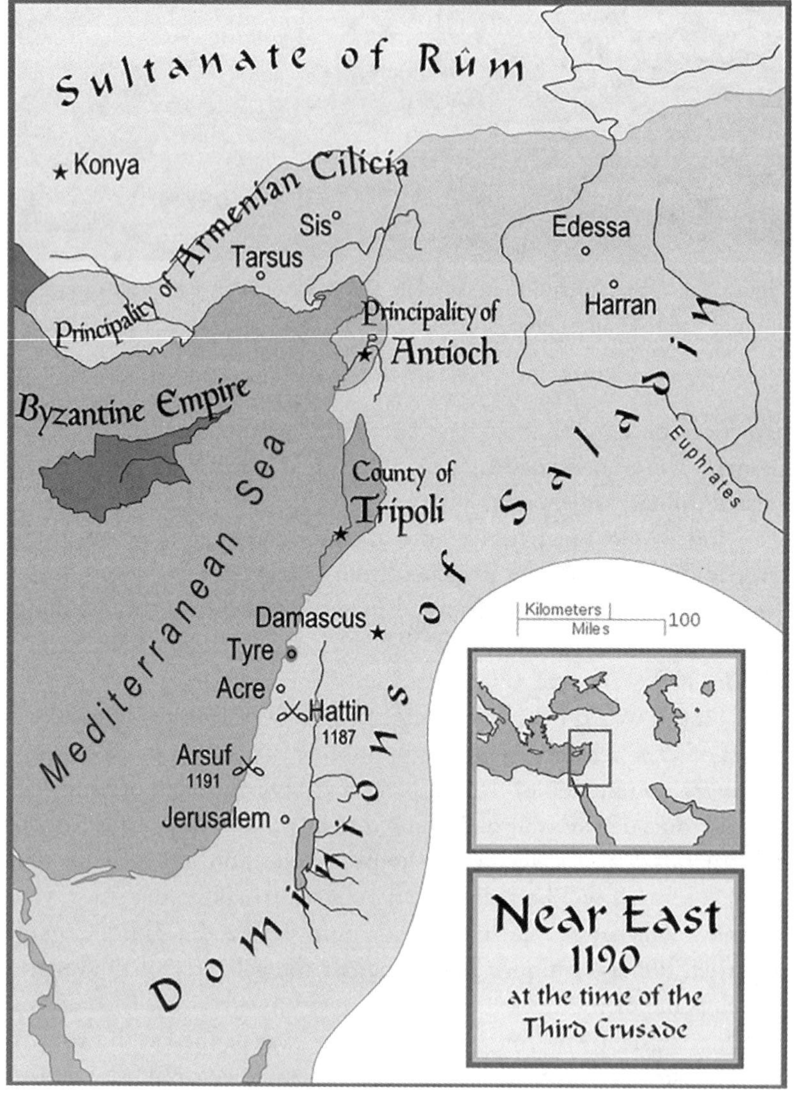

Figure 3.2. Theater of the Third Crusade.

Christian reflection more centered on inward discovery than outward conquest.[21]

But reading of this nature, and the lessons that came with such reading, would have to await the return of the kings. Now was the time to act (fig. 3.2).

Invasion of Cyprus

THE FLASH POINT of the Crusader attack was in Acre, a siege led by Guy, who was intent on redeeming himself from the disaster at Hattin. After a delay in Sicily, King Philip was the first to offer support to the siege. Richard, however, made an unplanned stop at the way station of Cyprus. The lives of the island's Orthodox Christians, Theodore and Neophytos among them, would be forever altered by Richard's arrival, as would the history of art. With this conquest, the conditions for the creation of the first surviving Virgin of the Passion began to emerge.

"When Richard's contemporaries called him 'Coeur de Lion,'" wrote Winston Churchill, "they paid a lasting compliment to the king of beasts."[22] Churchill's encomium is memorable, but the view from Cyprus was quite different. "The English king, the wretch," complained Neophytos, "landed in Cyprus, and found it a nursing mother."[23]

The island, to be sure, was ripe for defeat. Isaac Komnenos (ca. 1155–95/96), a usurper from Byzantium's Komnenian imperial family, helped facilitate King Richard's commandeering of the island. In the hopes of eventually ruling the entire empire, Isaac had been tyranniz-ing Cyprus for a number of years. When a storm sent a few ships from Richard's massive Palestine-bound fleet unwillingly to Cyprus, Isaac seized what he thought to be his moment, claiming the treasure of the wrecked ships and imprisoning the English crew. Anchored cautiously nearby was an additional ship bearing Richard's fiancée, Berengaria of Navarre (ca. 1165–230), who was then beckoned by an ill-intentioned Isaac to come ashore.

When Richard arrived, however, and the rest of his fleet with him, Isaac lost much of his swagger.[24] In a series of skirmishes, the king of England took on what was left of the Byzantine Empire in Cyprus and prevailed. Guy de Lusignan even arrived in time to lend a hand to Richard's island conquest. Having promised not to place the conquered Isaac in irons, Richard amused himself and his chroniclers by placing Isaac in shackles of silver instead.[25] Between the battles, the Lionheart treated Berengaria to a Mediterranean wedding. Aphrodite's isle was a fitting place for the occasion; but afterward, the new queen of England was granted a honeymoon of war.

Richard did not keep Cyprus for long. Hearing that King Philip was succeeding in breaking Saladin's hold upon Acre, Richard "gave a great and heartfelt sigh, [saying] 'God forbid that Acre should be won in my absence.'"[26] (Dante had yet to pen the *Purgatorio*, but his commentary "Envy's bellows pushes breath into your sighs" describes Richard well.[27]) The Lionheart departed for Acre, but not before selling the entire island to the Knights Templar.

These "defenders of the Catholic Church and attackers of the enemies of Christ," as Pope Innocent III put it, were named after their headquarters in the presumed temple of King Solomon on the Temple Mount in Jerusalem, which they were charged to protect.[28] The knights were granted a remarkable range of privileges in the Levant, including the right to tax without being taxed themselves.[29] They had also developed an impressive banking enterprise, which is to say, they could afford Cyprus.[30] The island was sold for a modest sum, for which Richard received a down payment before he was off, having now added Isaac's ships to his fleet.[31] For the king of England, Cyprus had proven a lucrative landfall indeed.

Within a year, however, the Knights Templar had grown dissatisfied with their purchase, and the Orthodox population, forced to shave their identifying beards, grew dissatisfied as well.[32] Perceiving the weak position of their new landlords, numbering by some accounts only twenty knights, the Orthodox islanders revolted against the "rapacious and unpopular" Templar rule the day before Easter, April 4, 1192.[33] The Knights retreated to a castle in the central town of Nicosia, from which they sought to arrange for a safe departure. But the angry islanders did not grant their request.[34] Their hand forced, the Templars burst from their fortress to slaughter the Orthodox population. It is unsettling to consider that their deadly emergence very well could have been coordinated with the ringing of church bells and the first rays of that year's Easter dawn.[35]

The Templars were through with Cyprus, and they weren't even offered a refund.[36] They eventually gave the island back to Richard, who in turn sold it again. The customer this time was none other than Guy de Lusignan. Neither Guy's heroics at Acre nor his assistance in conquering Cyprus had been able to cleanse the deep stain of his failure at Hattin. Moreover, when Guy's wife, Sibylla, died, his claim to the crown lost even more of its power. Which is to say, as the dust settled from the multiple claimants to the royal post of Jerusalem, Guy emerged crownless.

Even after his successor was promptly assassinated, Guy was still not entrusted the throne of Jerusalem, which went to Henry, the Count of Champagne. Guy was, however, granted a consolation prize: the right to purchase the island of Cyprus himself. He paid Richard the same price as the Knights Templar. In this way, Cyprus became Guy's compensatory kingdom—a proxy Jerusalem for the man responsible for losing the city in the first place.

The French rule of Cyprus that came with Guy's Lusignan family was much more enduring than the brief rule of the island by the Knights Templar. Bringing with them refugees from the Crusader states, the Lusignans controlled Cyprus for nearly three hundred years.[37] In Cyprus's francophone phase, all the Western monastic orders—Benedictine, Franciscan, Dominican, Cistercian, and the Knights Hospitaller and Templar as well—crowded onto the island.[38]

Each of these orders built in the Gothic style. It was an effective symbol of the new French rule—that is, the Western Latin rule—of Cyprus (fig. 3.3). We might, therefore, call these buildings "colonial

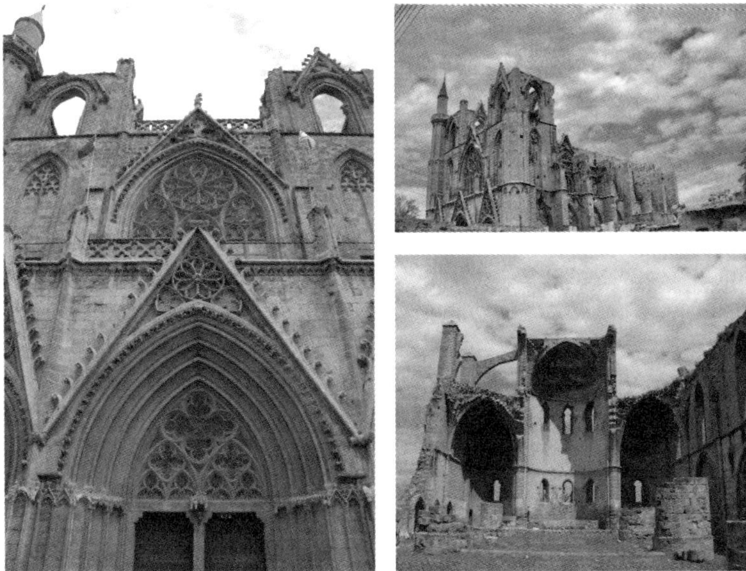

Figure 3.3. French Gothic style in Famagusta, Cyprus, was so dominant that even the Orthodox church in town (bottom right) employed it.

Gothic." Flying buttresses and pointed arches spread across the island like a Parisian garment, accounting for the architectural mélange that marks the island's urban centers to this day, whether in the modern capital of Nicosia or in Famagusta.

Eventually, even the Orthodox—whose urban bishops had been subordinated to the Latin church hierarchy—found themselves imitating the French architectural style (fig. 3.3).[39] But not in the hills. There, the humble beauty of the Orthodox church interior, each corner crammed with custom Orthodox saints, held its sacred ground.

Theodore Apsevdis, champion of the Orthodox style, was not about to carve in intricate French Gothic patterns. He had mastered not the chisel but the brush. He had visualized the sanctity of a recluse, and now he would find another patron, one who had been overthrown by the island's invasion by Richard. This patron, whose name was Leon, marshaled Theodore's talent to paint a lamentation for an island. Under these conditions, Theodore's training and his experience in Constantinople would be activated in ways that never could have come forth at Neophytos's Hideaway. Now, Theodore would be painting not to celebrate a saint but to grieve an unimaginable loss, one that the entire Byzantine world would eventually experience as well. For what had just happened to Cyprus would happen to Constantinople in just over a decade. But not before Theodore would replicate his own, more modest Hagia Sophia under hostile conditions, in which the first Virgin of the Passion would appear.

A century before Guy's disastrous career, the first ruler of Crusader Jerusalem, Godfrey of Bouillon, had refused to be named king in the city where Christ had worn a crown of thorns. Henry of Champagne, the new ruler of Jerusalem, similarly shunned the title that had caused so much rancor. Guy, by contrast, having been stripped of his crown and exiled to Cyprus, insisted on being called king of Jerusalem still.

But had Guy the opportunity in his remaining years at Cyprus to visit the church in the mountain village of Lagoudera, painted by Theodore Apsevdis, the Lusignan would have seen a painting that encapsulated centuries of Byzantium's hard-won political lessons—lessons that much of Latin Christianity had yet to learn. The Virgin of the Passion there would have offered a tonic to Guy's thwarted ambition and told the truth about his failures, though whether Guy would have deigned to enter a church belonging to the Christians he had conquered is difficult to say.

PART II

THE FRESCO

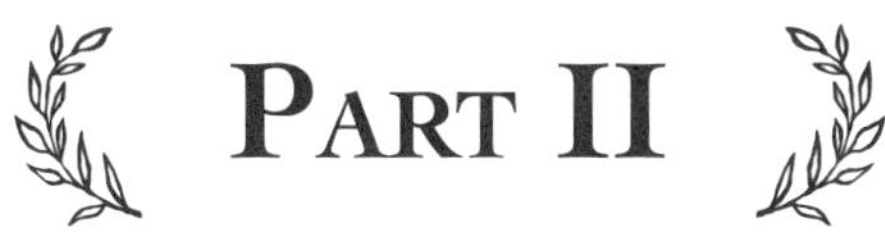

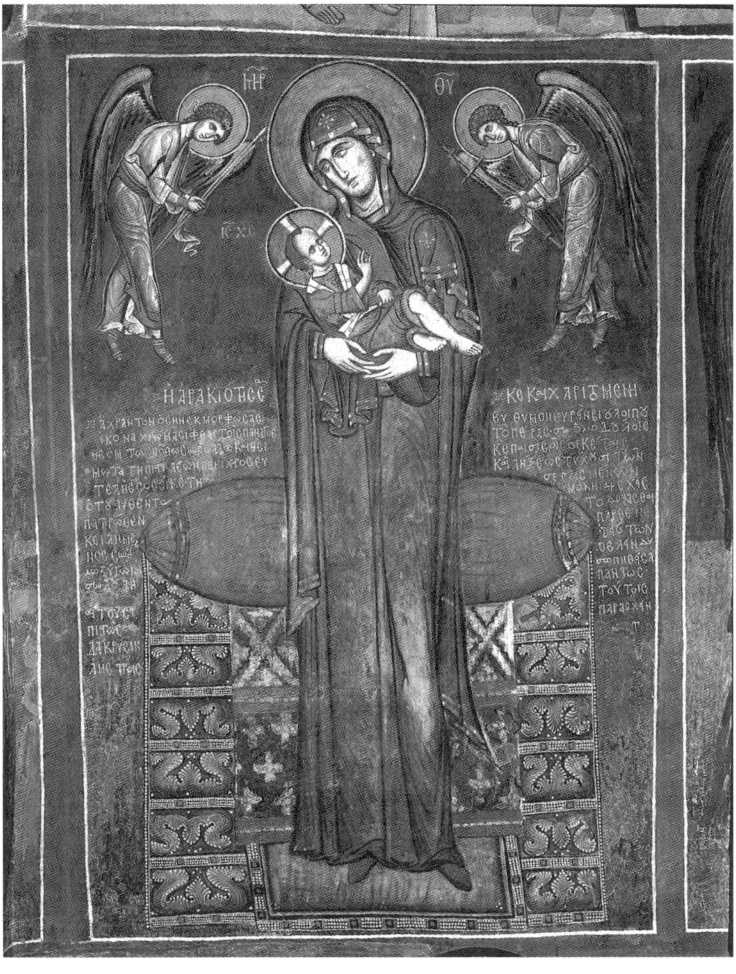

❧ **4** ❧

A TRUER CROSS

So many of our ostensible "goals," so many of the things we think we want, turn out to be the masks behind which our real desires hide; they are symbols for the actual values and qualities for which we hunger. They are not reducible to physical or material things.

—Robert Johnson, *We*

Our prayers are answered, then, by an enlargement of our capacity to suffer and accept suffering as an indelible part of our lives and the lives of others.

—Ann Belford Ulanov, *Primary Speech*

Byzantium always knew how to be humble in the end . . . even if it boasted about this to the Barbarians.

—Hans Georg Beck, *Byzantinistik heute*

The True Cross

THERE IS ANOTHER reason why it would have been especially poignant if the failed Crusader king Guy de Lusignan had wandered into the Virgin of the Vetches church painted by Theodore Apsevdis in the mountains of Cyprus. For in this church, built by the Greek-speaking Christians that Guy's Lusignan family had displaced, he would have found that which he—and all the Crusader armies—was seeking. As much as Guy must have hated his exile to Cyprus, wishing instead he had been granted permanent kingship of Jerusalem, he had been sent to an island that contained a painted answer to his catastrophic life. The sight of the Virgin of the Passion—with angels hovering above Jesus bearing the cross, spear, and sponge—could indeed have rectified Guy's failure, for the cross is what Guy de Lusignan had lost (fig. 4.1).

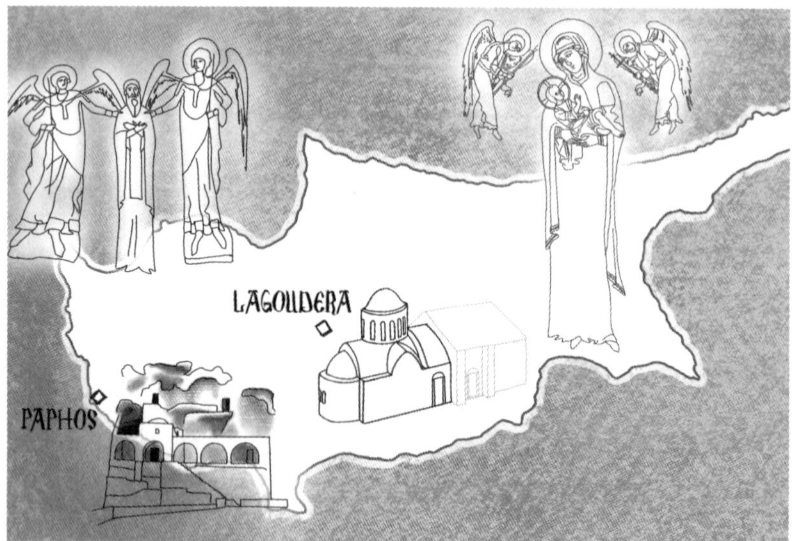

Figure 4.1. Neophytos's portrait and the Virgin of the Passion on Cyprus.

He had literally lost it, in fact. Recovering the "True Cross," the central relic of Christendom, had been one of the chief reasons for the Crusades in the first place. The word we use to describe these missions today, *crusade*, itself derives from *crucesignati* (those signed by the cross).[1] Moreover, the fusion of the red crosses that emblazoned the Templar armor with the recovery of the actual cross itself was understood as the culmination of their mission.[2] After they captured Jerusalem in 1099, the earlier Crusaders had achieved this objective. They had captured the True Cross upon which Christ had been crucified, presumably by torturing some Orthodox priests to get them to reveal its location.[3] Moreover, the recovery of the Holy Lance of Longinus, assumed to be the same one that pierced Christ's side, is what enabled those in the First Crusade to escape the Siege of Antioch in 1098. The discovery of the lance had filled the Latin Christians trapped in that city with such unexpected confidence that when they burst through the gates of Antioch, the Muslims—fearing some kind of trap—had let them pass.[4]

Accordingly, as Guy de Lusignan's army moved toward its destruction in 1187 at the Horns of Hattin, at its center was the Latin bishop of Acre astride his horse. He carried above him the True Cross the Crusaders had recovered. This relic, a testimony to Christ's great failure before his resurrection, could not fail them. Surely they were expecting another miraculous victory such as the kind that had been granted at Antioch. So great was their confidence that they flaunted the relic in view of Saladin himself.

But after the defeat at Hattin, the bishop of Acre was found dead, and the True Cross went missing, "raising the military disaster into a spiritual catastrophe."[5] Part of Pope Gregory VIII's appeal to launch the Third Crusade, which resulted in the sack of Cyprus, was to rectify "our ignominious alienation from our possession of the vivifying Cross."[6] Rumors swirled about its survival, and occasionally some Muslims claimed to be in possession of it, a claim that—when negotiating with Crusaders—was a very effective bargaining chip.[7] However, this large piece of the True Cross, to this day, has never been found.[8]

As much as the Battle of Hattin was a disaster for Latin Christendom, it was compounded by the loss of the True Cross, a disaster equal in the eyes of many to the ensuing capture of Jerusalem itself. Both of these failures rested on Guy's head. He was the reason Saladin had triumphed. Surely this was why Guy longed for the crown of Jerusalem. The chance at vindication that came with it might assuage the heavy burden on his brow. But it would not be so. What might have assuaged Guy's burden, however, was the message painted instead at the Virgin of the Vetches church. What required curing was the fever for the "True Cross" that had long gripped Christendom, a fever that the first Virgin of the Passion helped to break.

The angels that bear the cross and lance in the Virgin of the Passion restore to these instruments their earlier roles: not goads toward military success but emblems of a dignified defeat, one that was followed by a triumph—the resurrection—that transcended the merely political (fig. 4.2). In short, Theodore's cross was truer than the "True Cross" that evaded Guy's ambitions.[9] Painted as a mourning response to the Crusader conquering of Cyprus, it was tethered not to victory but to the redeemed failure that the original cross represented and that Guy's life—had he allowed it—might have represented as well.

The Cross in the East

THE BYZANTINE EMPIRE, far from being innocent of such a bellicose approach to the relics of the passion, had in fact created this attitude in the first place.[10] They suffered from the same fever, only they had suffered it earlier. Byzantine legend related that, after the famous vision of the cross that gave the emperor Constantine victory over his rivals, the

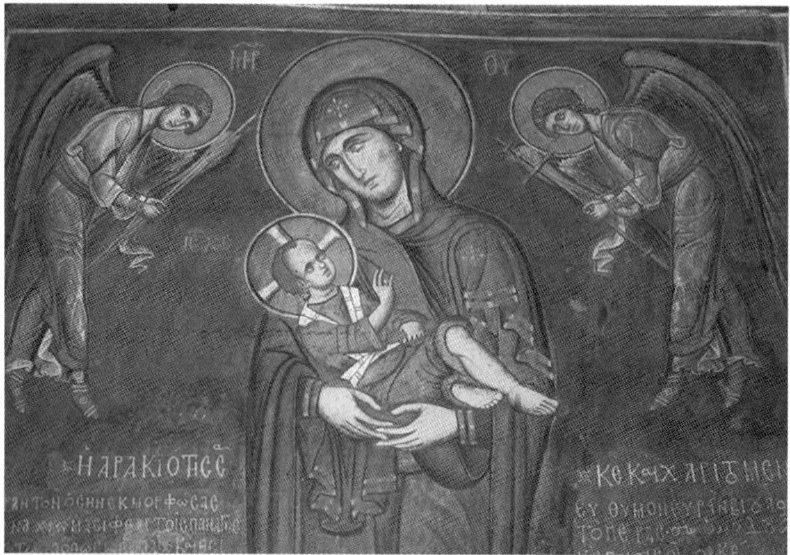

Figure 4.2. The Virgin of the Passion at the Virgin of the Vetches church.

True Cross was found in Jerusalem by Constantine's mother, Helena.[11] Very quickly, these legends were fused with an anti-Jewish polemic. Hearing that the local Jews refused to disclose its location, Helena's persuasion tactic was torture: a week's starvation in a pit.[12]

Moreover, when its hiding place was at last disclosed, the instruments of the passion were immediately weaponized. Legend relates that one nail from the passion was used as the bit in the bridle of Constantine's horse.[13] Immediately thereafter, Helena "stirred up a large persecution against the nation of the Jews and gave orders that they should be expelled from Judea."[14] So it was that the saving power of the cross was encrusted with the saving power of the empire. The largest chunk of the True Cross was kept in Jerusalem, where it had been deposited by Emperor Heraclius in 630 after he had reclaimed it from the Persians.[15] This was the considerable fragment that was recovered by the Crusaders and lost at Hattin.

But another piece was kept (and still is kept) in a mountaintop monastery in Cyprus named Stavrovouni, where Cypriot lore insisted it had been deposited by Helena herself.[16] Somehow, probably from this monastery, Neophytos had been granted his own smaller piece of the True Cross. It was the perfect addition to his enclosure, which was completed on the Feast of the Exaltation of the Cross (September 14, 1160) and was named after the Holy Cross as well.[17] The display of this fragment required an embellished presentation (fig. 4.3). This was another feature of Neophytos's Hideaway that a later artist, not Theodore himself, had painted. Right next to the cross was a picture of Constantine and Helena, a reminder of the fusion of the True Cross with political and military ambition.

Neophytos would later write that this cross was "the pride of the Orthodox and the fall of those of the wrong faith." The Byzantine Empire alone held the cross as its "most holy scepter" and "undefeatable trophy." It assured the destruction of the "infidel nations" as the "weapon of peace, with which the *basileis* [emperors] are armed for salvation, and hoards [*sic*] of enemies are quickly destroyed."[18] But almost as if to correct such triumphalism, Neophytos, contemplating his own mortality, imagined his coffin enhanced with wood that deliberately matched the wood of the cross.[19]

Standard as such thought might be for a Byzantine ascetic, Neophytos's approach to his piece of the True Cross is a far cry from the spirit of the first surviving Virgin of the Passion, painted by Theodore Apsevdis. It is possible now to imagine the humble Virgin of the Passion as a complement to the angels that flanked Neophytos's fragment of the

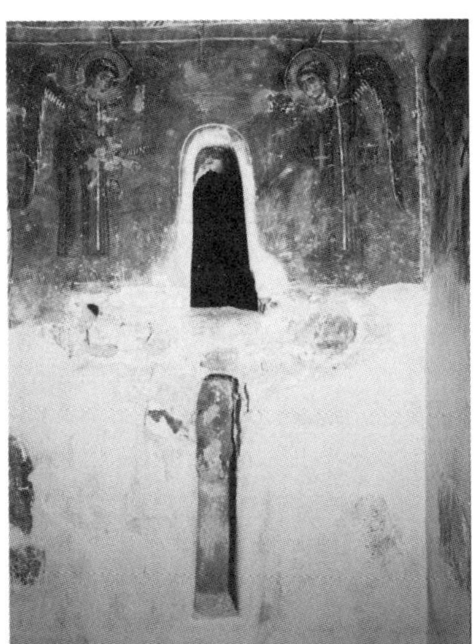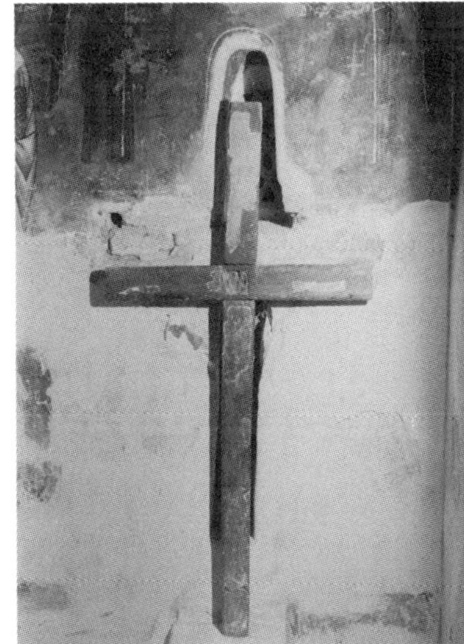

Figure 4.3. Neophytos's niche for his piece of the True Cross with flanking angels.

True Cross, offsetting political grandiosity with a humility more fitting for a saint. Even so, illuminating as such contrasts might be, it would be misleading to suggest this was all the enlightened notion of Theodore himself. He was not a war-protesting hippie in the disguise of a Byzantine painter offering us the twelfth-century equivalent of a "Make love not war" placard. Instead, Theodore was transmitting, perhaps unconsciously, a hard lesson that the Byzantine tradition had learned over centuries of devastating military defeat.

"To Lament Does Not Suit You": Byzantium's Early Mary

THE MESSAGE OF the Virgin of the Passion, in other words, had been percolating for nearly a thousand years. Although Byzantium had been intoxicated with political triumph earlier in its long life span, an intoxication emblemized by its devotion (imitated in turn by Latin Christians) to the True Cross, the Virgin Mary had long been tutoring the empire in a more excellent way. It is almost as if she was preparing the empire for its ultimate defeat and consequent resurrection in the form of the multinational Orthodox tradition that thrives to this day.[20]

The empire's slow progress from hubris to humility—which was, of course, never completed—is well illustrated by a different monument on Cyprus: the scepter-bearing angels surrounding Mary and Christ in the mosaic that still fills the apse of the sixth-century Panagia Angeloktistis (built by the angels) church (fig. 4.4).[21] If he had toured the island, Theodore might have seen it. Mary and Christ are here unassailable, their universal rulership emphasized by two orbs, not simply one. This unflappable early Mary is beautiful and dignified, to be sure, but less capable of responding to the sufferings of Theodore's island after the Easter morning slaughter of the Knights Templar.

The Virgin at Angeloktistis brings Byzantium's most confident centuries to mind. These were the years when Empress Pulcheria (d. 453), who had managed to marry without breaking her vow of virginity, went so far as to directly associate the Virgin Mary with her own virginal status. Pulcheria personally opposed those who would not grant Mary the title Theotokos (Mother of God).[22] Pulcheria was remembered to have founded three churches devoted to Mary in the imperial city—the Chalkoprateia, the Hodegoi, and the Blachernae—which would become the main Marian shrines of Constantinople, stationed like armed guards around the city walls.[23] The city's unofficial title even

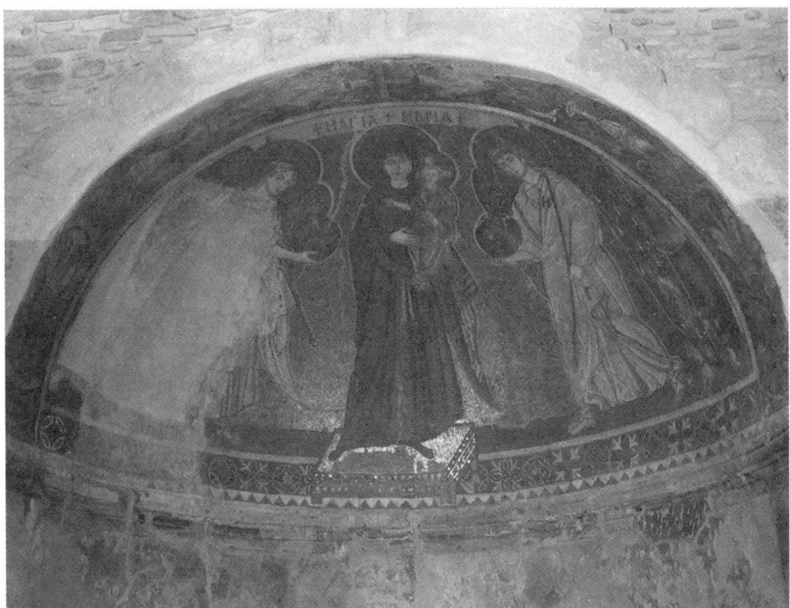

Figure 4.4. Early Byzantine mosaic showing a confident Virgin Mary at Angeloktistis in Cyprus.

became *Theotokopolis*, city of the Mother of God.[24] One of these shrines, the Blachernae, later became famous for its icon of the Mother of God (known as the Blachernitissa). In this image, Christ is exposed in Mary's womb as if in a modern ultrasound: a pregnant Mary marshaled to make a city impregnable.

Among the earliest foes in the empire's long line of enemies were the Avars. They were defeated next to the Blachernae shrine to the Virgin Mary in 626. A smaller confrontation near the Pege monastery, also dedicated to the Virgin, favored the Byzantines as well.[25] Indeed, this was the era when pagan temples such as the Parthenon in Athens and the temple of Cybele at Kyzikos became churches dedicated to Mary; it is not, therefore, surprising that Mary took on some pagan characteristics herself.[26]

But it was by her compassion that Mary conquered, something that is difficult to imagine coming from Athena. Perhaps to subvert well-known accounts of Athena's protective power, seventh-century Byzantine poet George of Pisidia wrote, "She [Mary] destroyed them by water, not by the spear," words important enough to be inscribed on stones at the site of the Avar defeat.[27] He continued, "As she gave birth without a seed, in the same way she now gives birth to salvation with no weapons."[28] Likewise, George writes of Mary, "She alone can triumph forever over nature, first in her conception and second in battle."[29] Such rhetoric may have functioned as a subtle critique, not a facile absorption, of the pagan warrior-goddess inheritance. Even in early Byzantium, "victory had nothing to do with how anyone fought and everything to do with prayer, compassion, and repentance."[30] But scandalous as that might be to militaristic logic, soon the great Marian shrines would be associated not only with victory but also with defeat.[31]

Anticipations of Theodore's Virgin of the Passion

WHEN THE ANGELOKTISTIS church was constructed, the Byzantine Empire could still imagine the time of Emperor Justinian (r. 527–65), who constructed Hagia Sophia. But the crisis the Byzantine Empire faced in the seventh century alone was nothing less than "the greatest series of conquests in the shortest period of time that the world has ever seen."[32] It was an onslaught, first by the Persians and then by Islam, "more rapid and more wide-ranging than those of Alexander the Great, more long-lasting than those of the Huns in the fourth and fifth centuries or the Mongol empire in the twelfth and thirteenth centuries."[33] It is no surprise that such an apocalypse would leave an indelible impression on Byzantine Mariology. The empire, after all, was facing new challenges that Mary the protectress could not address. New calamities were causing the Byzantines to bring forth valences of the Virgin that were hitherto muffled.

Under these new conditions, Mary was used not only to endorse emperors and empresses but to oppose them. Sophronius of Jerusalem, archbishop of his city from 634 to 638, was a fierce opponent of Emperor Heraclius, who had captured the True Cross from the Persians, safely depositing it in Jerusalem.[34] Sophronius appeared less than grateful for this imperial favor, however, and resisted the emperor's attempt to meddle in theological disputes.[35] In Sophronius's lengthy homily on the Annunciation, Mary appears to be deployed to critique imperial power:

> *You have demonstrated that the seats of the Thrones are second to you;*
> *You have reduced the loftiness of the Dominations;*
> *You have outstripped the leaders of the Principalities;*
> *You have strained the strength of the Powers.*[36]

Sophronius's most famous disciple, Maximus the Confessor, also emphasized this disjunction between ecclesial and political power, offering a "radical repudiation of the imperial ideological edifice."[37] Which is to say, long before James Madison, Byzantine mystics like Maximus had argued for the separation of church and state.

In the eighth and ninth centuries, when emperors endorsed the iconoclastic (image-breaking) cause to the chagrin of the monasteries, the cleavage between the imperial and ecclesial kingdoms widened.[38] Mary emerged as a quintessential dimension of the iconophile (icon-loving) cause.[39] If emperors had dared to remove or even deface images of Mary, the monks and nuns had preserved them. Byzantium, therefore, emerged on the other side of this artistic struggle (726–843) further saturated with Marian devotion but now very much in the form of images.[40] Imperial attempts to deny the populace their pictures of the Virgin proved ultimately futile. It is true that emperors and empresses after iconoclasm frequently depicted themselves on coins with the Virgin Mary beside them, her hands on their crowns. But it is difficult to escape the sense that these were crowns she might also be threatening to remove (fig. 4.5).[41] Depictions of the emperor with Mary and Christ were not just "propaganda"; they were petitions—a hope that thereby the emperor would gain the blessing of the heavenly court, which no emperor could control.

The Mary that was depicted in the apse of Hagia Sophia in 867, partly to celebrate the vindication of icons, is—in marked contrast to depictions of her in Western, Latin Christianity—devoid of imperial attributes (fig. 4.6).[42] She bears no crown or scepter or the dangling jeweled regalia indicative of imperial power, the *loros*.[43] Instead, a new maternal role is emphasized, a "special Middle Byzantine flavour" of motherly affection.[44] But this was more than just sentimental piety. Instead, this new Mary bore a deeper weight: the "universal potential of human nature . . . to suffer the divine."[45]

These new developments infused sermons. The Protevangelium, a companion piece to the Gospel of Luke, suggested that Mary, in compensation for the pains of childbirth that had afflicted Eve, had been spared any pains in labor.[46] But in the ninth-century sermons of George of Nicomedia, Mary's pains returned with a vengeance. Not in childbirth, however, but at Calvary. George the passionate preacher saw in the cross, spear, and sponge the delayed birth pangs that Mary had originally been spared.[47] In these sermons, it almost seems as if George is illustrating the

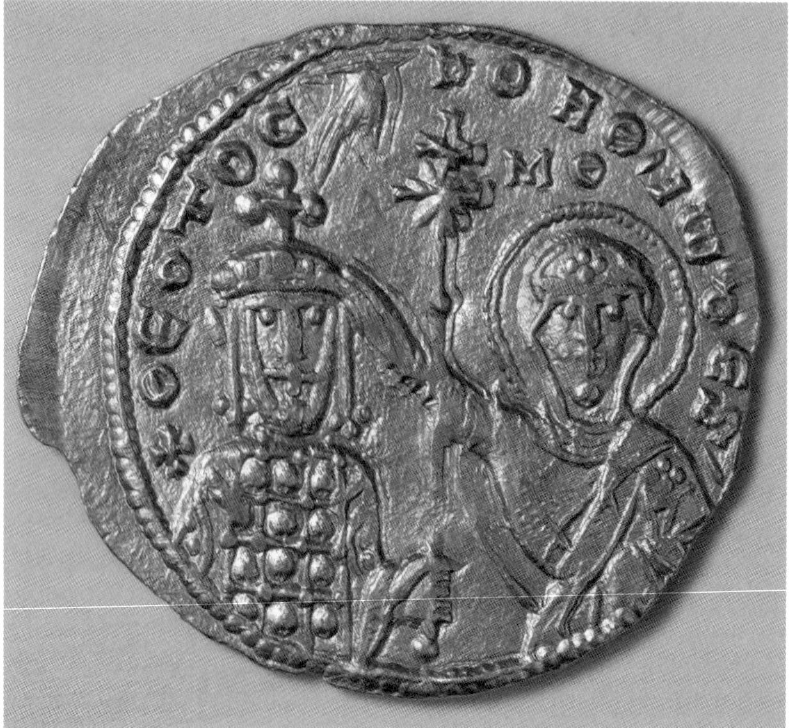

Figure 4.5. Gold coin of Mary with Emperor John Tzimiskes, 969–76.

Virgin of the Passion that was yet to come. The ancient Greek tradition of lamentation was finding new and unexpected expressions.[48]

In the tenth century, Symeon Metaphrastes contrasted Mary's joy at the Annunciation with her pain at the cross.[49] A sermon by Nikephoros Basilakes from the next century seems to allude to the reclining child in Mary's arms, similar to the Virgin of the Passion painted by Theodore Apsevdis: "Many times you slept on my breast as an infant, and now you have fallen asleep there as a dead man."[50] As is the pattern in Byzantine art, these homiletical and liturgical developments opened the way for new artistic depictions.[51] Such soundings were visualized in the mourning Virgins in twelfth-century Byzantine painting cycles throughout the empire, especially in the Balkans.[52] At Nerezi, to choose just one example, George of Nicomedia's sermons are graphically, even shockingly illustrated. Mary straddles her son, hugging him with her knees as if to give birth to him again with her pain (fig. 4.7).

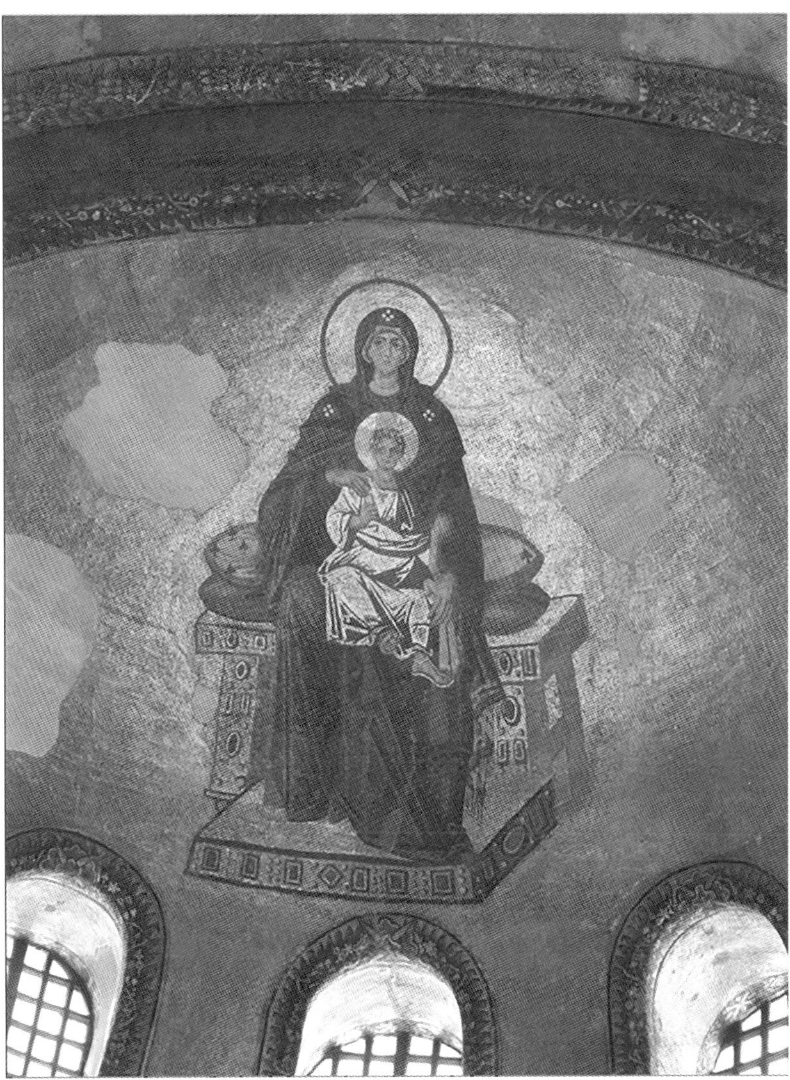

Figure 4.6. Apse at Hagia Sophia showing Mary lacking imperial regalia.

Unexpected as such a depiction may be, perhaps the most dramatic of these developments is the *Life of the Virgin*, which is attributed to Maximus the Confessor but appears to have been penned considerably later by John Geometres (ca. 935–1000).[53] For the author of the *Life of the Virgin*, not only does Mary's pain at the cross equal that of her Son—outrageously, it surpasses it.[54] "Take off, Mother, take off your

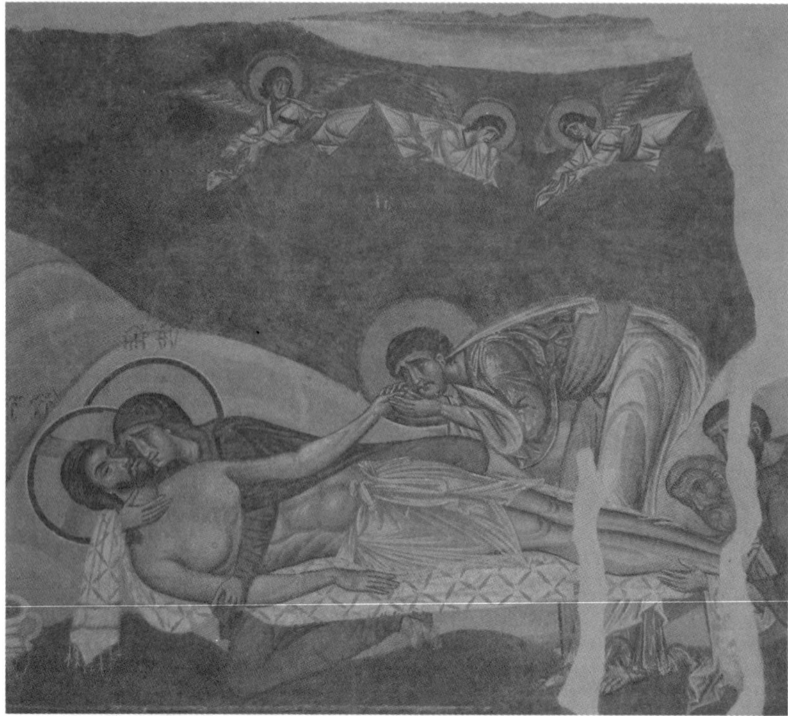

Figure 4.7. The lamenting Mary straddling Christ at Nerezi (1164).

mourning!" cried Christ to his mother in the sixth-century poetry of Romanos.[55] But centuries later, in poetry emerging from the very same church, Mary was finally given full permission to mourn.[56]

In the *Life of the Virgin*, as the disciples flee the scene of the crucifixion, Mary endures: "She was pierced in her heart because everyone had turned away all at once and become useless . . . mentally she was tortured and crucified with him."[57] The streams of blood from his wounds are paired with the fountain of tears from Mary's eyes. She hopes in vain to substitute herself for her son, and the painless delivery she enjoyed at the birth of her son is again reversed: "As her birthing was beyond nature, so also her sorrow."[58] Christ's cry of dereliction is even matched with Mary's own: "She stretched forth her hands, beat her breasts, and groaned from the depths of her heart, and she endured her torments and drenched the earth with her tears."[59]

It should not be surprising, therefore, to learn that in Byzantium's middle years, she bore associations not only with victory but also with loss. In the *Alexiad*, the Byzantine princess Anna Komnene reports that on one occasion—when her father, Emperor Alexios I Komnenos (1081–1118), was heading into battle—the weekly Marian miracle surrounding a famous icon of the Virgin at the Blachernae palace failed to occur, forcing the emperor to return.[60] On another occasion, Alexios attempted to take one of Mary's protective garments with him to battle, imitating his imperial predecessors, but the result was an embarrassment. Alexios stuffed Mary's veil into a tree and retreated.[61] Mary's power, once corralled by the emperors, began to (quite literally, in this case) evade the imperial grasp.[62]

These hard-won Byzantine lessons in humility, encapsulated in the Virgin Mary's transformation over centuries from residual warrior goddess to suffering mother, were not just curious episodes; they were codified in prayer and would have been transmitted to Theodore Apsevdis through the liturgy.[63] When he came to Cyprus, Theodore carried these lessons with him, lessons that he embedded in a conquered island's mountain church. The medicine for a suffering empire, and even for suffering souls like Guy de Lusignan's, was not the reclamation of the True Cross but instead the cross that loomed over the troubled Virgin Mary and her vulnerable divine son. There was a cure for vainglory and for any addiction to political glory as well. The tonic had already been concocted. Theodore's job was merely to administer the dose.

At the Virgin of the Vetches church in Cyprus, Theodore offered no false prophecy of impending Byzantine revival. The Byzantine Empire was finished on Cyprus; but centuries of deepening Marian reflection had ensured Cyprus was prepared for this defeat. Instead, Theodore gave us a postimperial cross, the Virgin of the Passion, an icon that would increasingly saturate an empire in retreat.

In the Virgin of the Passion, the same artist who used angels to depict the mortal Neophytos as divine was about to use angels to depict the divine Jesus as mortal. The contrast between the angels triumphantly flanking the recluse and the mourning angels in the Virgin of the Passion painted nearly a decade later is striking. The contrast between the angels flanking Neophytos's relic of the True Cross and Theodore's depiction of the cross hovering above Mary and Jesus is more striking still. The contrast between the bishop of Acre's procession of the True Cross in a failed pursuit of victory and Theodore's Virgin of the Passion that lamented certain loss is the most striking of all.

❧ **5** ☙

THE MEETING IN THE TEMPLE

[Byzantine artists] had great rational capabilities of expressing content by pictorial means with remarkable precision, thus conveying religious truths in conformity with the accepted theology of orthodoxy.

—Kurt Weitzmann, "Byzantine Art
and Scholarship in America"

The donor's grief is perceived through the transformation of the Virgin's image.

—Sophocles Sophocleous, *Panagia Arakiotissa*

The peculiar nature of Marian mediation is not that it takes the mediatory function on itself but rather that it only points to it, leaving space for it to be conceived, and experienced, and accepting and accommodating its humanity while paying full witness to its divine aspect.

—Giuseppe Fornari, *Dionysus, Christ,
and the Death of God*, vol. 2

[Byzantine images offer] the most subtle art and the most theologically complex pictures because they do not simply represent theology but enact it.

—Rico Franses "When All That Is Gold
Does Not Glitter"

IN THE SAME year of the Knights Templar's Easter slaughter, 1192, Theodore—a now marooned artist from Constantinople and the one-time painter of Neophytos's Hideaway—was summoned to paint again. Deep in the forested hills of Cyprus, beyond the reach of the island's new Latin rulers, the artist landed himself a job. We know the name of his employer—a dispossessed and devastated Byzantine governor named Leon, son of the authentes (i.e., governor).[1] Retreating into the mountains, Leon found refuge at the monastery that had been built by his father in a village called Lagoudera. The monastery's small church was known as the Virgin of the Vetches (Panagia tou Arakos), a name that derives from the wildflowers that grow in the region to this day. Besides two painted icons, this church, along with Neophytos's Hideaway, is all that remains of Theodore's work.[2] Leon could not have found a more fitting artist for the task. Centuries of development toward the mourning Virgin Mary in Byzantium were set to culminate in this tiny mountain church through Theodore's brush (fig. 5.1).

Perhaps Theodore's patron, Leon, had witnessed the revolt and massacre in Nicosia that year. Perhaps Leon had suffered some kind of personal tragedy in addition to losing his position as governor. Theodore had once been recruited by an imperially connected monk to bring his talent to a cave chapel, one among dozens of commissions that dotted a well-funded island. Now, he had been hired by a former governor to repaint what might even be called the Cypriot Byzantine Empire's tomb. There, in an act of mourning mixed with the paradox of praise, Theodore would paint not dreams of political glory but a faith that could endure the reality of imperial collapse.

Scenes from an earlier fresco series survive in the apse of the same church where Theodore painted the first surviving Virgin of the Passion. These paintings, limited to the eastern part of the church, evoke the earlier, more confident Mary of Byzantium's "magnificent age [of]

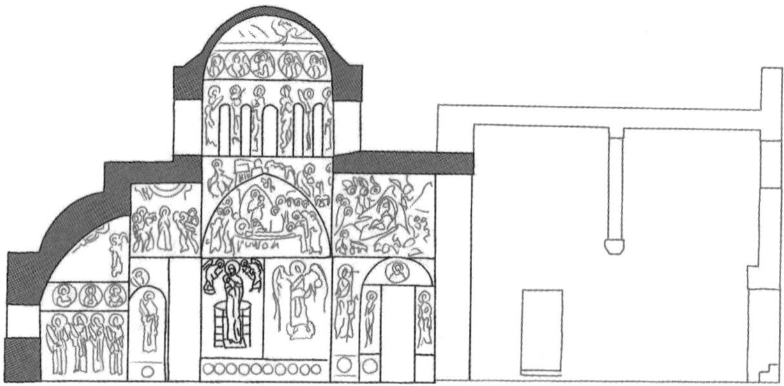

Figure 5.1. Plan of the Virgin of the Vetches church.

knowledge and prosperity . . . [and] courtly splendor."[3] Christ, seated on his maternal throne, is flanked by angels just as cherubim once flanked triumphant Israel's treasure—the ark of the covenant itself (fig. 5.2). Indeed, the apse resembles the sixth-century mosaics of Angeloktistis on Cyprus as well. Theodore no doubt had great respect for this painting that preceded him. He did, after all, leave it untouched. Perhaps his patron insisted that the suffering Virgin Mary need not eclipse the earlier one. Even so, Theodore's Virgin Mary would need to be different, for conditions on the island had dramatically changed.

Theodore painted the Virgin of the Passion on the south wall of the church in view of the earlier depiction of Mary in the apse. She summons any visitor to the church in her direction, inviting them to contemplate with her the fate of her son. Subtle allusions to the passion had long haunted Byzantine depictions of the Virgin and Child. Outstretched arms or crossed legs could anticipate Calvary; a sleeping posture could evoke the sleep of death.[4] Even Mary's heavy eyes alone could anticipate the cross. However, what was once allusion is made unavoidably explicit in the Virgin of the Passion, which displays the instruments of torture

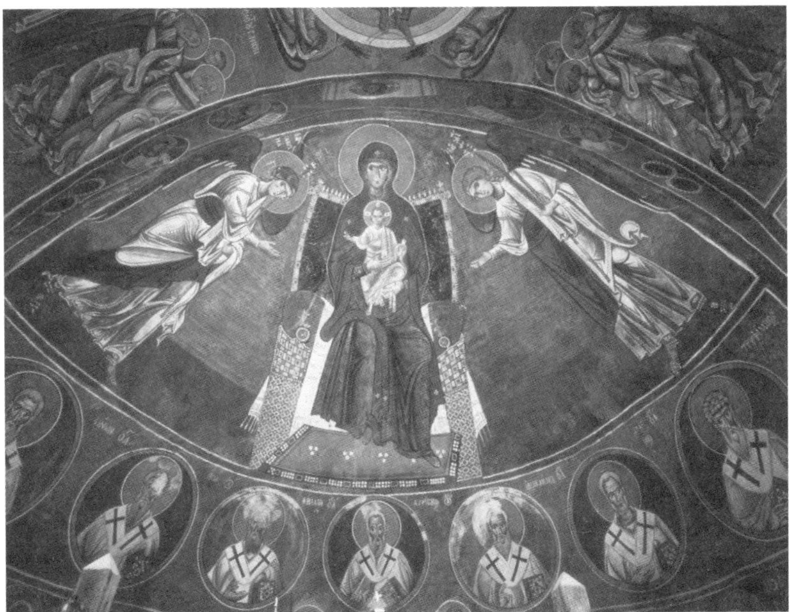

Figure 5.2. Apse at the Virgin of the Vetches painted before Theodore's intervention (before 1192).

themselves. The shock of a conquered Cyprus required nothing less. The passion is here not hinted at but heralded. The angel Gabriel had brought tidings of joy earlier in Mary's life, and indeed, he is depicted doing so in the arch of the same fresco series in view of the Virgin of the Passion. But this particular annunciation is not a happy one. Two angels in this case—Gabriel and Michael together—team up as if to ease the burden of such an unwelcome task. They are like police officers at midnight, burdened with informing unsuspecting family members of the loss of a loved one, reluctantly approaching a residential door.

On the right, the cross-bearing Gabriel announces tragedy to the infant who manages, impressively enough, to raise a consenting, blessing hand. His soon-to-be-pierced foot portends that he knew the disaster was coming. The foot also alludes to his ultimate betrayal ("Even my close friend in whom I trusted, who ate my bread, has lifted his heel against me" [Ps 41:9]).[5] His exposed leg is a subtle evocation of the recipe for the Passover lamb ("roast it over a fire—with the head [and] legs" [Exod 12:9 NIV]), showing him to be the long-prophesied lamb of God.[6] His crossed-nimbus, reclining posture and crossed legs allude to death, further assuring the immortal angel that this is news for which the child was prepared.[7] The cross is not his doom but his destiny. On the left, Mary nervously eyes the spear that hovers with uncomfortable closeness, calling to mind the words prophesied to Mary by the ancient, temple-dwelling Simeon in the Gospel of Luke: "A sword will pierce your own soul too" (Luke 2:35 NIV).[8] Indeed, to look at the Virgin of the Passion is to see with the eyes of Simeon himself, who Theodore deliberately painted just across the nave.

The Presentation of Christ in the Temple (i.e., "the Meeting")

ALTHOUGH THE VIRGIN of the Passion was destined to become a single icon, its first surviving instance is in fact part of a wider artistic conversation within the original church, requiring an intimate understanding of the Old Testament as well as the New. In the Hebrew Bible, in order to commemorate the Passover when the firstborn children of the Egyptians were slain, the book of Exodus decrees that Israelites "shall set apart to the Lord all that first opens the womb" (Exod 13:12). The ritual of dedicating the firstborn was known as the redemption. The purification of women after childbirth appears to have been a different ceremony, described in Leviticus chapter 12. Following a prescribed time of purification, "she shall bring to the priest at the entrance of the tent of meeting a lamb a year old for a burnt offering, and a pigeon or a turtledove for a sin offering, and he shall offer it before the Lord and make atonement for her" (Lev 12:6–7).[9] In the New Testament, the Gospel of Luke efficiently fuses these two moments (the redemption and the purification) when describing the meeting of Mary and Simeon in the temple.[10]

Luke then describes "a man in Jerusalem, whose name was Simeon," who the Spirit had promised would one day see the Messiah before his death (Luke 2:25–26). Accordingly, Simeon arrived at the temple when Joseph, Mary, and Jesus arrived to fulfill the customs of the law. Simeon was permitted to hold the Christ child, and while holding him, he proclaimed his famous prayer known as the *Nunc Dimittis*, which prophesied the sword of grief that would pierce the Virgin (Luke 2:35).[11]

Such biblical themes resounded in the Byzantine world, and a feast for celebrating the meeting of Simeon and Mary, originating in Jerusalem, became one of the twelve great feasts of the Orthodox church.[12] While not unknown in Byzantium's earliest centuries, iconography for the meeting of Mary and Simeon became much more common in the ninth.[13] There are visual depictions of the meeting that take place outside of the temple, which archaeologically would be more in accord with Jewish practice.[14] But in Byzantine versions, the meeting of Simeon and the presentation of the child are fused.[15] This fusion was justified by the mid-second- to early third-century Protevangelium of James, a "prequel" of sorts to the Gospel of Luke, which was nearly canonical for Eastern Christians.[16] The Protevangelium asserts that Simeon was the priest who took the high priest Zechariah's place after he was murdered by Herod's soldiers.[17] Unsurprisingly, this led to a nearly universal inclusion of an altar in depictions of the meeting in Byzantine art.

Theodore not only inherited this iconography but made a contribution to it at Lagoudera that constitutes a remarkable innovation. First off, he placed Simeon directly beneath Zechariah, tidily conveying the priestly lineage of the Protevangelium (fig. 8.3). But Theodore also went so far as to solve an iconographical quandary surrounding the meeting of Mary and Simeon that had been vexing Byzantine iconographers for hundreds of years.

Byzantine artistic experimentation with meeting iconography in the ninth century and beyond gave us a tug-of-war between Mary and Simeon with the Christ child caught in between. Sometimes Mary would hold the Christ child, and sometimes he would be held by Simeon (fig. 5.3).[18] Such

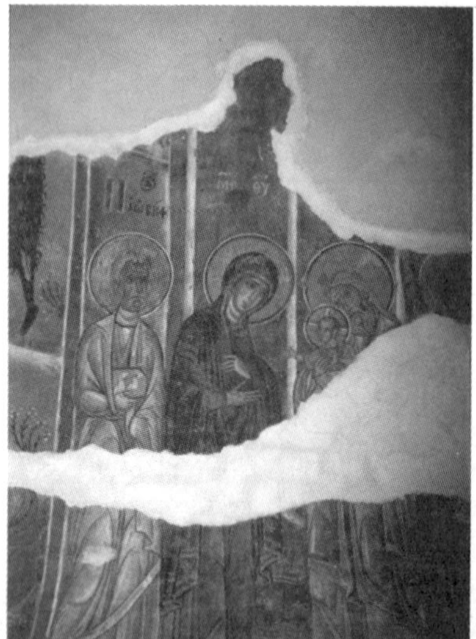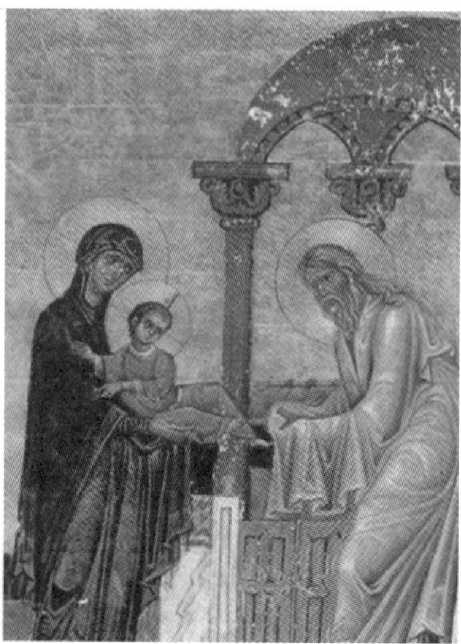

Figure 5.3. Wall painting of the meeting at Amasgou in Cyprus, manuscript of the Menologion of Basil II.

variation would finally be resolved, however, in the "final" version of the meeting iconography, where Simeon ends up with the child and Mary's hand is raised above the temple gates, which resemble the royal doors of the Byzantine church from which the Eucharist emerges.[19]

Still, long before this iconographical resolution, Theodore's unique approach to the problem took an entirely different turn. Instead of choosing a side in the tug-of-war between Mary and Simeon, he gave the Christ child to both of them (fig. 5.4). The altar in this case is not depicted because it is enacted in the actual sanctuary between the two figures when the liturgy takes place. Theodore Apsevdis produced a "split" meeting that offered a solution to this iconographical dilemma.

"The Meeting Is Ours"

IF THE SERENE Jesus in Mary's arms in the Virgin of the Passion courageously offers his consent, the Jesus in Simeon's arms shows fear. He grabs Simeon's garment; he kicks his legs in protest. If the famous icon of Cyprus, the Virgin of Kykkos, showed Christ in such a posture in the arms of his mother, now the genders switch, and Simeon is the one who struggles to calm the terrified child.[20] Christ may be simply acting as a toddler would when given to a stranger, but he also may be reacting

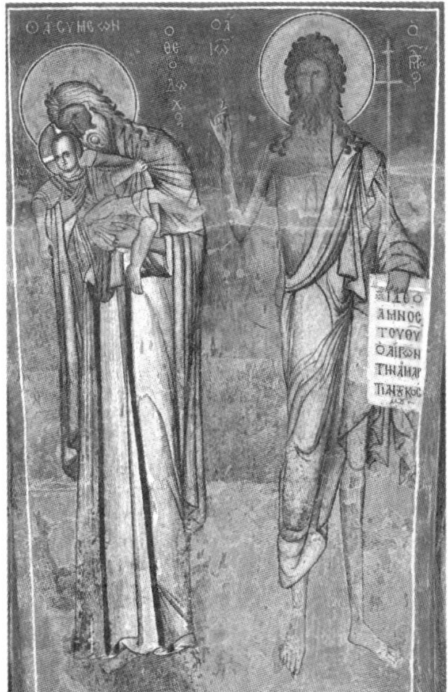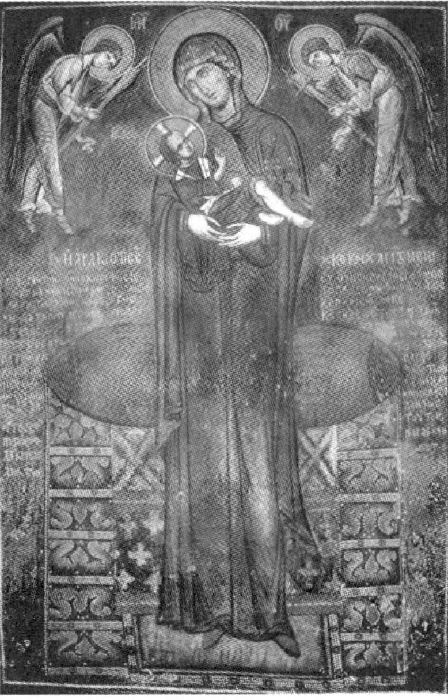

Figure 5.4. The "split" meeting at the Virgin of the Vetches church in Cyprus painted by Theodore Apsevdis.

to the sight of the cross that Simeon sees across the nave or even to the words of John the Baptist unfurled next to him, "Behold, the lamb of God, who takes away the sin of the world" (John 1:29). Centuries earlier, the desert abbot John Climacus had written, "Christ is frightened of dying but not terrified, thereby clearly revealing the properties of His two natures."[21] And now, in the conversation between Mary and Simeon, Theodore confirms this intuition in paint.

There are other clues to what might have given rise to such an unusual depiction of this biblical event. As mentioned, long before the active imagination of Jungian psychology or Ignatian spirituality, Neophytos the recluse had guided his listeners into imagining themselves inhabiting key biblical events, including the meeting of Mary and Simeon in the temple.[22] "Closing our sensory eyes for a little while, let us lift our inward vision and contemplate in our minds the pure Mother of God," Neophytos advised his listeners, "for she comes into our minds like a living Heaven, carrying the Sun of righteousness in her arms."[23] Perhaps Theodore had personally heard a version of such demanding sermons from Neophytos. Perhaps, just as likely, Theodore had learned such meditative techniques himself and was now giving them painted form.

The result is that Theodore's depiction of the meeting does far more than illustrate the fine points of biblical and theological nuance. It also makes the event present and immediate, offering comfort to his troubled patron Leon. If God in the arms of Simeon had feared, Leon the displaced governor could fear as well. If God in the arms of Mary consented to his fate, so could Leon. Ready to surrender her son to a horrible trial, here was a Mary to whom a displaced governor could relate.

And not only the governor; Neophytos's strategy of active meditation became, thanks to the paintbrush of Theodore, inescapable. "You see, beloved ones, how the Mother of God manifests herself to your minds today," announced Neophytos in his guided meditation session.[24] But Theodore ensured she manifested to the physical eyes as well. Theodore's unique arrangement means that not just meditating monks but anyone who stands before the Virgin of the Passion "becomes the Simeon—or as the case may be, the Anna: The meeting is ours."[25] The nave of the Virgin of the Vetches admits no voyeurs. The desire of scholars or neutral observers (as if there were such a thing) to view the Virgin of the Passion dispassionately is scrambled. Mary presents her son to you.

The Inscription

TO THE LEFT of the first surviving Virgin of the Passion is the word *Arakiotissa*, a reference to the church itself from the Greek word for vetch (*arakos*). Also in large letters to the right is *Kecharitomene*, "full of grace" (a reference to Luke 1:30). This title gives us possible reason to think the original Virgin of the Passion might be connected to another icon that bore that title, "Full of Grace," in Constantinople.[26] It was located in the very monastery where the Byzantine princess and historian Anna Komnene (1083–1153) retired to write her history, the *Alexiad*.[27] Perhaps the princess contemplated a similar icon as she ruminated upon the rudeness of the Crusaders, intimating the fate of the empire she had come to know. "For verily God has made me the repository of many sorrows," her great history concludes.[28] Still, nothing of this icon, or the monastery it was within, has survived other than written records. The Virgin of the Passion on Cyprus may be the closest we can get to what the princess saw.

Considerable portions of an elaborate prayer addressed to Mary accompanied the Virgin of the Passion at the Virgin of the Vetches.[29]

If Theodore wrote this prayer, then in contrast to his self-assertion in previous monuments, he now empties himself to become the voice of, and intercessor for, his suffering patron:

> *All pure mother of God, he who has portrayed*
> *your immaculate image in perishable colors*
> *with great yearning and most ardent faith,*
> *Leon, your poor and worthless servant,*
> *called after his father Authentes,*
> *together with his consort and fellow servant* [the name of Leon's
>   wife does not survive]
> *request faithfully with countless tears*
> *to find a happy conclusion to the rest of their life*
> *together with their fellow slaves and children, your servants,*
> *and receive the death of the saved.*
> *For you alone, Virgin, are able to be glorified*
> *When entreated to provide people with . . . t . . .*[30]

Whether Leon attained his petition—a happy conclusion to the rest of his life—is not known. Leon would certainly never regain his position of authority as a Byzantine governor in Lusignan Cyprus, nor was Theodore going to offer him false consolations of impending Byzantine renewal. Like the angels in Theodore's painting, Leon had traded his scepter for the spear, sponge, and cross.[31] Like Christ, Leon was both fearful and still somehow—in his better moments, at least—filled with faith. Like Mary, there was no part of him that welcomed the heavenly visitors that prophesied the end of his comfort, but he was prepared to consent to them nonetheless.

Beyond Balm

THERE IS MUCH more to the Virgin of the Passion than just suffering, just as there is more to the image than a complex illustration of the meeting of Mary and Simeon in the temple. Consolation is, in fact, only a small part of an elaborate showcase of Byzantine art and theology in the Virgin of the Vetches church, all of which radiates from the Virgin of the Passion icon. Leon, in other words, was not about to be defined by his misfortunes alone.

One modern admirer wrote of the Virgin of the Passion icon, "If I stand before this Image, I seem to see a sea, an ocean of ideas."[32] Many explorers of this ocean thus far, however, have hugged the sentimental shoreline, limiting the icon's lessons to maternal tenderness, failing to venture into the dark-blue waters of its underestimated theological depth. Exploring these waters necessitates a return to Constantinople, to the streets that Theodore Apsevdis would have once walked.

In the mid-twelfth century, the city was filled not only with icon painters but with quarreling theologians seeking the solution to a vexing, and not unimportant, question. The matter was finally settled, moreover, not only with arguments but with art. Theodore brought that art with him to Cyprus, where it infused his frescos at the Virgin of the Vetches church at Lagoudera and thereby infused the first Virgin of the Passion as well. The icon offers not only the depths of consolation but the heights of theological contemplation as well.

❦ **6** ❦

A THRONE PREPARED

The death of Jesus on the cross is God in three persons acting together, with one will, for one purpose—to deliver humanity from the curse of Sin and its not-so-secret weapon, the Law.

—Fleming Rutledge, *The Crucifixion*

No "part" or aspect of God—surely no divine person—wants to see me damned while another wants to see me saved. Not at all! God—the triune God whose essence is holy love—is *for* us.

—Thomas McCall, *Forsaken*

The mystery of the Cross of Christ lies in a contradiction, for it is at the same time an offering freely consented to and a punishment undergone entirely against his will.

—Simone Weil, *Notebooks*

Thou on earth both Priest and Victim in the eucharistic feast.

—W. Chatterton Dix, *Alleluia, Sing to Jesus* (1866)

THE THEOLOGICAL CONTROVERSY that so richly informed the first Virgin of the Passion was noteworthy enough—like many controversies in Byzantium that preceded it—to ultimately embroil the emperor himself. The row culminated in the years 1156 and 1157, making it one of the last great doctrinal battles that took place before Constantinople's destruction at the hands of Crusaders in 1204.[1] To explore the intricacies of this theological debate is to explore the ideas that directly gave shape to the first Virgin of the Passion in Cyprus. Wherever the icon has spread throughout the globe today, this answer has accordingly accompanied it as well.

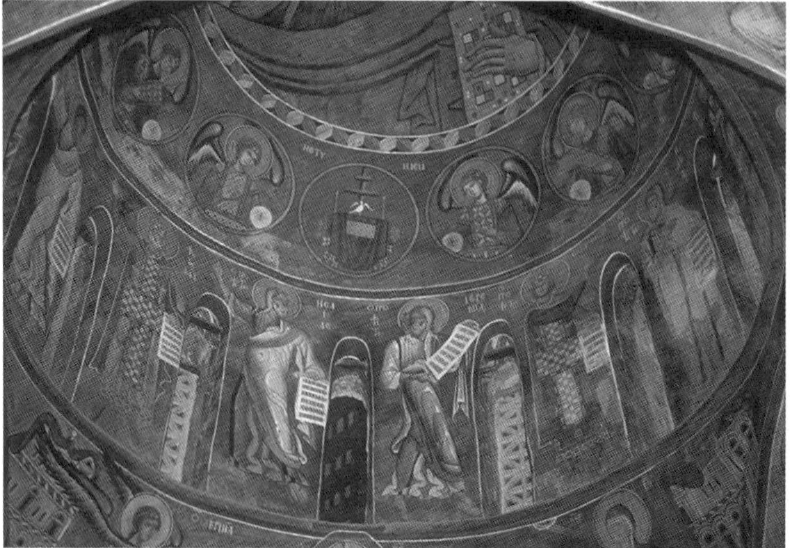

Figure 6.1. The Prepared Throne in the dome of the Virgin of the Vetches church.

Controversy in Constantinople

THE CITY THAT Theodore knew—with its competing monastic enclo-sures inhabited by educated, liturgically fluent monks—seemed almost designed to nurture theological skirmishes. Truth was at stake, of course, in these urgent wranglings, but other dynamics inevitably inserted themselves as well: a veiled jousting for prominence, the plea-sure of stimulation that comes with refined intellectual dispute, and the thrill of seeing a combatant's reputation vindicated or destroyed. While burning heretics at the stake was largely a Western Christian enterprise, losing parties in theological disputes could still be faced with imprison-ment, blinding, or exile.[2] Theology in Byzantium was a dangerous game.

Insofar as we can piece together the story from surviving records, the dispute that helped shape the Virgin of the Passion was ignited by a deacon named Basil, who appears to have been faced with some hecklers during one of his sermons.[3] Furthermore, these were not hecklers who could be easily bested. They were deacons by the names of Michael and Nicephorus; one was a professor of rhetoric who lectured on the Gospels at Hagia Sophia, and the other was a skilled rhetorician and man of letters who was an expert on the Epistles.[4] Basil had made himself some particu-larly learned enemies, and they chose one of Basil's sermons at the church of Saint John the Theologian, just outside Constantinople, to strike. For comparison, imagine two Harvard professors making a trip to the Boston suburbs to shout down a pastor during a routine Sunday sermon.

During the sermon, Basil declared something rather uncontroversial from a traditional Christian point of view—namely, that the Son of God and the Holy Spirit each received the sacrifice of the Eucharist along with the Father. Basil's logic was straightforward enough and can be easily reconstructed: Christians, although they worship the Father, Son, and Holy Spirit, are not polytheists. They worship a community of Persons in unified love, and this is a mystery that analogies from the reality with which we mortals are more familiar can only approximate. To divide the actions of the Trinity would therefore be to sunder a mandated unity, positing one or another member as a rogue agent of sorts. If creation, for example, was performed by the Father apart from the Holy Spirit, or if salvation was procured by the Son independently of the Father, then the harmony of God's work would be compromised, the bond of love broken. It therefore follows, Basil naturally concluded, that each member of the Trinity received the eucharistic sacrifice that was offered during the liturgy.

Uncontroversial as this might seem, it is here where Basil's learned—and obnoxious—opponents intervened.[5] They contested Basil's Trinitarian thought with a dilemma drawn from another branch of theology—namely, Christology.[6] Basil's opponents were well aware, as all Orthodox thinkers would have been, that the person of Christ represented both divine and human natures at once.[7] Which is to say, Christ encapsulates whatever it means to be human and whatever it means to be God as well. A less-than-divine or less-than-human savior, all sides would have concurred, made the rescue of fallen humanity less than complete. As Gregory of Nazianzus (d. 390) famously put it, "That which He has not assumed He has not healed. . . . If only half Adam fell, then that which Christ assumes and saves may be half also; but if the whole of his nature fell, it must be united to the whole nature of Him that was begotten, and so be saved as a whole."[8]

But at the same time, alongside Christ's dual nature, it was paramount for Christ's person to be understood as singular, lest Christ be viewed as some kind of ontological centaur or a divine-human amalgam such as Perseus or Heracles. The Council of Chalcedon (451), whose declarations were a nonnegotiable starting point for any theological dispute in the Byzantine tradition, had made the unity of Christ's personhood uncompromisingly clear.[9] This, Michael and Nicephorus contested, was the weak point in Basil's suggestion that the entire Trinity received the eucharistic sacrifice. Christ had to either offer the sacrifice or receive it. To suggest he did both would be to divide the person of Christ into offering and receiving parts.[10] "If one [Person of the Trinity] was sacrificed," Michael and Nicephorus inveighed against Basil from the peanut gallery, "the other received the sacrifice."[11]

It might seem a small matter for two academic types to register such an arcane objection in a suburban church—a mere dustup among deacons. But the charge was a serious one, and it called the integrity of the liturgy, and even the unity of Orthodoxy itself, into question. The Nicene Creed (325/381) had established the doctrine of the Trinity, and Chalcedon, meeting in 451, had established the unity of the two distinct natures of Christ. Now, however, Michael and Nicephorus, in order to humiliate Basil, had pitted Chalcedon against Nicaea, thereby threatening a rift in Orthodox thought. The controversy became public. Reports of a fresh theological melee, no doubt amplified by rumors and hearsay, rippled through the city's monastic ranks.

Looming Latin Christians to the west already questioned the validity of Orthodox worship, as did the Muslims who threatened from the east. Accordingly, the matter had to be settled fast, especially considering the fact that the visiting bishop of Kyiv demanded an answer before he left the city, lest any confusion spread abroad.[12] A synod therefore gathered in Constantinople in January of 1156 to put the prying questions of Michael and Nicephorus to rest. There it was affirmed that the "life-giving sacrifice" was offered to all three members of the Trinity. At this synod, Michael the deacon, and another supporter who had come alongside him, recanted.[13] Nicephorus the deacon, however, only dug in his heels, which resulted in his winning a powerful ally, Soterichos Pantevgenos.[14] Originally a deacon at Hagia Sophia, Pantevgenos had risen to become patriarch-elect of Crusader-occupied Antioch, and he came to Nicephorus's defense.[15] Pantevgenos, moreover, was whipsmart. The synod, in other words, had backfired.

Trinitarian Transactions

IT IS ADMITTEDLY difficult to reconstruct Pantevgenos's theological position, for as is usually the case in Byzantine theological disputes of such importance, records of the losing side's arguments are scarce.[16] But from what can be gathered, Pantevgenos appears to have penned a learned reply to the January 1156 synod in the form of a Platonic dialogue. Pantevgenos was not just intelligent—his arguments were considered formidable even by his opponents—but entertaining as well. With considerable style and flourish, Pantevgenos appears to have insisted upon a Trinitarian division of labor, with the Father receiving the Eucharist and the person of Christ offering it.[17]

But Pantevgenos, like many smart people, did not know when to stop. In order to maintain consistency, he then went on to make some rather bizarre, and even troubling, suggestions. Pantevgenos asserted that the Trinity rescued humanity in two discrete acts of reconciliation, one that unified divinity and humanity in the incarnation and another where the incarnate Son, on the cross, offered himself to the Father alone. In his attempt to rationalize the mystery of the Eucharist, Pantevgenos—it was charged—had now created a tripartite process of salvation. Humanity had first to be accepted by Christ, and only then with the self-offering of Christ would humanity be adopted by the Father, whereupon humanity was finally accepted by the Holy Spirit.[18] The love of God had been segmented into stages.

It did not help his case that Pantevgenos also appears to have supported his complex theology by suggesting the self-sacrifice of Christ in the Eucharist took place in mind and image only, which is to say, symbolically.[19] This move put undue pressure on the priest to reenact the passion in Christ's memory, as opposed to Christ officiating through the priest.[20] Finally, Pantevgenos's segmentation of the Trinity even entailed his denial that the liturgy could be celebrated in honor of the Trinity, since he claimed it was an offering of Christ to the Father alone.[21]

It is not difficult to imagine that the learned Pantevgenos had argued himself into a corner. His Trinity seemed rather transactional as opposed to a community of harmonized love. His liturgy became a juridical sacrifice as opposed to an act of free forgiveness and reconciliation.[22] His arguments seem a distant ancestor of those today that divide the Trinity by suggesting that God the Father, hot with wrath against humanity, was appeased by the comparatively compassionate actions of Christ on the cross.[23] In reply, theologians today rightfully posit the unified action of the Trinity in conferring salvation on the human race.[24] In the words of John Stott, "God does not love us because Christ died for us; Christ died for us because God loved us."[25] But helpful as such modern proclamation may be, a similar and far earlier answer to partitions in the Godhead came from Byzantium's collective response to Pantevgenos, a response that included color and song.

Beauty over Brains

ULTIMATELY, IT WAS the Orthodox liturgy and its art that settled this verbal theological skirmish. The answer would come not from logical deduction alone but from the hallowed tradition of praise, making this occasion a particularly fitting illustration of the famous phrase *lex orandi, lex credendi* (the law of prayer is the law of belief). Beauty would best these learned objections. Art and music would heal the divisions introduced by cleverly wielded words. Basil the deacon, it turns out, had ample support for his position in the divine service itself, even in one of its central moments.[26] This song was known as the Cherubic Hymn (a.k.a. the "Cherubikon") because it compares worshippers to angels.[27]

To exalt humanity to the level of angels recalls the fresco commissioned by Neophytos and the potential for undue exaltation that comes with it, especially for the presiding priest. Accordingly, the Cherubic Hymn was immediately preceded by a prayer, to be recited by the priest alone, that references human unworthiness.[28] In this prayer, Christ himself is entreated, who is—Pantevgenos appears to have forgotten—the one who is officiating at the service *through* the priest. In its earliest form, the prayer reads, "For You, Christ our God, are the Offerer and the Offered, the Hallower and the Hallowed."[29] This prayer, soon to be illustrated in frescos as well, was the answer to the brilliant Pantevgenos.[30]

If the actions of Christ—whether as priest, as victim, or as God who receives the offering—are unified, then the sacrifice of the Eucharist is indeed offered to the entire Trinity, including Christ. Nicholas of Methone emerged as the personality who drove this point home against Pantevgenos in defense of the prayer of the Cherubic Hymn.[31] To translate Nicholas's argument into grammatical terms, he claimed that the unified person of Christ, along with the entire Trinity, is at once the subject (the divine offerer), the direct object (the offering), and the indirect object (the divine receiver) of a single mysterious act.[32] As always in orthodox Christian reflection, the logical mind's tedious tendency to manage divine action is thwarted, surrendering instead to a register beyond logical control.

Even so, Pantevgenos demanded an imperial audience to air his views, and the request was granted.[33] At this gathering, Nicephorus the deacon at last recanted, but Pantevgenos gave one last gasp, which prompted the emperor to engage him in debate personally.[34] At last, Pantevgenos relented, presumably convinced by the argument that the persons of the Trinity would not exclude one another from honor.[35]

The upshot of the synod's decision, decreed in 1156 and then reasserted in 1157, was that salvation was less a complex transaction than a freely given gift from a merciful God. What were two separate parties for Pantevgenos (the Father and the Son) were, for Nicholas of Methone, conjoined in a single act of redemptive love. According to Nicholas, God "did not have to receive anything from us, [and] we did not go to him [to make an offering] but he condescended toward us and assumed our nature, not as a condition of reconciliation, but in order to meet us openly in the flesh."[36] The notes of unmerited grace in this statement should not be missed.

Needless to say, the now vindicated prayer of the Cherubic Hymn, "For You, Christ our God, are the Offerer and the Offered," was emphasized with new vigor in the decades and centuries to come.[37] Accordingly, this is how the prayer reads in the Orthodox liturgy today: "For you are the one who offers and is offered, who receives, and is distributed."[38] We can imagine the smile on more than a few priests' lips as they prayed the prayer of the Cherubic Hymn, perhaps a bit louder than the mandated whisper, following these tempestuous debates. They needed no longer be troubled by Pantevgenos's intellectual gymnastics, however impressive they may have been. The response to God's saving act of love was not the pedantic dissection of divine functions but praise.[39]

Still, the resolution to a controversy in icon-soaked Byzantium would not be complete without its visual dimension. Pantevgenos's tedious textbook of heavenly mechanics would be responded to with freshly beautified church interiors. This is where the Virgin of the Passion enters the story.

Artistic Ramifications of the Synod

LIKE A BEST-SELLING book in the present that soon becomes a film, the decision of the synods of 1156/57 would soon be reinforced in paint.[40] The question became how to articulate this fresh understanding of redemption in visual form. An easy enough approach would be to literally write out the prayer of the Cherubic Hymn on a scroll held by Basil the Great himself (to whom the prayer was attributed) and paint this in a church, a move that indeed becomes standard in Byzantine art just after 1157.[41] Indeed, a reference to this prayer is included, painted onto the scroll of Basil the Great, in the apse at the Virgin of the Vetches church in Cyprus, painted by the artist who preceded Theodore Apsevdis.[42]

Another development, however, was riskier. This move entailed somehow depicting the Trinity, a mystery that, by necessity, exceeds human vision.[43] Fortunately, there was one motif that was reserved enough to make this move responsibly. It is known as the Prepared Throne (Hetoimasia). This motif reverently "depicts" the invisible Father as an empty throne, lest God be mistaken (as God too often is) for a bearded male.[44] It represents the Son as a Gospel book and (occasionally) the instruments of the passion, and it symbolizes the Holy Spirit as a dove. This was the path pursued by Theodore himself in the sections of the church that he painted in Cyprus. Theodore placed this image of the Trinity—the Prepared Throne—prominently in the fresco program at Lagoudera, just below Christ in the dome. It is hard to imagine anyone making the point of the entire Trinity receiving the eucharistic sacrifice more directly than this (fig. 6.1, 6.2).

But the connections to the synods of 1156/57 are not exhausted by Theodore's dutiful inclusion of the Prepared Throne at a strategic point in the program. Theodore was not just a mindless stenographer; rather, he offered an impressive theological contribution of his own.[45] The painter also imbued the entire church with the spirit of the synods. It is almost as if Theodore the painter was trying to outdo Nicholas of Methone and the emperor's response to the sophistry of Pantevgenos.

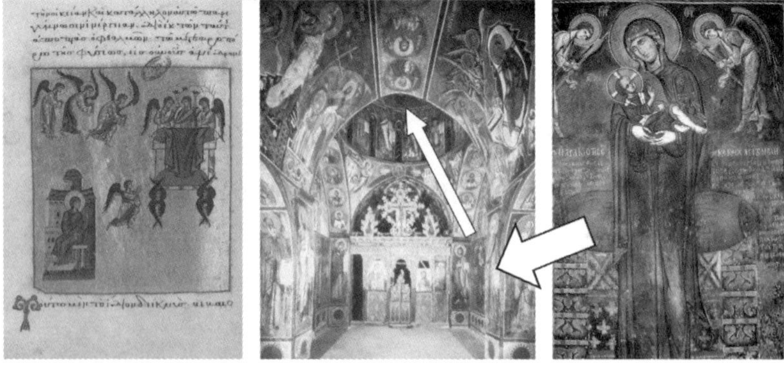

Figure 6.2. *Left*: Mary paired with the Prepared Throne (Vat. gr. 1162, 130v). *Center*: View of the Virgin of the Vetches church with the Prepared Throne and the Virgin of the Passion connected. *Right*: The Virgin of the Passion at the Virgin of the Vetches church.

Surely in conversation with his patron and other learned souls at the Virgin of the Vetches church, Theodore offered an unexpected Marian solution to the controversy that embroiled the city he knew so well.[46]

Theodore did this by connecting the Prepared Throne in the dome above to the Virgin of the Passion below it. Mary was frequently referred to as a throne in Byzantine rhetoric. As the famous Akathistos hymn puts it, "Hail, since you [Mary] are the chair of the king."[47] When depicting the Annunciation, Byzantine artists sometimes paired the empty throne of God with the throne of the Virgin. One scene captures the moment just after the Annunciation as Gabriel—having proclaimed the Word made flesh to Mary—heads back to God's vacated chair (fig. 6.2).[48] But Theodore connected these dots more explicitly. The drama at play in the miniature is enacted in the church itself but—reflecting the new political situation on Cyprus—with the added dimension of the instruments of the passion.

Unlike in the theology of Pantevgenos—where the love of Father, Son, and Spirit was compartmentalized and possibly even in conflict—in the Virgin of the Vetches church, the love of the Father, Son, and Spirit for humanity worked not in discord but in concert, "on earth" (the walls) "as it is in heaven" (the dome). God's throne had been prepared beforehand not to extract slavish obedience from fawning subjects but for humble service. His throne was not a majestic chair of a distant king but his mother's lap and ultimately Calvary itself.

How fitting, moreover, that Christ's compassionate throne-ship would be freshly emphasized when the Byzantine emperor on Cyprus had been unseated himself. The original choice of early Christians to emphasize Christ's throne was in direct refutation of the imperial claims of Caesar.[49] And here Byzantine art, after centuries of imperial grandstanding, was appealing to that original insight again. The Prepared Throne painted by Theodore Apsevdis, enacted in the Virgin of the Passion, alludes to a decision made before time began. Christ was "the lamb slain from the foundation of the world" (Rev 13:8 KJV). It is an insight, moreover, that political theorists today may find of help.[50]

This use of the Prepared Throne, however, unfurls even further dimensions of the original image, which requires exploring another far more consequential theological debate, all of which resonate in the original Virgin of the Passion and in its innumerable global copies in the present as well.

❦ 7 ❦

MARY AS WISDOM

[The Virgin of the Passion] is as complex as an entire sermon, but its theological arguments end in a presentation of a human ethos that accepts and transcends predetermined human destiny.
    —Hans Belting, *The Image and Its Public in the Middle Ages*

Sophia is the Memory of God, in the holy depths of which is all that is and outside of which is Death and Madness.
    —Pavel Florensky, *The Pillar and Ground of the Truth*

As in the first generation, the Creation, so in the regeneration, our re-creating, he begins with that which was necessary for that which follows, Mercy before Judgement. Nay, to say that mercy was first, is but to post-date mercy; to preferre mercy but so, is to diminish mercy; The name of first or last derogate from it, for first and last are but ragges of time, and his mercy hath no relation to time, no limitation in time, it is not first, nor last, but eternal, everlasting.
    —John Donne, *Sermon on the Evening of Christmas-Day*, (1624)

The Divine Eucharist is the sacrificial, crucified Sophia, the sacrifice of God Himself, and God Himself is the Sacrifice.
    —Sergius Bulgakov, *The Eucharistic Sacrifice*

WHEN IT COMES to refuting heresies, the Virgin of the Passion is at least two for one. The image does more than offer an answer to the transactional theology of the all too clever Pantevgenos that segmented the Trinity. The Prepared Throne painted by Theodore Apsevdis in the dome of the Virgin of the Vetches church, reflected in his Virgin of

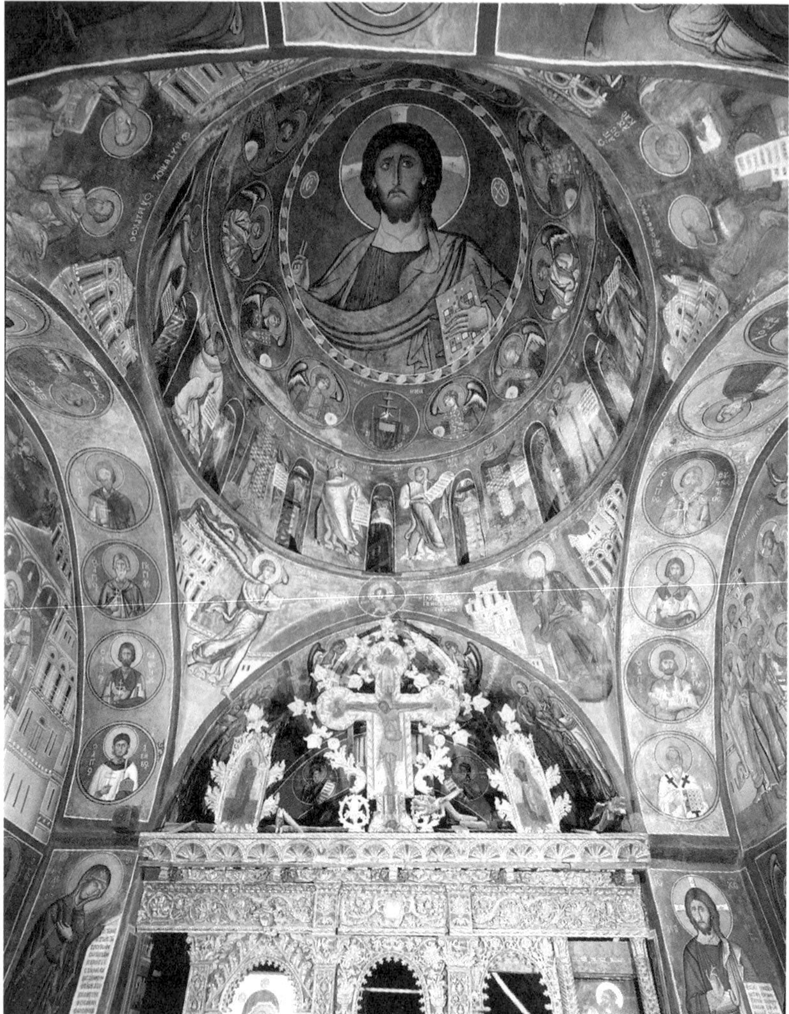

Figure 7.1. The dome at the Virgin of the Vetches church at Lagoudera in Cyprus painted by Theodore Apsevdis. The Prepared Throne is below Jesus, and the Virgin of the Passion is just below the Dormition to the right.

the Passion below, also drew upon a much earlier, and much more noteworthy, theological battle. The Virgin of the Passion also refutes the logic of Arius (d. 336), who famously denied the full deity of Jesus Christ, thereby generating the response of the Nicene Creed. This creed—the most important and universal in all of Christian history—is adamant that Christ is no underling. Jesus of Nazareth is not God's subordinate but God's equal, "God from God, Light from Light, true God from true God, begotten not made, of one being with the Father."[1] The debate that led to the Nicene formulation revolved around the female figure of Wisdom in the Old Testament book of Proverbs. In addition to the divine Jesus and human Mary, the Virgin of the Passion, it turns out, subtly evokes this Wisdom figure as well. Centuries before the figure of Wisdom was recovered by contemporary avant-garde and feminist theologians, the Virgin of the Passion ensured such Wisdom would be transmitted, however much that transmission went unnoticed by the modern world.[2]

The Battle for Wisdom

THE LIBYAN THEOLOGIAN named Arius may have had compelling pastoral reasons for his claim that Christ was less than God.[3] Arius was a shepherd of souls, and to expect his flock to follow a Jesus who was fully divine—it may well have seemed to him—was to set the bar impossibly high. A less-than-divine Jesus might at least give Arius's less-than-divine congregants a fighting chance at successful imitation of Christ. In addition, Arius, in tune with the Neoplatonic philosophical rhythm of his age, appears to have preferred a God who was placidly unperturbed, not eternally embroiled in relationship as the doctrine of the Trinity proclaimed.

Combing the Scriptures for proof of his understanding of Jesus, Arius seized upon a passage in Proverbs: "The Lord possessed me [Wisdom] at the beginning of his work, the first of his acts of old. Ages ago I was set up, at the first, before the beginning of the earth" (Prov 8:22–23). This passage was Arius's proof text par excellence, and the debate over its interpretation is what launched the controversy that culminated with the Nicene Creed.[4] By Arius's reckoning, the passage showed that Wisdom—which Arius interpreted to be Jesus—was not eternal but created at a certain moment in time. Jesus, as a result, could not be fully divine and was even "alien in essence" to God.[5] Proverbs 8 offered evidence, Arius inveighed, that God in purest form was a solitary monad.[6] Which is to say, even if Jesus was the first act of God, he was still an act, rather than sharing the being of God. In short, long before Pantevgenos, Arius had also driven a wedge between the love of Jesus and the distinct love of the Father per se.

If Nicholas of Methone was responsible for refuting Pantevgenos in twelfth-century Constantinople, it was the church father Athanasius

(d. 373), among others, who offered the definitive arguments against Arius and his followers. It would be a mistake to simplistically assume that this was because Athanasius had imperial backing. On the contrary, Athanasius was banished by emperors repeatedly, and it was often the Arians who enjoyed imperial support.[7] A fairer interpretation is that Athanasius was representing an already long-standing Christian commitment to Christ's divinity, one that was in place long before Christianity was even a legal religion at all.[8]

Informed by this already ancient tradition, Athanasius contested that Arius's pastoral logic was in fact disastrous, in part for the same pastoral reasons. A less-than-divine Jesus meant that humans were offered less-than-divine help. Instead, they only received the assistance of a semi-divine messenger who—because he was created "before the beginning of the earth" (Prov 8:23)—was not entirely human either.[9] If God had only sent a second-string messenger, Athanasius argued, then God had not bothered to personally solve the problem of human finitude and mortality but had only sent a glorified errand boy, however exalted this subordinate might be in comparison to mortals. Moreover, by assuming there was a time when Jesus was created, Arius projected a temporal understanding onto God, who was necessarily beyond time.[10]

To make his case against Arius, Athanasius had to grapple with Arius's prize proof text, the beachhead of his claim that Christ was not divine: "The Lord possessed me [Wisdom] at the beginning of his work, the first of his acts of old. Ages ago I was set up, at the first, before the beginning of the earth" (Prov 8:22–23). Athanasius, who preferred to read Proverbs with hermeneutical flair, accused Arius of a wooden literalism.[11] The passage had to be more than a simple evocation of Jesus. Athanasius pointed to the rather obvious fact that Wisdom in this passage is in fact female, which mitigated against a flat insistence that it referred to Christ.[12] In short, the "first of his acts of old," for Athanasius, was not simply a person but a plan. The Wisdom in question was God's blueprint of salvation, established in Christ before the world was made.[13] In the spirit of the ninth chapter of Proverbs ("Wisdom has built her house" [Prov 9:1]), Athanasius used an architectural analogy to make his point: just as a wise architect would first design a rebuilding plan for a given house in case it was destroyed, "so in the same manner our salvific renewal was established in Christ before we existed, in order that we may be enabled to be created anew in him."[14]

So it was that a robust understanding of the Old Testament figure of feminine Wisdom, not strictly identified with Jesus, became wedded to Christian orthodoxy, even if Christian orthodoxy has often kept Sophia discreetly out of sight.[15] But all such theological nuances, amazingly enough, would be reflected in Theodore's fresco program, where

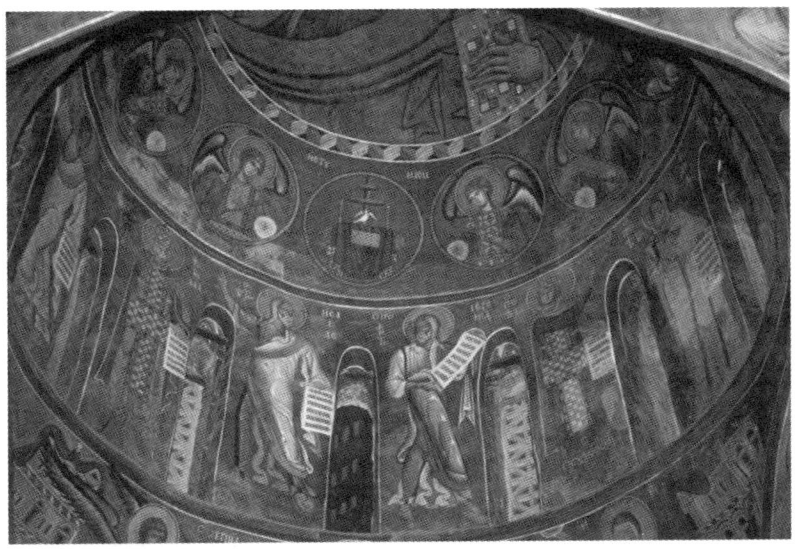

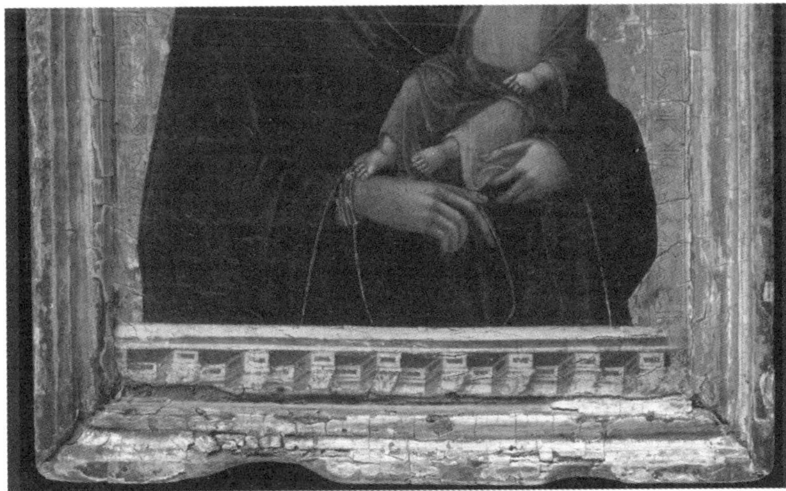

Figure 7.2. Dome at the Virgin of the Vetches church and Duccio's Madonna and Child parapet (ca. 1300).

the first Virgin of the Passion appeared. Such nuances would appear in all subsequent Virgin of the Passion icons as well. Indeed, it is possible that the Virgin of the Passion could be understood as Sophia in disguise, making it among the earliest instances of this iconography in the Christian tradition and certainly one of the most pervasive.[16] When the vast proliferation of the Virgin of the Passion icon is considered, Wisdom was not as far from sight as many have supposed.

The Wisdom of the Passion

THEODORE'S BRILLIANT DECISION to paint a jagged blue-and-red band just above the Prepared Throne in the dome at the Virgin of the Vetches church does far more than dismantle the still-widespread misconception that Eastern Orthodox artists did not know how to paint three-dimensional illusions. Instead, this band conveys the difference between the uncreated and created dimensions—that is, between God and what God has created. If Western artistic illusionism such as Duccio's could mark the transition from "the world we inhabit into the fictional world of the artist," Theodore Apsevdis used the same motif, more than a full century beforehand, to enable us to pass from the world we inhabit into the realm of God (fig. 7.2).[17] In other words, the jagged band tidily conveys the subtle Nicene distinction between the begotten and the born.[18]

Christ, who is God, necessarily inhabits the realm above this line, for—contra Arius—Christ has always been. Beneath this jagged band, naturally enough, would be the "first of his acts of old," the Prepared Throne. Indeed, the word *prepared* in the term Prepared Throne was directly connected, in Byzantine art, to this primordial understanding of God's plan of salvation.[19] And it quite clearly is evoked near the first Virgin of the Passion at the Virgin of the Vetches church in Cyprus, with the words "Prepared Throne" (Hetoimasia) inscribed on either side of the image in the dome. The message is this: even before creation as we know it, God's first move was to ensure that if anything was to go wrong in the "very good" (Gen 1:31) creation, the rescue plan—namely, the passion evoked by the cross on the throne—would be firmly in place. Perhaps the most interesting, albeit suggestive, evidence that Theodore had this Athanasian understanding in mind when he painted the program is that the fresco restorers at Lagoudera have suggested that the Prepared Throne would have been the first medallion painted in the church, at least in that particular section.[20] Perhaps Theodore Apsevdis wanted to start the fresco program where God did: in the beginning.

Fittingly, it is only angels who accompany the Prepared Throne just below the jagged band. For Byzantine thinkers like Basil the Great, angels, although created, nevertheless inhabit the timeless realm with God.[21] Which is to say, angels are not bound to time as we are. But below the narrow strip of red in the dome, time as we know it begins (fig. 7.3).[22] Here we meet the prophets, whose messages conveniently illustrate how God's time and human time begin to intersect. Moses's scroll reads, "In the beginning, God created the heavens and the earth" (Gen 1:1). Solomon bears a scroll from Proverbs reading, "Many women have done excellently, but you surpass them all" (Prov 31:29), perhaps evoking not only Mary but the Wisdom of Proverbs 8 as well. Jeremiah touches the same notes: "He found the whole way to knowledge, and gave her to Jacob his servant and to Israel whom he loved" (Bar 3:36). But the future is referenced among these prophets as well. The scrolls in the dome held by Jonah, Gideon, Elijah, Elisha, and Daniel bear eschatological messages.[23] Both past and future are here deliberately referenced, for as John of Damascus puts it, "With His divine, all seeing, and immaterial eye [He sees] all things at once, both present and past and future, before they come to pass."[24]

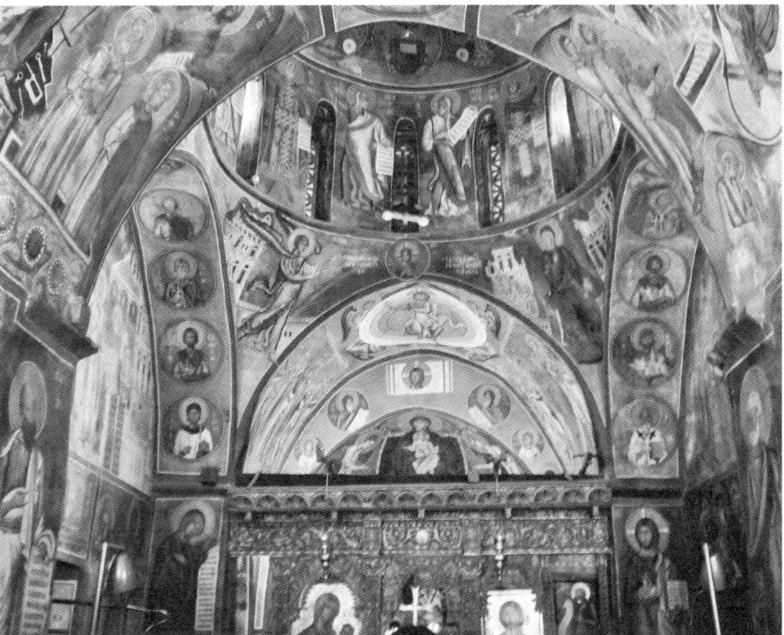

Figure 7.3. The Virgin of the Vetches church showing the descent of Christ.

But as Theodore's program moves downward, the viewer is more and more enmeshed in time. The great descent of Christ in the dome at Hagia Sophia is replicated here in miniature. The moment of the Annunciation stretches across the pendentives, illustrating the uncreated one's descent into creation. The medallion enclosing the Christ child reads "Immanuel," which means "God with us." Accordingly, the Mary who receives this message on the right is the time-bound Mary of Nazareth (fig. 7.3).

But the Virgin of the Passion below her on the south wall offers additional valences. Having examined Athanasius's response to Arius, it is now possible to see that the angels with the instruments of the passion evoke the Wisdom of Proverbs 8 as well. Here, Mary is not only Mary but Sophia—Wisdom herself: God's plan of salvation finally realized. To emphasize this point, the embroidered ends of the cushion of Mary's throne in the Virgin of the Passion deliberately resemble the embroidered ends of the Prepared Throne above. Mary's garment in the Virgin of the Passion is the same color as the fabric that covers the Prepared Throne above. Christ's garment is the same color as the Gospel book above, emphasizing that he is the living Word (fig. 7.4).

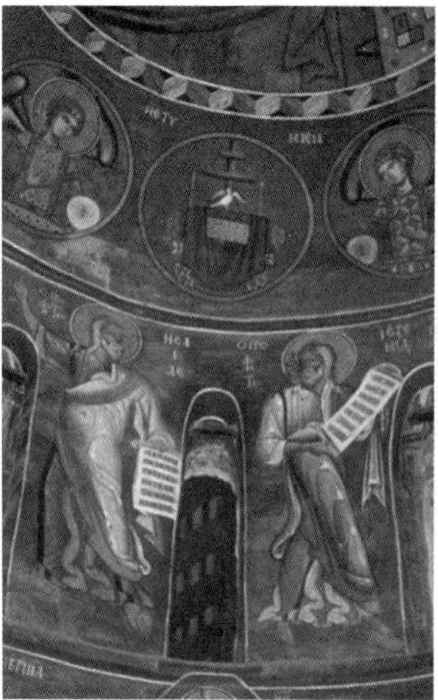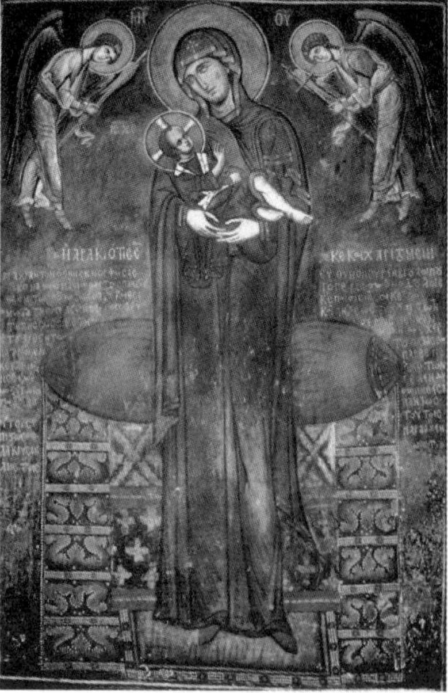

Figure 7.4. Comparison of the Prepared Throne and the Virgin of the Passion.

But most poignantly, Mary—who here is also Wisdom—is not seated as she would normally be depicted. Instead, she stands, she responds, she represents God's refusal to address the matter of broken humanity while comfortably sitting down.[25] She is God's wise plan of salvation activated at last. As Proclus, a fifth-century Byzantine preacher, put it, "In order to mend the primal robe, Wisdom herself took to the loom that was set up in the virginal workshop, weaving for herself a garment with a shuttle propelled by divine power."[26]

The Predestination of All

THESE WISDOM RESONANCES are not incompatible with the more straightforward interpretation of Mary as a woman who was called to deliver and rear the Son of God and bear her own personal cross of discipleship.[27] The Byzantines felt no need to choose between different interpretations of the Virgin Mary. Multiple meanings could be operative at once. As the *Life of the Virgin* explains regarding Mary, "For words spoken by the Holy Spirit should not be understood only in one way but in many ways, for they are a treasure house of good things."[28]

Indeed, once the Virgin of the Passion is understood not only as Mary but as Wisdom, an additional level of meaning opens as well: she symbolizes the salvific destiny of all humans, collectively understood as the church.[29] God's wise plan is not just an abstract proposition; it would be inhabited by innumerable beloved souls. This is a very ancient understanding. A second-century Christian text, *The Shepherd of Hermas*, depicted a mysterious elderly woman. The text's author wonders about the figure's identity, thinking perhaps she is a sibyl, an ancient prophetess. It is then revealed, however, that the figure is the church: "She was created the first of all things. For this reason she is old; and for her sake the world was established."[30] In time, such motifs, which drew upon Proverbs 8, crystallized in the figure of Mary. "The Virgin Mary is a symbol of the Church," proclaimed Ephraim the Syrian. "We call the Church by the name of Mary, for she deserves a double name."[31] After all, if the church is the body of Christ (1 Cor 12:27), it is in Mary's womb where that body was made.[32] As one Byzantine author put it, "The couch prefigured primarily the all-holy Mother of God, and then the soul of each one to be saved."[33]

The Virgin of the Passion therefore symbolizes not simply a plan but a richly populated, personalized one. The Virgin of the Passion evokes the predestination of rescued humanity. This is not to limit the icon to those associated with Christianity's institutional expressions nor to eliminate such associations. Mary symbolizes the church in a wide, mystical, and collective sense. In his understanding of God's plan of salvation, Athanasius showed "wise silence . . . concerning the destiny of individuals as such,"[34] choosing to emphasize the predestination of all humans in Christ. There is no trace in Athanasius of the notion that would later torment so many—namely, the possibility that God would have chosen beforehand a portion of humanity to be damned apart from God's designs for human salvation as a whole.[35] Instead, there is only the election in Christ before the world was made, let alone before the introduction of human sin. Athanasius offers only the ringing clarity of the book of Ephesians, humanity unified in God's primordial decision for good: "He chose [elected] us in him before the foundation of the world" (Eph 1:4). To look at the Virgin of the Passion, therefore, is to see oneself and to see Christ reach out to bear the consequences of sin that we are incapable of bearing ourselves.

There is no such thing, the image announces, as a human soul predestined by a loving God to everlasting damnation, that influential idea that would sadly eclipse Athanasius's understanding.[36] There is no *decretum horribile* here.[37] The icon instead announces that there has only ever been one primordial decision: God's decision to collectively judge and redeem all humanity in Christ.[38] This is "the wrath of the lamb, the wrath of redeeming love. As such the very wrath of God is a sign of hope, not of utter destruction."[39]

The combined message is this: despite God's sorrow over sinful humanity—a sorrow eloquently conveyed by Christ's averted gaze in the dome—and despite our warfare and wickedness, our betrayals and brutality, our hubris and hatred, God was prepared to act.[40] The Prepared Throne conveys that there was never a time-bound moment when God's plan to rescue humanity was not already being enacted.[41] On the wall below, the instruments of the passion hovering above Mary and Christ convey that the rescue has been realized. To reassert: Mary is not just Mary in this image but Sophia, the church, all of humanity at once, and your own self-portrait as well.

The meaning of the image is perfectly summarized by the Silesian cobbler and mystic Jacob Boehme (1574–1624), who somehow—though he lacked formal schooling and quite likely never saw the image—came to understand it perfectly: "When God saw and took notice of our miserable Fall, he did illustrate himself by the holy Eternal Virgin of his

Wisdom in the Eternal Wonders, in mercy which always floweth out of his heart, and did comprehend with his speculation the Throne [made in Time], and did further illustrate himself in the Throne into many millions without number, and established his Covenant with his Oath therein, with his precious promise of the Woman's Seed."[42]

But the icon's ocean of meaning has deeper levels still.

❦ **8** ❧

MARY AS PRIEST

Mary is not the "model" only for women, the prototype of submissive, passive, and oversweet femininity. . . . Mary is not a goddess either. . . . Mary is fully human and represents all of humanity. . . . She is a sign, the anticipation of a human person entirely given to the Lord.
  —Elisabeth Behr-Sigel, *The Ministry of Women in the Church*

Activity is not specifically masculine; nor is receptivity distinctively feminine; rather, to be a person is to be both active and receptive.

  —William Witt, *Icons of Christ*

[Mary] represents the extremes of both femininity and masculinity in her person: in short, this larger-than-life figure embodies aspects of both genders.
  —Mary B. Cunningham, *The Virgin Mary in Byzantium*

Mary doesn't simply present what comes from the Father; she offers what she authors, which is the flesh.
  —Annemarie Weyl Carr, "Thoughts on the Economy of the Image of Mary"

THE CONNECTION OF the Virgin of the Passion to predestined humanity—that is, to the church—widens the image's original range of meaning further still. For it turns out that Theodore Apsevdis had even more to contribute to the debate that embroiled Constantinople in the mid-twelfth century. Beyond evoking the Trinity and Wisdom through the Prepared Throne, he also went so far as to illustrate the very prayer that upended the arguments of Soterichos Pantevgenos—that is, the prayer of the Cherubic Hymn: "For you are the one who offers and is offered, who receives and is distributed." In so doing, Theodore associated Mary intimately with priesthood.

Such a move, however, is really not all that surprising considering what was waiting for him in the earlier layer of painting at the Virgin of the Vetches church. When Theodore first stepped inside the building that he would so dramatically repaint, Mary the priest was already present. The mysterious cloth held by Mary in the apse, painted by the artist who preceded Theodore, is not a tea towel for performing domestic chores (fig. 8.1).[1] Nor is it an innocuous handkerchief to dry tears or stop

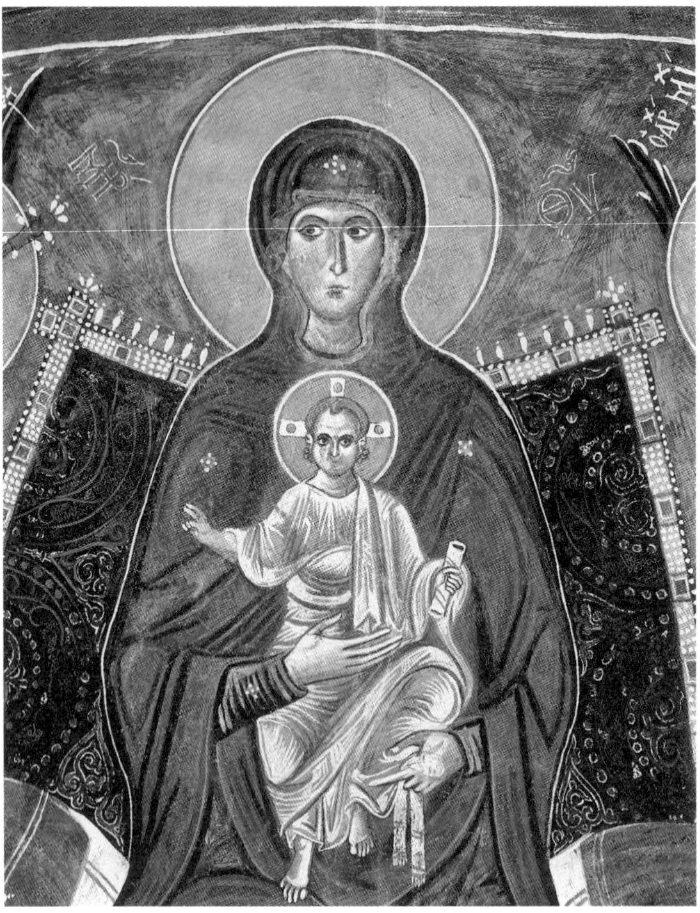

Figure 8.1. Mary with a eucharistic cloth indicating priesthood in the apse in the first layer of painting (pre-1192) at the Virgin of the Vetches church in Lagoudera, Cyprus.

a runny nose.[2] The cloth instead may associate Mary with priesthood.[3] Known in the East as an *encheirion* (literally, a "handy") and later as an *epigonation*, this cloth is "a sign of one's participation in the liturgy . . . a link with the highest sacraments."[4] This eucharistic cloth is attested early in Christian art. It appears to have evolved into a more elaborate embroidered diamond cloth still worn by bishops today.[5]

Rather than overriding such sacramental associations when he repainted the main section of the mountain church, Theodore intensified them. As if responding to his artistic predecessor, Theodore went so far as to associate Mary with priesthood in each of the sections of his program. The entire building itself emerges as a visualized prayer of the Cherubic Hymn, with Mary playing the role of the humble, whispering priest through whom her son officiates. Understanding the full extent of how this prayer imbues the program—and consequently, the Virgin of the Passion icon as well—necessitates understanding the full range of the Virgin Mary's life as it was understood in the Byzantine world.

Looking North: The Proto-Gospel

THE BYZANTINES WERE not satisfied with the sparse information on offer in the Gospels about the Mother of God. They wanted to know the

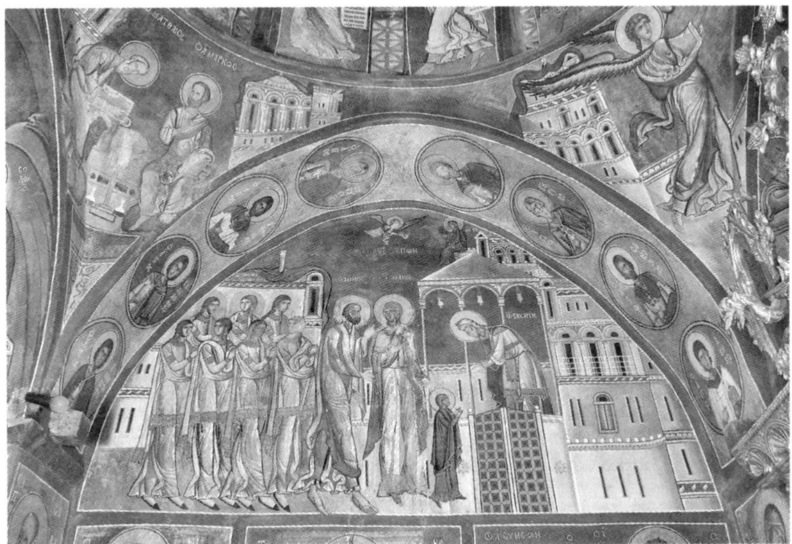

Figure 8.2. The presentation of Mary in the temple, north wall of the Virgin of the Vetches church at Lagoudera.

stories about her childhood and the stories about her funeral. Such stories, moreover, were on offer in some of the earliest surviving nonbiblical Christian texts. Such accounts need to be understood not as competing with the biblical canon but as making commentary upon it, just as a sermon, poem, novel, or film today might reverently fill in the details that were understandably left out of brief biblical accounts. Accounts of Mary's childhood and old age were elaborated upon and refined over time, complete with pictures—the fond and faithful editing of a grand family album.

The second-century Protevangelium (already briefly discussed) was among the earliest and most beloved of these apocryphal texts.[6] Though condemned by Jerome (d. 420) and Pope Innocent I (d. 417), the document enjoyed near biblical authority in the East, providing comparatively fertile ground for Mary's association with priesthood.[7] A feast celebrating the presentation of Mary in the temple appeared in Jerusalem lectionaries by the eighth century, and the first surviving artistic depictions of the event surface in a tenth-century ivory.[8] In the Protevangelium, Jesus's grandparents Joachim and Anna, the parents of the Virgin Mary, mourn their earlier barrenness and, in a moving petition, plead to God for a child. Echoing the first chapters of Genesis, Anna complains that the birds of heaven, the beasts of the earth and the waters, and the earth itself are fruitful, while she remains fruitless. An angel appears to grant her request, and Anna shows her gratitude with a promise: "*As the Lord my God lives*, if I bear a child, whether male or female, I will *bring it as a gift to the Lord my God*, and it shall *serve him all the days of its life.*"[9]

Interestingly enough, the child's gender offers no barrier to temple service.[10] Like modern parents debating the right age to send their child to school, Joachim and Anna argue as to when Mary should be dropped off at the temple. Joachim's suggestion that two years old is a sufficient age is rebuffed by Anna's insistence that they wait until Mary is three, and Joachim assents.[11] In the meantime, Mary had not walked seven steps before Anna lifted her off the ground, promising, "*As the Lord God lives, you shall walk no more upon the earth until I bring you into the temple of the Lord,*" a line that perhaps accounts for Theodore's choice to have the young Mary hover in the scene of Mary's presentation in the temple at the Virgin of the Vetches church (fig. 8.2).[12] Or perhaps Theodore was referring to the moment in the Protevangelium when Mary the toddler, having been presented for temple service, signals her assent by joyfully dancing, a clear echo of the dancing David, whose lineage—through Joseph (Matt 1:16; Luke 1:27)—Mary shares.[13]

Concerned, however, that his daughter might not be eager to enter temple service, Joachim insists that the undefiled daughters of the Hebrews join them, each with lamps burning, "in order that the child may not turn back and her heart be enticed away from the temple of the Lord."[14] Theodore depicts these accompanying daughters even while he seems to be playing with the motif of hesitation by having some of them turn their heads. The author of the Protevangelium deftly adds that Mary's parents praised and glorified almighty God "because the child did not *turn back*," which may be a subtle allusion to Lot's wife, who did.[15] Perhaps to highlight this dynamic, Theodore made a late twist in the head of Anna.[16] Mary faces the temple like flint, while her mother (understandably!) prevaricates.[17] Adding even more of a common touch, Theodore may have deliberately made Joachim and Anna resemble his patron, Leon, and his wife.[18]

The Protevangelium suggests that it was Zechariah, the future father of John the Baptist, who received Mary in the temple. Theodore may be reminding us of this by depicting John the Baptist just below his father (fig. 8.3). The impenetrable walls of the temple above John seem to evoke the grizzly Baptist's contrasting wilderness vocation. By becoming a desert-dwelling prophet, John the Baptist refused the priestly lineage of both his mother, Elizabeth, who was in the priestly line of Aaron, and his father, Zechariah, who was in the lesser priestly line of Abijah (Luke 1:5). It might be possible, therefore, to read the temple-dwelling Mary of the Protevangelium as the means of granting Zechariah the priestly offspring he never had. Though Zechariah's future son would not enter the temple service, Mary—to whom he was related via his wife, Elizabeth—did. Such connections emerge not only from a reading of the Protevangelium but from Theodore's visual choices at the Virgin of the Vetches as well.

The Protevangelium then relates that "Mary was in the temple nurtured like a dove and received food from the hand of an angel."[19] Accordingly, Mary appears a second time in the same scene at Lagoudera, sitting dovelike on the roof in her more traditional Marian blue wimple and red maphorion. As if to illustrate her occupation of the sanctuary, the angel hovers above the inscription that reads "Holy of Holies," in which this girl centrally resides.[20]

When viewing Theodore's illustration of the Protevangelium, the Marian rhetoric of the ninth-century preacher George of Nicomedia

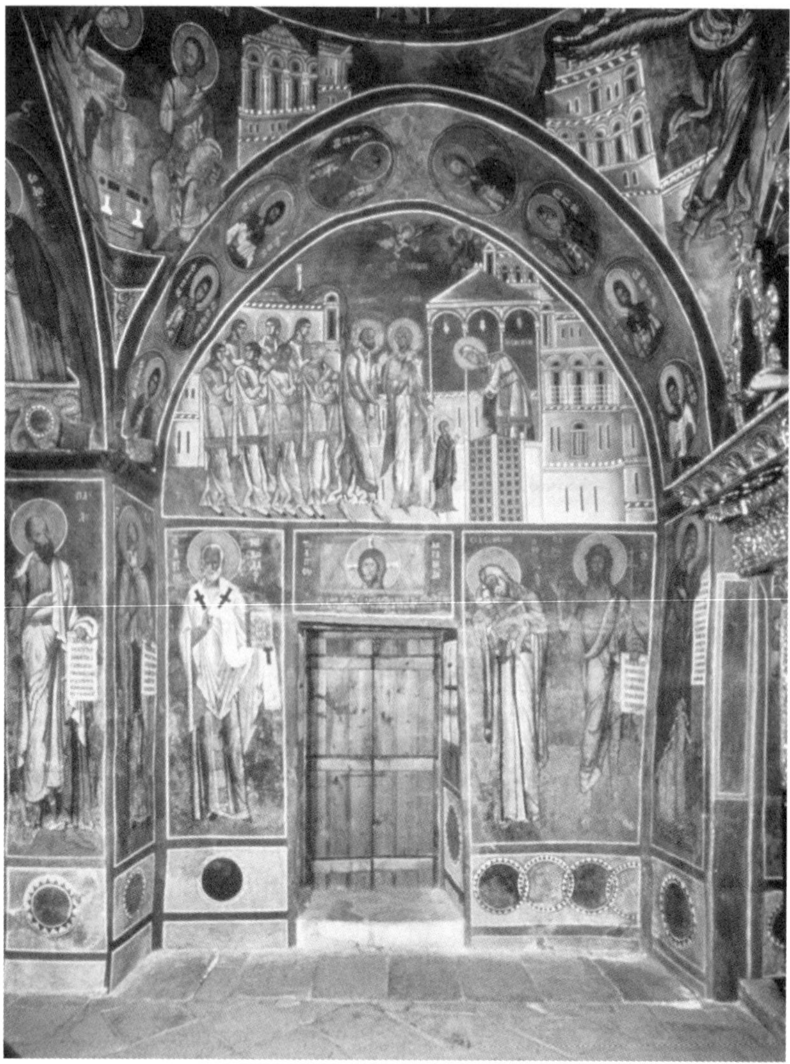

Figure 8.3. Simeon the priest and John the Baptist below the temple, north wall of the Virgin of the Vetches church at Lagoudera.

is immediately understood: "Temple of God, she enters the Temple."[21] From a strictly historical vantage point, it may be dubious for the Protevangelium to permit a child to reside in the holy of holies.[22] But what is not dubious is the historical fact that illustrations of the Protevangelium, such as Theodore's, consistently visualized a woman occupying the domain of the high priest.

But the true extent of Mary's connection to priesthood in Theodore's program comes with his unexpected inclusion of the prayer of the Cherubic Hymn, "For you are the one who offers, and is offered." This requires considering what lies directly beneath the scene of Mary's presentation in the temple. There, as previously mentioned, Simeon the priest, in the lineage of the priest Zechariah just above him, offers the struggling Christ child. The fact that Christ is being offered by Simeon below, and Mary is being offered by her parents above, is no coincidence. This is one step in the illustration of the contested prayer of the Cherubic Hymn. But this illustration is only fully fathomed when one considers the Dormition on the south wall, just above the Virgin of the Passion.

Looking South: The Dormition

THE BYZANTINES WERE not content with the stories of Mary's upbringing alone. They wanted to know the stories of the end of her earthly life. Mary's "falling asleep"—that is, her Dormition—has been celebrated since the sixth century on August 15.[23] In early narratives of the event, Mary—sensing her earthly life coming to a close—summons all of the disciples to her funeral. But it was not only *her* funeral. Meditation on the Dormition also served as a meditation on the death of every believer. "This is *our* frame that we celebrate today—*our* formation, *our* disintegration," announced Andrew of Crete in a homily on the Feast of the Dormition. The "Mystery of the Virgin, now being accomplished . . . is our lot too."[24] With this in mind, perhaps Theodore's portrait of Neophytos flanked by angels at the Hideaway can be read as a Dormition as well.

Fittingly, Dormition depictions were often at the exit of churches, evoking the exit of all of us from earthly life, and in line with this tradition, the Dormition is near an exit at the Virgin of the Vetches church as well.[25] Mary may have once held Christ as a baby, but in classic Dormition images, the situation is reversed. Here it is Christ who tenderly holds the soul of Mary, an image of adult children who are often summoned to hold their elderly parents. The message is this: as Christ holds Mary at the end of her life, Christ will tenderly hold the souls of dying believers as well.

In Theodore's program, the ministering angel painted just above Mary's soul echoes the angel that ministered to Mary the toddler just across the nave. It is almost as if Theodore was illustrating the words from the Dormition homilies: "For if she had received nourishment from angels in the Lord's temple, while she was still a child, how much more should she be served by the powers on high after she had become herself the Lord's temple!"[26] (fig. 8.4).

But the Dormition is not without its priestly aspects as well. Indeed, homilies associated with the Dormition have long been suffused with Mary's desire to make an offering of her own body to the Lord. "Bring me a censer," Mary says in one of the earliest Dormition accounts, "because I want to make an offering to God, our Lord Jesus Christ, who is in heaven."[27] This could well be a reference to the temple offering of incense, which was the privilege of only the high priest.[28] It is easy to overlook that the gathering of the male apostles in this great apocryphal event occurred because of *Mary's* desire to make an offering.[29] It might be possible to understand the bishop hovering so close to Mary with a censer in Theodore's depiction as a reflection of her request, "Bring me a censer."[30]

As with the presentation of Mary in the temple, the full extent of Theodore's contribution is only understood when one looks just below. There in the Virgin of the Passion, Mary holds the serene Jesus, who extends his hand in consent to the angel who hovers with the cross. But with the all-important prayer of the Cherubic Hymn in mind, it is now possible to see that the image of Christ offering himself can be paired

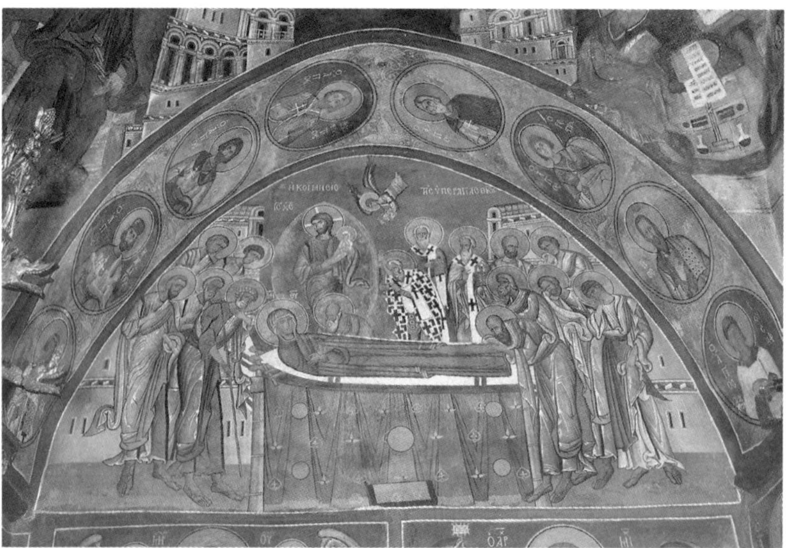

Figure 8.4. The Dormition at the Virgin of the Vetches church (1192).

with Mary, who offers herself above as well. The self-offerings of Mary and Christ combine.

These dynamics of offering are crowned by the Prepared Throne in the dome above, which represents the receiving Trinity. With this, the entire fresco program falls into place (fig. 8.5). If the synods of 1156/57 had accentuated the importance of the prayer of the Cherubic Hymn, the Virgin of the Vetches church did so even more. On the south wall, just as a serene Jesus offers himself in the arms of the Virgin, so Mary offers her own body to Christ in the Dormition directly above. Together they evoke the prayer: "You are the one who offers." And on the north wall, just as the struggling Christ child is offered by Simeon, so Mary is offered by her parents above. Together they complete the prayer: "and is offered." Rather than being a surprising innovation, this iconography grew naturally from the rich soil of Byzantine art and theology. The contrast between Christ's fear and courage was long established.[31] Christ being his own offering was a pervasive visual theme.[32] However the contested text in Geometres's *Life of the Virgin* is rendered, the visual milieu of the Virgin of the Vetches church communicates how Christ's self-offering operates through the Marian ecclesial matrix remarkably well.[33]

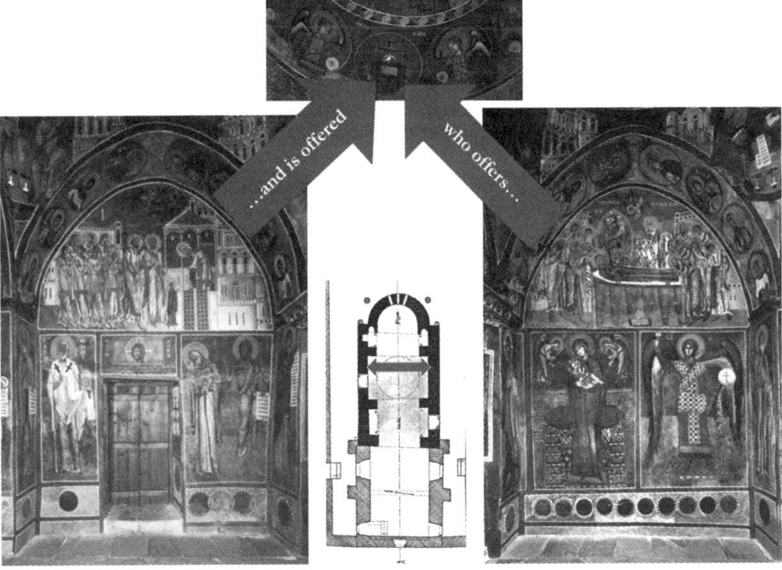

Figure 8.5. The prayer of the Cherubic Hymn at the Virgin of the Vetches church.

The aim of the prayer of the Cherubic Hymn is to remind the priest that it is Christ who is offering himself *through* the priest. Likewise, at Lagoudera, it is Christ below who offers himself and is offered *through* Mary, who—of course—represents the church, an offering received by the entire Trinity referenced in the Prepared Throne above. Nearly all the scholars who have examined this painting see rich eucharistic connections.[34] It has long been argued that the gesture of Mary in the Virgin of the Passion at Lagoudera is saturated with eucharistic symbolism, even to the point where her arms deliberately resemble the liturgical spoon used in the Orthodox church.[35] As noted previously, the exposed leg of Christ references the eucharistic lamb, an artistic echo of the accentuating of the legs in biblical descriptions of the Passover (Exod 12:9). These connections can be pressed even further. Paired with the exposed skin of the struggling Christ child in the arms of Simeon across the nave, the entire nave "emphasize[s] the fleshly and eucharistic aspects of Christology."[36]

In sum, the Virgin of the Passion, in its original setting in Cyprus, encapsulates a complex theological tradition with ingenious efficiency.[37] The image simultaneously illustrates the wisdom of God's good plan of salvation, tethered to the Prepared Throne above, and conveys the eucharistic dimensions of the famous prayer, "You are the one who offers and is offered." Mary, herself in a priestly lineage, is placed in temple service from a young age, she lifts up her eucharistic son, and at the end of her life, she makes a priestly offering. The priesthood of Christ operates through her.[38] It is no wonder that pseudo-Epiphanius (d. 680) could write,

> *I call the Virgin both priest and altar,*
> *she, the "table-bearer"*
> *who has given us the Christ,*
> *the heavenly bread for the forgiveness of sins.*[39]

Neophytos, the Cyprus recluse, likewise proclaimed in his sermon on the meeting of Mary and Simeon, "She comes as a table, having upon it the bread of life. . . . She comes as a grapevine bearing the cluster so that new wine may slake the faithful."[40] The dimensions of Mary's priestly ministry, even her preaching and apostolic ministry, only expanded as Byzantine Marian reflection matured.[41] Theodore's Virgin of the Passion gave such resonances visual form.

When considering Mary as both as preacher and priest, it is possible to think of the Virgin of the Passion icon as a full-scale religious service in itself, containing both a sermon (the message of the eternal Word's mission to save) and a meal (the Eucharist). The global destiny of the Virgin of the Passion icon, moreover, ensured that these theological and liturgical dimensions would be transmitted into the modern world. Just as the plumage of a caged tropical bird reflects the environment of the jungles in which it evolved and from which it was captured, so did the Virgin of the Passion icon convey the resonances of its natural theological habitat in Cyprus wherever it was destined to appear.

How this eucharistic icon began its spread throughout the world is the subject to turn to next.

PART III

THE ICON

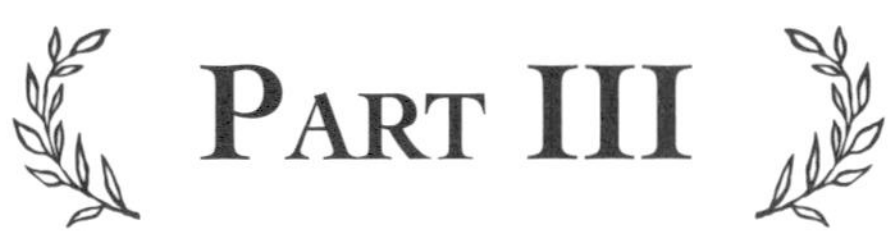

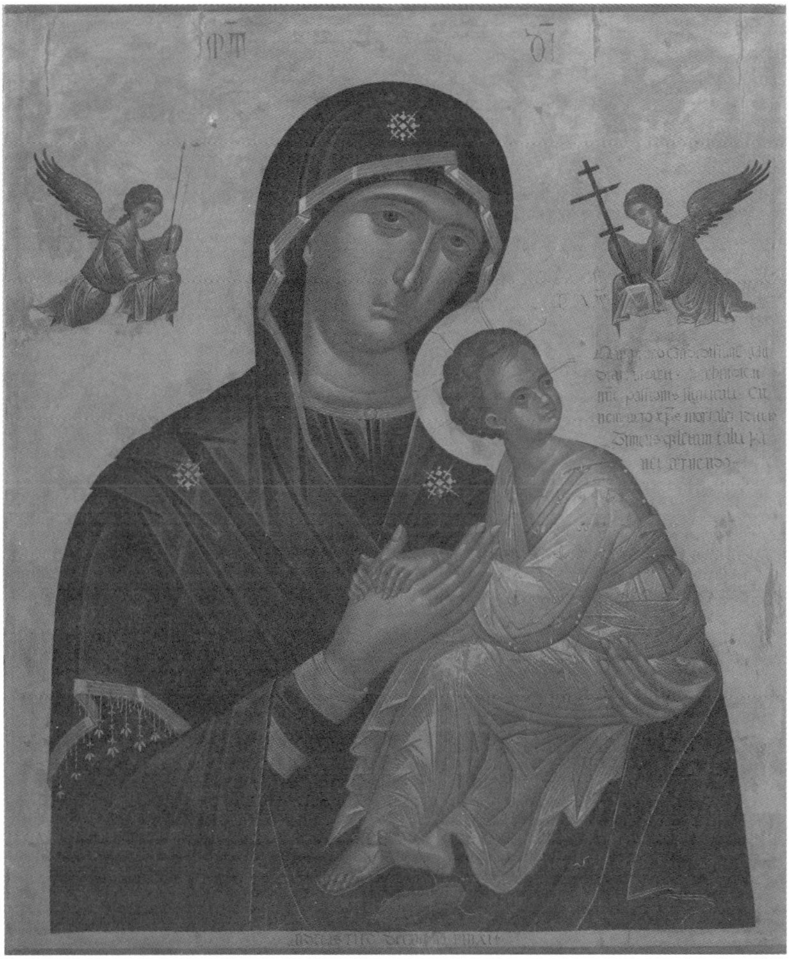

9

THE VIRGIN OF DEFEAT

When the battle did not go well for him, [the Sumerian king Enmerkar] understood that [the goddess] Inanna had deserted him.

—Tikva Frymer-Kensky, *In the Wake of the Goddesses*

As Alcibiades . . . understood . . . an open defeat—even one of minor strategic importance—signified loss of favor of the Mother of the Gods.

—Mark Munn, *The Mother of the Gods, Athens, and the Tyranny of Asia*

The signs of her rule are not that she has at her disposal crowns such as the masses will never touch, nor choice gems, ornaments and fabrics, nor regal costume different from the attire of common people. Such things were invented for those kings who cannot rise above what is earthly, and whose clothes reign rather than their souls.

—Gregory Palamas, *Second Sermon on the Entry of the Mother of God into the Holy of Holies*

THE VIRGIN OF the Passion may well have functioned as a worship service in miniature, including allusions to a complex sermon and the eucharistic feast. But a Christian worship service is intended to energize a congregation for service in the world, and the Virgin of the Passion performed this function as well. As the icon spread beyond its original setting in Cyprus—appearing on pillars and walls and icons throughout the Mediterranean and beyond—it was on a mission of mercy to minister to an empire, one that was soon to suffer the same fate as Cyprus as a whole. While Latin and Greek Christians were battling over icons labeled "The Virgin of Victory," a different icon was coming into view:

the Virgin of the Passion, poised to leave her traces wherever the bloodshed of the Crusades—or of Byzantium's emerging rival empire, the Ottomans—increased.

The Crosses of Zara

AFTER HIS CAPTURE of Cyprus, following some military success, Richard the Lionheart negotiated the possibility of Christian pilgrims visiting Jerusalem's Church of the Holy Sepulchre again, where they could visit Golgotha and the empty tomb of Christ.[1] On one such visit, Jerusalem's occupying Muslims permitted one Christian pilgrim, the bishop of Salisbury, to see the True Cross—but only to see it.[2] In short, Richard brokered a treaty with Saladin but did not defeat him, nor did Richard recapture the largest portion of Christendom's chief relic.[3] The dream of holding the True Cross accordingly lived on, and it was still powerful enough to generate the next Crusade.

A preacher known as Martin the Hermit would inspire what has come to be known as the Fourth Crusade just as Bernard of Clairvaux had inspired the Second. Martin claimed, audaciously enough, to be speaking for Christ himself: "The words are not mine. . . . The most sacred and venerable Cross of wood . . . is locked and hidden away by persons to whom the word of the Cross is foolishness, so that no Christian might know what was done with it or where to look for it."[4] This renewed hunt for the True Cross would ultimately lead to the infamous sack of Constantinople in 1204.[5]

This Crusade departed not from Vézelay but from Venice, the capital of the maritime empire known as *La Serenissima*, "the most serene republic." The lagoon city's elderly leader, Doge Dandolo (r. 1192–1205), agreed to lead the enterprise himself.[6] Seeing the old man publicly take the cross, joining the ranks of his grandfather and uncle who had been Crusaders before him, inspired many others to join the mission; but there were certainly not as many soldiers, or funds, as had been hoped for.

In October of 1202, a decade after Theodore painted his response to the previous Crusade, the Virgin of the Passion, the fleet set off. The mission was led by Dandolo's galley, which flew under Venice's flag of Saint Mark, the winged lion.[7] Each nobleman from various regions of Europe commandeered his own ship, their crosses color coded to reflect their regions. But the cross is what unified them all. Trumpets blasted and clerics chanted *Veni creator spiritus* (come, Creator Spirit) from towers attached to the fronts of each vessel.[8]

The Fourth Crusade was immediately complicated by the doge's dodgy plan to sack the city of Zara (Zadar in present-day Croatia) along the Adriatic Sea. Venice had long hoped to gain control of this wealthy and well-fortified city, which had cast off the yoke of Venetian authority, robbing Venice of tax revenue and crucial access to Dalmatian forests necessary for the construction of fleets.[9] Zara, however, was under the control of King Emico of Hungary, who was himself a Crusader, and the current pope, Innocent III (r. 1198–1216), had forbidden the Crusaders from attacking any Christian city.

Hearing that the doge planned to sack Zara, a papal letter was hurried to the city by a Cistercian abbot of a monastery south of Paris. It was read aloud as the fleet arrived: "My lords, in the name of the Pope of Rome, I forbid you to attack this city, for the people in it are Christians, and you wear the sign of the cross."[10] Faced with this proclamation, some French knights refused to join the siege, infuriating the doge.

Still, the warnings were not successful, and the papal letter was concealed from any knights who had not heard it read lest it deter them.[11] Doge Dandolo considered his financial agreements with his fellow Crusaders, to whom he had offered considerable loans, to supersede the papal command. As a result, the siege took place anyway. The crosses that the citizens hung over their walls to indicate their status as Christians offered no deterrent.[12] After all, the precedent of Cyprus, of Christians sacking Christians, had already cleared the way.[13]

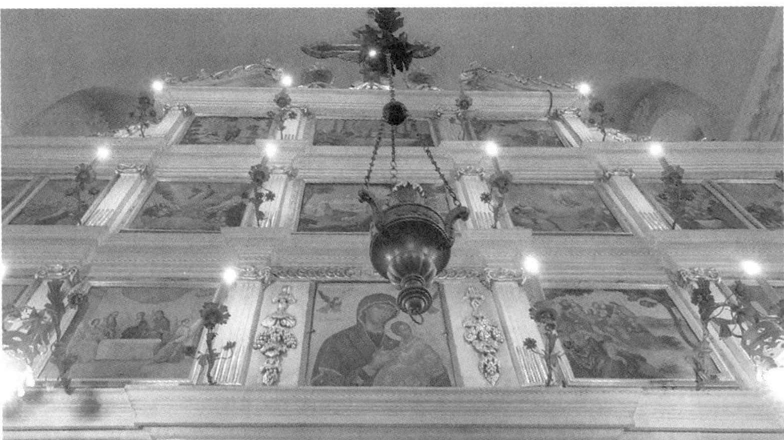

Figure 9.1. Virgin of the Passion at Zara (modern Zadar).

Following the sack of Zara, Martin, the same hermit who had preached the Crusade, was so disgusted that he begged, unsuccessfully, to be released from his vow to complete the mission.[14] Pope Innocent III's ensuing excommunication of the army for its actions also had no effect.[15] This is the way the story of the Fourth Crusade is told, and the story is not untrue.

But if Theodore Apsevdis responded to the Third Crusade with the Virgin of the Passion, the Christian residents of Zara appear to have done so as well, even if this visual retort came centuries afterward. Anyone who visits Zara (Zadar) today, entering the central Church of Saint Elias, will find the Virgin of the Passion to be the confident centerpiece of the iconostasis. The crosses of Zara, pitifully unfurled over the city walls to deter the Crusaders, may have failed, but the cross on offer in the Virgin of the Passion icon did not (fig. 9.1).

That being said, as far as the soldiers of the Fourth Crusade were concerned, Zara, like Cyprus, had been conquered, and Constantinople—even if the Crusaders did not originally intend to vanquish that city—was next.

Guy de Lusignan Revisited

IN THE EARLY thirteenth century, Constantinople was the largest metropolis in Christendom, with a population roughly six times that of Venice or Paris.[16] The aims of the Crusaders' visit to this city were resupply, a solidification of alliances, and possible profit. But upon their arrival, soon the visiting Crusaders became embroiled in politics. The City of Gold was not helped by its recently crowned opportunistic Byzantine emperor, Alexius IV, who was willing to negotiate with the Crusaders for his own gain, promising them he could convince the Orthodox church to submit to Rome.[17] It was a clever tactic, as the goal of unifying the Eastern and Western branches of the church, divided since 1054, might even please the pope enough to cause him to lift his excommunication of the Crusade. Nevertheless, Alexius IV was mistrusted by his own people, and his leadership was further contested by his blinded father, Isaac II Angelos, who, faced with the crisis of visiting Crusaders, had resorted to soothsayers and astrologers.

Compounding the instability still more, leadership was then wrenched from both Alexius IV and Isaac II in a palace coup by Alexius IV's son Alexius V, nicknamed Mourtzouphlos, a Greek word that referenced both his gloomy disposition and the massive tangle of eyebrows indistinguishably unified above his ever-calculating eyes. Mourtzouphlos's aim was not to cooperate with or mollify the Crusaders, as his father had done, but to destroy them. Even so, Mourtzouphlos was faced with a lack of confidence from the threatened population he ruled, who preferred other imperial contenders. Mourtzouphlos was prepared, therefore—like Guy de Lusignan before him—to win the confidence of his threatened citizens in battle.[18]

The Crusaders, stationed outside the city, soon ran out of supplies. A band of them accordingly set off to conquer a nearby castle. This was the moment Mourtzouphlos chose to strike. His army advanced, accompanied by Constantinople's Orthodox patriarch on horseback, who carried a bejeweled icon of the Virgin. Which is to say, they employed the same strategies used by the Latin bishop of Acre who had processed the True Cross at Hattin in 1187. Among the relics encrusted within this icon was a piece of the spear that had pierced Jesus.[19] If the Holy Lance had galvanized the first Crusaders at Acre, another piece of what was claimed to be the same lance was now being used against them.

One Byzantine mercenary was so confident in this divine protection that he galloped forward wearing only a crown, some of which must have been buried into his skull as the sword of Henry of Flanders crashed down on his unprotected head.[20] The Crusader army, already tested at Zara, made short shrift of Mourtzouphlos's warriors. The patriarch himself was struck by Peter of Bracieux, representing the sword-wielding bluster of his apostolic namesake well. Still, Peter was less interested in the patriarch than in the icon of the Virgin that he carried.[21] One Crusader, Robert of Clari, boasted, "They have so great faith in this icon that they fully believe that no one who carries it in battle can be defeated, and we believe that it was because [Mourtzouphlos] had no right to carry it that he was defeated."[22] In fact, Mourtzouphlos—who survived the confrontation—was so ashamed by his defeat that he claimed to have won the battle, insisting the icon had been stored away for safekeeping. To contest these rumors that spread through the city in the days after the battle, the Crusaders humiliated Mourtzouphlos by steering a ship near the city walls, in full view of the population, and there unfurling—with accompanying trumpets—both the imperial standard that they had captured and the captured icon of Mary.[23]

So proud were the Crusaders of this success that even though the whereabouts of this exact Marian icon are uncertain, centuries later, the Venetians found a similar icon and claimed this to be the one that

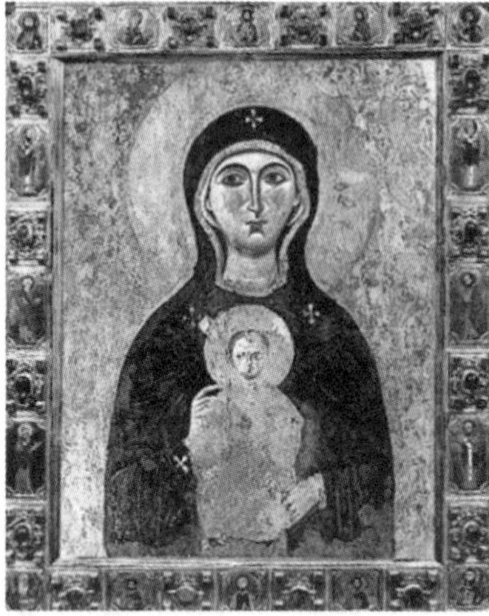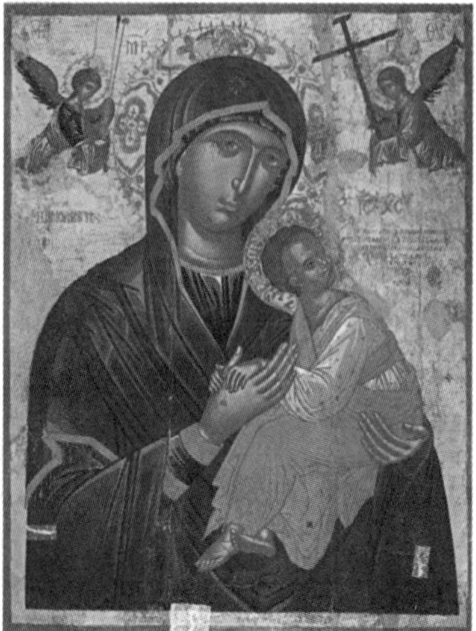

Figure 9.2. Nicopeia icon, San Marco, Venice; the Virgin of the Passion, Venice.

had humiliated Mourtzouphlos.[24] She is known as the Nicopeia, the Virgin of Victory, and she can be visited in the south transept of San Marco in Venice to this day.[25]

Still, not far away from San Marco in Venice today is the Museum of Icons, where the Virgin of the Passion challenges her rival, the Nicopeia.[26] Likely brought to Venice by Greek refugees coming into the city in the wake of Ottoman expansion, she offers a different version of Christianity that remains, for so many, concealed from view (fig. 9.2).

The Spread of the Virgin of the Passion

ON THE TERMS of finding the True Cross, the Fourth Crusade in part succeeded. Following the defeat of Mourtzouphlos, when the Crusaders breached the walls and ransacked the city of Constantinople, the loot was plentiful indeed. In the Pharos (lighthouse) chapel of the imperial palace, they acquired a different piece of the cross to make up for the larger piece seized by Saladin. They found another piece in the treasury of Hagia Sophia.[27] Additional compensation for their trouble came when the Crusaders also discovered one of the nails used to crucify Christ. These precious relics now "belonged to Rome, no matter what sinful processes had removed them from Constantinople and scattered them across Western Christendom."[28] The renown—and the revenue—that came with these relics when they made their way westward was extreme.

But the spread of the *Virgin* of the passion would ultimately outpace the spread of the looted *relics* of the passion. Through wall paintings and, above all, through icons, the image was moving like a deep ocean current beneath the surface disturbances of the Crusades. We only know of the spread of the image through chance survivals, but the survivals are frequent enough to merit the case that the icon was prevalent in the wake of Constantinople's defeat.[29]

One such survival is in the region of what is now Serbia. There at a church called Žiča is a Virgin of the Passion that dates to the early fourteenth century.[30] Christ, held by his mother, recoils at his fate, represented by a single freestanding angel bearing the cross beside them. The Ottoman Empire was consolidating in the region, presenting a new threat to what was left of the Byzantine Empire and to any rival Serbian rulers as well. Faced with fresh threats, a fearful Christ and his mother offered fresh consolation. Perhaps these painters were even unconsciously reminding their patrons that the Serbian power would be limited, just as the Byzantine Empire had been (fig. 9.3).

Another fourteenth-century Virgin of the Passion also appears in the Balkans, at the church of Hosios David in Thessaloniki.[31] Accordingly, right next to an ancient Christian mosaic of the boy Christ enthroned is a church that hearkens to the original Christian wisdom of a power beyond all thrones. Moreover, the image is located near the locus of eucharistic consecration, as if to suggest that the icon's liturgical resonances were still very much sensed.

One of the most dramatic instances of the Virgin of the Passion came in the late fourteenth century in Serbia at King Marko's monastery.[32] King Marko was a Serbian ruler (r. 1371–95) who had been crowned as a "New David," and the Virgin of the Passion was painted on a church alongside many other images to celebrate this event in 1372. The Virgin of the Passion appears directly above the south entrance to the church, set against a dark-blue backdrop. The previous year, the Serbians had been defeated at the Battle of Černomen (also known as the Battle of Maritsa) in 1371.[33] Accordingly, the royal Hebrew kings, with unfurled banners including classic Psalms referencing the Virgin, are intruded upon by the terrified Christ child and a cross-bearing angel (fig. 9.4).[34]

As Theodore Apsevdis had done at the Virgin of the Vetches church in Cyprus, the Virgin of the Passion was once more summoned to navigate defeat, anticipating the future Ottoman victory at the Battle

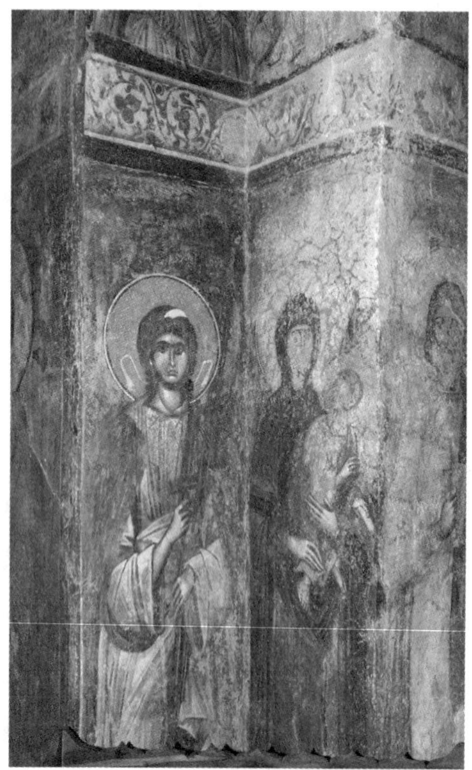

Figure 9.3. The Virgin of the Passion at Žiča.

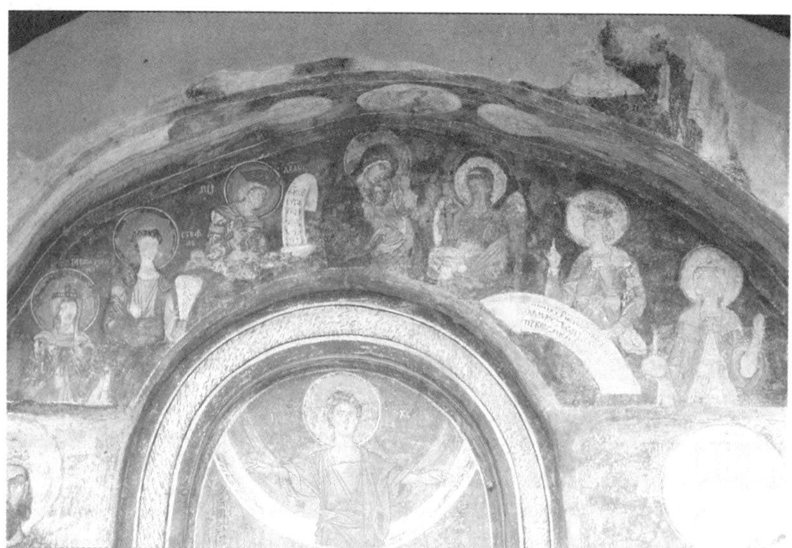

Figure 9.4. The Virgin of the Passion at Marko's Monastery (1372).

of Kosovo in 1389. In short, the image acknowledges military failure but evokes a power beyond political boundaries as well.

But important as these wall paintings may be, the Virgin of the Passion saturated threatened Orthodox territories all the more through portable icons. In one of these images that survives at Saint Catherine's Monastery on Mount Sinai, the Greek inscription reminds fearful Christians that this was an emotion shared by their Lord: "And Christ, clothed in mortal flesh, seeing the signs of death, was afraid (fig. 9.5)."[35]

A Virgin of the Passion icon can be found in the Byzantine lake town of Kastoria as well.[36] On the back of the image of the deposition (the removal of Christ from the tomb), an artist painted an image of the confident Mary and child, but—reflecting the conditions in the Balkans—the Virgin of the Passion was included flanking the image on the lower right (fig. 9.5).[37] Interestingly enough, in this icon, Theodore Apsevdis's precise arrangement at the Virgin of the Vetches church endures. On the right column of images surrounding the main icon, the Virgin of the Passion is just below a depiction of the Dormition, evoking the priestly prayer "You are the one who offers." On the left of the main icon, the presentation of Mary in the temple is portrayed just above Simeon, completing the prayer, "and is offered." The priestly resonances from Virgin of the Vetches church on Cyprus, it seems, were more than just a local oddity.

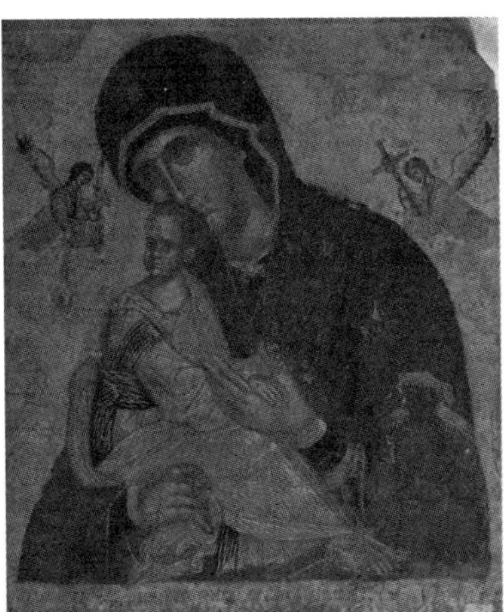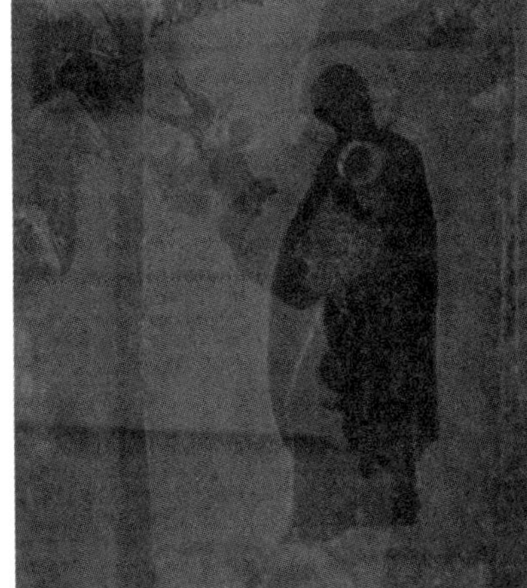

Figure 9.5. Virgin of the Passion icon at Saint Catherine's Monastery on Mount Sinai; detail of the Virgin of the Passion flanking the Virgin Pantanassa in Kastoria, Greece.

An equally rich association of the Virgin of the Passion to the Eucharist came when she replaced, in several instances, the traditional Annunciation on the royal doors of the sanctuary, through which the Eucharist emerges.[38] Mary and a frightened Jesus appear on the right-hand door, while a single angel with the cross appears on the left-hand door. The associations with the prayer "You are the one who offers and is offered" here continue. These images, however, also seem to be intimating that the entire empire might be offered up as well.

Another portable Virgin of the Passion at the Saint Anastasia Museum in Rhodes, dating to the mid-fifteenth century, makes for a particularly poignant connection to defeat, for the image appears to have been painted as the Knights of Rhodes were furiously at work defending the island from Ottomans. In this icon, Mary is seated on a throne, and an angel in a bright-orange tunic, as tall as the seated Virgin, stands bearing the instruments of the passion.[39]

She is a far cry from the island's most well-known surviving sculpture, the *Nike of Samothrace* of the mid-second century BCE, expertly chiseled from the marble of Rhodes and now displayed at the Louvre. This "last great victory dedication of the Hellenistic Age" may be the delectable summit of Greek art.[40] But the Virgin of the Passion had carved an alternative, even if this was something that the Crusaders, Mourtzouphlos, the Knights of Rhodes, or the Ottomans could not fathom (fig. 9.6).

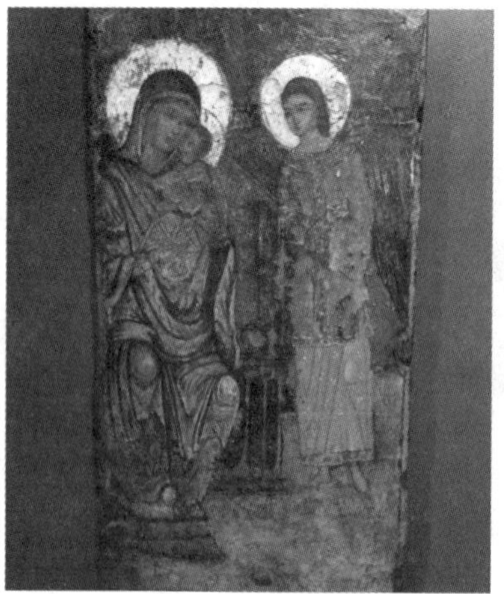
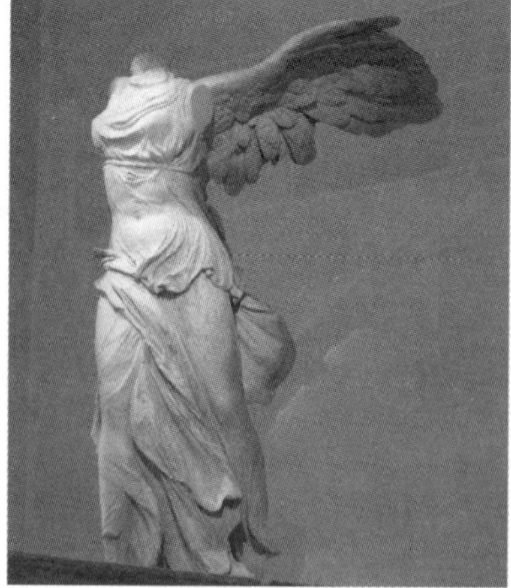

Figure 9.6. The Virgin of the Passion at Rhodes and the *Nike of Samothrace* made from Rhodian marble.

Reverse Dominion

THE VIRGIN OF Victory that had been captured by the Latins in the Fourth Crusade, it turns out, was a decoy. The Virgin of the Passion was far more difficult to apprehend. Indeed, besides her peaceful occupation of Zadar and Venice today, already mentioned, the icon would lovingly apprehend all of the Byzantine Empire's attackers. The Virgin of the Passion has colonized Richard's England, appearing in every corner of what we would today call the United Kingdom, from the heart of London to the Scottish moors.[41] Moreover, in the streets of Nicosia, just steps from the castle where the Knights Templar emerged to butcher the Orthodox locals, nuns from Sri Lanka have recently unfurled a banner illustrating the same icon. The entire domain of modern France, warred over by Philip and Richard, would eventually be dotted with thousands of churches housing this icon.[42] Paris's jewel-box church of Sainte-Chapelle, the storehouse for the relics taken from Constantinople in the Fourth Crusade, is itself ringed by shrines to the Virgin of the Passion in the form of *Notre-Dame du Perpétuel Secours*. There is even a large church dedicated to the image just a short walk from the Metro stop named after Philip Augustus.[43] Even in the labyrinthine alleys of the city of Cairo once ruled by Saladin, she appears in curtain veils and makeshift altars too numerous to count (fig. 9.7).

The prerequisite for this full dominion, however, was a singular event: the final collapse of the Byzantine Empire itself.

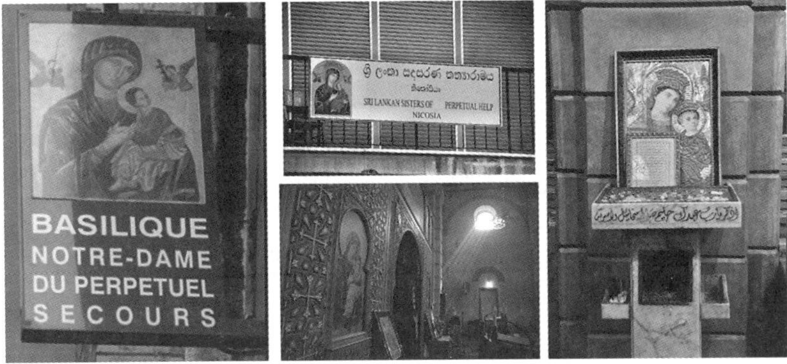

Figure 9.7. Sign for a Parisian Basilica, the Sri Lankan Sisters of Perpetual Help banner in Nicosia, and Virgins of the Passion in contemporary Cairo's Coptic sector.

❧ **10** ☙

PEACEFUL CONQUEST

The maxim of illusory religion runs: "Fear not; trust in God and he will see that none of the things you fear will happen to you"; that of real religion, on the contrary, is "Fear not; the things that you are afraid of are quite likely to happen to you, but they are nothing to be afraid of."

—John Macmurray, *Persons in Relation*

[The Fall of Constantinople] was a moment of recovery and rebirth. . . . [It was] a moment that provided the beginnings of an ongoing consolidation of a new, and largely unified, Christian identity in the East . . . unified as never before.

—K. E. Fleming, "Constantinople:
From Christianity to Islam"

Vivas to those who have fail'd!
And to those whose war-vessels sank in the sea!
And to those themselves who sank in the sea!
And to all generals that lost engagements, and all overcome heroes!

—Walt Whitman, *Song of Myself*

Byzantine cultural influence expanded almost in inverse proportion to its political strength.

—Judith Herrin, *Byzantium*

A City's Rise and Fall

IT WAS THOUGHT that the famous Hodegetria icon might prevent the empire's expiration. On August 15, 1261, the Feast of the Dormition of Mary, the Byzantine Empire had formally recovered from Latin occupation, and much of the credit was given to the Hodegetria. After he evicted the Crusaders, Emperor Michael Palaiologos (r. 1261–82) had made arrangements to enter Constantinople through its famous Golden Gate, with the icon leading the way. As one source from the time puts it, "It was on this icon that Michael Palaiologos had reposed his hopes of recapturing the Byzantine capital" (fig. 10.1).[1] And recapture it he did.

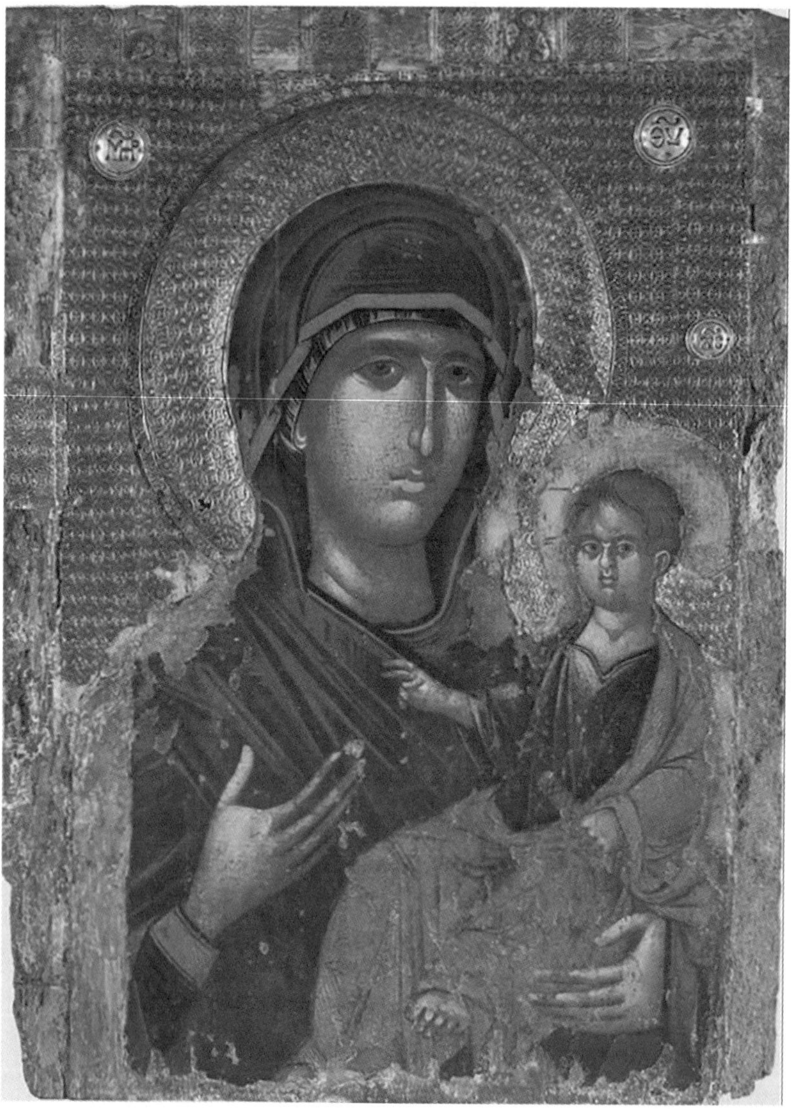

Figure 10.1. The Hodegetria icon (fourteenth-century copy), National Museum of Serbia.

The tradition of the Hodegetria's Tuesday procession, where the icon lent her hallowed presence to a variety of the city's monasteries, was resumed.[2] Laywomen followed in the Hodegetria's train carrying candles and wearing dresses of pure white silk, as if they were participating in a wedding. The laymen followed along in reverence, their voices offering a buzzing bass tone to the songs that were chanted before the icon at each church along the way. The image's weight required a group of men, the confraternity of the Hodegetria—with matching purple garments and headdresses—to lift her high, along with an umbrella that shielded her from the sun. The thuribles would have been packed with incense far beyond the level required for an interior procession and were no doubt waved with additional flair. After all, the entire city, during such processions, became a church. Even so, I expect the thuribles sent up enough sweet smoke of incense on these occasions to remind some elderly observers of the fire that had consumed the city during the siege of the Crusaders just over fifty years before.[3]

Imperial hope, and trust in this icon, was ultimately not fulfilled. With the rise of the Ottoman threat, the emperor of Constantinople soon became, as a well-known saying goes, more of a mayor than an emperor. Aside from the holdout of the fortress of Mystra in southern Greece, Constantinople would soon become all that was left. As outside threats increased, the Hodegetria icon, Byzantium's great protector, was moved from the Hodegon to the Chora monastery near the city's massive land walls, which was thought to be more secure. The monastery had already been covered with some of the most splendid flowerings of late Byzantine art. These mosaics, lovingly created in the empire's twilight, must have welcomed the famous Hodegetria icon with solemnity and deference. And it was here that Constantinople's official palladium, her invincible protector, failed.

The nineteen-ton cannon, nicknamed "Basilica," capable of firing an eight-hundred-pound projectile, could not be interminably resisted. On May 29, 1453, the Ottomans at last breached the land walls of Constantinople, walls that had stood strong for over one thousand years. The Janissaries—that is, kidnapped Christian children who had been raised to become the sultan's elite force—entered the Chora monastery and, after casting lots for the jewels in which the Hodegetria was encrusted, famously hacked the image to pieces with an axe.[4] It happened on a Tuesday, no less, the same day as the icon's famous weekly procession. If the point of the Hodegetria was mere protection, she was ultimately pointless.

Some argued that the destruction of the idolatrous Hodegetria occurred because Islam was destined to triumph over Christianity.[5] Others have gone so far as to blame the destruction of the Hodegetria on the obstinacy of the Orthodox in refusing to submit to the papacy.[6] Still others might suggest that any appeal to protective icons is part of a vanished religious past, and such images should now be bequeathed to the secular domain of art historians and museum curators who can neutralize them lest they cause further religious conflict.[7]

But there is another way of perceiving the same event. As Byzantium's late spiritual masters, the hesychasts, put it, Mary's power was of a higher kind, and she "showed what it meant to be a heavenly subject instead of an earthly one."[8] The Hodegetria could permit this disaster because her successor, the Virgin of the Passion, was strong enough to endure.[9] As the first Virgin of the Passion arose from the outpost of Cyprus, the Virgin of the Passion this time would arise from the outpost of Crete (fig. 10.2).

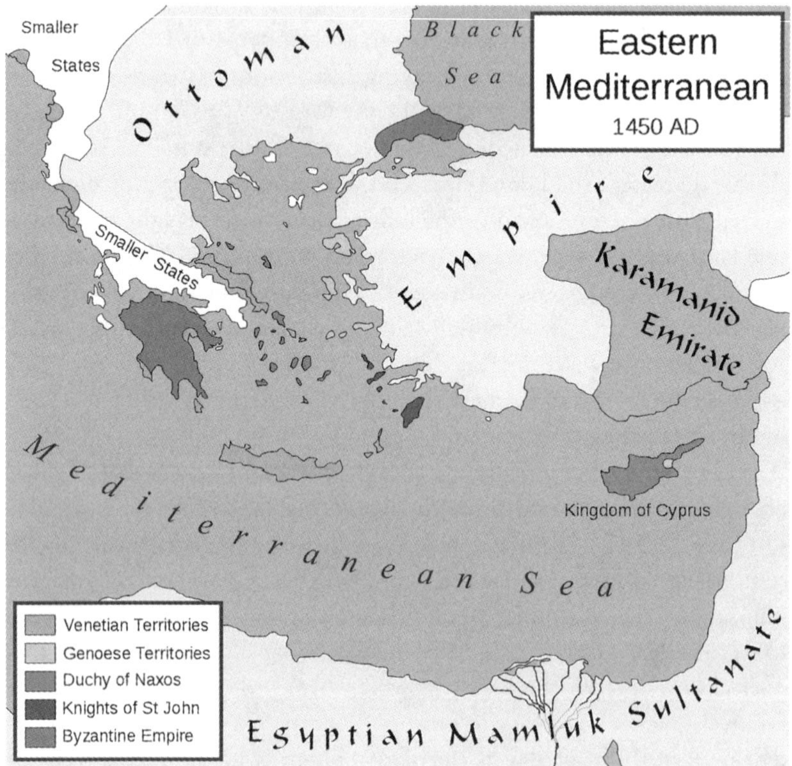

Figure 10.2. Eastern Mediterranean ca. 1450.

The Crossbow and the Brush

WHEREAS ORTHODOX CYPRUS was colonized by the Lusignans in the 1190s, Orthodox Crete was taken by the Venetians shortly after the Fourth Crusade.[10] In the centuries since the Venetian victory, the island's Greek Orthodox population had settled into a smoldering discontent, periodically breaking out in revolt. Like Cyprus, Crete's mountains hosted the holdouts, while the urban centers were given over to the Latin monastic orders. Gothic arches predominated, as did Dominican, Franciscan, and Augustinian monks. Orthodox priests were permitted to exist, but only with clipped wings. The Orthodox church on Crete was stripped of its power to ordain, lest its ministers escape Latin Christian surveillance.

But the threat of the Ottomans in the fifteenth century did much to unify Candia's Latin and Greek Christians. Venetian Crete sent reinforcements to Constantinople to resist the Ottomans, ships that carried Latin and Greek alike. One such Greek Christian from Crete, Nikolas Ritzos, is on record as having served on one such Venetian ship. A surviving document reveals that Nikolas Ritzos was enlisted as a crossbowman. He had also rented an expensive suit of armor, and his son Andreas, himself an icon painter, guaranteed the total value of his father's suit in case of a loss.[11]

But what the father was unable to accomplish with a weapon, his son Andreas was able to do with a brush. Naval missions to defend Constantinople were doomed to fail, but the artistic production from the island of Crete was destined for hitherto unimaginable success. Artists had emerged on Crete as distinguished individuals, enjoying considerable amounts of education, prestige, and wealth.[12] And among these artists, Andreas Ritzos in particular was responsible for codifying the form of the Virgin of the Passion that would spread throughout the globe.

The diverse earlier examples of the Virgin of the Passion would, thanks to Andreas Ritzos, be simplified and streamlined. Moreover, this new form of the icon would be affordable. Just as Theodore Apsevdis had translated the imagery of mosaics into the less expensive medium of fresco painting, now artists were translating fresco paintings into the more affordable and accessible mode of icons.[13] Which is to say, just as the Hodegetria was being hacked to pieces, her replacement was being produced on an almost industrial scale.[14]

Andreas Ritzos and the Final Formulation

HIGHLY EDUCATED, RITZOS was informed not only of the complex differences between Latin and Greek Christianity but even by the Jewish mysticism of the Kabbalah.[15] He took this education and refined artistic training, freighted now with the weight of a long-anticipated Mediterranean catastrophe, and poured it into his work. If Augustine had written *City of God* to provide a theological account for the fall of the Roman Empire, Andreas Ritzos would do the same thing for the fall of the Byzantine Empire—but with a paintbrush instead of a pen. Ritzos must have lamented his father's failed military venture; he surely witnessed the flood of Orthodox refugees pouring into his home island. Under these new conditions, the mere allusions to suffering that haunted the icons of Andreas's artistic predecessors would no longer be adequate.[16] Centuries beforehand, Theodore Apsevdis had moved beyond allusions on Cyprus, for the suffering of the island required that the instruments of the passion be painted directly. And now, Andreas Ritzos would replicate this precise evolution again (fig. 10.3).

In addition to the angels bearing the cross, spear, and sponge, Ritzos included Christ's upturned foot as Theodore did on Cyprus. But to

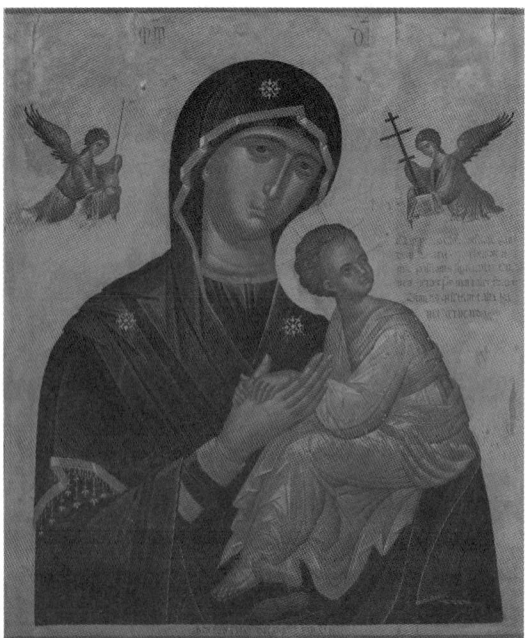

Figure 10.3. Virgin of the Passion by Andreas Ritzos.

emphasize Christ's vulnerable humanity even more, his sandal—which a future John the Baptist would dare not loosen—dangles.[17] Ritzos also added the charming detail of Christ gently grasping his mother's thumb at the icon's precise center, in the region of Mary's heart.[18] The child's face is wrenched away to engage the angel with the cross. This balances the tenderness of the united hands of Jesus with a stark severity.[19] Still, Christ lacks the panic manifested in other Virgins of the Passion such as those in the Balkans. The result is an equipoise between fear and confidence that surrenders to neither. In other words, both the north wall (Simeon holding the struggling Christ child) and the south wall (Mary holding a confident Jesus) painted by Theodore Apsevdis in Cyprus are at play in this icon. The icon's priestly associations, therefore, are consequently intensified; at the same time, Christ's human and divine nature both receive subtle visual appeals. The golden tassels on Mary's garment (her maphorion) may evoke her priesthood as well, recalling the pomegranate and bell-lined priestly garments of Aaron (Exod 28:31–35).[20]

Andreas Ritzos would sign his name in both Greek and Latin to reach out to both Orthodox and Catholic clientele.[21] In addition, a Greek or Latin inscription is frequently affixed to the image to appeal to a bilingual range of customers. The inscription reads,

> *The one who previously hailed the Virgin*
> *Now the symbols of the Passion shows.*
> *Christ having robed Himself in mortal flesh*
> *Looks at them apprehensively in fear of death.*[22]

Clearly, Ritzos struck a nerve, for with the Fall of Constantinople, the popularity of this particular icon dramatically expanded. An oft-cited contract from 1499 lists an order of seven hundred Cretan icons, five hundred "*a la latina*" and two hundred "*a la greca*."[23] This demand would peak in the 1560s and 1570s, corresponding with the zenith of Venetian power.[24] Not all of these icons were Virgins of the Passion in the Ritzos formulation, but many of them would have been. The result is that at the same time that the Virgin of Victory (Nicopeia) icon was retroactively, even nostalgically, connected by Venetians to the sack of Constantinople in 1204 with much pomp and splendor, the Virgin of the Passion—in a new form—was quietly stealing the show.[25]

Even when Western artistic influence, such as one-point perspective and naturalized blue skies, encroached upon this icon type, the

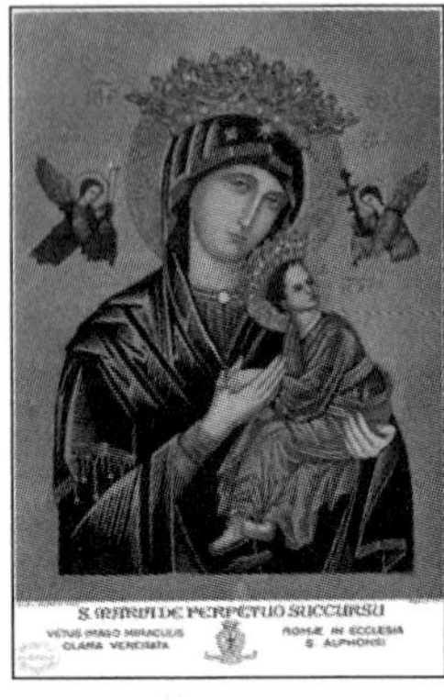

Figure 10.4. Our Lady of Perpetual Help.

Virgin of the Passion as defined by Ritzos seems to have been almost untouchable.[26] The type, with two angels bearing the instruments, the conjoined hands of mother and son, the tilted head of Christ, and a dangling sandal, was set.[27] Christ looks to the angel with the cross, seemingly unaware of its meaning. The knowing, heavy eyes of Mary, which engage the viewer, betray that she does (fig. 10.4).

Miraculous Verification and Global Proliferation of the Ritzos Type

THE FAME OF the icon, already widespread thanks to the artists of Crete, would gain an additional boost when it was connected to reports of a miracle.[28] It is a story that has been propagated as widely, and with as little variation, as the icon itself. It is not the only miraculous story associated with the icon.[29] But it is the most widespread and is for that reason worth reciting in full.[30]

At the height of the Venetian icon trade, one sailor stole a Virgin of the Passion from a church in Crete and absconded with it to Rome (fig. 10.5). During a storm at sea, the image was credited with the ship's safe passage. Upon arrival in Rome, the thief held on to the image until— upon falling ill—he mended his ways, requesting to a friend that the icon be placed in a church. Rather than follow these instructions, the friend was convinced by his wife to keep the impressive image for himself. The family's daughter subsequently received a vision in which Mary demanded that the picture be placed in the Church of Saint Matthew, located between the churches of Santa Maria Maggiore and the Basilica of Saint John Lateran in Rome. Mary revealed herself in this vision as *Mater de Perpetuo Succursu* (Mother of Perpetual Help), and this in turn became the origin

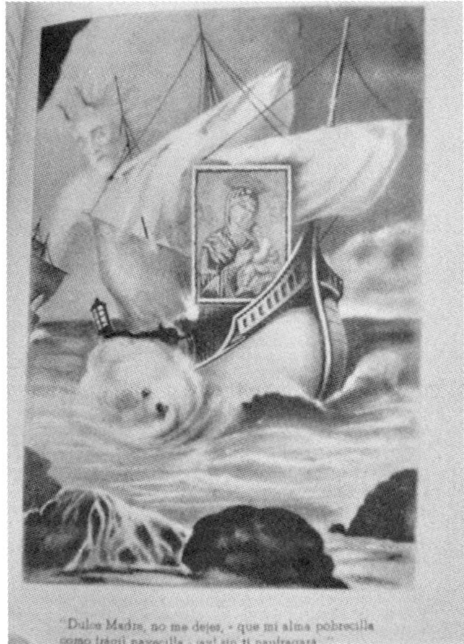

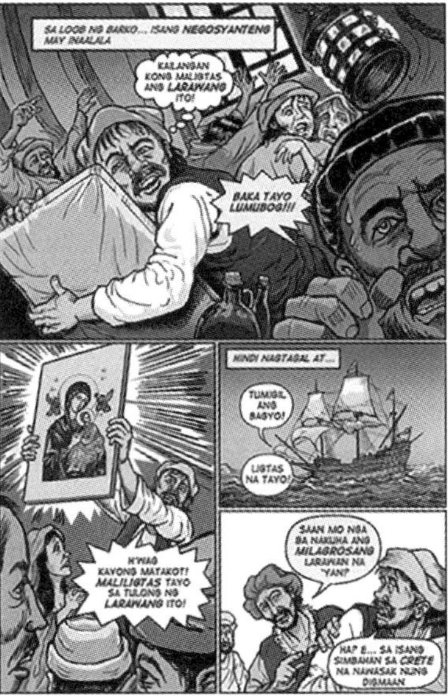

Figure 10.5. Legend of Our Lady of Perpetual Help related by a Spanish story-book (Epifanio Moran's *Esclavos de "La Esclava,"* Madrid, 1946) and comic in Filipino (Ang Larawan ng Ina ng Laging Saklolo).

of the icon's second name. The parents yielded to their daughter's wishes, and the image was placed in the Church of Saint Matthew at Merulana in Rome on March 27, 1499—near the high-water mark of Cretan icon production. So it was that "devotion to Our Mother of Perpetual Help began to spread throughout the city of Rome."[31]

Soon, the fate of this originally Byzantine icon would be connected to modern empires as well, specifically Napoleon's. When the Church of Saint Matthew was destroyed in 1798 during the French invasion of Rome by Napoleon's army, the icon was moved to another church and was nearly forgotten.[32] Oral tradition, however, kept the memory of the icon alive, and a generation later, the whereabouts of the image was rediscovered.[33] The former site of the Church of Saint Matthew was now inhabited by the global order of Redemptorist priests, who named their new church after their founder, Saint Alphonsus Liguori (d. 1787). When these Redemptorists learned that an icon had once been kept at the site of their new headquarters, they petitioned Pope Pius IX (head of the church from 1846 to 1878) to have the image entrusted to them. Not only did this famous pope grant the request, but he also insisted in 1865 that the Redemptorists "make Her known throughout the world."[34]

So it was that the newly discovered icon made its modern debut, becoming the prototype for worldwide proliferation as Our Lady of Perpetual Help.[35] If the icon's expansion on Crete was nearly industrial in scale, now its reproduction would be industrial without qualification. The image's machine-aided replication in the nineteenth and twentieth centuries, including medals, prayer books, short tracts, official reproductions, and even comic books, dwarfed any earlier multiplication.[36] Ritzos's—and only Ritzos's—Virgin of the Passion was reproduced at a staggering rate; gaining the world, according to one of the icon's admirers, "by peaceful conquest."[37] So as not to only privilege those with vision, the variety of these reproductions is such that there is even one book that offers novenas to the image in braille (fig. 10.6).

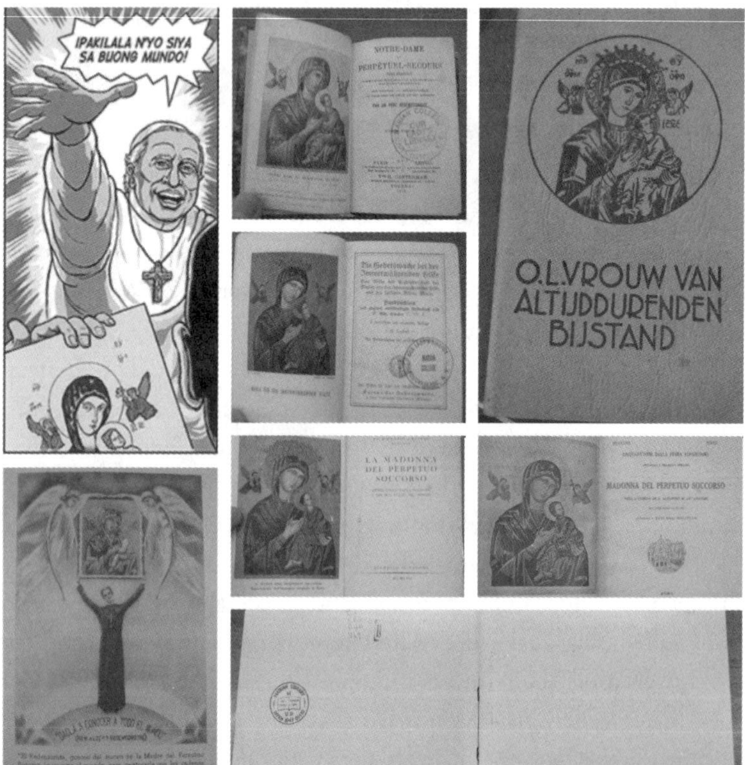

Figure 10.6. Our Lady of Perpetual Help devotional manuals.

Peaceful Conquest

BUT WHEREVER THIS icon went, its original connection to suffering and loss would not remain far from view. When Napoleon's troops conquered Rome, they may have sent a miraculous Virgin of the Passion, now dubbed Our Lady of Perpetual Help, into hiding. But they also inadvertently set up the conditions for the same icon's rediscovery and global expansion sixty-five years later, an expansion that would occupy so much of the territory that Napoleon fleetingly sought to conquer himself.

Moreover, when Pope Pius IX chose this icon as the image to be disseminated globally by the Redemptorist order, his choice was more fitting than he could have known. He was, after all, quickly losing the Papal States. Pius IX had personally blessed the swords of those who would defend his once ample territory, even as they used the old Crusader battle cry, "God wills it."[38] He was not about to yield to the status of the patriarch of Constantinople, with only the ability "to pray and to bless."[39]

Still, the papacy, willingly or not, was shifting from a military to a more spiritual role.[40] In 1870, months after the proclamation of papal infallibility, canons bombarded the gates of Rome and the Papal States were annexed completely, bringing a more than one-thousand-year temporal reign (754–1870) to an end.[41] In the following year, the Virgin of the Passion—with Mary and Jesus now crowned—was formally placed on the high altar of Saint Alphonsus, the base of its global replication as Our Lady of Perpetual Help.[42] What had happened to Cyprus and Constantinople had happened to Rome.

The Virgin of the Passion became the heir of the Hodegetria, but to spread not ultramontanism (as has been argued) but mercy.[43] The Tuesday processions of the Hodegetria in Constantinople may have been impressive, but after the city's collapse, the Virgin of the Passion would reach far beyond the walls of the city itself in a global procession through lands of which the most learned Byzantine was not yet even aware. Which is to say, the Virgin of the Passion guarantees not the glories of Christendom but the subtler glories that lie on the far side of its collapse. Perhaps she even anticipates new micro-Christendoms to come, less wedded to the powers of this world and all the stronger for it.

CONCLUSION

A MADONNA OF THE FUTURE

We must not jump over the missing feminine to embrace the appealing image of androgyny, an identity beyond male and female. What kind of solution can that be? The feminine has been neglected for centuries, and now it is not to matter any more; we are beyond it. There must be a time—and I think our is the time, with all our anger and hurt, with all our raised fists and our open palms—when the feminine can have its chance to be herself, her many selves, together and differently.

—Ann Belford Ulanov, *The Wisdom of the Psyche*

I am not saying that suffering exists in order for God to reveal himself. I am only saying that where suffering exists and is consciously accepted, there divine love shines forth brightly. . . . Our jagged and hard-edged earth plane is the realm in which this mercy is the most deeply, excruciatingly, and beautifully released. That's our business down here. That's what we're here for.

—Cynthia Bourgeault, *The Wisdom Jesus*

The Marian sense of being overwhelmed from outside by the presence of the other's pain is one of the things that displaces the ego and its self-oriented projects—including the self-oriented project of "doing good" or "serving the neighbour."

—Rowan Williams, *Looking East in Winter*

The story of Christ's sacrifice belongs not to an economy of credit and exchange but to the trinitarian motion of love, it is given entirely as gift—a gift given when it should not have needed to be given again, by God, at a price that *we* imposed upon *him*. As an entirely divine action, Christ's sacrifice merely draws creation back into the eternal motion of divine love, for which it was fashioned.

—David Bentley Hart, *The Beauty of the Infinite*

IN THE MID-NINETEENTH century, the French writer and poet Théophile Gautier (1811–72) visited the crumbling walls of Istanbul, once Constantinople, a sight that he counted as the most austere and melancholic in the world. Walking along the mighty empire's once impregnable barrier, he noticed how earth and seed had found their way into the gaps in the masonry. Shrubs, he observed, had taken the place of battlements, growing into trees: "The thousand tendrils of parasitical plants sustained the stone which would otherwise have fallen; the roots of trees, after acting as wedges to introduce themselves between the joints of stones, became chains to confine them (fig. C.1)."[1]

Such was the role of the Virgin Mary in the Byzantine Empire and perhaps in other empires as well, a role so exquisitely communicated in

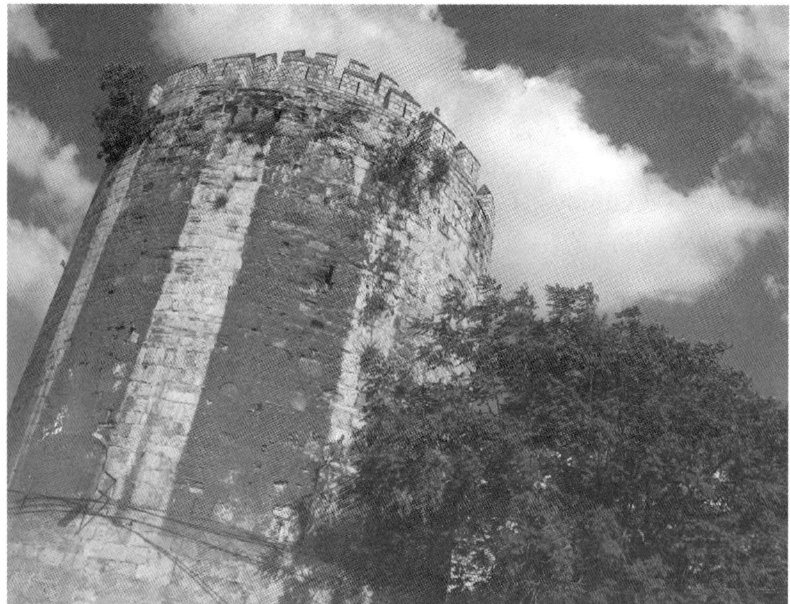

Figure C.1. The walls of Constantinople.

the Virgin of the Passion icon. Where the empire's walls had fallen, her tendrils sustained the stone and outlasted it. What has been said about Christianity in regard to antiquity can be said of the Virgin of the Passion in regard to Byzantium: "It has long survived the collapse of the empire from which it first emerged."[2] The Virgin of the Passion is at once among Byzantium's "most enduring legac[ies] . . . and the index of its utter transformation."[3] It may have been in Byzantium where Mary was linked to imperial power, but it was also in Byzantium where this link was severed. In short, Mary did not save the empire from destruction; instead, she taught the empire how to be gracefully destroyed and how to transcend that destruction as well.

For some, this conclusion may seem unsatisfying. After tracing the bloodshed in the wake of the 1389 Battle of Kosovo, Rebecca West (1892–1983), the great chronicler of the Balkans, found this Christian concession, the choice for a heavenly over an earthly kingdom, pitiable. This "impulse towards defeat" makes of the whole world "a vast Kosovo, an abominable blood-logged plain, where people who love go out to fight people who hate, and betray their cause to their enemies, so that loving is persecuted for immense tracts of history, far longer than its little periods of victory."[4] West concludes that "until there is a kind Caesar every child of woman is born in peril."[5] But God himself, born in peril under an unkind Caesar, knows such conditions himself. Sadly, West's tour guide on her visit to King Marko's monastery was too rushed and failed to point out the Virgin of the Passion painted on its wall.[6] The icon represents the repudiation of the kind of Atonement theology Rebecca West abhorred.[7] The image does not value suffering and defeat for its own sake; still less does it mock those called to nation building, protective service, or legitimate defense. It only teaches us how to bear suffering when, despite our legitimate efforts to forestall it for ourselves or for others, suffering finds us still.

Mary among the Goddesses

THE ISLANDS OF Cyprus and Crete—hailed today, however dubiously, as the homeland of innocent goddess worship—were, in fact, the islands that promulgated the pagan logic of sacrifice.[8] Until, that is, such logic was overturned, a reversal represented by the Virgin of the Passion that emerged from those same islands.[9] It is not that Mary, in this remarkable icon, delivered what previous goddesses such as Astarte, Isis, Aphrodite, or Artemis promised. She did not compete on those terms. In place of the child sacrifice sponsored by Astarte, Mary offered up the lamb of God, the priestly sacrifice that rendered future ones, whether human or animal, unnecessary.[10] In place of Isis, a fourth-generation deity, Mary represents the Wisdom that is the first (not fourth) of God's acts of old.[11] In place of phallus-centered Egyptian religion, where a solitary male God masturbates the world into existence, the Virgin of the Passion presents the only-begotten son, born with no intervention from the phallus at all.[12] In place of the temple prostitution of Aphrodite, Mary offered a less salacious beauty, cultivated by artists like Theodore Apsevdis and Andreas Ritzos, who never required Mary to strip.[13] In place of the security promised by Artemis—promised but not delivered—Mary offered a faith that could survive devastation intact.[14]

In short, what was said about Mary a generation ago—that she merely endorses the status quo of men—is far more credibly assigned to the pagan goddess tradition that Mary replaced.[15] The status of regular women under Christianity has also been checkered, of course, for patriarchy is a many-headed hydra. But Christianity offers unique resources to combat it.[16] Epiphanius of Salamis (d. 403) may have railed against female participation in the Christian liturgy from the island of Cyprus in addition to arguing that women are, by definition, "unstable, prone to error, and mean-spirited."[17] Arguing against women in ministry, he thundered, "If it were ordained by God that women should offer sacrifice or have any canonical function in the church, Mary herself, if anyone, should have functioned as a priest in the New Testament. . . . But it was not God's pleasure [that she be a priest]."[18]

Yet an enormity of visual and verbal references to Mary as a priest in the Byzantine tradition, especially on the island of Cyprus, suggest otherwise. Neophytos's statement is worth repeating: "She comes as a table, having upon it the bread of life. . . . She comes as a grapevine bearing the cluster so that new wine may slake the faithful."[19] Neophytos also used the motif of a woman, the Virgin Mary, breaking a taboo to dwell in the holy of holies as a symbol of men finding redemption.[20] At the Virgin of the Vetches, Theodore depicted such a vision in paint.[21] The Virgin of the Passion icon represents this Marian priesthood that emerged from the heart of Orthodox Christianity. Scholars who resist Mary's priestly aspects, whether from secular-feminist or traditional Christian approaches, agree that Mary cannot be associated with the Eucharist.[22] She would certainly not appear on altars.[23] But Mary represents the church, so it could not be otherwise. Accordingly, the Virgin

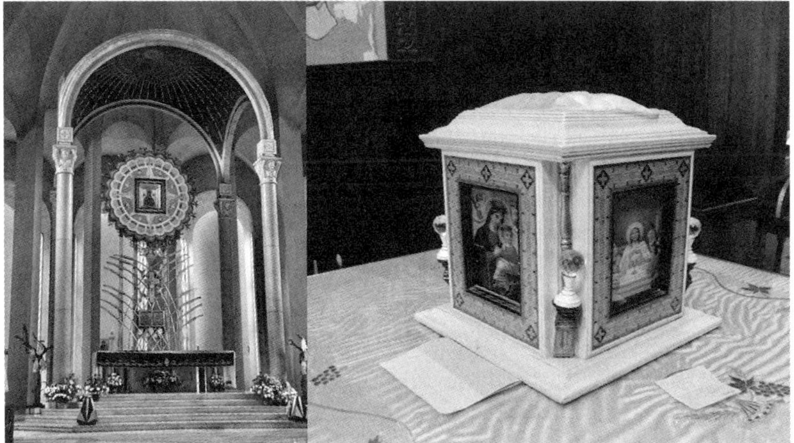

Figure C.2. Virgin of the Passion in eucharistic altar contexts at the Baclaran Church and Saint Damian in Boulaq, Cairo.

of the Passion regularly appears both near altars and on them.[24] She can be found dripping with brass grapes atop a tower of eucharistic sheaves at her famous shrine in the Philippines or casually perched on the high altar in the sanctuary in the churches of Coptic Cairo (fig. C.2). Representing the resolution of the eucharistic controversy of 1156/57, the Virgin of the Passion testifies to the undivided Trinity that—in the eucharistic banquet—overcomes all orders of sacrifice, debt, punishment, and exchange, freely inviting all of creation to feast.[25]

Mary and Christian Violence

OR SO IT could have been. More often than not, the fractured church ostensibly formed by this feast has failed to absorb its central message. A church formally beholden to Christ's teaching of love even for one's enemies—obviously enough—should have been far less violent than its record reveals.[26] Christians must therefore look the criticism that their faith fosters aggression and violence, the paradigmatic case being the Crusades, squarely in the eye. Historical context, important as it may be, and the theoretically legitimate use of defensive force do not cause legitimate moral complaints against Christianity to evaporate.[27]

Still, the Virgin of the Passion and its enormous global popularity afford a noteworthy response to such charges. Even while violence in the name of Christianity endures, modern representatives of the military orders of the Knights Templar or the Knights Hospitaller are not easily found. The former was (however cruelly) suppressed, and the latter survives only in a variety of chivalric orders that offer modern relief work.[28] But the Virgin of the Passion, born from the Easter morning slaughter by the Knights Templar in 1192, suffuses the globe as possibly the most enduring visual result of these missions of Christian violence. The Truer Cross borne by the angels in this image has surpassed the obsession with the "True Cross" that generated the Crusades.

The icon, thanks to its Athanasian reference to Wisdom, also offers an answer to the violent theology of double predestination, the chilling prospect that God ordained some to salvation and others to an irrevocable, predetermined damnation. "In spite of its great richness this [Athanasian] insight had little or no influence upon the later development of the doctrine of predestination," inveighed Karl Barth in the twentieth century.[29] And yet, while it may have been ignored in verbal theology, this Athanasian perspective on predestination did inform the visual theology of Byzantium, specifically through the motif of the Prepared Throne and—because of the icon's connection to this motif in its original setting—in the Virgin of the Passion icon as well.[30]

As if in response to such amnesia, throughout the cities where major debates about predestination occurred—Boston, Princeton, and St. Louis, in particular—major shrines to the Virgin the Passion offered, and still offer, a corrective.[31] Such icons, proclaiming God's eternal decision for and not against us, surely put the *perpetual* in Our Lady of Perpetual Help. Mary, when we include her aspects as Wisdom and the collective humanity of the church, represents us all. Not only is the Wisdom offered by this icon orthodox, but to deny such Wisdom is to flirt with the clearly heretical prospect that Jesus is not fully divine. It is time to bring this Sophia, too long outsourced to fringe traditions, in from the cold.[32]

Just as importantly, the icon also corrects those who would underestimate the deity's bliss by projecting violence onto God. Classical Christian theology posits that God is perfect innocence. Select currents of modern theology, however, inject "the finite, the fragile, the weak, the negative . . . within God himself."[33] But the Virgin of the Passion avoids this error, adhering as it does to the jagged demarcation in Theodore's program between created and uncreated, beyond which human minds cannot speculate.[34] In the Virgin of the Passion icon, God surely takes on our grizzly finitude, a fact represented unambiguously by the cross.[35] But the original representation in Cyprus—connected as it is to the majestic Christ in the dome above—is anchored to the infinite plenitude of Christ's divine nature as well.[36] Which is to say, the God of the Virgin of the Passion, however freighted with grief, is at the same time "the inexhaustible fountainhead of life and light and beauty, a God of infinite ontological health."[37]

Finally, the image also mitigates violence between Christians. Although the icon has been viewed as a triumphant possession of Catholicism against a stubborn Orthodox church that has failed to submit to the papacy, another way of seeing the image, because it encapsulates the Nicene faith, is as a unifier of divided Christianity.[38] The image calls Christians to look not only backward to some ideal Christian moment of unity but forward to the sixteen hundredth anniversary of the split from the Church of the East in 2031 or to the one thousandth anniversary of the split between East and West in 2054.[39] Looking to the Latin and Greek leaders united underneath this Madonna in one illustration (fig. C.3), the image serves as an emblem of ecumenism.[40] If, as some have suggested, we are entering a new "Age of Mary," it is paramount that it be not the pet project of one branch of the Christian tradition but a global effort of the entire church.[41] The Virgin of the Passion is already embraced by Eastern Orthodoxy, Roman Catholicism, and Oriental Orthodoxy.[42] But it beautifully encapsulates Protestant theology as well.[43] The Redemptorists of Belfast, under the patronage of the icon, have worked for peace between Protestants and Catholics.[44] The icon's global presence, moreover—unconnected to any one Christian confession, still less to imperial politics—makes it particularly suited as an expression of global faith. "The association of the Christian religion with Roman civilization adversely disassociated non-Roman kingdoms with Christianity," claims one recent study of global Christian faith.[45] If so, perhaps only an expressly postimperial image like the Virgin of the Passion can be a banner for global Christianity in the present. An *image*, as opposed to an abstract verbal declaration, may be the most immediate path to unifying the long-entrenched verbal kingdoms of divided Christianity.[46] Perhaps, moreover, this unity has already been visually achieved and has only failed to be noticed. How fitting if an image born of Christian violence against Christians would be recognized as an icon of unity par excellence.

In sum, Theodore Apsevdis succeeded in replicating the theological and liturgical heritage of the Church of Holy Wisdom, Hagia Sophia, on the island outpost of Cyprus, while being free from the entanglements of imperial power. As the Crusaders pursued the True Cross, the

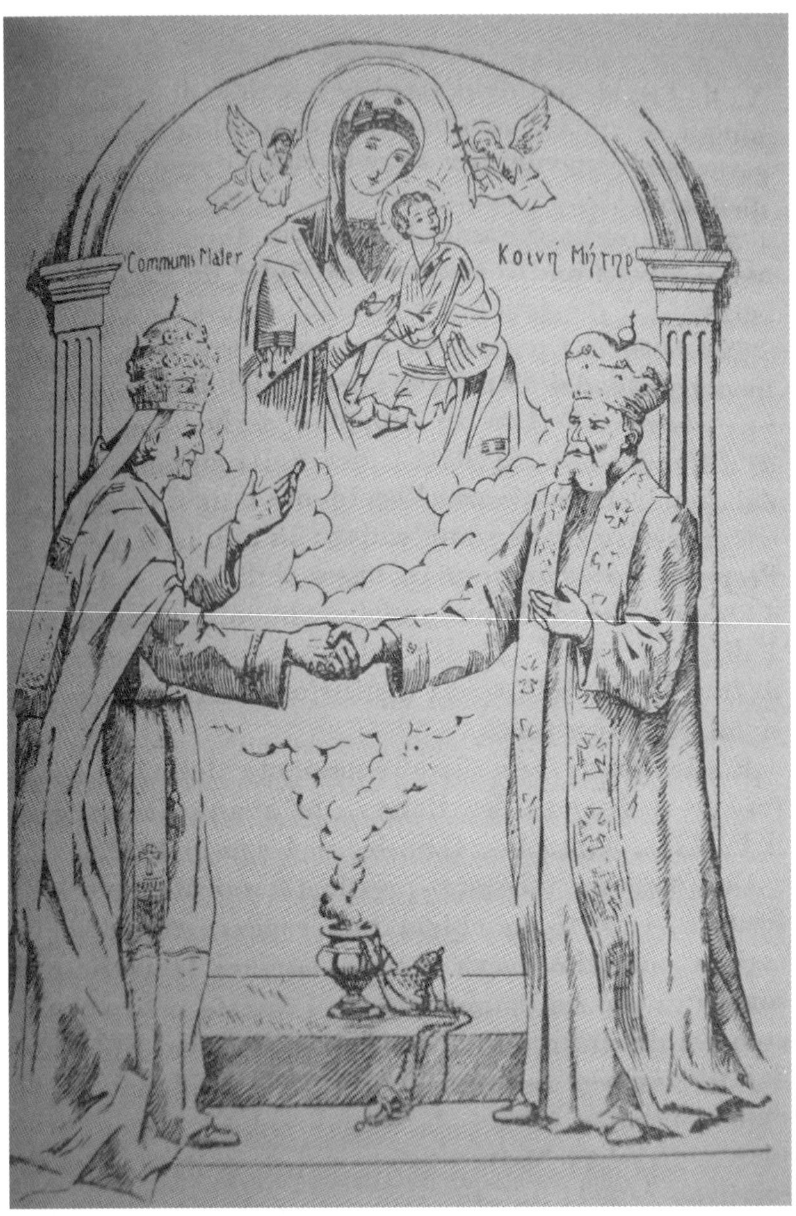

Figure C.3. Our Lady of Perpetual Help unifying the Catholic and Orthodox churches in a modern devotional manual.

Wisdom of the Virgin of the Passion gently pursued the Crusaders. Centuries later, as the Ottomans conquered Constantinople, including Hagia Sophia, the Virgin of the Passion's mission to disseminate such Wisdom was renewed by Andreas Ritzos, who, along with those who copied him, produced innumerable Hagia Sophias in miniature.[47] The Mary in the Virgin of the Passion icon answers Christian violence with the lamb of peace, she offers the eucharistic lamb once and for all, and she answers divisive speculation about predestination with the "lamb slain from the foundation of the world" (Rev 13:8 KJV). The Virgin of the Passion, truly the "icon of love," communicates all of these complexities in an instant.[48]

The story this global icon tells is, therefore, the great story of redemption, a story that outranks and outlasts all other stories, including all stories that remain to be told as well. Nothing precedes the contents of this icon, "neither death nor life, nor angels nor rulers, nor things present nor things to come, nor height, nor depth, nor anything else in all creation" (Rom 8:38–39). For if this icon's Wisdom did not precede such stories, she would not be the "first of his acts of old" (Prov 8:22). To speak in modern terms, the Virgin of the Passion both precedes and includes the stories of physics, astronomy, geology, and biological evolution, including any future advances in such fields. The icon antedates and transcends all stories of power, whether of the Byzantine Empire or any other empire, nation, federation, conceptual schema, or economic system. Naturally, the story of this icon anticipates and encompasses our own personal stories as well. For in the words of Thomas Aquinas, "this nativity [i.e., Wisdom] is the beginning of every other nativity."[49]

A Global Tour

FOR ALL THEIR ambitions, no Crusader king or Ottoman sultan would have dared to imagine a reign as expansive and long lasting as the reign of the Virgin of the Passion. From the crypts of private chapels to the peaks of mountain cathedrals, she has enveloped the world in a clandestine network of compassionate sorrow. Often she is not noticed. Or at least not noticed until the travails of life are acute enough to shake an observer into noticing she is already there.

She contests contemporary political corruption in the Philippines from her base at the Baclaran Church (fig. C.4). The crutches piled up next to the image at the Our Lady of Perpetual Help Basilica in Boston, a testimony to healings, almost seem to tease Harvard Medical School, located only a few city blocks away (fig. C.4). She holds her place at Moscow's Pushkin Square, where the Strastnoy Monastery dedicated to her had long stood. In the Soviet era, it was commandeered as a museum for antireligious propaganda until it was destroyed by Stalin in 1937 and renamed Pushkin Square. In turn, the same square hosted Russia's first McDonald's in 1991.[50] There is now a strong movement for the monastery's reconstruction among Russians who appear dissatisfied with communism and capitalism; the Virgin of the Passion offers a challenge to both.[51] While Mary has been marshaled anew for nationalism by some Russians, she has just as frequently been marshaled against abusive state power. The Virgin of the Passion exemplifies this spirit.[52]

The shrines to Nuestra Señora del Perpetuo Socorro (her Spanish title) throughout Mexico are an affront to the Conquistadores who took a different Mary, entitled *"La Conquistadora,"* as their emblem.[53] But she also challenges Indigenous theologies. In the very region where the famous Olmec greenstone sculpture the Las Limas Monument (1000–600 BCE) was discovered, possibly testifying to child sacrifice,

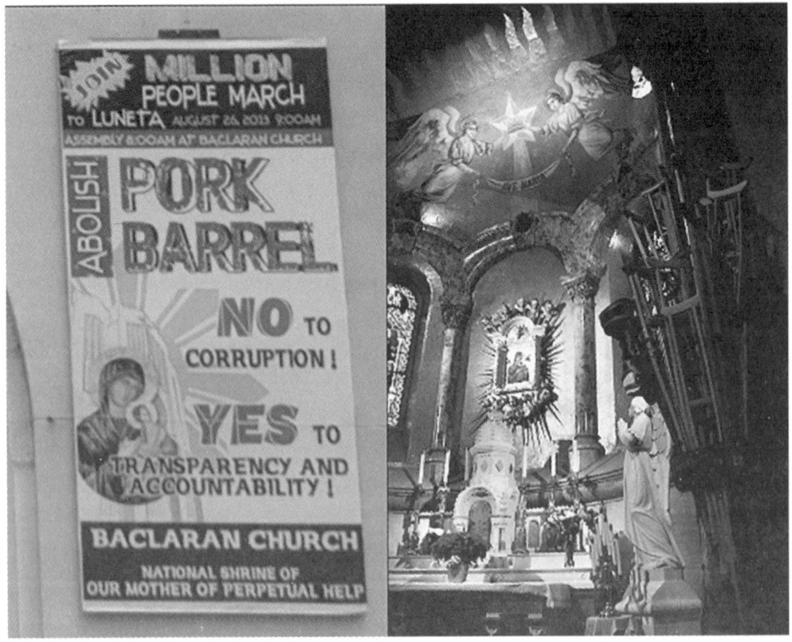

Figure C.4. Sign at the National Shrine of Our Mother of Perpetual Help in Manila and Our Lady of Perpetual Help shrine with crutches in Boston.

shrines to the Virgin of the Passion can now be found as well. She testifies to the cessation of sacrifice.[54]

In the Black Hills of South Dakota, she remains an emblem of Native American displacement.[55] The Virgin of the Passion icon emerged as a result of English, and then French, colonization of Cyprus, in turn becoming an emblem of the Indigenous population's original habitation of the island. In the same way, North America has itself been colonized by competing French and English interests, and the First Nations of the continent appear to have taken a liking to the icon in its form as Our Lady of Perpetual Help. Churches dedicated to this icon hover over battlefields where Indigenous people fought for their territory.[56] Moreover, the famous First Nations artist Norval Morrisseau (1932–2007), founder of the Woodland School, was depicted with this icon, reminding his secular admirers of just how intertwined Indigenous identities are with Christianity.[57] She is the titular icon of Rapid City, South Dakota, and Oklahoma City, Oklahoma, two cities that are major sites of Indigenous life. At the latter, Indigenous saints Kateri Tekakwitha and Juan Diego are depicted, alongside representatives of other Indigenous communities, under the banner of Our Lady of Perpetual Help (fig. C.5).[58]

In the parishes of St. Louis and Chicago, this image is embraced by African American communities. At Chicago's Church of the Holy

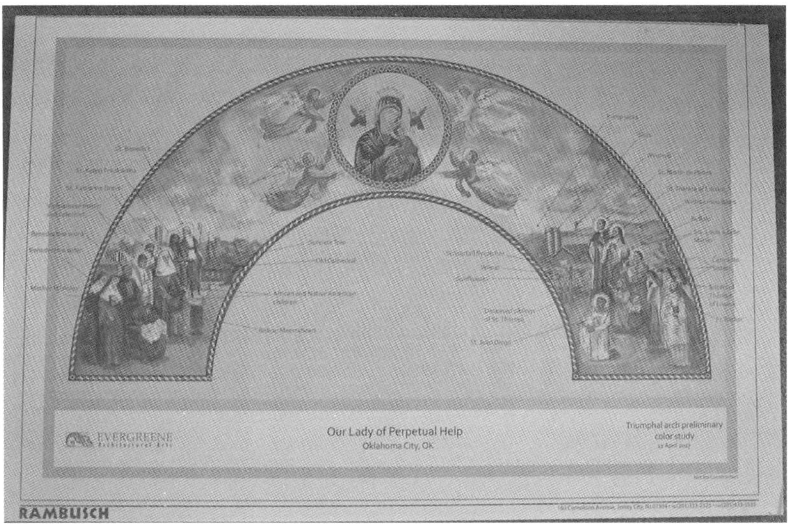

Figure C.5. Plans for Our Lady of Perpetual Help mural, Oklahoma City, OK.

Family, one example of Our Lady of Perpetual Help—credited with saving the church from the Great Chicago Fire of 1871—has been enthusiastically adopted by a predominantly African American church. The choir still rehearses by the icon with seven lights, in fulfillment of one priest's vow to burn them before the icon forever in gratitude for the church's survival. On my visit to the parish, the sermon centered on Marion Perkins's Black *Man of Sorrows* at the Art Institute of Chicago, and the sorrows of Mary in the icon and those of the Black Christ sculpted from Chicago's architectural fragments seemed to combine.

Moreover, in the Church of Saint Alphonsus Liguori in the heart of St. Louis, nicknamed "the Rock," visitors will find a fully Africanized Gothic environment.[59] Black saints, Coptic iconography, and African drums have graced the space but without any need to displace its famous icon, Our Lady of Perpetual Help.[60] Perhaps this is because as the patroness of Haiti, the icon is directly connected to the only successful slave revolt in human history.[61] Or perhaps it is because Mary, as one Black theologian suggests, "may hold the key to turning pain and contempt into maternal grace."[62] The image of Moses the Black next to a Virgin of the Passion in Koutloumousiou Monastery on Mount Athos, it turns out, was prescient (fig. C.6).

But all such North American depictions, impressive as they may be, seem eclipsed by her manifestations in Asia. Just a fifteen-minute drive away from a prominent temple to the goddess of prosperity in

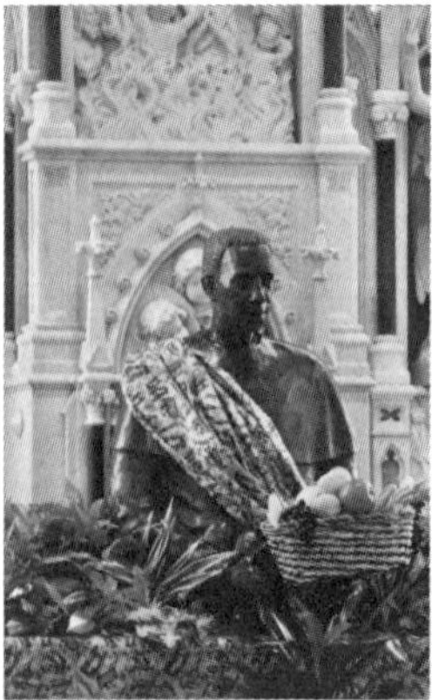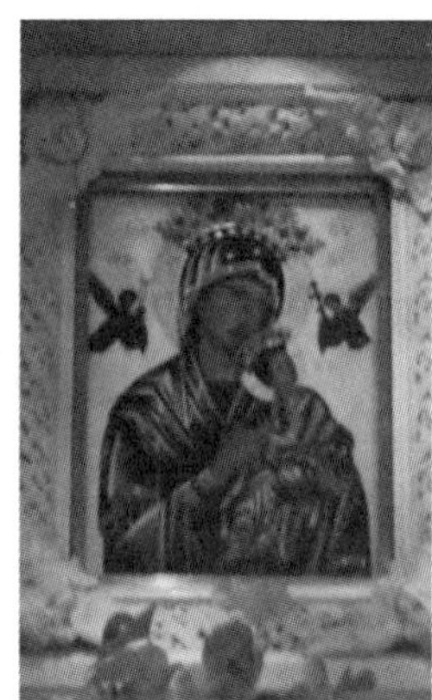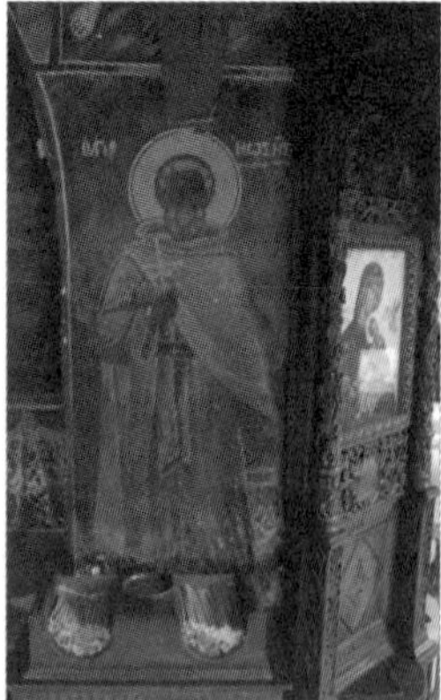

Figure C.6. East and west transepts at the Saint Alphonsus Liguori "Rock" Catholic Church in St. Louis and the Koutloumousiou Monastery shrine on Mount Athos with Moses the Black.

Chennai, India, there is a rival shrine to Our Lady of Perpetual Help.[63] A small shrine to Our Lady of Perpetual Help in Hong Kong seems to complement the large statue of the Buddhist goddess Guanyin, reminding the famous female bodhisattva of the Marian influence upon her.[64] In Singapore, the massive church of Our Lady of Perpetual Succour, featuring the icon, seems to do the same to the Kwan Im (Guan Yin) Thong Hood Cho Temple nearby. The Japanese American Catholic artist Daniel Mitsui has also made his own Virgin of the Passion that responds to Buddhism (fig. C.7).[65]

Indeed, the three-dot *çintamani* pattern on Christ's garment, which frequently appears in the Ritzos version of the icon (fig. 10.3), recalls the ancient Buddhist symbol of enlightenment.[66] Without obfuscating the crucial differences between Christianity and Buddhism, perhaps the angels bearing the instruments of the passion above can be understood as aids to meditation—canceling distracting thoughts, evoking the "mind descending to the heart" of Christian mystics.[67] Mary's right forefinger in the classic icon points to exactly the place that Orthodox sages suggest is the domain of the heart.[68] Indeed, the words of the spiritual masters of the Christian East for advanced states of silent prayer sound like a description of the icon itself: "The intellect mystically offers up the lamb of God upon the altar of the soul."[69] Stirred by the challenge of Buddhism, the ancient practice of Christian contemplation appears to be awakening again.[70] Perhaps the Virgin of the Passion can light the way ahead.[71]

Not that the icon stays put with the religiously minded. Sometimes the image encroaches upon, or even appears to challenge, the ostensibly secular turf of the modern museum. The meal of the Eucharist, presided over by Mary in this icon, had been served at Brooklyn's massive Basilica of Our Lady of Perpetual Help long before Judy Chicago's *The Dinner Party* (1974–79) was added to the Brooklyn Museum.[72] Our Lady of Perpetual Help has long been honored at Saint Patrick's Church just across from Frank Gehry's dramatic architectural innovations at the Art Gallery of Ontario in Toronto.[73] Within the museum, moreover, a 1957 self-portrait of William Kurelek prominently displays Our Lady of Perpetual Help.

The pervasiveness of the original icon can be easily tested. Wherever you find yourself, if you plug "Our Lady of Perpetual Help" (or its equivalent in any language) into a search map, you are likely to realize you are surrounded by churches dedicated to this image. But the

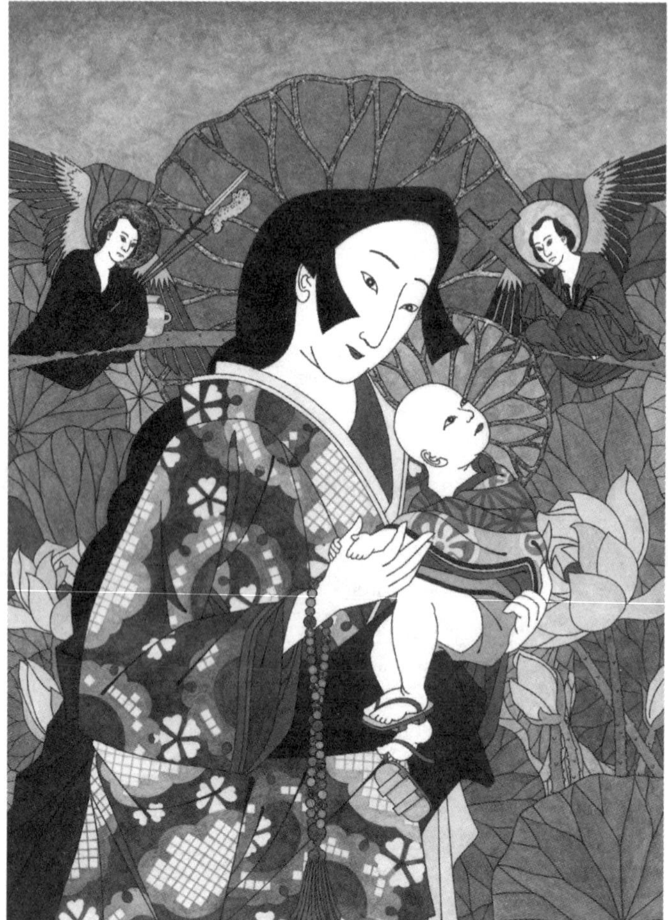

Figure C.7. Our Lady of Perpetual Help by Daniel Mitsui (2020).

companies that enable the detection of such proliferation are haunted by this Virgin as well.[74] Cyberspace has not eclipsed this icon but only enabled new variations on the image to freshly surface, from digital shrines to tattoos.[75] The icon's recent appearances in Hollywood films or Netflix series, the irreverent *Our Ladies of Perpetual Succour* play and film, or even the Our Lady of Perpetual Hops brewery might be construed as desecrations of the image, or perhaps such manifestations are just further evidence of her invincible pervasiveness.[76] Indeed, having begun this book with a reference to the September 11, 2001, terrorist attacks, just as I completed it, the Saint Nicholas Orthodox church at the site of the former towers was dedicated. The church itself is intended to resemble an abstracted Byzantine mosaic of the Virgin herself from Hagia Sophia.[77] If this is combined with the two depressive marks from the World Trade Center now just beyond the church, the site might also be considered a Virgin of the Passion as well.

Still, other references are more direct. A recent fresco in Cyprus is a reminder that the Virgin of the Passion is anything but art history. In contemporary Cyprus, not far from the border where Turkish soldiers advanced in their invasion of the island, Theodore Apsevdis's Virgin of the Vetches church appears again, reverently remixed by contemporary icon painters, including the indispensable ingredients of Simeon and the Prepared Throne. There, she testifies to the continual suffering, and resilience, of the island from which she first emerged (fig. C.8).

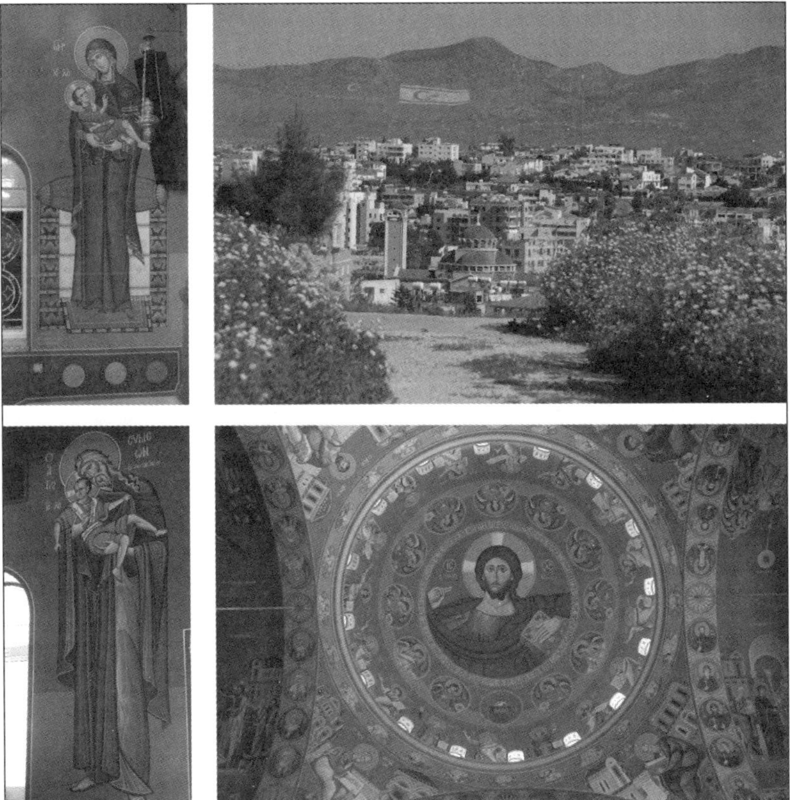

Figure C.8. Panagia Pallouriotissa church in Nicosia, Cyprus.

Another recent appearance of the icon, however, is a reminder that Mary—suffused as she is with compassionate sorrow—is also mother of the risen Lord and is not only connected to defeat. At the 2012 Summer Olympics, after winning the gold medal in the five-thousand-meter race, the Ethiopian Orthodox athlete Meseret Defar broadcast the icon to the world yet again (fig. C.9).[78] Upon her victory in London, a city once ruled

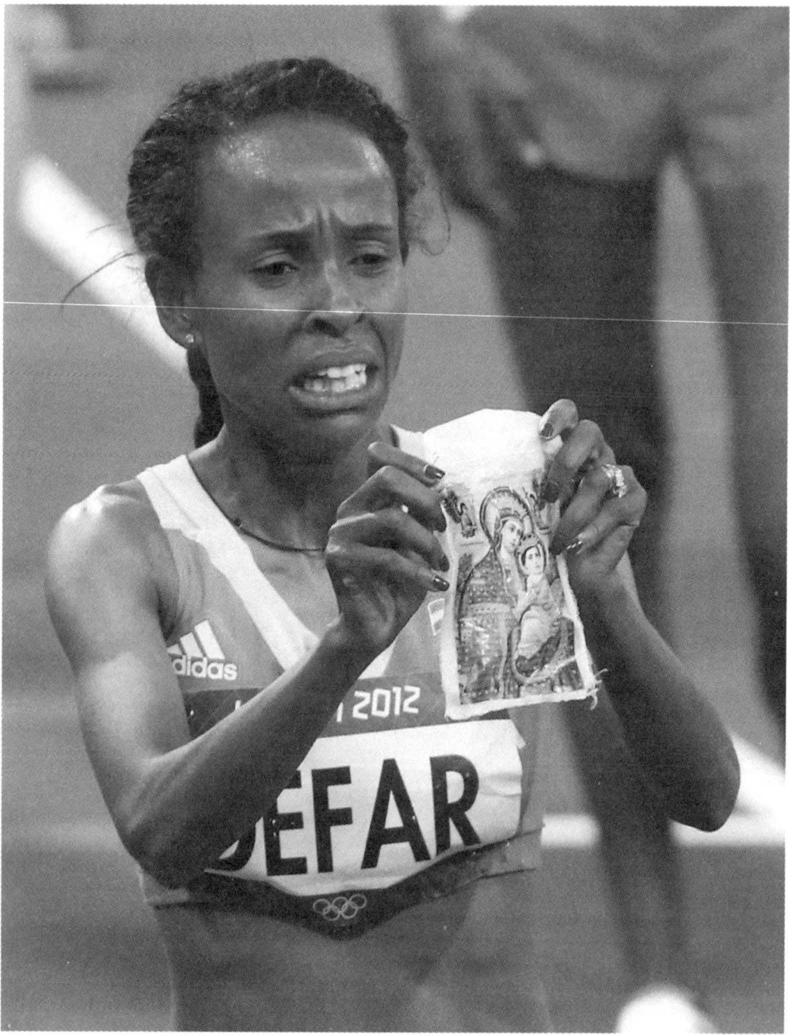

Figure C.9. Meseret Defar with the Virgin of the Passion after her victory at the 2012 Olympics.

by Richard the Lionheart, the weeping athlete pulled a woven Virgin of the Passion from her jersey and placed it upon her face, with sweat operating as an adhesive. The moment came more than eight centuries after the icon's first known appearance, and it is likely that the people who saw the image in that one moment surpassed the number of people in all of Europe when the image was first painted.[79] Which is to say, the history of the Virgin of the Passion icon has only just begun.[80]

When Defar peeled the icon from her face and lifted it to the world, a sports announcer was prompted to remark, "There's obviously a message in there somewhere, isn't there?"

Indeed, there is: "Hail, Mother of the Lamb."[81]

APPENDIX

THE NAME OF THE ARTIST

[The] paintings [at Lagoudera] are the work of the best Byzantine painters active around 1200, undoubtedly coming from Constantinople. In the case of Lagoudera, this appears to have been Theodore Apseudes, in all likelihood brought to Cyprus from Constantinople by Basil Kinnamos, Bishop of Paphos, ca. 1183, to work in the Enkleistra of St. Neophytos, where his signature has survived on his work, and from where he may have been brought to Lagoudera by Leon of Authentes, around 1192.

> —Slobodan Ćurčić, "Architecture of
> Panagia Arakiotissa, Lagoudera"

There is no doubt that a single painter had the main responsibility for the drawings, most of the execution, and the final appearance of the paintings. . . . When compared to the wall paintings of other Byzantine churches of the same period, the painted ensemble in the church of the Panagia tou Arakos [the Virgin of the Vetches] is clearly superior in respect to the final impression it calls forth.

> —Chara Konstantinidi, "Byzantine Painting in the
> Church of the Panagia tou Arakos"

[The Byzantines] elevated the status of the work of art to the realm of theology and effectively cast the artist in the role of theologian.

> —Charles Barber, *Figure and Likeness*

THERE IS LITTLE reason to doubt that a Cretan artist named Andreas Ritzos gave us what became the most recognized form of the Virgin of the Passion. But this book has also proceeded on the assumption that we know the name of the artist of the first surviving Virgin of the Passion, painted in 1192 at the Virgin of the Vetches church in Cyprus, to be Theodore Apsevdis. This is an exciting suggestion and would make him among the earliest, possibly *the* earliest, Byzantine monumental painters on record in Byzantium whose name endures.[1] Envious of the named artists of the Italian Renaissance, admirers of Byzantine art have long attempted to invent their own "Greek Giotto" or "Raphael," even to the point of inventing a name.[2] But the name Theodore Apsevdis, there is very good reason to believe, is an authentic artist's signature.

As already discussed, at the Hideaway (Enkleistra) of Neophytos on Cyprus, a signature survives that reads "The Enkleistra. . . . was painted by the hand of Theodore Apseudes [Apsevdis] in the 6691 [1183]."[3] At the Virgin of the Vetches, moreover, where the first Virgin of the Passion can be seen, there was an inscription that may have once read *Theodoros*, which is in the same hand as the 1192 paintings themselves. What survives of the inscription today can be read at the bottom left of an image of the Baptism of Christ. The inscription is submerged in baptismal waters, so to speak, near Christ's left foot. It appears to read "Remember your slave . . . a monk . . . o." Beneath this inscription, both inside the church proper and lining the outside of the church, are two parallel tombs. Based on this connection, and extreme stylistic similarities, most (but not all) scholars have attributed portions of both monuments to Theodore Apsevdis, the same artist who painted Neophytos's Hideaway.[4]

Similarities between the paintings of the Hideaway and the Virgin of the Vetches church include the same plastering techniques, the same way of burnishing thick black paint on the decorative borders, the same technique for simulated pearls with white blobs of paint, the use of white highlights in garments with "spidery lines coming out of the blob, one of them ending in a hook," and a "general air of similarity that is hard to define."[5] There is even a correspondence with the places in both monuments where the artist seems to have shown fatigue. Comparing the image of the ascension of Christ in both programs, for example, one scholar sees both a "sketchy finish" and "perfunctoriness of line."[6]

In other words, the painter of both monuments not only painted in the same manner but relaxed his approach in a similar manner as well. Comparisons of the handwriting of both monuments, carefully considered, are frequently a near-perfect match.[7] Sometimes the similarities are exact, sometimes they diverge. But these divergences can be easily explained if the artist employed assistants. Overall, I take it that the easiest explanation is that both monuments are painted by the same artist. And because he signed the first one, we know his name was Theodore Apsevdis and that he may have, the Virgin of the Vetches inscription suggests, become a monk.

Even so, a compelling minority report has recently been offered.[8] In this case, the artist at Lagoudera is not Theodore but is named, more tenuously, the "Painter of Leon," after Leon, the patron who commissioned the work. This painter, in turn, was himself an apprentice of the "Painter of Authentes," after Authentes, an earlier patron presumed to be Leon's father. An apprenticeship relationship has been suggested between the "Painter of Authentes" (1170–78), who painted the earlier part of the Virgin of the Vetches church, and the "Painter of Leon," who painted the rest of it, including the Virgin of the Passion.[9] According to this interpretation, the monk in the inscription beneath the Baptism at the Virgin of the Vetches is taken to be a reference to Leon's father, Authentes, not the painter himself. This interpretation therefore assumes that it was in fact Authentes who took the habit later in life and that it is he who is buried beneath the signature.[10] The similarities between the Enkleistra and Lagoudera, moreover, can—according to this interpretation—be attributed to separate artists within the same painterly school.[11]

This interpretation, however, has issues of its own. It seems strange to me (but not impossible) for Leon, having honored his father, Authentes, in the church's most prominent inscription ("Leon, your poor and worthless servant, called after his father Authentes"), would then ask the artist to also have his father's name included in a comparatively inauspicious place as well, only there to reveal that his father was a monk.[12]

Based on architectural analysis, a different candidate for the second burial, in addition to the patron Leon of Authentes, is the artist himself, Theodore Apsevdis. The artist/monk—this hypothesis suggests—was buried parallel to Leon but outside the church proper (i.e., beyond the sanctuary itself, closer to the outer wall). Theodore, having been buried in a suitably less auspicious location, but still near his patron Leon, was possibly "given the privilege of placing this personal votive inscription."[13] What commends this interpretation is the precedent for such placements in Byzantine art at the time, with people of differing levels of importance closer to the church interior and less important people lining the exterior.[14] But even this hypothesis is more speculative than the simple possibility that has guided this study: the same Theodore painted both the earlier portions of the Hideaway and the later portions of the Virgin of the Vetches. And in both cases, he signed his name.

The fact that there is an "upward trajectory" in artistic development between the Hideaway (1183) and the Virgin of the Vetches (1192) does not nullify the connection between the two monuments; rather, it helps establish it.[15] Mango and Hawkins suggest that Theodore was just getting used to monumental painting at the Hideaway.[16] It is not unreasonable to conclude that a decade later, he had grown in his ability, as most good artists do. There is nearly universal evidence that competent painters, from Fra Angelico to Federico Zuccari, develop their skills over time. This would be even more the case when an artist moved from the squat conditions of the Hideaway to the more expansive and well-lit interior of the Virgin of the Vetches, to say nothing of the suffering of the island that summoned the artist to paint in a manner suitable to the patron's more serious need.[17]

In "the absence of unequivocal documentary proof," this leaves us with (at least) three positions about the painter Theodore Apsevdis:[18]

1. The signature reading "Theodore Apsevdis" at the Hideaway, its stylistic similarities to the Virgin of the Vetches church, and the (no longer surviving) inscription of *Theodoros* are sufficient to establish a connection between the two monuments (including their portable icons[19]) by the same artist who, later in life, may have become a monk and who had grown in his artistic ability over the ensuing decade.[20]

2. It is safer to call the artist of the later phase of the Virgin of the Vetches church the "Lagoudera master" or a "nameless artist" whose style was very close to that of the Hideaway artist.[21] The connection between the two monuments is unprovable, but "there are enough similarities of color and technique . . . to warrant the view that the Encleistra and the church at Lagoudhera contain paintings by the same masters who were trained in the same workshop."[22]

3. The "Painter of Leon" at Lagoudera was apprenticed to the "Painter of Authentes" in the same monument; it was Authentes who

became a monk, and any stylistic connection between this artist and the Hideaway of Neophytos is attributable to schools.[23]

With respect for the two other positions, I have taken the first one in this book.

All three hypotheses are admittedly tenuous, and the coiner of the third admits that it too is constructed on "indirect testimony."[24] What unifies the views is more important than what divides them: each concurs that a singular painter of considerable ability, in all likelihood from Constantinople, was responsible for the later paintings at the Virgin of the Vetches.[25] Proponents of each position name the paintings a "perfect union of form and content," a "masterpiece of the language of Byzantine religious painting" offering "the highest level of artistic depiction in its age."[26] I, along with the majority of scholars, simply add to this consensus—thanks to the survival of two fragmentary inscriptions—that we have evidence of the artist's development *toward* this level of attainment and that we know the artist's name.

In any event, there is certainly more evidence to establish Theodore to be the painter of both monuments than there was to establish a more famous "named" Byzantine artist, Manuel Panselinos, to be the painter of the Protaton, the central church of Mount Athos.[27] The name "Manuel Panselinos" was not connected to that monument until four centuries after its completion.[28]

Recently, during the restoration of the Protaton, new evidence emerged: a fragmentary inscription that *does* tell us the precise name of one of the Protaton painters (in fact, it was Michael Astrapas).[29] This information does not nullify the rich lore around the figure of Manuel Panselinos. Instead, the name Panselinos—even though it was an invention—functioned as a placeholder of sorts until more information was revealed. Likewise, should new evidence emerge to dispute what I believe to be the well-founded claim that Theodore Apsevdis painted both the Hideaway and the Virgin of the Vetches, I trust my efforts in this book will not be wasted either.

In the meantime, however, there is not enough evidence for anyone to be indisputably right. "Hermeneutics is always a wager," and my money is on the traceable career of Theodore Apsevdis.[30] I suggest this, moreover, not because I am succumbing to the Renaissance obsession with the achievements of individual artists. Though I believe Theodore to have painted both monuments, the Virgin of the Passion—I have attempted to argue—is not the invention of any one particular artist but the late flower of a remarkable civilization, a bloom sorely needed for what remains of ours.

In short, there is no need to invent a Byzantine Giotto when one already exists. Or perhaps Giotto might be understood as the Renaissance Apsevdis!

ACKNOWLEDGMENTS

ART HISTORY ON the island of Cyprus is often accomplished in pairs. Couples, such as the Stylianous and the Winfields, published their research together. Likewise, my wife, Denise, has been an untiring companion in this investigation from start to finish. She stood with me before the frescoes at the Virgin of the Vetches church, where it was clear to me that her understanding of the Virgin of the Passion transcended my own, even if I was the one to write it all down. Denise and our children, Peter and Polly, have happily accommodated themselves to a life in which at least one image of the Virgin Mary inhabits every room. This book is as much for them as for our lost family member, Clement.

Beyond such constant support, the additional gratitude I have accumulated in the course of finishing this project is enormous. I thank the late Slobodan Ćurčić, who kept the door open in the art history department for a student wandering in from a theological seminary. I thank Nikolas Bakirtzis and Rachel Iannacone for hosting me in Cyprus, and Dimitri Gondikas, the Program in Hellenic Studies, and Stanley Seeger for making the journeys possible. I thank Patricia Fortini Brown for sharing her love for Venice and its colonies with her students. I thank AnneMarie Luijendijk and Kathleen McVey for their kind initial feedback. I thank Howard and Roberta Ahmanson profusely for the leave and hospitality that made finishing this book possible. I am grateful to the Institute for Advanced Studies in Culture at the University of Virginia (especially James Davidson Hunter, Paul Nedelisky, and Ty Buckman) for hosting me for this project's completion.

Thanks especially also goes to John Walford, Nino Zchomelidse, Peter Brown, Lou Ruprecht, Nancy Ševčenko, Bill Borror, Karfried Froehlich, Rusty Reno, Matthew Aragon Bruce, the late Robert Jenson, George Hunsinger, Bruce McCormack, John Behr, Brian Daley, George Parsenios, Scott Moringiello, Mark Edwards, John Drury, Keith Johnson, Tim Larsen, Jim Beitler, Alan Jacobs, Daniel Treier, Rick Gibson, Sarah Hinlicky Wilson, Diane Schulte, the late Susan Lehre, Marilyn Hansen, Shari Kenfield, Trudy Jacoby, Alyson Williams, Catherine Jolivet-Lévy, Jason Long, Tim Taylor, Thomas Pfau, Timothy

Verdon, Annemarie Weyl Carr, Dragan Vojvodić, Robin Jensen, and Arthur Versluis. I am grateful for discussions with the late Lois Drewer, Jelena Bogdanović, Nebojša Stanković, Katherine Marsengill, Marius Hauknes, Jelena Trkulja, Val MacIntyre, Martin Johnson, John Wilson, Michael Martin, Xenophon Moniaros, Robert Nelson, Scott Johnson, Garnette Cadogan, Athanasios Papageorghiou, and especially Ally Kateusz. I thank the nuns at the Hagios Ioannes Prodromos Monastery outside of Serres, Greece. Father Carl Hoegerl at the Redemptorist headquarters in Brooklyn produced archival gems that he was kind enough to entrust to me. Father Justin and Father Porphyrios at Saint Catherine's Monastery at Mount Sinai were likewise incredibly helpful in giving me access to the most important Byzantine icon collection in the world. Father Tarasios at Koutloumousiou Monastery on Mount Athos and Father Fred Brinkmann at the Church of Saint Alphonsus in Rome were also very generous with their time. Additional funding from Princeton's Department of Art and Archaeology, the Princeton Graduate School, and the Princeton Institute for International and Regional Studies helped make my research abroad possible. The Center for the Study of Religion hosted a graduate discussion group led by John Gager that was invaluable. The Collegeville Institute and Michael McGregor generously offered kind and encouraging support. I thank Karen Lee and Michael Wilder at Wheaton College for approving the leave that made this book possible, my fantastic colleagues in the Art Department of Wheaton College, and Emily King at Fortress Press for reaching out to me because of an article I wrote on bourbon, which resulted in reviving my languishing dissertation. The quality of her guidance, along with Elvis Ramirez, has been an unanticipated gift.

I especially thank John and Katherine Milliner, John and Linda Hawkins, Abbie and Brian Killeen, Tommy and Dominique Hawkins, David and Susie Holmes, Michael Tarwater, Kevin Heimann, David Oakley, Kerry Haps, Jerry Root, Dan Haase, Bryan McGraw, Rita George-Tvrtković, Neil Morrison, and those in Owen Sound, Ontario, who prayed so faithfully for this project. Thanks especially for the invigorating comradery of F3 Wheaton. Thanks to my dear friends on the board of Bridge Projects: Jonathan Anderson, Ann Hirou, Jane Milosch, Cara Lewis, and Linnéa Spransy. Thanks also to all the students in the Virgin Mary class I teach with Amy Peeler. The privilege of journeying with the Peeler family, both Amy and Lance, in our explorations of the Virgin Mary has been a singular blessing. I thank Ryan Kemp for so kindly volunteering to read an early chapter and George Kalantizis for his journey to the Baclaran shrine in Manila, which he lovingly photographed. I thank my students Elise Colón and especially Kathleen Parker for their assistance with different phases of this book and Sharon Dunbar for her remarkable illustrations that brought the narrative to life. Profound gratitude to Tina Beattie, Maria Evangelatou, and Natalie Carnes, my profligately generous readers who vastly improved this project, even while I am completely to blame for any of its remaining deficiencies. Thanks to my wonderful colleagues at the Mediterranean Encounters group (Anthi Andronikou, John Landsdowne, Maria Parani, Georgios Markou, Justin Wilson and Magdalene Breidenthal among them). In sum, the debts of gratitude listed here have dispelled any illusion that writing is solitary work.

Am I allowed to thank the Virgin Mary herself? Doing so seems a breach of both academic protocol and that of the Protestant institution where I teach. But both are learning otherwise, and so yes, thank you Mary, and all the more thanks (of course) to the one in your arms. Finally, I thank the woman who had the temerity to shout out "Our Lady of Perpetual Help!" after I was asked about the Virgin of the Passion icon at the Princeton University Art Museum. I tried to go and meet her afterward, but she was gone.

Epiphany 2022
LAND OF THE ANISHINAABE

NOTES

Introduction

1 Helen C. Evans, *Byzantium: Faith and Power (1261–1557)* (New Haven, CT: Yale University Press, 2004). We call the empire "Byzantine" today, but its residents would have understood themselves as Roman. The term *Byzantium* was coined in the sixteenth century and became standard around 1850 (Anthony Kaldellis, *Romanland* [Cambridge, MA: Harvard University Press, 2019], 15). Considering the dramatic nature of Christianization, I do not find this division point arbitrary, even while I see considerable Byzantine continuity with Roman tradition that came before it (as evidenced by the goddess tradition that preceded the Virgin Mary and that the Virgin Mary transformed). Some argue for the term "Eastern Roman Empire" or "Romanland" (from *Romanía*). I will, nevertheless, retain the term "Byzantine Empire" in this book, although I am well aware of its complexities. As Kaldellis himself asserts, "We will not solve [the problem of what to call the Byzantine Empire] by making a word taboo" (xv).

2 A fascinating anecdote is related by Jacob Needleman on a visit to Mount Athos in conversation with Father Vassilios, an abbot of Stavronikita: "I risked exaggerating the success of Eastern religion in America because I was now sure that Father Vassilios did not fully grasp the need that was being felt in America—in California—for a new quality of psychological experience. But he interrupted me with a quiet laugh, and startled both me and my interpreter. 'I could tell you of things a thousand times better than your Yoga,' he said." Jacob Needleman, "The Used Religions," in *Sacred Tradition & Present Need*, ed. Jacob Needleman and Dennis Lewis (New York: Viking, 1975), 9. Needleman's *Lost Christianity* (New York: Jeremy P. Tarcher, 1980) remains a classic account of the contours of this hidden Christian tradition. See also Robin Amis, *A Different Christianity* (Chicago: Praxis Institute Press, 2009, 2016). Profound inner experience and traditional Christianity need not be opposed.

3 I do, on the other hand, believe the beings depicted in the icon, which wood and pigment can successfully mediate, are, in fact, more alive than I am. This seems to be a much quicker way of achieving what proponents of object-oriented ontology or new vitalism are after. See David Joselit, Carrie Lambert-Beatty, and Hal Foster, eds., "A Questionnaire on Materialisms," *October* 155, no. 155 (Winter 2016): 3–110. At the same time,

C. A. Tsakiridou asserts that "in Orthodox terms, we can speak of a deified form in art in the same way that we can speak of the deified appearance of an ascetic." C. A. Tsakiridou, *Icons in Time, Persons in Eternity: Orthodox Theology and the Aesthetics of the Christian Image* (Farnham, UK: Ashgate, 2013), 22. Though she also cites Maximus the Confessor: "All visible things (*phainomena*) need a cross, that is, a capacity which holds back their participation of what is active in them according to sense" (Tsakiridou, 179). The Virgin of the Passion icon, indicating both presence (Mary and Christ) and absence (the cross), nicely articulates this balance.

4   Half a century ago, the art historian Hans Belting wrote that "it is precisely [the] process of adapting and transforming Byzantine models on which research will have to concentrate." Hans Belting, review of "Byzantine Art and the West," by Otto Demus, *Art Bulletin* 54, no. 4 (December 1, 1972): 544. David Freedberg later concurred, "The study of copies . . . remains one of the great tasks of the history of images." David Freedberg, *The Power of Images: Studies in the History and Theory of Response* (Chicago: University of Chicago Press, 1991), 121.

5   Richard P. McBrien, ed., *The Catholic Encyclopedia* (San Francisco: Harper-Collins, 1995), 650. An extensive study of the icon as it emanated from its base, Rome, has been compiled by the Redemptorist priest Fabriciano Ferrero, *Nuestra señora del Perpetuo Socorro: Proceso histórico de una devoción Mariana* (Madrid: Editorial el Perpetuo Socorro, 1966). Ferrero concludes, "Together with the apparitions of Lourdes and Fatima, the image of the Passion, Our Lady of Perpetual Help, the Mediatrix of all graces, the Co-redemptrix, spread rapidly throughout the world, bringing relief and consolation in illnesses, in suffering of the soul and of the spirit, and in all the circumstances in which the human heart may encounter pain" (231; author's translation). See also Fabriciano Ferrero, *Santa Maria del Perpetuo Socorro: Un icono de la Santa Madre de Dios "Virgen de la Passion" con el Presagio gloriosa Cristo* (Madrid: Editorial el Perpetuo Socorro, 1994). A helpful English translation of some of Ferrero's 1994 volume can be found in Fabriciano Ferrero, *The Story of an Icon*, ed. Michael McGreevy (Cambridge: Redemptorist, 2001).

6   The concept of "power" has permeated Byzantine art history's most prominent book covers and museum exhibitions, but rarely is it discussed or defined. Steven Lukes's conclusion in one of the more influential anthologies is not encouraging: "Every attempt at a single general answer to the question [of power] has failed and seems likely to fail." Steven Lukes, *Power* (Oxford: Blackwell, 1986), 17. "Power is everywhere," declares Foucault, "not because it embraces everything, but because it comes from everywhere." Michel Foucault, *The History of Sexuality: An Introduction*, vol. 1, trans. Robert Hurley (London: Penguin, 1990), 93. Sarah Coakley suggests

that recent academic debates over the meaning of the term *power* "rival in complexity—and arguably replicate in secular form—the debates that might in a pre-modern age have been held over the nature and purpose of divine 'acts.'" Sarah Coakley, *Power and Submissions* (Oxford: Blackwell, 2002), xv. She then asks for proof of the existence of power as an atheist might ask for proof for the existence of God: "Is power a force, a commodity, a hereditary deposit, a form of exchange, an authority, a means of 'discipline,' sheer domination, or a more nebulous 'circuit'? Must it necessarily involve intentionality, imply resistance, suppress freedom, or assume a 'hierarchy'? And where does it reside: in individuals, in institutions, in armies or police forces, in money, in political parties, or more generally and democratically in every sort of subtle societal exchange?" (xv–xvi). Coakley concludes that "there is no answer to these questions which is not also an implicit ideology, or at least a *recommendation*" (xvi), citing Foucault's exchange with Habermas as a perfect instantiation of such metaphysical presumptions at work. The history of the Virgin of the Passion, connected not to triumph but to disaster, unsettles facile appeals to "power." Which is to say, her "power," to recall the words of Saint Paul, was made perfect in weakness (2 Cor 12:9). It blossomed, perhaps most fully, in collapse.

7 Bissera Pentcheva, *Icons and Power* (University Park: Penn State University Press, 2005), 11. Pentcheva has since gone far beyond political power in her approach to the Virgin Mary in Byzantium, appealing to power of a different kind. As she puts it in a later publication, "Mary's moving gaze sent a current through my body. For the first time, I experienced what we easily call 'object' as living and present." Bissera Pentcheva, *The Sensual Icon: Space, Ritual and the Senses in Byzantium* (University Park: Penn State University Press, 2013), 5.

8 Vasiliki Limberis, *Divine Heiress: The Virgin Mary and the Creation of Christian Constantinople* (London: Routledge, 1994), 140–41.

9 Pentcheva, *Icons and Power*, 2.

10 Hans Belting, *Likeness and Presence: A History of the Image before the Era of Art*, trans. Edmund Jephcott (Chicago: University of Chicago Press, 1994), 36.

11 Belting, 36. Pentcheva likewise remarks, "Subsuming the functions of the empress, Victoria and Tyche, the Theotokos emerges as the most potent guarantor of victory." Pentcheva, *Icons and Power*, 21. See also Stephen J. Shoemaker, *Mary in Early Christian Faith and Devotion* (New Haven, CT: Yale University Press, 2016), 177–78.

12 Pentcheva, *Icons and Power*, 2.

13 Artemis, for example, was unable to prevent the natural and political disasters visited upon her chief sanctuary. Guy Maclean Rogers, *The Mysteries of Artemis of Ephesos: Cult, Polis, and Change in the Graeco-Roman World* (New Haven, CT: Yale University Press, 2012), 271, 275. Artemis, moreover, was

not one to linger to offer any consolation. "Farewell," Artemis says to the dying Hippolytus in Euripides's play of that name. "I may not watch man's fleeting breath, Nor strain mine eyes with the effluence of death." Euripides, *Hippolytus*, trans. Gilbert Murray, Harvard Classics 8 (New York: P. F. Collier & Son, 1909), 347.

14   I am well aware, and appreciative, of the large turn in Crusades scholarship that combats popular misconceptions by understanding the crusading enterprises on their own terms as defensive missions against Islamic conquest. Rodney Stark has popularized much of this research in *God's Battalions: The Case for the Crusades* (New York: HarperOne, 2010). But however important it may be to contextualize the Crusades, I still believe it possible to discern, with Christian moral hindsight today, that they were—on the whole—not necessarily a good idea. Erasmus's "irenicism" (as opposed to outright pacifism) is instructive in this regard. Erasmus, *Collected Works of Erasmus*, vol. 27, ed. A. H. T. Levi (Toronto: University of Toronto Press, 1974), 316. The Virgin of the Passion may have been making this point long before Erasmus picked up his pen.

15   I thank Dick Ohman for this formulation.

16   Even the latest specialized volume on the frescoes painted by this artist varies the spelling between "Apseudes" and "Apseudis." Athanasios Papageorghiou, Charalambos Bakirtzis, and Christodoulos Hadjichristodoulou, eds., *The Church of Panagia tou Arakos* (Nicosia: Leventis Foundation and Bank of Cyprus Cultural Foundation, 2018), 44, 84. I am choosing *Apsevdis* to articulate the modern Greek pronunciation of this name as it is spoken to this day on the island.

17   That the artist's name was Theodore Apsevdis is not certain, but it is probable. Those interested in the varieties of scholarly theories about Theodore can consult this study's appendix.

18   For Carol Christ's account of her pilgrimages to Crete, see *Odyssey with the Goddess: A Spiritual Quest in Crete* (New York: Continuum, 1995); and *A Serpentine Path: Mysteries of the Goddess* (Cleveland, OH: FAR Press, 2016). The latter reveals that Christ has now led over five hundred women on forty goddess pilgrimages to Crete (172). "The serpentine path continues to unfold" (174), and one of its twists, in my own reading at least, is that these very personal pilgrimages to sacred Marian sites in Crete may, in fact, be encounters not with the goddess in the disguise of the sacred shrines to the Virgin Mary but with the Virgin Mary in disguise as the goddess (see, e.g., 33–37, 127–28). Christ explains that the root of the goddess movement was her dissatisfaction with the Christianity that she once practiced and was due in part to the Vietnam War, which she traced to the warlike images of the Hebrew Bible. Carol Christ, "Why Women, Men and Other Living Things Still Need the Goddess: Remembering and Reflecting 35 Years

Later," *Feminist Theology* 20, no. 3 (2012): 242–55. However, the goddess tradition also invokes this warlike spirit in both the past and present. See Bettany Hughes, *Venus and Aphrodite: A Biography of Desire* (New York: Basic Books, 2020), 75, 146. Aphrodite was the "*progenitrix* of the Julio-Claudian imperial line . . . mother of the Roman Empire." Laura Salah Nasrallah, *Christian Responses to Roman Art & Architecture* (Cambridge: Cambridge University Press, 2010), 252. If protest of the Vietnam War helped launch the goddess movement, it is worth pointing out that devotion to an Indigenous Vietnamese Mary, Our Lady of La Vang, is rapidly spreading through the country that once invaded her today.

19 Lucy Goodison and Christine Morris, "Beyond the 'Great Mother': The Sacred World of the Minoans," in *Ancient Goddesses: The Myths and the Evidence*, ed. Lucy Goodison and Christine Morris (London: British Museum Press, 1998), 113–32. Goodison and Morris assert, "While some [goddess figurines from Crete] might be seen as divine, we are far from a static unitarian picture of a 'Goddess.' The evidence about life in these early [Cretan] communities is too sparse to give further clues about the meanings the figures may have had for the people who used them" (115). Likewise, Frymer-Kensky pleads, "There was not one Goddess, there were many goddesses; they were not enshrined in a religion of women, but in the official religion of male-dominated societies; they were not evidence of ancient mother-worship, but served as an integral part of a religious system that mirrored and provided the sacred underpinnings of patriarchy." Tikva Frymer-Kensky, *In the Wake of the Goddesses: Women, Culture, and the Biblical Transformation of Pagan Myth* (New York: Free Press, 1992), vii.

20 The icon's name means "health of the Roman people" but is understood to mean "salvation" or "protectress of the Roman people" as well. See Gerhard Wolf, *Salus Populi Romani: Die Geschichte römischer Kultbilder im Mittelalter* (Weinheim, Germany: VCH Acta Humaniora, 1990).

21 Metropolitan Museum of Art, *The Vatican: Spirit and Art of Christian Rome* (New York: Harry N. Abrams, 1982), 334–35.

22 Athonite legend relates that Saint Gabriel himself, disguised as a monk, first added this formula in prayer before the icon, *Axion Estin* ("it is truly meet," or "it is worthy"). The phrase also became the title of the epic poem by the modern Greek poet Odysseus Elytis, who—not without reverence—intermingled the motif with modern concerns in Odysseus Elytis, *Axion Esti*, trans. Edmund Keely and George Savidis (Pittsburgh, PA: University of Pittsburgh Press, 1974). The two icons—the "Dreaded Protection" (the name of the Virgin of the Passion at Koutloumousi) and the *Axion Estin*—are linked processionally. On the Monday after Easter, the *Axion Estin* is carried forward to Koutloumousi and returned that evening. The next day, the "Dreaded Protection" icon returns the favor and is carried

to the Protaton and then returned. R. M. Dawkins, *The Monks of Athos* (London: George Allen & Unwin, 1936), 206–7.

23 Matushka Constantina Palmer, "Axion Esti Icon Arrives in Thessaloniki from Mount Athos," YouTube video, accessed November 17, 2021, https:// www.youtube.com/watch?v=OInVuA3pBXY&t=216s. I do not point this out to condemn military processions of all kinds. A case might be made that the presence of the icon is a restrainer of violence.

24 This is not to suggest a facile dichotomy between peaceful pre-Constantinian Christianity and power-hungry post-Constantinian faith. Power can be used for good, such as when Constantine extended legal protections to those unprotected by Roman law. Peter Leithart, *Defending Constantine* (Downers Grove, IL: IVP Academic, 2010), 212. The freedom of religion offered by Constantine's advisor Lactantius is exemplary: "We grant both to Christian and to *all men* the freedom to follow whatever religion each one wished." Robert Louis Wilken, *The First Thousand Years* (New Haven, CT: Yale University Press, 2013), 85. However, this understanding was not necessarily embraced by Constantine's successors.

25 Though I do contrast the political and transpolitical aspects of the Virgin Mary in Byzantium in this book, I do not mean to pit these elements entirely against one another. Powerful Byzantine emperors and empresses had every right to venerate the Virgin as well. It is not wrong to ask for protection or to enjoy it when granted. Proper devotion to the Virgin Mary does not mean actively courting military defeat as if that is the only way the humility of Christ can be fathomed. I only mean to suggest that the Virgin of the Passion relativizes protection and victory, showing that the Virgin Mary and the Christianity she represents cannot be limited to this role alone. As Pauline Allen puts it, "'Any history of the cult of the Virgin would have to allow for multiple developments' . . . [even] some degree of paradox in the evidence." Pauline Allen, "Portrayals of Mary in Greek Homiletic Literature (6th–7th Centuries)," in *The Cult of the Mother of God in Byzantium: Texts and Images*, ed. Leslie Brubaker and Mary B. Cunningham (Burlington, VT: Ashgate, 2011), 85. If the side of Byzantine Mariology that focuses on her protective role has been overemphasized, this is not to suggest the Virgin of the Passion is the entirety of the story.

26 Friedrich Nietzsche, *Twilight of the Idols*, trans. Richard Polt (Indianapolis: Hackett, 1997), 6; Rainer Maria Rilke, *Selected Poems of Rainer Maria Rilke*, trans. Robert Bly (New York: Harper & Row, 1981), 106.

27 To summarize a vast debate, "demasculinizing" the Trinity by swapping out traditional language for God (e.g., exchanging "Creator, Redeemer, Sustainer" for "Father, Son, and Holy Spirit") and simply assigning a feminine gender to the Holy Spirit are ultimately dissatisfying options that underestimate the complexity of Trinitarian gender dynamics. See, for example,

Sarah Coakley, "'Femininity' and the Holy Spirit?," in *Mirror to the Church: Reflections on Sexism*, ed. Monica Furlong (London: SPCK, 1988); Cynthia Bourgeault, "Why Feminizing the Trinity Won't Work," in *The Holy Trinity and the Law of Three* (Boulder, CO: Shambala, 2014), 13–21; and Janet Martin Soskice, *The Kindness of God: Metaphor, Gender, and Religious Language* (Oxford: Oxford University Press, 2008). William Witt's understanding strikes me as correct: "In God's own nature, God is neither transcendent nor immanent, but Trinitarian and relational. The diviner persons are both active and receptive. . . . Activity is not specifically masculine, nor is receptivity distinctively feminine; rather, to be a person is to be both active and receptive." William Witt, *Icons of Christ: A Biblical and Systematic Theology for Women's Ordination* (Waco, TX: Baylor University Press, 2020), 289–90. I take a "strategic essentialist" position regarding gender (as opposed to mere essentialist or pure constructivist positions), which involves critiquing how gender has constellated in expected "roles" of men and women in the past without abandoning male and female categories wholesale. See Serene Jones, *Feminist Theory and Christian Theology* (Minneapolis: Fortress, 2000), 42–48. Christianity, accordingly, "both affirms and denies that our sexuality has eternal significance." Tina Beattie, *The New Catholic Feminism* (London: Routledge, 2006), 310. The way forward, it seems to me, is "not a theology that validates truth against the unreliable benchmark of women's experience, or indeed of any human experience, but rather . . . the opening up of a mystical space, illuminated by the doctrines and traditions of the Catholic faith [and Orthodox and Protestant as well] wherein all benchmarks disappear in the sublime encounter between the bodily human and the incarnate God." Tina Beattie, *Theology after Postmodernity* (Oxford: Oxford University Press, 2013), 8. When it comes to gender, the roof appears to be higher in the church than in the relatively cramped, immanentized sexuality elsewhere. Even if the church's roof needs to be raised higher still, she has the necessary tools for the job. The aim is neither to fossilize nor to obliterate our recieved notions of gender but to redeem them.

28 "The Mother of God . . . is so closely united to the sacrifice of her divine Son that she has been called the Virgin Priest by the Fathers of the Church." Pius IX, preface to Mgr. Van den Berghe, *Marie et le Sacerdoce*, 2nd ed. (Paris: Louis Vivès, 1875), vi. See also Michael O'Carroll, *Theotokos: A Theological Encyclopedia of the Blessed Virgin Mary* (Wilmington, DE: Michael Glazier, 1983), 293. Following Pius IX's assertion, "St. Pius X commissioned two Cardinals to compose a prayer to *Virgo Sacerdos* and then indulgenced it for the universal Church (9 May, 1906)" (O'Carroll, 122). In 1913, however, this direction changed, and images of the Virgin Mary with priestly vestments were forbidden followed by a ban on devotions to her as priest in 1927 (O'Carroll, 122).

29   Pius IX's utterance appears to have been what prompted René Laurentin's collation of evidence. René Laurentin, *Maria, ecclesia, sacerdotium: Essai sur le développement d'une idée religieuse* (Paris: Nouvelles Éditions Latines, 1952); and René Laurentin, *Marie, l'eglise et le sacerdoce: Etude théologique* (Paris: Nouvelles Éditions Latines, 1953). Laurentin quarantined the evidence he compiled on p. 131 of the latter volume by bifurcating the capital priesthood of Christ (the order of the means of grace) and the assistant priesthood of Mary (the order of the personal life of grace). The former is principal, constituting the sacrifice, and the latter is a dependent, spousal, and cooperative role. The former is a sacrifice of the man-God for humanity, and the latter is a sacrifice of humanity as if united to the sacrifice of Christ. But to anticipate chapter 6 of the present volume, this seems strangely similar to Pantevgenos's "doctrine of humanity's double-staged salvation, first through the physical incorporation of the Logos-Son, the second by means of the self-offering to the Father." Alexander P. Kazhdan and Ann Wharton Epstein, *Change in Byzantine Culture in the Eleventh and Twelfth Centuries* (Berkeley: University of California Press, 1985), 160–61. For a similar suggestion of how Manfred Hauke's gender symbolism leads to Apollinarianism, see Witt, *Icons of Christ*, 284–85. Tina Beattie's logical extension of Laurentin's argument in favor of female priesthood that does not neutralize female sexuality is formidable. Tina Beattie, *God's Mother, Eve's Advocate: A Gynocentric Refiguration of Marian Symbolism in Engagement with Luce Irigaray* (London: Continuum, 2002), 194–207; Beattie, *Catholic Feminism*, 302–11.

30   There is no need to choose between traditional calcification or progressive liquefaction of gender. As Sarah Coakley explains, "Gender does indeed 'matter' . . . but gender is not static, not fixed into the seemingly immovable stuckness of what secular theory gloomily calls 'the gender binary.' Rather, it is made redemptively labile—subject to endless reformulations one can scarcely imagine at the beginning of the spiritual journey. And this occurs precisely by its submission to something more fundamental: the interruptive desire of the trinitarian God for fallen creation." Sarah Coakley, *God, Sexuality, and the Self: An Essay "On the Trinity"* (Cambridge: Cambridge University Press, 2013), 59. The textual and art historical record appear to suggest that just such a labile reformulation has occurred *within* the mainstream Christian traditions through Mary's pervasive priesthood. Sisto's nuanced read of Sergius Bulgakov is equally instructive. Discarding the subordinationism that "unnecessarily complicates [Bulgakov's] thought," Sisto is inspired by Bulgakov's Mariology to "retain . . . the differentiation of the sexes but reject . . . the traditional patriarchal structure of Marian theology that has tended to delimit women to passive roles in the Church." Walter Nunzio Sisto, *The Mother of God in the Theology of Sergius Bulgakov:*

The Soul of the World (Oxfordshire: Routledge, 2018), 212. See also note 46 in this introduction and note 38 in chapter 8 of this book.

31 Timothy Kelly and Joseph Kelly, "Our Lady of Perpetual Help, Gender Roles, and the Decline of Devotional Catholicism," *Journal of Social History* 32, no. 1 (Autumn 1998): 14.

32 There is a tradition of comparing Abraham's and Mary's sacrifices on the island of Cyprus, where the Virgin of the Passion first appeared. Annemarie Weyl Carr argues that the sacrifice of Abraham that appears on the south side of the triumphal arch at Asinou, which flanks Mary in the apse, is "surely Eucharistic in content," thereby "joining Eucharistic typologies with the Annunciation." Annemarie Weyl Carr, "Iconography and Identity: Syrian Elements in the Art of Crusader Cyprus," in *Religious Origins of Nations? The Christian Communities of the Middle East*, ed. Bas Ter Haar Romeny (Leiden: Brill, 2010), 148. Perhaps the warning issued to Abraham after the promise ("dreadful and great darkness fell upon him" [Gen 15:12]) could be compared to Simeon's prophecy to Mary ("a sword will pierce through your own soul also" [Luke 2:35]).

33 A sense of the scale of output can be gained from the fact that Sarah Jane Boss, ed., *Mary: The Complete Resource* (Oxford: Oxford University Press, 2007), was soon followed by Chris Maunder, ed., *The Oxford Handbook of Mary* (Oxford: Oxford University Press, 2019). In the field of Byzantine studies alone, a series of volumes has poured forth since the turn of the millennium, which was marked by Maria Vassilaki, ed., *Mother of God: Representations of the Virgin in Byzantine Art* (Milan: Skira, 2000). A single-volume overview that clearly explains how the Marian timeline of early Christianity has shifted is Shoemaker, *Mary in Early Christian Faith*. Because gauging the extent of renewed popular devotion would be an enormous task, I will limit it to an example local to myself. Visits to the nearby Guadalupe shrine in Des Plaines, Illinois, reach into the hundreds of thousands annually. Kori Rumore and Laura Rodríguez Presa, "Why 200,000 People Travel Each December on Foot, by Horse, and Even Semitruck to Visit the Shrine of Our Lady of Guadalupe in Des Plains," *Chicago Tribune*, December 11, 2019.

34 For cases of Mary as an avenger, see Jane Baun, "Apocalyptic Panagia: Some Byways of Marian Revelation in Byzantium," in Brubaker and Cunningham, *Cult of the Mother*, 199–211. Baun compares these stories to the vengeance psalms. They "reveal what believers *really* wanted Mary to do" (207). A very important study showing Mary's warlike characteristics is Rita George-Tvrtković, *Christians, Muslims and Mary: A History* (Mahwah, NJ: Paulist, 2018). See also Amy G. Remensnyder, *La Conquistadora: The Virgin Mary at War and Peace in the Old and New Worlds* (Oxford: Oxford University Press, 2014).

35 Cleo McNelly Kearns argues that "Mary does not act, even in the imaginary, as [a eucharistic] agent or celebrant, nor is she depicted as elevating, blessing, or breaking the elements of bread and wine as a priest might do." Cleo McNelly Kearns, *The Virgin Mary, Monotheism, and Sacrifice* (Cambridge: Cambridge University Press, 2008), 275. Likewise, Nancy Jay's extensive study on women and sacrifice insists that women and the altar are like oil and water, a necessary proof of patriarchy that extends across cultures. Nancy Jay, *Throughout Your Generations Forever: Sacrifice, Religion, and Paternity* (Chicago: University of Chicago Press, 1992), xxiii. I respond to these claims in this book's conclusion.

36 In the original novel, Catch-22 (the number twenty-two was chosen randomly) signifies a situation from which there is no escape: "Orr would be crazy to fly more missions and sane if he didn't, but if he was sane, he had to fly them. If he flew them, he was crazy and didn't have to; but if he didn't want to, he was sane and had to." Joseph Heller, *Catch-22* (New York: Simon & Schuster, 1996), 55.

37 Ihnat communicates this dilemma with special force: "The recalcitrant Jews who refused to acknowledge Mary brought out the reverse of her merciful side, for she made sure they suffered the consequences." Kati Ihnat, *Mother of Mercy, Bane of the Jews: Devotion to the Virgin Mary in Anglo-Norman England* (Princeton, NJ: Princeton University Press, 2016), 182. By attempting to address this problem, I am not suggesting that Mary was not used in these ways or that such research is inaccurate. Instead, I aim to show ways that Mary can offer better models for the present. This is possible because the tradition of the Virgin Mary is so polyvalent.

38 Hence, in contrast to Sarah Jane Boss's "cosmic maternal vision" of the Virgin in *Mary: New Century Theology* (New York: Continuum, 2004), Elizabeth Johnson attempts to bring Mary down to earth in *Truly Our Sister: A Theology of Mary in the Communion of Saints* (New York: Continuum, 2006). Both, however, are possible.

39 G. K. Chesterton, *Orthodoxy* (New York: Doubleday, 1959), 83. Christianity (and Mary) combines "furious opposites, but keeping them both furious" (96).

40 For example, Jeanette Favrot Peterson concludes her magnificent study of Guadalupe with this: "Images of the Virgin of Guadalupe institutionalized the imperial agenda and then, in a stunning reversal, helped to catalyze the movements that would dispossess the colonizer." Jeanette Favrot Peterson, *Visualizing Guadalupe: From Black Madonna to Queen of the Americas* (Austin: University of Texas Press, 2014), 274.

41 Averil Cameron, "Introduction: The Mother of God in Byzantium: Relics, Icons, Texts," in Brubaker and Cunningham, *Cult of the Mother*, 5. Mary Cunningham similarly argues, "Although [Mary in Byzantium] became an increasingly compassionate and human interlocutor for Christian devotees,

she encompassed in her person a full spectrum of theological, devotional and even polemical reflection that had developed over more than a millennium." Mary B. Cunningham, *The Virgin Mary in Byzantium, c.400–1000* (Cambridge: Cambridge University Press, 2021), 6.

42 This is a title given to Mary (among hundreds) in the Byzantine Akathistos hymn: "Hail, mother of the lamb and the shepherd; Hail, fold of spiritual sheep." Leena Mari Peltomaa, *The Image of the Virgin Mary in the Akathistos Hymn* (Leiden: Brill, 2004), 9. Mary is also called "Mother of the living Lamb" in the Syriac liturgy. See Samuel Thykoottam, *The Mother of God in the Syriac Tradition* (Kerala, India: St. Ephrem Ecumenical Research Institute, 1989), 17.

43 Ross Douthat, *The Decadent Society: How We Became the Victims of Our Own Success* (New York: Simon & Schuster, 2020).

44 Simone Weil, *Simone Weil Reader*, ed. George A. Panichas (New York: David McKay, 1977), 467.

45 Biblical Wisdom literature, penned by Jews who were surrounded by the cult of Isis in Alexandria, offered a vigorous response to the goddess. For a clear layout of competing theories as to Wisdom's emergence, see James L. Mays, ed., *Harper's Bible Commentary* (San Francisco: Harper & Row, 1988), 501–2. Accordingly, Wisdom offers a vigorous Christian response to a revived goddess culture today, though I connect it (in chapter 7) more directly to the orthodox Christian tradition than do some of Wisdom's contemporary advocates. Robust embraces of Wisdom by feminist theologians include Elizabeth Johnson, *She Who Is: The Mystery of God in Feminist Theological Discourse* (New York: Crossroad, 1994), 86–87, 92; Elizabeth Schüssler Fiorenza, *Jesus: Miriam's Child, Sophia's Prophet*, 2nd ed. (London: Bloomsbury T&T Clark, 2015). But it is often forgotten that the Wisdom tradition has long flourished in all three main branches of the Christian tradition. An efficient overview of an Orthodox approach can be found in Sergius Bulgakov, *Sophia: The Wisdom of God; An Outline of Sophiology* (Hudson, NY: Lindisfarne, 1993); a Roman Catholic historical outline is on offer in István Cselényi, *The Maternal Face of God? Explorations in Catholic Sophiology* (Kettering, OH: Angelico, 2017). The relatively neglected (yet massive) Protestant contribution to these developments is well covered by Arthur Versluis, *Wisdom's Children: A Christian Esoteric Tradition* (Albany: State University of New York Press, 1999). Two anthologies offer helpful overviews of the primary literature: Arthur Versluis, ed., *Wisdom's Book: The Sophia Anthology* (St. Paul, MN: Paragon, 2000); and Michael Martin, ed., *The Heavenly Country* (Kettering, OH: Angelico, 2016). Wisdom (both created and uncreated) is not a fourth member of the Trinity as much as the Trinity's pervasive ground, "distinct from the hypostases, though it cannot exist apart from them and is eternally hypostacized in them" (Bulgakov,

Sophia, 34). Far from being heterodox, this understanding of Wisdom is an underestimated safeguard *against* heresy. Although Wisdom is referred to in female terms in the Bible, Wisdom is not stereotypically female any more than God the Father is stereotypically male. Wisdom accordingly manifests as both Christ and Mary in the iconographical tradition—a fact that betrays not confusion but insight and is well expressed in the Virgin of the Passion icon. Equivalent to God's glory, or Shekinah, she "unites God with the world as one common principle" and expressly avoids subordinationism of various kinds, including Arianism (Bulgakov, *Sophia*, 74). Even so, theological precision in this arena is necessarily elusive: "Sophianic insight—though always informed by scripture, liturgy, and the traditions of the Church—is arrived at experientially, mystically, artistically and, as such, proves an uncomfortable fit in the strictures of theological examination." Michael Martin, *The Submerged Reality: Sophiology and the Turn to a Poetic Metaphysics* (Kettering, OH: Angelico, 2015), 140.

46 Luke 1:51–52, as rendered by *The Book of Common Prayer* (New York: Church Hymnal Corporation, 1979), 65. For mainstream evidence for Mary's priestly status, in addition to Laurentin (note 29 in this chapter), see Alexei Lidov, "The Priesthood of the Virgin Mary as an Image-Paradigm of Christian Culture," *IKON* 10 (2017): 9–26; Maria Evangelatou, "Krater of Nectar and Altar of the Bread of Life," in *The Reception of the Virgin in Byzantium: Marian Narratives in Texts and Images*, ed. Thomas Arentzen and Mary B. Cunningham (Cambridge: Cambridge University Press, 2019); Anne L. Clark, "The Priesthood of the Virgin Mary: Gender Trouble in the Twelfth Century," *Journal of Feminist Studies in Religion* 18, no. 1 (Spring 2002): 5–24; Ally Kateusz, "Introduction to Mary as High Priest in Early Christian Narratives and Iconography," in *Mary, the Apostles, and the Last Judgment*, ed. Stanislava Kuzmová and Andrea-Bianka Znorovszky, Trivent Medieval Series (Budapest: Trivent, 2020); Matthew J. Milliner, "Visual Cherubikon: Mary as Priest at Lagoudera in Cyprus," in Kuzmová and Znorovszky, *Last Judgment*; and esp. [Pseudo-]Maximus the Confessor, *The Life of the Virgin*, trans. Stephen Shoemaker (New Haven, CT: Yale University Press, 2012). In short, if Hans Urs von Balthasar famously argued that Mary was "without any pretensions to apostolic power; she has other and greater powers" (cited in Pope John Paul II's *Mulieris Dignitatem*), increasing evidence suggests she has apostolic power as well. Whether Mary's well-attested priesthood has been holding the place for women to be ordained today is a matter I leave readers (and churches) to decide for themselves. Whatever one makes of these ongoing debates, the Virgin of the Passion, so directly associated with priesthood and with Christ's priesthood in particular (a claim unfurled in chapter 8), may be the most pervasive global manifestation of Mary's priestly dimensions.

Chapter 1

1 Annemarie Weyl Carr offers an important corrective to the tendency to
dismiss later Lusignan art in favor of the Byzantine in *Asinou across Time:
Studies in the Architecture and Murals of the Panagia Phorbiotissa, Cyprus*,
Dumbarton Oaks Studies 43 (Washington, DC: Dumbarton Oaks, 2013).
But I still have a hard time escaping judgments of artistic merit in this
particular case. Cyril Mango and Ernest J. W. Hawkins suggest that, as
the standards of the day go, Theodore was "not a first-class artist—he was
a little weak at compositions—and he may even have been a beginner at
monumental painting." Cyril Mango and Ernest J. W. Hawkins, "The Hermitage of St. Neophytos and Its Wall Paintings," *Dumbarton Oaks Papers*
20 (1966): 206. Yet they confirm that he was in all likelihood brought from
outside Cyprus. More recently, Chara Konstantinidi asserts that "when
compared to the wall paintings of other Byzantine churches of the same
period, the painted ensemble in the church of the Panagia tou Arakos is
clearly superior in respect to the final impression it calls forth." Chara Konstantinidi, "Byzantine Painting in the Church of the Panagia tou Arakos,"
in Papageorghiou, Bakirtzis, and Hadjichristodoulou, *Panagia tou Arakos*, 85.

2 Slobodan Ćurčić claims that monuments such as Studenica in the Balkans
and Lagoudera in Cyprus are "the work of the best Byzantine painters
active around 1200, undoubtedly coming from Constantinople." Slobodan
Ćurčić, "Architecture of Panagia Arakiotissa, Lagoudera," in Papageorghiou,
Bakirtzis, and Hadjichristodoulou, *Panagia tou Arakos*, 42.

3 I refer to Latin Christians as shorthand for the complex theater of Western
Christianity, where the liturgy was in Latin versus the Greek liturgy of
Eastern Orthodox Christianity.

4 On the eve of the Fourth Crusade, Constantinople was "the most powerful
and wealthy state in the Christian world. To be sure, it had fallen on hard
times, but it was within living memory that Manuel II had manipulated
the kings of Europe like pawns as he bought them off with his superior
wealth. Indeed, Byzantium had been until very recently the gold standard
of Christian empire and Christian society." George E. Demacopoulos, *Colonizing Christianity: Greek and Latin Religious Identity in the Era of the Fourth
Crusade* (New York: Fordham University Press, 2019), 9.

5 Psalm 27:4 NASB (which would be Psalm 26:4 in the Septuagint). The
Psalter was the "backbone of personal devotion" in Byzantium, and the
emperor himself was sometimes known to "spend the whole night without
sleep, in prayer and psalmody, holding the Psalter and reading from it."
Georgi R. Parpulov, "Psalters and Personal Piety in Byzantium," in *The Old
Testament in Byzantium*, ed. Paul Magdalino and Robert Nelson (Washington, DC: Dumbarton Oaks Research Library and Collection, 2010), 80.

6   "Christianity is not monotheistic and neither is it polytheistic. Its God is beyond form and matter, and forms and matter are reconciled with one another beyond the primal cut of philosophical castration through their union within the being of God in the fully human and fully divine natures of Christ. . . . The mystery of the Trinity is a reconciliation between the one and the many, form and matter, creator and creation." Beattie, *After Postmodernity*, 355.

7   Eunice Dauterman Maguire and Henry Maguire, *Other Icons: Art and Power in Byzantine Secular Culture* (Princeton, NJ: Princeton University Press, 2007), 131, 161, 103. We know of these because Niketas Choniates lamented their destruction by the Crusaders (107).

8   Hughes, *Venus and Aphrodite*, 100–101. The most express admiration of such statuary came in the work of the late Byzantine author Manuel Chrysoloras, who was himself familiar with Italian art (134).

9   Anastasia Lazaridou, *Transition to Christianity: Art of Late Antiquity, 3rd–7th Century AD* (New York: Alexander S. Onassis Public Benefit Foundation, 2011), 148.

10   Nanette Solomon, "Making a World of Difference: Gender, Asymmetry, and the Greek Nude," in *Naked Truths: Women, Sexuality, and Gender in Classical Art and Archaeology*, ed. Ann Olga Koloski-Ostrow and Claire L. Lyons (New York: Routledge, 1997), 197–99. Laura Nasrallah claims that "by the Roman period, [Aphrodite] cannot prevent the rapid proliferation of the images of her body, which multiply her literal exposure." Nasrallah, *Christian Responses*, 294. Björn Kurtén similarly asserts, "There is a straight line from Ice Age art . . . to the Playboy bunnies of later days." Björn Kurtén, *How to Deep-Freeze a Mammoth* (New York: Columbia University Press, 1986), 112–13. Which is to say, carving a cross on a nude image of Aphrodite need not but could be understood as a defense of actual women.

11   Cyril Mango, Michael Vickers, and E. D. Francis, "The Palace of Lausus at Constantinople and Its Collection of Ancient Statues," *Journal of the History of Collections* 4, no. 1 (1992): 89–98.

12   Hughes, *Venus and Aphrodite*, 101.

13   "There was a man," claimed the desert ascetic John Climacus, "who having looked upon a body of great beauty, at once gave praise to its Creator, and after one look was stirred to love God and to weep copiously." John Climacus, *Ladder of Divine Ascent*, trans. Colm Luibheid and Norman Russell (Mahwah, NJ: Paulist, 1982), 179. As Peter Brown comments, "It was not because men like Cassian, Dorotheos of Gaza, and John Climacus feared sexual temptation more than any other. It was rather that the body, in which sexuality lurked with such baffling tenacity, had come to be viewed in the searching light of a new, high hope." Peter Brown, *The Body and Society* (New York: Columbia University Press, 1988), 239.

14 "Unless we have some sense of the implications of the trinitarian God's 'proto-erotic' desire for us, then we can hardly begin to get rightly ordered our own erotic desires at the human level. Put another way, *we need to turn Freud on his head.*" Sarah Coakley, *The New Asceticism* (London: Bloomsbury Continuum, 2015), 96.

15 As Dionysius the Areopagite, whose theology informs the splendor of Hagia Sophia, put it, "Beauty unites all things and is the source of all things. It is the great creating cause which bestirs the world and holds all things in existence by the longing inside them to have beauty." *Divine Names* 704 A, cited in Nadine Schibille, *Hagia Sophia and the Byzantine Aesthetic Experience* (Farnham, UK: Ashgate, 2014), 195. Schibille shows how Dionysius differed from Neoplatonism by also including divine darkness in his rich theology of light: "God is simultaneously absolute light and complete darkness. . . . Such a synthesis is indeed evident in the interior design and illumination of Hagia Sophia in Constantinople" (196–97).

16 Symeon the New Theologian, *Divine Eros: Hymns of Saint Symeon the New Theologian*, trans. Daniel K. Griggs (Crestwood, NY: St. Vladimir's Seminary Press, 2010), hymn 30, 242.

17 The surpassing of Solomon was a common motif in Byzantine tradition. Justinian even had a statue of Solomon erected nearby that looked at Hagia Sophia in despair. Victoria Gerhold argues that the motif was "not only meant to praise the material qualities of the church, but also to symbolize, in more general terms, the spiritual triumph of Christianity over Judaism." Victoria Gerhold, "*Defeating Solomon*: Intertextuality and Symbolism in the Legend of Hagia Sophia," *Scripta Mediaevalia* 11, no. 1 (2018): 14. Such supersessionist rhetoric has fortunately been discarded in more recent Christian reflection. See Carl E. Braaten and Robert W. Jenson, eds., *Jews and Christians: People of God* (Grand Rapids, MI: Eerdmans, 2003).

18 In the *Alexiad*, penned by Princess Anna Komnene (1083–1153), we have extended commentary on the Byzantine royal attitude toward the Crusaders. Even their scholars, with their poorly pronounced Greek, were considered boorish and uncultured. For a recent account, see Loulia Kolovou, *Anna Komnene and the Alexiad: The Byzantine Princess and the First Crusade* (Philadelphia: Pen & Sword History, 2020).

19 Though the tensions had long been stewing, Christianity formally split into the Greek-speaking East and Latin-speaking West in 1054. It took more than a millennium for these mutual anathemas (curses) of the rival branches of the faith to be formally rescinded (in 1965), and even this "gesture of justice and mutual pardon is not sufficient to end both old and more recent differences between the Roman Catholic Church and the Orthodox Church." "Joint Catholic-Orthodox Declaration of His Holiness Pope Paul VI and the Ecumenical Patriarch Athenagoras I," Libreria

Editrice Vaticana, December 7, 1965, https://www.vatican.va/content/
paul-vi/en/speeches/1965/documents/hf_p-vi_spe_19651207_common
-declaration.html.

20   Bissera Pentcheva, *Hagia Sophia: Sound, Space and Spirit in Byzantium* (University Park: Penn State University Press, 2017).

21   To speculate about Theodore's thoughts as I do here is just that, speculation. But it is informed speculation. If I take the gamble of imagining Theodore's own thoughts, I am following the counsel of others. R. G. Collingwood claims, "It is by historical thinking that we re-think and so rediscover the thoughts of Hammurabi or Solon, it is in the same way that we discover the thought of a friend who writes us a letter, or a friend who crosses the street." R. G. Collingwood, *The Idea of History* (Oxford: Clarendon, 1993), 219.

22   Dante, *Paradiso*, trans. Robert Hollander and Jean Hollander (New York: Anchor, 2008), canto 26, line 62.

23   As Gregory Palamas would put it later in Byzantine history, "Impassibility does not consist in mortifying the passionate part of the soul, but in removing it from evil to good, and directing its energies toward divine things . . . one must offer to God the passionate part of the soul, alive and active, that it be a living sacrifice." Gregory Palamas, *The Triads* (Mahwah, NJ: Paulist, 1983), 19–20.

24   "The 'region' of eternity is that of *intensity*, which surpasses the measures of quantity that we employ in time and space." [Valentin Tomberg], *Meditations on the Tarot* (New York: Penguin, 1985), 180.

25   As Lidov explains, "Within the space of Justinian's Hagia Sophia, which originally did not have any figurative images, the image of God was created by the most sophisticated system of lighting, including natural light of the sun, moon and stars, reflected by the golden mosaics, marble decorations, silver furnishings and vessels, as well as by the fire burning in innumerous, sometimes moving, lamps and in thousands of candles visible through the transparent smoke of incense. . . . A glittering and blinking cloud of light hung over the [original] cupola." This cloud was "the original Judeo-Christian proto-icon which did not break the Second Commandment and, therefore, was the ideal image of God . . . the luminous and fiery cloud was combined with the anthropomorphic image of Christ." Alexei Lidov, "The Aerial Icon of Heavens: Kaavod-Doxa-Slava Bozhia and the Luminous Clouds in the Domes of Byzantine Churches," in *Air and Heavens in the Hierotopy and Iconography of the Christian World* (Moscow: Russian Academy of Arts, 2019), 26–27.

26   Writing of the marble at Hagia Sophia, Paul the Silentiary says this soon after its second consecration in 563: "Yet who even in the thundering strains of Homer, shall sing the marble meadows gathered upon the mighty

walls and spreading pavement of the lofty church? Mining [tools of]
toothed steel have cut these from the green-flanks of Carystus and have cleft
the speckled Phyrgian stone, sometimes rosy mixed with white." He goes
on to list colored stone from the Nile, Libya, and Celtic regions that were
collected in the great church. Cyril A. Mango, ed., *The Art of the Byzantine
Empire 312–1453: Sources and Documents* (Toronto: University of Toronto
Press, 1985), 85–86.

27 On the eve of its conquest in 1204, "Constantinople was indisputably the
greatest metropolis in the Christian world. Its huge population—estimated
at 375,000–400,000—dwarfed every city in the West. In comparison, Paris
and Venice probably had about 60,000 inhabitants each." Jonathan Phillips,
The Fourth Crusade and the Sack of Constantinople (New York: Penguin,
2004), 144.

28 The arguments are well rehearsed in John of Damascus (for the first stage of the
iconoclastic controversy) and Theodore the Studite (for the second, more
refined stage). The ultimate decision was that icons were allowed so long as
they did not claim too much for themselves, a fact that Byzantium often
forgot. The best way of engaging this fascinating episode is by reading John
of Damascus himself. John of Damascus, *Three Treatises on the Divine Images*,
trans. Andrew Louth (Crestwood, NY: St. Vladimir's Seminary Press, 2003).

29 This form of art deserves the name fresco: "It is clearly misleading to claim
that fresco painting on plaster patches is an innovation or an invention of
Italian painters in the thirteenth century. The technical difference in fresco
method that Italian painters evolved was that they began to paint a whole
scene piece by piece on fresh plaster sections, whereas Byzantine painters began all except the largest scenes with a complete plaster patch and
then modified it." David Winfield and June Winfield, *The Church of the
Panaghia tou Arakhos at Lagoudera, Cyprus: The Paintings and Their Painterly
Significance* (Washington, DC: Dumbarton Oaks, 2003), 324.

30 Catia Galatariotou, *The Making of a Saint: The Life, Times and Sanctification
of Neophytos the Recluse* (Cambridge: Cambridge University Press, 1991), 134.

31 Peter W. Edbury, *The Kingdom of Cyprus and the Crusades, 1191–1374*
(Cambridge: Cambridge University Press, 1991), 2–3. For an examination
of Constantinople's views of Cyprus during this period, see Galatariotou,
Making of a Saint, 222–23. "There is in short no doubt that Constantinopolitan snobbery operated against the Cypriots; but at the very least it did so
no more than it did against other Greek Orthodox provincials; and indeed
there are hints that the very opposite might in fact have been the case"
(Galatariotou, 224). For the economic expansion of Cyprus at this time,
see Galatariotou, 59.

32 Theodore the Studite, *Writings on Iconoclasm*, trans. Thomas Cattoi (Mahwah, NJ: Paulist, 2015).

33   Rogers, *Artemis of Ephesos*, 271, 275. As we shall see, the Virgin of the Passion is herself the record of how devotion to the Virgin was not halted by, but survived, such disasters.

34   Vincent Scully, *The Earth, the Temple and the Gods*, rev. ed. (New Haven, CT: Yale University Press, 1979), 86. Dennis Hughes concludes that literary references to human sacrifice do not necessarily mean it took place, especially in the later centuries. Dennis Hughes, *Human Sacrifice in Ancient Greece* (London: Routledge, 1991), 191.

35   Tatian, "Address of Tatian to the Greeks," in *Ante-Nicene Fathers*, vol. 2, trans. J. E. Ryland, ed. A. Cleveland Coxe (Peabody, MA: Hendrickson, 2004), 77. A Christian disaffected with paganism like Tatian is admittedly a hostile witness to the rites of Artemis (if he did experience them). Even so, the gore was real, and the practice of sacrificial victims and reading of the entrails of victims had increased along with the cult's popularity at the time when Tatian was writing (Rogers, *Artemis of Ephesos*, 176). It is not difficult to imagine how someone might be not charmed but disillusioned by these rituals and their dissatisfying "secrets."

36   "Homily 1:1," in *Proclus of Constantinople and the Cult of the Virgin in Late Antiquity: Homilies 1–5, Texts and Translations*, trans. Nicholas Constas (Leiden: Brill, 2003), 137.

37   Shoemaker concludes that the Council of Ephesus in 431 was *both* a Christological proclamation *and* a clear concession to popular Marian devotion. Based on earlier evidence for Marian veneration, "we must abandon the older perspective that saw the Council of Ephesus as the primary cause and inspiration for the cult of the Virgin. The cult of the Virgin was instead already well established before the council ever met." Shoemaker, *Mary in Early Christian Faith*, 227–28. The process also involved a refinement of heterodox Christian approaches to Mary, which were only gradually more accepted among proto-orthodox Christians (232). Rogers's massive study on the cult of Artemis at Ephesus, which is itself quite critical of Christianity, nevertheless concludes, "Through Mary and the story of her suckling of Jesus, the all-powerful god was made human and humane." Rogers, *Artemis of Ephesos*, 285.

38   This may have been the very sculpture taken into custody by the Christian eunuch Lausos. Hughes, *Venus and Aphrodite*, 100.

39   Hughes, *Venus and Aphrodite*, 47–49. Hughes describes Aphrodite's regular prostitutes as "pitiful sex-slaves . . . weaving by day and being shagged by night—so cheaply, an *obol* at a time, that even slaves could afford to buy their wares" (45). While some high-class *hetaira* (professional courtesans) existed, the line between *hetaira* (courtesans) and *pornai* (common prostitutes) is blurry. This word for "prostitute," from which we get our word *pornography*, means "to sell." The category of *hetaira* seems to be a creation

of men to elevate their own behavior, but they could just as quickly demote these women back to the *pornai*. Such terminology offers "very little usable information about the 'real lives' of 'real women'; instead, they may allow us to see something of the needs and investments of the men who created them." Leslie Kurke, "Inventing the *Hetaira*: Sex, Politics, and Discursive Conflict in Archaic Greece," *Classical Antiquity* 16, no. 1 (April 1997): 107. See esp. chap. 7, "The Whore with the Golden Heart, the Happy Hooker, and Other Fictions," in Eva C. Keuls, *The Reign of the Phallus: Sexual Politics in Ancient Athens* (Berkeley: University of California Press, 1993), 187–203. Laura K. McClure adds, "Because we have no first person accounts from any ancient prostitutes, we will never know for certain their lived realities." Laura K. McClure, *Women in Classical Antiquity: From Birth to Death* (Hoboken, NJ: Wiley-Blackwell, 2020), 113. For the ways that Christianity radically transformed previous understandings of sexuality, see Kyle Harper, *From Shame to Sin: The Christian Transformation of Sexual Morality in Late Antiquity* (Cambridge, MA: Harvard University Press, 2016).

40 Theodore Apsevdis was "in all likelihood brought to Cyprus from Constantinople by Basil Kinnamos, Bishop of Paphos, ca. 1183, to work in the Enkleistra of St. Neophytos, where his signature has survived on his work, and from where he may have been brought to Lagoudera by Leon of Authentes, around 1192." Ćurčić, "Architecture of Panagia Arakiotissa," 42.

Chapter 2

1 For the icon of Kykkos, see Ephraim the Athenian, *A Narrative of the Founding of the Holy Monastery of Kykkos and the History of the Miraculous Icon of the Mother of God*, trans. Andreas Jakovljevic (Nicosia: Research Centre of Kykkos Monastery, 1996); and Annemarie Weyl Carr, "The 'Virgin Veiled by God': The Presentation of an Icon on Cyprus," in *Reading Medieval Images: The Art Historian and the Object*, ed. Elizabeth Sears and Thelma K. Thomas (Ann Arbor: University of Michigan Press, 2002), 215–27. In short, the general Manuel Voutomytis sent several icons to the monastery he founded as gifts. The abbot Isaias and other Cypriot monks had traveled to Constantinople and were aware that they were not getting the finest icons. They might have seen the Eleousa icon, which was held in the emperor's palace, and petitioned for that particular image. The icon can be seen—or rather, it can't be seen—in the monastery of Kykkos today. It has long been covered by revetment.

2 Mango and Hawkins, "Hermitage of St. Neophytos," 134.

3 Mango and Hawkins, 124, 205.

4 Mango and Hawkins, 123.

5 Robin Cormack, *Writing in Gold: Byzantine Society and Its Icons* (London: George Philip, 1985), 218.

6   The interpretation of Cyril Mango and Ernest Hawkins has been followed
    by many: "Industrious and devout as Neophytos undoubtedly was, he was
    also a man of quite remarkable vanity . . . [which] meets us at every corner
    of the Enkeistra. . . . In the Enkleistra Neophytos built a monument to
    himself." Mango and Hawkins, "Hermitage of St. Neophytos," 128–29.

7   Galatariotou, *Making of a Saint*, 232–35.

8   Galatariotou, 213–15.

9   Mango and Hawkins, "Hermitage of St. Neophytos," 115.

10 Galatariotou, *Making of a Saint*, 112–13. On another occasion, Neophy-
    tos compares an incident where he was saved from a dangerous fall to
    biblical events, specifically the Hebrews enduring the fiery furnace. Even
    so, Neophytos qualifies the comparison: "For even though there stands an
    immeasurable amount of time between then and now, and there is much
    difference [between the two cases], yet divine grace exists always timeless
    and unaltered" (Galatariotou, 112).

11 Cormack subtly argues that painting enabled Neophytos to proclaim his
    own ascendency, to which in writing he could only allude. Cormack,
    Writing in Gold, 241–42. Galatariotou suggests that Neophytos's writings,
    alongside his paintings, "represent two different but interlocked expressions
    of steps taken within one and the same process [of] self-sanctification."
    Galatariotou, *Making of a Saint*, 128–30.

12 Some who tried to sit in his own cell, Neophytos believed, were miraculously
    prohibited from doing so because of the "holy and pure icons." Galatariotou,
    Making of a Saint, 144.

13 Galatariotou, 185, 189, 201. "Despite Neophytos' rebukes of the people for
    their sins, his severest castigations are reserved for the rulers rather than the
    ruled" (189).

14 Galatariotou, *Making of a Saint*, 171–172. Even in death, Neophytos
    instructed his monks to build a wall before his tomb "to hide the place of
    his burial from strangers so that his body would remain undisturbed until
    the day of the last trumpet." Cormack, *Writing in Gold*, 227.

15 Galatariotou, *Making of a Saint*, 126. Galatariotou assumes that a dream
    of a "handsome, big book" placed by Neophytos's side along with a lit
    candle betrays that Neophytos felt "his writings are no less significant than
    St. Basil's" (125), sealing the case that "he is enlightened and equal to great
    ecclesiastical writers" (126).

16 Indeed, Galatariotou concedes that her diagnosing the dream as arrogance
    is not "the only possible interpretation of Neophytos's dream" (126). Even if
    one were to choose to deconstruct the dream, Freud is not the sole option.
    For the dream analysis of the desert father Evagrius of Pontus, see Evagrius
    of Pontus, "Dreams of Vainglory and Sadness," in *The Greek Ascetic Corpus*,
    trans. Robert E. Sinkewicz (Oxford: Oxford University Press, 2003), 173.

17 Kazhdan and Constable pushed against this common misunderstanding decades ago: "The martyrs who defended Christianity against their relentless enemies were no less heroic than Aeschylus's defender of Hellenic liberty. The difference between Byzantium and Antiquity is one not of humility and heroism, commonplace and classic, but of two different kinds of heroism and humility." Alexander Kazhdan and Giles Constable, *People and Power in Byzantium* (Washington, DC: Dumbarton Oaks, 1982), 3.

18 Nikolas Bakirtzis lists a variety of such figures in "Locating Byzantine Spatial Considerations and Strategies in Rural Landscape," in *Experiencing Byzantium*, ed. Claire Nesbitt and Mark Jackson (London: Routledge, 2020), 115–16. In Cyprus, near Neophytos's Enkleistra, other ascetics such as Euthymios showed the same pattern (118–20). Closer to Nicosia, the images of Saint Sozomenos "are part of the effort to establish the chapel as a cult center through the documentation of the saint's 'credentials' for sainthood." Nikolas Bakirtzis, "Revising the Monastic Legacy of Saint Sozomenos near Potamia," in *The Art and Archaeology of Lusignan and Venetian Cyprus (1192–1571)*, ed. Michalis Olympios and Maria Parani (Turnhout, Belgium: Brepols, 2019), 95.

19 "The spirit of vainglory is most subtle and it readily grows up in the souls of those who practice virtue. It leads them to desire to make their struggles known publicly, to hunt after the praise of men." Evagrius Ponticus, *The Praktikos & Chapters on Prayer*, trans. John Bamberger (Kalamazoo, MI: Cistercian, 1981), 19. Rebecca Konydyk DeYoung explains, "The prideful desire superiority, and the vainglorious the show of superiority, although these can easily be entangled in practice." (That fact partly explains, I think, why the two vices were merged into one on later lists of the seven deadly sins and why the English term *vanity* captures the flavor of both.) Rebecca Konydyk DeYoung, *Vainglory: The Forgotten Vice* (Grand Rapids, MI: Eerdmans, 2014), 8.

20 Mango and Hawkins, "Hermitage of St. Neophytos," 129. Mango and Hawkins dismiss the claim as demonstrably untrue based on their detection of Neophytos's vanity.

21 The sun of praise or the storms of criticism are indifferent to a house built on "the rock" (Matt 7:25) of loving divine regard. "If we live out of that view of ourselves, we will be able to appreciate and celebrate goodness in others without envy or competition. . . . If glory is both our reality and our destiny, then our calling is to acknowledge this in other as much as ourselves." DeYoung, *Vainglory*, 131.

22 St. John Chrysostom, *Commentary on the Gospel of St. Matthew* IV.18 (modified translation), cited in Jean-Claude Larchet, *Therapy of Spiritual Illnesses: An Introduction to the Ascetic Tradition of the Orthodox Church*, vol. 1 (Montreal: Alexander, 2012), 233.

23 John Climacus, *The Ladder of Divine Ascent*, trans. Norman Russell (Mahwah, NJ: Paulist, 1982), 123, 205. Admittedly, Byzantine monastic literature is also littered with excessive self-debasement. Observing the extreme asceticism of the "bedraggled, dirty, and verminous" penitents in "the Prison," John Climacus "came close to despair when [he] compared [his] own indifference with what they went through." Climacus, 125, 127. Roberts calls this "spiritual cannibalism," instead suggesting that humility is "a self-confidence so deep, a personal integration so strong, that all comparison with other people, both advantageous and disadvantageous, slides right off." Robert C. Roberts, *Spiritual Emotions: A Psychology of Christian Virtues* (Grand Rapids, MI: Eerdmans, 2007), 90. Fortunately, the Byzantine emphasis on divinization, especially evidenced in Neophytos, offers an important corrective to such self-despising trends.

24 In the early Byzantine artistic tradition, the only records we have are of saints *refusing* to be depicted. Daniel the Stylite was enraged by someone who attempted to paint his own likeness. He promptly removed the icons to spurn the "glory of men" (Galatariotou, *Making of a Saint*, 135). That said, Saint Theodore of Sykeon reluctantly consented when some monks secretly created an image of him. Saint Symeon the New Theologian commissioned a painting of his own living spiritual father, which was considered so untoward that it contributed to Symeon's own exile (Galatariotou, 135–36). But Neophytos boldly appears to have demanded a portrait of himself. Or perhaps it was demanded by his admirers. The words of Symeon himself might apply to the depiction of Neophytos by Theodore Apsevdis: "Those who say that now there are no men who could be . . . worthy of receiving the Holy Spirit . . . of being regenerated through the grace of the Holy Spirit and of becoming the sons of God with consciousness, practical experience and visions, overthrow the whole dispensation through the Incarnation of our Lord God and Saviour Jesus Christ and clearly deny the renewal of God's image or of human nature, corrupted and slain by sin." Symeon the New Theologian (Discourse 64), cited in Leonid Ouspensky and Vladimir Lossky, *The Meaning of Icons* (Crestwood, NY: St. Vladimir's Seminary Press, 1983), 49.

25 The words "May I join the community of these two angels by virtue of my 'angelic' habit" are written above the painting. Cormack, *Writing in Gold*, 242. The diptych in Greek can also be translated, "O holy two [angels], I fervently pray that this image should come true." The double meaning was probably intended. Galatariotou, *Making of a Saint*, 140–41.

26 This entails a "transformation, a transfiguration, of human beings . . . [involving] a kind of reconstitution of our humanity, a reshaping, a straightening out of all the distortions and corruptions that we have brought upon our humanity by misusing—abusing—our human capacities. . . . This reconstitution of human nature is something impossible

without the grace of God, without everything implied in God the Word's living out what it is to be human." Andrew Louth, "The Place of *Theosis* in Orthodox Theology," in *Partakers of the Divine Nature: The History and Development of Deification in the Christian Tradition*, ed. Michael J. Christensen and Jeffery A. Wittung (Madison, NJ: Fairleigh Dickinson University Press, 2007), 37.

27 St. Maximus the Confessor, *On the Cosmic Mystery of Jesus Christ: Selected Writings from Maximus the Confessor*, trans. Paul M. Blowers and Robert Louis Wilken (Crestwood, NY: St. Vladimir's Seminary Press, 2003), 108.

28 As Paul puts the same idea, "I have been crucified with Christ. It is no longer I who live, but Christ who lives in me. And the life I now live in the flesh I live by faith in the Son of God, who loved me and gave himself for me" (Gal 2:20). Thomas Merton uses the terms "false self" and "true self" to describe such dynamics: "My false and private self is the one who wants to exist outside the reach of God's will and God's love—outside of reality and outside of life. And such a self cannot help but be an illusion." Thomas Merton, *New Seeds of Contemplation* (New York: New Directions, 2007), 34.

29 Symeon the New Theologian, Hymn 30, trans. Alfeyev, 467–72, cited in Norman Russell, *Fellow Workers with God: Orthodox Thinking on Theosis* (Crestwood, NY: St. Vladimir's Seminary Press, 2009), 146. Famously, Symeon goes even further: "I move my hand, and my hand is the whole Christ since, do not forget it, God is indivisible in His divinity. . . . Do not accuse me of blasphemy, but welcome these things . . . both my finger and my penis are Christ." Symeon the New Theologian, *Divine Eros: Hymns of Saint Symeon the New Theologian*, trans. Daniel K. Griggs (Crestwood, NY: St. Vladimir's Seminary Press, 2010), 87 (15:165). Symeon is equally celebratory of female anatomy in the same hymn: "Look at Christ in the womb and notice the things in the womb, and escaping the womb, and from whence my God went out and passed through . . . *no one* imitating him need be ashamed" (Symeon the New Theologian, 89). If Kyle Harper concludes that the Late Antique Christian tradition is "anti-erotic to its very foundation" (*From Shame to Sin* [Cambridge, MA: Harvard University Press, 2016], 244), then Symeon's rhetoric suggests that in Byzantium, the ice was beginning to thaw.

30 Maximus the Confessor, *De ambiguis*, PG XXXI, 908 CD, cited in Vladimir Lossky, *The Mystical Theology of the Eastern Church* (Crestwood, NY: St. Vladimir's Seminary Press, 2002), 214.

31 Symeon the New Theologian, *Divine Eros*, 243.

32 I thank Maria Parani for this observation.

33 Galatariotou, *Making of a Saint*, 117.

34 St. John of the Cross, *The Poems of St. John of the Cross*, trans. Willis Barnstone (New York: New Directions, 1972), 77.

35   Mango and Hawkins, "Hermitage of St. Neophytos," 184; Cormack, *Writing in Gold*, 236.

36   For a contemporary psychological approach to active imagination, see Robert Johnson, *Inner Work: Using Dreams and Active Imagination for Personal Growth* (San Francisco: HarperSanFrancisco, 1986). Complementing Johnson's helpful guidance, G. C. Tympas—tending to the ancient history of this practice of active imagination—concludes that "there is a huge difference between Jung's active imagination, through which the ego encounters unconscious dynamics and aims the inner Self, and Maximus' compound psychic function that is able to directly experience the divine through prayer and spiritual contemplation." G. C. Tympas, *Carl Jung and Maximus the Confessor on Psychic Development: The Dynamics between the "Psychological" and the "Spiritual"* (London: Routledge, 2014), 166. It seems that Carl Jung acknowledged this debt to Ignatius that many of Jung's modern followers have missed. Kenneth Becker, *Unlikely Companions: Carl Gustav Jung and Ignatius Loyola* (Leominster, UK: Gracewing, 2002). For the ways that imaginative practices functioned well before Ignatius of Loyola, see Craig Harbison, "Visions and Meditations in Early Flemish Painting," *Simiolus: Netherlands Quarterly for the History of Art* 15, no. 2 (1985): 87–118. Neophytos's career shows that the practice of imaginative prayer stretches back even further. Moreover, Neophytos passed these imaginative techniques on to others though his sermons, which "both recreate the [biblical] event in the viewer's mind and install the viewer in the event so that it happens to him." Annemarie Weyl Carr, "The Presentation of an Icon at Mount Sinai," *Deltion* 17 (1994): 247. Other artists may have continued to capture Neophytos's prayer experiments after Theodore. The Deposition in the Hideaway—painted by other artists, but still during Neophytos's lifetime—appears to show Neophytos as Joseph of Arimethea. Other scenes in the naos also resemble Neophytos (the Last Supper and the Washing of the Feet), but as these were repainted in 1503, it is uncertain whether they accurately reflect the originals. Mango and Hawkins, "Hermitage of St. Neophytos," 144; Andreas Stylianou and Judith Stylianou, *The Painted Churches of Cyprus* (London: Trigraph, 1985), 364.

37   Carr, "Icon at Mount Sinai," 248.

38   Cormack relates Neophytos's (admittedly eccentric) contributions to a eucharistic controversy in Constantinople about which Neophytos, through the bishop of Paphos, was well informed: "Issues of theology were not only discussed at the centre; they were reworked and reformulated by isolated hermits in the outlying provinces. Even when the Byzantine empire was losing political control at its margins, the Byzantine world was bound together by its common concern for common religious problems." Cormack,

Writing in Gold, 224. As shall be seen, this will be the case at the Virgin of the Vetches church as well.

39 Myrtali Acheimastou-Potamianou, *Greek Art: Byzantine Wall Paintings* (Athens: Ekdotike Athenon, 1994), 238.

40 One in the Patriarchal monastery in Peć dating to 1345 reads, "God's is the gift, by the hand of Ioaannes." The name "Srdj the sinful" survives in Dečani from about the same time. Another at Rhodes dating to 1434/35 reads, "Alexios, the sinner, and so-called painter." Kalopissi-Verti, "Painters in Late Byzantine Society: The Evidence of Church Inscriptions," *CahArch* 42 (1994): 144.

41 Within her study of vainglory, Rebecca DeYoung insists that "humans are social creatures. We need to live in relationship with each other. If we are to be known and loved, we must be acknowledged, affirmed, and appreciated for who we are and for the good what we do—in fact, it is essential to our fullest well-being." DeYoung, *Vainglory*, 22.

42 +ιστοριθ [gap of 0.26 m] λειστρα δια χειρο[ς] εμου θεοδώρου του Αψευδους. Mango and Hawkins, "Hermitage of St. Neophytos," 183. The year 6691 corresponds to 1183 CE.

43 Neophytos the Recluse, *Concerning the Misfortunes of the Land of Cyprus*, trans. C. D. Cobham, 11, cited in Demetra Papanikola-Bakirtzis and Maria Iacovou, eds., *Byzantine Medieval Cyprus* (Nicosia: Bank of Cyprus, 1998), 25.

Chapter 3

1 Thomas F. Madden, *The New Concise History of the Crusades*, updated ed. (Lanham, MD: Rowman & Littlefield, 2005), 73.

2 James A. Brundage, *The Crusades: A Documentary Survey* (Milwaukee, WI: Marquette University Press, 1962), 148.

3 Amy Kelly, *Eleanor of Aquitaine and the Four Kings* (Cambridge, MA: Harvard University Press, 1950), 268–69.

4 "Tactically sound as it might be, guarded inaction was rarely popular with Latin soldiers." Thomas Asbridge, *The Crusades: The Authoritative History of the War for the Holy Land* (New York: HarperCollins, 2011), 327.

5 Madden, *Concise History*, 75.

6 Asbridge, *Crusades*, 353.

7 "The Lord hemmed in His people with the sword and, as a punishment for the sins of men, gave over His inheritance to slaughter and devastation." Kenneth Fenwick, ed., *The Third Crusade: An Eye-Witness Account of the Campaigns of Richard Coeur-de-Lion in Cyprus and the Holy Land* (London: Folio Society, 1958), 22.

8 Asbridge, *Crusades*, 352.

9 There are varying reports. Christopher Tyerman, *God's War: A New History of the Crusades* (Cambridge, MA: Belknap of Harvard University Press, 2006), 372.

10 Jessalynn Bird, Edward Peters, and James M. Powell, eds., *Crusade and Christendom: Annotated Documents in Translation from Innocent III to the Fall of Acre, 1187–1291* (Philadelphia: University of Pennsylvania Press, 2013), 8.

11 Jonathan Riley-Smith, *The Oxford Illustrated History of the Crusades* (Oxford: Oxford University Press, 2001), 67. Bernard did "persuade one *crucesignatus* to abandon the crusade for 'something far better,' 'that true Jerusalem,' the Cistercian order . . . [and] threatened them with excommunication if they attempted to join the expedition east." Tyerman, *God's War*, 178.

12 Martin B. Shichtman, "Politicizing the Ineffable: The *Queste del Saint Graal* and Malory's 'Tale of the Sankgreal,'" in *Culture and the King: The Social Implications of the Arthurian Legend*, ed. Martin B. Shichtman and James P. Carley (Albany: State University of New York Press, 1994), 164.

13 The tympanum might also be contemplated as an illustration of the claim that the Holy Spirit proceeds from the Father and the Son (*filioque*), the Western Christian insertion into the Nicene Creed long protested by Orthodox Christians so impacted by the mission the tympanum inspired. See Michael D. Taylor, "The Pentecost at Vézelay," *Gesta* 19, no. 1 (1980): 11.

14 It is important, however, to keep in mind that "the primary purpose of the tympanum was to reveal the divine ordination of both monastic customs and monastic claims," for monasticism was understood as a continuation of Pentecost (Taylor, 11). That said, Taylor, pushing against the well-established scholarly connection of Vézelay to the Crusades, still concedes the possibility "that the peripheral portions of the tympanum were evocations of the crusading ideal. . . . Some of Peter the Venerable's interest in reuniting the churches, converting Jews and Mohammedans, and securing the Holy Sepulchre may have been added to the ascetic ideals at the heart of the composition" (13).

15 Decades ago, Michael Camille compared twelfth-century cathedrals to "shimmering Postmodern towers of today's corporate headquarters; their advanced architecture and technical complexity was symbolic not only of the wealth within but also of power to exclude those without." Michael Camille, *Image on the Edge: The Margins of Medieval Art* (London: Reaktion, 1992), 77. More recently, Debra Higgs Strickland similarly argues that "figures of Muslims to some extent, and figures of Jews to a much greater one, are depicted in English medieval works of art from the twelfth century onwards as bestial and misshapen, engaged in sadistic behaviors. Sometimes they are rendered fully monstrous. . . . The protracted, bloody project of the Crusades, believed sanctioned by God against the Muslim 'heathen' . . . was fueled by pictorial images of Christian versus Muslim armies, in which the 'Saracen' warriors are rendered as gigantic, dark or otherwise physically distorted." Debra Higgs Strickland, "Monstrosity and Race in the

Late Middle Ages," in *The Ashgate Research Companion to Monsters and the Monstrous*, ed. Asa Simon Mittman and Peter Dendle (Burlington, VT: Ashgate, 2012), 377–78. Surely such sentiments lend new resonance to Bernard's famous critique of the *deformis formositas ac formosa deformitas* (deformed beauty yet beautiful deformity) of Romanesque art. Bernard particularly singled out depictions of *semihomines* (part man, part beast) for censure. Diane J. Reilly, "Bernard of Clairvaux and Christian Art," in *A Companion to Bernard Clairvaux*, ed. Brian Patrick McGuire (Danvers, MA: Brill, 2011), 279.

16 John Block Friedman, *The Monstrous Races in Medieval Art and Thought* (Syracuse, NY: Syracuse University Press, 2000), 178.

17 "When he kills a malefactor this is not homicide but malicide, and he is accounted Christ's legal executionaer against evildoers." Cited in Peter Partner, *The Knights Templar and Their Myth* (Rochester, VT: Destiny, 1990), 8. For Bernard's address in full, see Bernard of Clairvaux, *In Praise of the New Knighthood: A Treatise on the Knights Templar and the Holy Places of Jerusalem*, trans. M. Conrad Greenia OCSO (Trappist, KY: Cistercian, 2000).

18 Asbridge, *Crusades*, 374. Richard would later sell the sword to obtain additional ships.

19 Hugh of St. Victor, *De Arca Noe Morali*, cited in Hugh of St. Victor, *The Didascalicon of Hugh of St. Victor: A Medieval Guide to the Arts*, trans. Jerome Taylor (New York: Columbia University Press, 1991), 171.

20 Chrétien de Troyes, *Perceval; or, The Story of the Grail*, trans. Ruth Harwood Cline (Athens: University of Georgia Press, 1985), xvi.

21 It was after this discovery that Robert de Boron composed his famous meditation on Joseph of Arimathea and the Grail legend. Pierre Le Gentil, "The Work of Robert de Boron and the *Didot Perceval*," in *Arthurian Literature in the Middle Ages: A Collaborative History*, ed. R. S. Loomis (Oxford: Clarendon, 1959), 268.

22 Winston Churchill, *A History of the English-Speaking Peoples*, vol. 1 (New York: Dorset, 1956), 229.

23 Neophytos the Recluse, *Concerning the Misfortunes*, 10–11.

24 Western sources suggest that Isaac Komnenos had an alliance with Saladin. Peter Edbury explains that while Muslim authors do not confirm this, they do confirm an alliance between Saladin and Isaac II Angelos, who was officially the Byzantine emperor during the seizure of Cyprus. Suffice it to say, there was sufficient reason for Isaac Komnenos to be mistrusted, and without Constantinopolitan endorsement, his position was already weak. "We shall never know the full story." Peter W. Edbury, "Crusaders and Pilgrims: The Conquest of Cyprus in 1191," in Papanikola-Bakirtzis and Iacovou, *Byzantine Medieval Cyprus*, 29.

25 Fenwick, *Third Crusade*, 27.

26 Fenwick, 55.

27 The full quotation reads: "Because your appetites are fixed on things that, divided, lessen each one's share, envy's bellows pushes breath into your sighs." Dante, *Purgatorio*, trans. Jean Hollander and Robert Hollander (New York: Doubleday, 2003), 305.

28 Pope Innocent II, *Omne Datum Optimum* (March 29, 1139), in *The Templars: Selected Sources*, ed. Malcolm Barber and Keith Bate (Manchester: Manchester University Press, 2002), 60.

29 Pope Innocent II, 61–62.

30 By 1150, the Templars owned more than forty castles and preceptories in Europe. It is estimated that eventually, the Templars possessed nine thousand estates in England and France. Malcolm Barber, *The New Knighthood: A History of the Order of the Temple* (Cambridge: Cambridge University Press, 1994), 22.

31 Edbury, "Crusaders and Pilgrims," 29. Edbury elaborates that one hundred thousand Saracen bezants (the Western version of the Muslim dinar produced in the Holy Land) was a bargain, as a knight could receive four hundred thousand bezants each year as a fief. Richard, in any case, received only half of it. The low price can be explained by his being in the area for only a year and needing to raise money quickly.

32 Fenwick, *Third Crusade*, 54.

33 Barber, *New Knighthood*, 119; Edbury, *Cyprus and the Crusades*, 7. For a discussion of the variety of sources behind this story, see A. Gilmour-Bryson, *The Trial of the Templars in Cyprus* (Leiden: Brill, 1998), 14.

34 Francesco Amadi, *Chroniques d'Amadi et de Strambaldi* (Paris: Imprimerie Nationale, 1891), 84–85. For a helpful discussion of the reliability of this source, see M. J. K. Walsh, N. Coureas, and Peter W. Edbury, *Medieval and Renaissance Famagusta: Studies in Architecture, Art and History* (Burlington, VT: Ashgate, 2012), 44.

35 Barber, *New Knighthood*, 119–20.

36 Edbury, *Cyprus and the Crusades*, 9.

37 Their rule lasted through 1489, after which the island experienced Venetian rule until 1571, when it was finally conquered by the Ottomans. Sir David Hunt, ed., *Footprints in Cyprus: An Illustrated History* (London: Trigraph, 1982), 175.

38 Hunt, 191.

39 Hunt, 194.

Chapter 4

1 The term *crucesignati* was used occasionally after the twelfth century to refer to "Crusaders." Madden, *Concise History*, 1.

2   "The discovery of the Jerusalem relic of the True Cross brought physical symbolism to the fulfilment of the journey of the bearers of the cross." Tyerman, *God's War*, 160.

3   Steven Runciman, *A History of the Crusades*, vol. 1 (Cambridge: Cambridge University Press, 1951), 294. Tyerman is more suspicious of this story, but he does not rule it out. Tyerman, *God's War*, 160.

4   "A scrap of metal found beneath an old, much renovated church after a day's digging does not stretch credibility or credulity. What mattered in June 1098 was the crusader's belief." Tyerman, *God's War*, 144.

5   Tyerman, 371.

6   Phillips, *Fourth Crusade*, 5.

7   This tactic was used by the sultan Al Kamil (ca. 1177–1238). Madden, *Concise History*, 155.

8   After it was captured by Saladin in 1187, the True Cross was mock-processed upside down through the streets of Damascus. Following the Crusaders' successful reclaiming of the city of Acre, the envoys of Richard the Lionheart had been permitted to inspect it, but Saladin did not return it. The sultan promised to return the True Cross, along with payment and Christian hostages, in exchange for the release of Muslim hostages. But when Saladin did not make his payment on schedule, hoping to wear down the Crusader army, Richard called the sultan's bluff. He ordered 2,600 members of the Muslim garrison executed in view of Saladin and his army, just as Saladin had executed the Knights Templar and Hospitallers following the Battle of Hattin. Tyerman, *God's War*, 455–56. Richard adds in his own account of this incident, "A few of the more notable were spared, and we hope to recover the Holy Cross and certain Christian captives in exchange for them" (456). Tyerman adds, "The sultan probably recognized the massacre for what it was, a deliberate act of policy for which his actions were in part responsible" (457). Even so, Richard's actions may give us reason to receive the legends surrounding his valor with skepticism.

9   Compounding this point, the Christ child's earring (fig. 4.2) may indicate that this is a true image and no idol, for unlike the jewelry surrendered to generate the golden calf (Exod 32:24), this gold is withheld.

10   George E. Demacopoulos, "War, Violence, and the Feast of the Holy Cross in Byzantium" (inaugural lecture for Fr. John Meyendorff & Patterson Family Chair of Orthodox Christian Studies, Fordham University, October 5, 2015). I thank the author for sharing this yet-to-be-published paper with me. For a book that explores the Holy Cross and its relation to Cyprus in particular, see Andreas Stylianou and Judith Stylianou, *By This Conquer* (Nicosia: Zavallis, 1971).

11   The legend appears to have first developed in the second half of the fourth century to account for the presence of the cross, which was venerated by an increasing flow of pilgrims into Jerusalem. Helena was known, via the court historian Eusebius, to have visited Jerusalem. Jan Willem Drijvers, *Helena Augusta: The Mother of Constantine and the Legend of Her Finding the True Cross* (Leiden: Brill, 1992), 138–41.

12   These new valences appear in the Judas Cyriacus legend that dates to the fifth or sixth century, which in turn became the most popular version, especially in the Latin Middle Ages (Drijvers, 165). When the Jew Judas Cyriacus refused to disclose the location of the True Cross, Helena replied, "'I swear by Christ, who was crucified, that I shall torture you with hunger and thirst if you do not tell the truth.' And when she had said these things, she ordered Judas to be thrown into a dry well for seven days and that he should stay there without food." Judas finally relented and disclosed the location (Drijvers, 168).

13   In the Judas Cyriacus legend, Helena explains that this is so that the horse "will be an invincible weapon for [Constantine] against all his enemies because now the victory belongs to the king and he will have peace instead of war. In this way the saying of the prophet Zechariah will be fulfilled, who said, It will happen on that day that the bridle of the horse will be called holiness unto the Lord [Zech 14:20]." See also Stylianou and Stylianou, *By This Conquer*, 8. As mentioned, George Demacopoulos has explored how the hymns surrounding what became the Feast of the Exaltation of the Cross in the seventh and eight centuries reflect imperial more than theological concerns. Demacopoulos, "War, Violence." Demacopoulos points out that Heraclius was remembered by the West as the first Crusader. He rightly contends that the theological and imperial elements of the Feast of the True Cross (September 14) should be disentangled.

14   The Judas Cyriacus legend, cited in Drijvers, *Helena Augusta*, 168.

15   Tyerman, *God's War*, 35. Tyerman, however, adds an important distinction between Byzantine military attitudes and that of the Crusaders: "Byzantine warfare remained a secular activity, for all its divine sanction, never a penitential act of religious votaries" (35). See Judith Herrin, *Byzantium: The Surprising Life of a Medieval Empire* (Princeton, NJ: Princeton University Press, 2007), 84–85.

16   Stylianou and Stylianou, *By This Conquer*, 98.

17   Mango and Hawkins, "Hermitage of St. Neophytos," 123–34.

18   Galatariotou, *Making of a Saint*, 242. In this case, Neophytos was referring to the contest between the Orthodox and the Latins. This was a representative attitude at the time.

19   Galatariotou, 108.

20   This is not, of course, to suggest that Orthodox nationalism is a thing of the past. To anticipate the present book's conclusion, Mary's lesson

is always one that stands to be learned again, and the Virgin of the Passion—in Pushkinskaya square in Moscow, among other places—is fortunately there to teach it.

21 Stylianou and Stylianou, *Painted Churches*, 51. The main body of the church dates to the eleventh century, but the sixth-century apse survives.

22 The result was that "anyone who challenged Pulcheria's legitimacy on the grounds that she was a woman risked insulting the New Eve." Nicholas P. Constas, "Weaving the Body of God: Proclus of Constantinople, the Theotokos, and the Loom of the Flesh," *Journal of Early Christian Studies* 3, no. 2 (Summer 1995): 188. Constas suggests that "images of Pulcheria and the Virgin were so close that an attack on the one could, and was perhaps supposed to be seen as an offense to the other" (188). The oft repeated story of Pulcheria opposing Nestorius's prohibition of her in the sanctuary with the words "Have I [my gender] not given birth to God?" only emerges in the nineteenth century. Nevertheless, "we should not write Pulcheria out of the picture, even if we are left with a somewhat less colorful portrait of her involvement in the Nestorian controversy than we once thought." Shoemaker, *Mary in Early Christian Faith*, 217.

23 Shoemaker's reasoning connecting the foundations to Pulcheria is convincing. Shoemaker, *Mary in Early Christian Faith*, 220–21.

24 Cyril Mango, "Constantinople as Theotokopoulis," in Vassilaki, *Mother of God*, 17–25.

25 Mango, "Constantinople," 21; Shoemaker, *Mary in Early Christian Faith*, 177.

26 Mango, "Constantinople," 22. More extensively, see Anthony Kaldellis, *The Christian Parthenon: Classicism and Pilgrimage in Byzantine Athens* (New York: Cambridge University Press, 2009); Limberis, *Divine Heiress*, 140–41.

27 Pentchceva, *Icons and Power*, 62. For more recent examinations of Mary's role in warfare, see Leena Mari Peltomaa, "Role of the Virign Mary at the Siege of Constantinople in 626," *Scrinium* 5, no. 1 (2009): 284–99; and Martin Hurbanič, *The Avar Siege of Constantinople in 625: History and Legend* (Cham, Switzerland: Palgrave Macmillan, 2019).

28 Pentcheva, *Icons and Power*, 65.

29 Annemarie Weyl Carr, "The Mother of God in Public," in Vassilaki, *Mother of God*, 330.

30 Anthony Kaldellis, "'A Union of Opposites': The Moral Logic and Corporeal Presence of the Theotokos on the Field of Battle," in *Pour l'amour de Byzance: Hommage à Paolo Odorico*, ed. Christian Gastgeber et al. (Frankfurt: Peter Lang, 2010), 131–44. Kaldellis's subtle reading of these famous war texts reveals that Byzantine writers were never quite comfortable with Mary in warfare: "Power is subverted, even—and this is crucial—in the case of the Theotokos. It remains exclusively in the hands of God" (144).

31 The first record we have of a high-ranking Byzantine noble going to
    the Hodegon monastery, which would later be associated with the famous
    Hodegetria icon, resulted not in triumph but in disaster—the supplicant
    was assassinated: "On the eve of his intended departure for his campaign
    against the Arabs in 866, Caesar Bardas went to the Hodegon to pray. As
    he entered the church, his cloak slipped from his shoulders and Bardas was
    overwhelmed by ominous feelings, which were fulfilled by his assassination
    on the following day." Christine Angelidi and Titos Papamastorakis, "The
    Veneration of the Virgin Hodegetria and the Hodegon Monastery," in
    Vassilaki, *Mother of God*, 375. Although it occurs in the Hodegon monas-
    tery, there is no icon mentioned in this particular passage.

32 John Haldon, *The Empire That Would Not Die: The Paradox of Eastern
    Roman Survival, 640–74* (Cambridge, MA: Harvard University Press,
    2016), 294. See also John Haldon, *Byzantium in the Seventh Century: The
    Transformation of a Culture* (Cambridge: Cambridge University Press,
    1997), 450. Such were the conditions that gave rise to apocalyptic literature
    such as the *Vision of the End* and to a general shift from what was essentially
    a late-Roman society into a Byzantine one.

33 Haldon, *Eastern Roman Survival*, 294.

34 Sophronius "had come to look beyond any direct association between sec-
    ular empire and Christian salvation . . . [believing] successful and thriving
    Christian community could be envisaged independently of the Roman
    [i.e., Byzantine] state." Haldon, *Eastern Roman Survival*, 92, 98. Haldon
    adds that these views were "highly damaging to the internal cohesion of
    the state and community" and were, "in the end, marginalized by main-
    stream Christian Roman thinkers in the seventh and eighth centuries."
    Haldon, 98. This cleavage between church and state fostered the condi-
    tions for the hesychastic movement that did much to prepare Byzantium
    for its political end.

35 In particular, Sophronius was a chief opponent of Heraclius's attempt to
    end discussions on the theological issue of Monothelitism. His *Ekthesis* of
    636 or 638 attempted to prohibit further discussion, which only hardened
    Sophronius's resolve. Haldon, 92, 98.

36 Allen, "Portrayals of Mary," 75. Of course, Sophronius would have had the
    "spiritual forces of evil in the heavenly realms" (Eph 6:12 NIV) in mind as
    well, but this does not rule out imperial associations in the passage, espe-
    cially considering Sophronius's hostility toward Emperor Heraclius.

37 Phil Booth, *Crisis of Empire: Doctrine and Dissent at the End of Late
    Antiquity* (Berkeley: University of California Press, 2013), 341. Famously,
    Maximus paid for this resistance with his life.

38 "Kings," declared the defender of icons John of Damascus, "do not possess
    the authority to legislate for the church . . . for the business of kings is political

administration; ecclesiastical governance pertains to pastors and teachers." Cited in Jaroslav Pelikan, *The Spirit of Eastern Christendom (600–1700)* (Chicago: University of Chicago Press, 1977), 108. After iconoclasm, "caesaropapism was replaced by a diarchy of emperor and patriarch." Gerhard Ladner, "Origin and Significance of the Byzantine Iconoclastic Controversy," *Medieval Studies* 2 (1940): 142. Jaroslav Pelikan endorses Ladner's view. Jaroslav Pelikan, *Imago Dei: The Byzantine Apologia for Icons* (Princeton, NJ: Princeton University Press, 1990), 38. Pelikan argues that a degree of caesaropapism certainly remained in Byzantine society after the iconophile triumph, but it was significantly weakened. Perhaps a rough parallel can be drawn between the iconoclastic controversy and the snows of Canossa, where Holy Roman emperor Henry IV did penance before Pope Gregory VII in 1077.

39 Iconophiles could "artfully cover their confession of faith in icons under their confession of faith in the Theotokos." Niki Tsironis, "The Mother of God in the Iconoclastic Controversy," in Vassilaki, *Mother of God*, 38. For a massive revision of the traditional accounts of Byzantine iconoclasm, see Leslie Brubaker and John Haldon, *Byzantium in the Iconoclast Era, c. 680–850: A History* (Cambridge: Cambridge University Press, 2011). Jaś Elsner offers a helpful review, pointing out that there is nevertheless "every possibility that [early Christian] images were put to private devotional use." Jaś Elsner, "Iconoclasm as Discourse: From Antiquity to Byzantium," *Art Bulletin* 94, no. 3 (2012): 372.

40 Shoemaker reminds us that this shift should not be overplayed, because imagery emphasizing Mary's special bond with her son predates the iconoclastic period as well, especially in Egypt, which was spared the worst of iconoclasm. Stephen Shoemaker, "The (Pseudo?-)Maximus *Life of the Virgin*," *Journal of Theological Studies* 67, no. 1 (April 2016): 135.

41 For the mainstay of Byzantine art, imperial dress in the heavenly court denotes second rank, while the same dress in the earthly court denotes first rank. Christ and Mary, therefore, have no need for imperial regalia, although their angelic consorts do have such a need. In short, the Byzantine separation between the heavenly and earthly powers always followed distinct visual codes. The fact that Mary appears on coins and seals with the emperors is not only, therefore, evidence of a flat conflation of the heavenly and earthly powers but also evidence of their distinction. Such depictions are "at the same time a statement of the emperor's present political power and a prayer for his reception into the court of heaven." Henry Maguire, "The Heavenly Court," in *Byzantine Court Culture 829–1204*, ed. Henry Maguire (Washington, DC: Dumbarton Oaks, 1997), 250.

42 By contrast, Mary in late antique Rome appears in imperial garb "as if to compensate for the lack of an imperial family." Judith Herrin, "The Imperial Feminine in Byzantium," *Past and Present* 169, no. 1 (November

2000): 14. In Byzantium, however, the empress had a corner on the market of imperial imagery. It is for this reason that Mary wears her humble attire: a head covering and no jewelry to speak of. "From the earliest surviving monuments that record her presence," explains Herrin, "the Virgin wears this deeply unregal costume" (15–16).

43 Pentcheva, *Icons and Power*, 26.

44 Jane Baun, "Discussing Mary's Humanity in Medieval Byzantium," in *The Church and Mary*, ed. R. N. Swanson (Woodbridge, UK: Boydell, 2004), 66. Baun adds, "Authors, theologians, and artists of the [Middle Byzantine] period begin to ponder how the most traumatic event in the life of the divine family, the Crucifixion, affected its relationships" (66). For a classic articulation of this shift, see Ioli Kalavrezou, "Images of the Mother," *Dumbarton Oaks Papers* 44 (1990): 165–72. Kalavrezou argues for a Middle Byzantine shift to maternal imagery, an argument she reaffirms in "The Maternal Side of the Virgin," in Vassilaki, *Mother of God*, 41–45. More recently, Pauline Allen summarizes the turn in this way: "Once she has attained this stature, her humanity can be comfortably show-cased, as it is in eighth-, ninth-, and tenth-century Greek homiletic literature where she is portrayed encomiastically as enduring in a human fashion her Son's Passion and death, and where her maternal tenderness is clearly linked to the economy of salvation." Allen, "Portrayals of Mary," 84. Likewise, Henry Maguire argues that "pre-iconoclast art was more concerned with presenting the *external* evidence of Christ's humanity. Post-iconoclastic art, on the other hand, showed the *internal* evidence, the human feelings that enabled the viewer to experience the Incarnation not only intellectually, but also emotionally through an engagement with the inner life of the Virgin." Henry Maguire, "Body, Clothing, Metaphor: The Virgin in Early Byzantine Art," in Brubaker and Cunningham, *Cult of the Mother*, 51.

45 Fr. Maximos Constas, "The Story of an Edition: Antoine Wenger and John Geometres' *Life of the Virgin Mary*," in Arentzen and Cunningham, *Reception of the Virgin*, 334.

46 Edgar Hennecke, *New Testament Apocrypha*, vol. 1, ed. Wilhelm Schneemelcher, trans. R. McL. Wilson (Philadelphia: Westminster, 1963), 383–85.

47 "What did she feel when the sponge was pressed to His mouth? What did she feel when the vinegar touched His pure lips? I will tell you: searing flames of fire penetrating her womb. . . . The fire lighted within me is beyond anything natural, and by far exceeds the pain of childbirth." George of Nicomedia, cited in Fr. Maximos Constas, *And a Sword Shall Pierce Your Own Soul (Lk 2:35): The Kenosis of Christ and the Mother of God in Orthodox Iconography* (Allston, MA: Holy Resurrection Orthodox Church, 2013), 32. By contrast, the birth of Christ was, according

to Byzantine tradition dating to the mid-second- to early third-century Protevangelium, painless. See Stephen J. Shoemaker, "A Mother's Passion: Mary at the Crucifixion and Resurrection in George of Nikomedia's Passion Homilies," in Brubaker and Cunningham, *Cult of the Mother*, 53–68.

48 Over time, the lamentation rituals of the pre-Christian Greek world were gradually absorbed and refined by Christianity, which offset despair with the hope of the resurrection. For the classic account, see Margaret Alexiou, revised by Dimitrios Yatromanolakis and Panagiotis Roilos, *The Ritual Lament in Greek Tradition*, 2nd ed. (Lanham, MD: Rowman & Littlefield, 2002). Alexiou explains, "As time went on, the Church fathers objected less frequently and less vehemently to the evils of lamentation" (29). For an illuminating account of what Aphrodite's lament of Adonis meant for the women of classical Athens, see Ronda R. Simms, "Mourning and Community at the Athenian Adonia," *Classical Journal* 93, no. 2 (December 1997–January 1998): 121–41. I thank Maria Evangelatou for informing me about the Adonia.

49 "I received from the angel pledges of joy, and I took away all tears from the face of the earth, but now these tears are increased by my own." Symeon Metaphrastes, cited in Fr. Maximos Constas, *Kenosis of Christ*, 30.

50 Henry Maguire, *Art and Eloquence in Byzantium* (Princeton, NJ: Princeton University Press, 1081), 99.

51 Further liturgical parallels to the Virgin of the Passion have been suggested by Mirjana Tatić-Djurić, "Iconographie de la Vierge de Passion: Genese du Dogme et des Symboles," *De Culto Mariano: Saeculis XII–XV*, Acta Congressus Mariologici Mariani Internationalis Romae Anno 1975 Celebrati, vol. 6 (Rome: Pontificia Academia Mariana Internationalis, 1981), 163n143. Pallas connects the shape of Mary's hands at Lagoudera to the eucharistic spoon based on a sermon from Methodius. D. I. Pallas, *Die Passion und Bestattung Christi in Byzanz: Der Ritus—das Bild* (Munich: W. & I. M. Salzer, 1965), 177.

52 In particular, this can be seen at the churches of Kastoria in Greece and in the church of Studenica in Serbia. Earlier art historians assumed such iconographical innovations were the result of a new Good Friday service added in the late eleventh century, but such developments now appear to be more deeply rooted in normative Byzantine culture: "If we pick apart this 'new' Good Friday service, we find that it is not something all that new, but rather a modification of three extant and overlapping [daily, weekly, and annual] liturgical cycles." Nancy P. Ševčenko, "The Service of the Virgin's Lament Revisited," in Brubaker and Cunningham, *Cult of the Mother*, 251.

53 Attractive as the thesis may be that Maximus the Confessor was the author of the *Life of the Virgin*, which exhibits an especially mournful Mary,

scholarly opinion seems now to have shifted to attributing it to the Middle Byzantine period, specifically to John Geometres (ca. 935–1000). Constas, "Story of an Edition," 340. Christos Simelidis persuasively argues that the text was composed by Geometres (in 976–79 or 987–89) and was then simplified and translated into Georgian by an Athonite monk named Euthymios, after which a later scribe (or Euthymios himself) conferred authority on the text by attributing it to Maximos the Confessor, who was especially trusted in Georgia. Christos Simelidis, "Two Lives of the Virgin: John Geometres, Euthymios the Athonite, and Maximos the Confessor," *Dumbarton Oaks Papers* 74 (2020): 158.

54   "I would say, even though it is a bold statement, that she suffered more than him and endured sorrows of the heart: for he was God and Lord of all things, and he willingly endured suffering in the flesh. But she possessed the frailty of a human being and a woman." [Pseudo-]Maximus, *Life of the Virgin*, 101. Such statements both illustrate and simultaneously challenge the standard misogyny of the medieval world.

55   Thomas Arentzen, *Virginity Recast: Romanos and the Mother of God* (Lund, Sweden: Lund University Press, 2014), 206. Mary does indeed weep in Romanos's poetry, but she then remains stalwart even at the cross: "For Mary gazed at him on the wood and said: Although you submit to the Cross, you remain *my son and my God*" (Arentzen, 206).

56   Interestingly, both poets, Romanos and Geometres, were associated with the church of the Theotokos *ta Kyrou* in Constantinople, which is where Romanos was buried. Geometres appears to have been inspired by Romanos's poem "On Mary at the Cross." Simelidis, "Two Lives," 136.

57   [Pseudo-]Maximus, *Life of the Virgin*, 104.

58   Maximus, 109, 111. The classic Christian tradition famously spares Mary the pain of childbirth, which is the result of sin (Gen 3:16). But even as pain engulfs her life as never before during Christ's torture, it is Christ who enables her to withstand: "How could you bear to behold such a dreadful sight, unless the grace and power of your son and Lord strengthened you and confirmed for you the glory of his mercy." Maximus, 106.

59   Maximus, 107.

60   E. R. A. Sewter, trans., *The Alexiad of Anna Comnena* (Harmondsworth, UK: Penguin, 1969), 395, quoted in Annemarie Weyl Carr, "Threads of Authority: The Virgin Mary's Veil in the Middle Ages," in *Robes and Honor: The Medieval World of Investiture*, ed. Stewart Gordon (New York: Palgrave, 2001), 59–93. While this is sometimes taken as evidence that emperors always participated in the usual miracle, Carr suggests, "We have no evidence that Alexios (or any other emperor) ever participated in the 'usual miracle.'"

61   Sewter, *Alexiad*, 227. Perhaps with these events in mind, patriarch John Oxeites castigated Emperor Alexios for his impiety, citing the invincible veil

of Mary and (by implication) his inability to use it properly. Paul Gautier, "Diatribes de Jean l'Oxite centre Alexis ler Comnene," *Revue des etudes Byzantines* 28 (1970): 38–39, cited in Carr, "Threads of Authority."

62 In addition, the twelfth-century chronicle of Choniates tells of a vision related to the Battle of Myriokephalon in 1176, a pivotal military defeat for the Byzantine Empire that was the beginning of the end, leading to the irreversible process of losing Anatolia. In the account, a bilingual man named Mavropoulos approached the emperor Manuel I Komnenos (1143–80) and related a dream from the previous night. Mavropoulos had entered a church and petitioned an icon of the Mother of God, which replied, "The emperor is now in the utmost danger, who will go forth in my name to assist him?" An unseen voice replied, "Let [Saint] George go." Mary responded, "He is sluggish." "Let [Saint] Theodore set forth," responded the voice, but Mary rejected him as well. "And finally," the chronicler concludes, "came the painful response that no one could avert the impending evil." H. J. Magoulias, *O City of Byzantium: Annals of Niketas Choniates* (Detroit: Wayne State University Press, 1984), 107–8, quoted in Pentcheva, *Icon and Power*, 69.

63 See note 52 in this chapter.

Chapter 5

1 Our knowledge of the rank of Leon, son of Authentes, is limited to the term αὐθέντης, reserved for high-ranking Byzantine families. The Winfields suggest that Leon was possibly a regional governor. Winfield and Winfield, *Panagia tou Arakos*, 51. Chara Konstantinidi uses these designations to name the painter of the first layer at the Virgin of the Vetches the "painter of Authentes" and the second phase the "painter of Leon." Konstantinidi, "Byzantine Painting," 60–85.

2 For the debate over the details of whether it was indeed Theodore Apsevdis who painted both monuments, see this book's appendix.

3 Konstantinidi, "Byzantine Painting," 60, 65.

4 Chrysanthe Baltoyianni, *Icons: The Mother of God in the Incarnation and the Passion* (Athens: Adams Editions, 1994), 79–142.

5 Baltoyianni, 133. But there is also a hint of the victory of redemption here: "And I will put enmity between you and the woman, and between your off-spring and hers; he will crush your head, and you will strike his heel" (Gen 3:15 NIV). Baltoyianni suggests that the upturned foot in such icons goes back to the ninth or tenth century (the Hodegetria of Tsikanli in Georgia). The dangling sandal in later examples of the icon in fifteenth-century Crete serves to highlight this motif, which also appears in late Byzantine sermons. Baltoyianni, 132–34.

6 Baltoyianni, 19.

7   In Byzantine homilies, the reclining posture could evoke death, a motif traceable to antiquity. Baltoyianni, 80–81.

8   Unlike Jesus's disciples, Simeon knew the Messiah's life would be fraught with pain.

9   Perhaps one can read this verse onto the Virgin of the Passion, seeing Christ the Lamb as redeeming not just Mary but all women from the lingering stain of patriarchy. For a history of how this passage has been interpreted, see Linda S. Schearing, "Double Time . . . Double Trouble? Gender, Sin, and Leviticus 12," in *Leviticus: Composition and Reception*, ed. Rolf Rendtorff, Robert A. Kugler, and Sarah Smith Bartel (Leiden: Brill, 2003); and Dorothea Erbele-Küster, *Body, Gender and Purity in Leviticus 12 and 15* (London: Bloomsbury T&T Clark, 2017), 53–54. I thank Amy Peeler for these references.

10   "And when the time came for their purification according to the Law of Moses, they brought him up to Jerusalem to present him to the Lord (as it is written in the Law of the Lord, 'Every male who first opens the womb shall be called holy to the Lord' [Exod 13:2, 12]), and to offer a sacrifice according to what is said in the Law of the Lord, 'a pair of turtledoves, or two young pigeons' [Lev 12:8]" (Luke 2:22–24).

11   This is from the Latin words for the prayer's beginning: "You may now dismiss your servant in peace" (Luke 2:29 NIV).

12   Allen, "Portrayals of Mary," 78. The stational liturgy associated with the meeting was viewed by the pilgrim Egeria in 381–84. Originally celebrated on February 14, it was changed to February 2 and introduced to Constantinople by Emperor Justianian in the sixth century. This feast, known as the ὑπαπαντή (meeting) is also frequently referred to as the presentation, referring to the presentation of Christ in the temple. I refer to it as the meeting to distinguish it from the presentation of Mary in the temple. Annemarie Weyl Carr gives an overview of scholarship in this area, with special attention to the Virgin of the Vetches church, in Carr, "Icon at Mount Sinai," 242–45. Simeon's prophecy of the sword makes him, for the Byzantines, the last of the prophets of Mary. Though interpreted as Mary's doubt earlier in Byzantium, with the sermons of George of Nicomedia, the sword began to be understood as the passion.

13   Henry Maguire, "The Iconography of Symeon with the Christ Child in Byzantine Art," *Dumbarton Oaks Papers* 34/35 (1980/1981): 261–69.

14   Dorothy C. Schorr, "The Iconographic Development of the Presentation in the Temple," *Art Bulletin* 28, no. 1 (March 1946): 21. Schorr points out that an "outdoor" altar against an architectural background corresponds most to the Jerusalem temple at the time of the birth of Christ. However, this would of course not have been known to the early Christian artists. The example she employs of the outdoor meeting is from Cod. Lat. 9448,

an antiphonary from Prüm (in modern Germany) dating to the eleventh century (Schorr, 23).

15 "In this [later] scene, the two episodes of the meeting with Simeon and the presentation of the Child at the altar are always synthesized." Schorr, 22.

16 The text will be further discussed in chapter 8.

17 Hennecke, *New Testament Apocrypha*, 387–88.

18 In the earliest description of the Presentation at Saint Sergius at Gaza, the orator Choricius says, "The mother is present, holding the child in her arms" (cited in Maguire, "Iconography of Symeon," 262). Other occasions where Mary holds the child include the pre-iconoclastic version at the Kalanderhane in Istanbul or in the Menologion of Basil II. A description of a destroyed illustration of the event at the Church of the Holy Apostles has Simeon holding Christ. The description is given by Constantine of Rhodes, written between 931 and 944. He describes the "old man Symeon carrying Christ as a baby in his arms." Maguire, "Iconography of Symeon," 262. Other occasions where Simeon holds Christ include the Chapel of Saint Eustathius in Cappadocia or at Amasgou in Cyprus.

19 Variations continued, such as Simeon holding the Christ child as Mary grieves or the Simeon Glykophilon, where he appears alone holding the Christ child. But Cretan icons and Dionysios's "Painter's Manual" evidence the fact that Simeon holding the child becomes standard. Dionysios's manual reads, "Candlemas. [The Presentation in the Temple]: A temple and a domed canopy. Saint Simeon the receiver of God holds the infant Christ in his arms, who gives him his blessing. The Virgin on the other side of the altar stretches out her arms to the child." Paul Hetherington, trans., *The "Painter's Manual" of Dionysios of Foura* (London: Sagittarius, 1981), 32.

20 For the Virgin of Kykkos, see Carr, "'Virgin Veiled by God,'" 221.

21 Climacus, *Divine Ascent*, 132.

22 See chapter 2, note 36 in this book.

23 Neophytos's sermon on the meeting of Mary and Simeon. Carr, "Icon at Mount Sinai," 245. "That an icon should engage the viewer in this kind of kinetic and participatory contemplation challenges the characteristic metaphors used in explaining icons—metaphors in which the icon becomes 'transparent,' 'like window,' or in some other way vanishes from view" (248). Carr also shows an icon of the transfiguration near the same time period that invites viewers to imagine themselves as the apostles.

24 Carr, 246.

25 Annemarie Weyl Carr, "Thoughts on the Economy of the Image of Mary," *Theology Today* 56, no. 3 (October 1999): 372.

26 R. Janin offers a description of the "full of grace" (Kecharitomene) monastery in Constantinople and describes its rule. It was founded by Irene Ducas, wife of Emperor Alexios I Komnenos (1081–1118). In addition

to the icon of the Annunciation within the monastery (no description is given), the monastery boasted a mosaic of Christ washing the feet of the disciples, perhaps because the monastery was connected to the Philanthropos ("love of man") monastery nearby. R. Janin, *La Géographie Ecclésiastique de L'Empire Byzantin*, vol. 3 (Paris: Centre National de la Recharche Scientifique, 1969), 188–91. Could it be that the monastery's relics of Saint Spyridon, a Cypriot saint, connected it to the island of Cyprus, where Spyridon was born? It is impossible to say. The fact that Theodore did not include the foot washing at the Virgin of the Vetches indicates that he was not merely imitating this monastery. Even if the Virgin of the Passion at the Virgin of the Vetches church in Cyprus evokes an original in Constantinople, it is possible that his angels of the passion were added to a preexisting model.

27 Neville pushes back at the scholarly assumption that Anna's stay in a monastery was necessarily forced. See chapter 8, "A Room of One's Own," in Leonora Neville, *Anna Komnene: The Life and Work of a Medieval Historian* (Oxford: Oxford University Press, 2016).

28 Anna Komnene, *The Alexiad*, trans. Elizabeth A. S. Dawes (independently published, 2021), 380.

29 In the vocative inscription, "Leon directs his prayer not to the image but to the Virgin herself . . . [the patron] assumes the third person. Visual and verbal grammar agree." Robert Nelson, "Image and Inscription: Pleas for Salvation in Spaces of Devotion," in *Art and Text in Byzantine Culture*, ed. Liz James (New York: Cambridge University Press, 2007), 110.

30 Winfield and Winfield, *Panagia tou Arakos*, 67–68. For an interpretation of the final portion, see Andréas Nicolaïdès, "L'église de la Panagia Arakiotissa à Lagoudéra, Chypre: Etude iconographique des fresques de 1192," *Dumbarton Oaks Papers* 50 (1996): 4–5. Robert Nelson explains in regard to Lagoudera and other monuments that "inscriptions and icons join to create holy space." Nelson, "Image and Inscription," 116.

31 We can even trace the troubles of Cyprus in the pigments, as evidenced by Theodore having run out of, in some of the upper backgrounds, the more expensive color blue. Winfield and Winfield, *Panagia tou Arakos*, 51.

32 The speaker is identified as "Father Beetz, counselor to the Archbishop of Freiburg." "Si coram hac Imagine sto, videor mihi mare videre, oceanum idearum." Clement Henze, *Mater de Perpetuo Succursu: Prodigiosae Iconis Marialis ita nuncupatae monographia* (Bonn, Germany: Collegium Josephinum, 1926), 28.

Chapter 6

1 The controversy is recorded in Nicetas Choniates, *Thesaurus orth. fidei* I, 24: *Synodus graecae ecclesiae de dogmate circa illa verba* "Tu es qui offers"

(PG 140, 137–202); John Kinnamos, *Deeds of John and Manuel Comnenus*, trans. Charles Brand (New York: Columbia University Press, 1976), 135–36.

2 Though sentenced to blinding in 1159 due to his views on the Eucharist, Michael Glykas was not dissuaded from theological debate, which he kept up until after 1185. Cormack, *Writing in Gold*, 223. For a nuanced view of Byzantine approaches to theological and religious diversity, see Averil Cameron, "Enforcing Orthodoxy in Byzantium," *Studies in Church History* 43 (2007): 1–24. Cameron suggests it is misguided to pursue modern notions of toleration in Byzantium, which inherited an understanding that religious conformity was state business.

3 Kinnamos, *Deeds of John*, 135. Admittedly, Kinnamos gives us one somewhat gossipy angle on a complex controversy. I have tried to reconstruct the events with caution.

4 Paul Magdalino, *The Empire of Manuel I Komnenos: 1143–1180* (Cambridge: Cambridge University Press, 2002), 279.

5 On the other hand, it may have been Basil who was the obnoxious one, sniping against these learned men in his sermons. It is difficult to reconstruct the cases from what is preserved. Magdalino, *Manuel I Komnenos*, 279.

6 Kinnamos says that they mocked him, as if the two were a Byzantine version of Statler and Waldorf from the *Muppet Show*. Kinnamos, *Deeds of John*, 135.

7 As mentioned, Theodore Apsevdis was also drawing upon this understanding when he contrasted the struggling Christ in the hands of Simeon with the assenting Christ in the hands of Mary at the Virgin of the Vetches church in Cyprus.

8 Gregory Nazianzen, *Nicene and Post-Nicene Fathers: Second Series*, vol. 7, ed. Philip Schaff and Rev. Henry Wallace (1893; repr., New York: Cosimo Classics, 2007), 440.

9 The famous definition of the Council of Chalcedon in 451 put it this way:

> We all with one voice teach the confession of one and the
> same Son, our Lord Jesus Christ: the same perfect in divinity
> and perfect in humanity, the same truly God and truly man,
> of a rational soul and a body; consubstantial with the Father
> as regards his divinity, and the same consubstantial with us as
> regards his humanity; like us in all respects except for sin;
> begotten before the ages from the Father as regards his divinity, and in the last days the same for us and for our salvation
> from Mary, the Virgin God-bearer as regards his humanity, one and the same Christ, Son, Lord, Only-begotten,
> acknowledged in two natures, which undergo no confusion,

no change, no division, no separation; at no point was the difference between the natures taken away through union, but rather the property of both natures is preserved, and comes together into a single person and a single subsistent being; he is not parted or divided into two persons, but is one and the same only-begotten Son, God, Word, Lord Jesus Christ.

Jaroslav Pelikan and Valerie Hotchkiss, *Creeds and Confessions of Faith in the Christian Tradition: Early, Eastern and Medieval,* vol. 1 (New Haven, CT: Yale University Press, 2003), 181.

10 This heresy is often called Nestorianism after Nestorius, archbishop of Constantinople from 386 to 450. Nestorius abided by the Nicene Creed, which is to say, he did not believe Mary was the mother of a mere human being (Anthropotokos). Still, he preferred to refer to Mary as Christotokos ("bearer of Christ"), making her the mother of the man in whom God dwelt, not of the deity itself. His opponents discerned that limiting Mary's maternity to Christ's human (as opposed to his divine) nature required a separation in the nature of Christ. The Council of Ephesus, without adding to the Nicene Creed, affirmed the term *Theotokos,* which effectively conveyed the "communication of properties" between Christ's two natures. Eventually, Nestorius was able to reconcile himself to the term *Theotokos,* in part "because its position in Christian worship was so firmly established as to be unassailable." Jaroslav Pelikan, *The Christian Tradition: A History of the Development of Doctrine,* vol. 1, *The Emergence of the Catholic Tradition (100–600)* (Chicago: University of Chicago Press, 1971), 242. Sebastian Brock is right to point out that "the association between the Church of the East and Nestorius is of a very tenuous nature, and to continue to call that church 'Nestorian' is, from a historical point of view, totally misleading and incorrect—quite apart from being highly offensive and a breach of ecumenical good manners." Sebastian Brock, *Fire from Heaven: Studies in Syriac Theology and Liturgy* (Aldershot, UK: Ashgate, 2006), 14. The Assyrian Church of the East, which did not consider Nestorius a heretic, has its own marvelous history: "We must never think of these churches as fringe sects rather than the Christian mainstream in large portions of the world. Among African and Asian Christians, these two strands of Christianity would certainly have outnumbered the Orthodox." Philip Jenkins, *The Lost History of Christianity* (New York: HarperOne, 2009), xi.

11 Kinnamos, *Deeds of John,* 135.

12 Karl Christian Felmy, "The Development of the Trinity Doctrine in Byzantium (Ninth to Fifteenth Centuries)," in *The Oxford Handbook of the Trinity,* ed. Gilles Emery and Matthew Levering (Oxford: Oxford University Press, 2011), 219.

13 The supporter's name was Eustathios of Dyrrhachion. Felmy, "Development of the Trinity," 218.

14 As with the name Theodore Apsevdis (also spelled Apseudes), I am spelling Soterichos Pantevgenos (also spelled Panteugenos) to reflect how it would be pronounced in modern Greek.

15 Kazhdan and Epstein, *Change in Byzantine Culture*, 160. This fact may have introduced a political twist into the proceedings. Antioch had at this point been taken by the Crusaders and was still haunted by a menacing Latin presence that questioned the legitimacy of Orthodox worship. To have an Orthodox bishop of that city, even if he was in exile, side with Basil's accusers might have risked destabilizing a Greek population threatened by the Latin church.

16 Taft gives sources for the dialogue in Choniates, *Thesaurus* I, 24 (*PG* 140, 140–48). Robert Taft, *The Great Entrance: A History of the Transfer of the Gifts and Other Pre-anaphoral Rites of the Liturgy of St. John Chrysostom* (Rome: Pont. Institutum Studiorum Orientalium, 1975), 135.

17 Kazhdan and Epstein, *Change in Byzantine Culture*, 160. Explicating the controversy, Aristeides Papadakis writes, "Any confusion between God's hypostatic characteristics and his actions or energies, or between the 'immanent' and 'economic' Trinity, was unacceptable . . . against [Pantevgenos's] breakdown of the saving work of Christ into a two-tiered process of salvation, Nicholas and the Church were to contend that the redemption of mankind was not only essentially a Trinitarian act, but a consequence of the totality of the divine economy which include not only Christ's incarnation, death and passion, but resurrection." Aristeides Papadakis, with John Meyendorff, *The Christian East and the Rise of the Papacy: The Church 1071–1453 A.D.* (Crestwood, NY: St. Vladimir's Seminary Press, 1994), 192–93.

18 Kazhdan and Epstein, *Change in Byzantine Culture*, 160–61; Felmy, "Development of the Trinity," 219. As Meyendorff puts it, reasserting the arguments against Pantevgenos in the present, "The hypostatic union is precisely what permits one to consider God as performing humanly in the act of offering, while remaining God by nature and, therefore, receiving the sacrifice." Meyendorff, *Byzantine Theology* (New York: Fordham University Press, 1979), 40.

19 At the same time, caution is important here, as Taft insists that "Soterichos did not deny that it is Christ whom we receive in the eucharist." Taft, *Great Entrance*, 137. It is the nature of that reception that seems to have been at stake.

20 Papadakis, with Meyendorff, *Christian East*, 191.

21 Felmy, "Development of the Trinity," 219.

22 John Meyendorff, *Christ in Eastern Christian Thought* (Washington, DC: Corpus, 1969), 199.

23   Fleming Rutledge systematically dismantles such crass misunderstandings over hundreds of pages: "We must emphatically reject any interpretation that divides the will of the Father from that of the Son, or suggests that anything is going on that does not proceed out of love. . . . The tradition taken as a whole is solidly behind the idea that the cross of Christ is an event undertaken by the Three Persons united." Fleming Rutledge, *The Crucifixion: Understanding the Death of Jesus Christ* (Grand Rapids, MI: Eerdmans, 2015), 163, 297.

24   As Thomas McCall puts it, "The Holy Trinity is completely unified in divine intentions and actions—unless there are multiple gods, we cannot believe otherwise. Some 'part' or 'parts' of God are not against me while another part is for me. The Son does not love me and bless me while the Father hates me and curses me (or *would like* to do so, and *would* do so, if not for the presence of the Son between us). Rather, it is *God* who is for us." Thomas H. McCall, *Forsaken: The Trinity and the Cross, and Why It Matters* (Downers Grove, IL: IVP Academic, 2012), 46. See also esp. 160–61. I thank Emily Hunter McGowin for this reference.

25   John Stott, *The Cross of Christ* (Downers Grove, IL: IVP Academic, 1986), 174. Similarly, Hart insists that "the violence that befalls Christ belongs to our sacrificial order of justice, an order overcome by his sacrifice, which is one of peace." David Bentley Hart, *The Beauty of the Infinite: The Aesthetics of Christian Truth* (Grand Rapids, MI: Eerdmans, 2003), 371.

26   Though "neither the date of its origin nor the stages of its development can be determined with precision" (Pelikan and Hotchkiss, *Creeds and Confessions*, 269), the Byzantine rite is "a hybrid of Constantinopolitan and Palestinian rites, gradually synthesized during the ninth to fourteenth centuries in the monasteries of the Orthodox world, beginning in the period of the struggle with Iconoclasm." Robert F. Taft, *The Byzantine Rite: A Short History* (Collegeville, MN: Liturgical, 1992), 16.

27   "We, who in a mystery represent the Cherubim and sing the thrice-holy hymn to the life-giving Trinity, let us now lay aside every care of this life. For we are about to receive the King of all, invisibly escorted by the angelic hosts. Alleluia, alleluia, alleluia." Greek Orthodox Archdiocese of Thyateira and Great Britain, *The Divine Liturgy of Our Father among the Saints John Chrysostom* (Oxford: Oxford University Press, 1995), 23. The Cherubic hymn became a part of the liturgy under Justin II (573–74). Taft, *Byzantine Rite*, 47. The most ancient manuscripts of the liturgy attribute the prayer to Basil the Great, which would certainly have offered comfort to Basil the deacon. Taft, *Great Entrance*, 131.

28   We might compare the prayer of the Cherubikon, therefore, to the comparatively humble portrait of Neophytos at the Enkleistra that offsets the triumphant portrait examined in chapter 2.

29 On the matter of the antiquity of the prayer, Felmy suggests, "This last part
of the prayer was changed, probably around the time of Emperor Manuel I
(1143–80), to read as it does today in the received text of the liturgy: 'For
You, Christ our God, are the Offerer and the Offered, the One who receives
and is distributed, and to You we give glory.'" Felmy, "Development of the
Trinity," 218. Even so, Taft confirms that at least in its earlier form, it was
well known in Constantinople at the beginning of the twelfth century, as
evidenced by the fact that Pantevgenos did not object to it, even accepting
it as attributed to Basil the Great. Taft, *Great Entrance*, 136. In addition,
an apocryphal homily attributed to Cyril of Jerusalem that may date to
the sixth century suggests something similar: "I see a child who brings to
Earth a sacrifice according to the Law, but who receives in heaven the pious
sacrifices of all. [I see him] on the cherubic throne, seated as is becoming to
God. He himself is offered and purified; he himself offers and purifies all;
he is the offering and he is archpriest." Christopher Walter, *Art and Ritual
of the Byzantine Church* (London: Variorum, 1982), 210.

30 The rule that Rowan Williams applies to Arius can be applied here as well:
"The history of theology [and possibly the liturgy as well] is a history of
such fertile and suggestive mistakes (revealing mistakes, we might say)."
Rowan Williams, *Arius: Heresy & Tradition*, rev. ed. (Grand Rapids, MI:
Eerdmans, 2001), 267.

31 Beck suggests that Nicholas of Methone, though disparaged by some
historians, is one of the most important theologians of his age. Hans-Georg
Beck, *Kirche und Theologische Literatur im Byzantinishcen Reich* (Munich:
C. H. Beck, 1959), 624. Though we know little about him, we do know
he was "an educated man so well-versed in dialectic as to dare undertake
a detailed refutation of the Neoplatonic philosopher Proclus." Athanasios
Angelou, "Nicholas of Methone: The Life and Works of a Twelfth-Century
Bishop," in *Byzantium and the Classical Tradition*, ed. Margaret Mullett and
Roger Scott (Birmingham, UK: Centre for Byzantine Studies, 1981), 143.
Meyendorff's gloss of Methone's argument is instructive:

> For all the actions of God *ad extra* are actions in which the three
> persons participate, the Father, the Son and the Holy Spirit; their
> participation remains, no doubt, personal, but the action is essen-
> tially one. [For example . . . the] Logos alone "becomes flesh," but
> the Father and the Spirit participate in the economy of salvation.
> One could therefore not imagine that the receiving of the offering
> could be a hypostatic characteristic of the Father alone, in which
> the Son would not participate: this reception is our very salvation
> accomplished by the one God, Father, Son and Holy Spirit.
> (Meyendorff, *Christ in Eastern Christian Thought*, 198)

32   Or as Karl Barth puts precisely the same idea independently, "The One who
reconciles the world with God is necessarily the one God Himself in His
true Godhead. Otherwise the world would not be reconciled with God."
Karl Barth, *Church Dogmatics*, vol. 4, pt. 1 (Edinburgh: T&T Clark, 1956),
193. Fleming Rutledge sees the same dynamic in Anglicanism in the preaching of Lancelot Andrewes, who "takes great pains to keep the persons of
the Trinity together so that we do not think of the Son as the victim of the
Father." Rutledge, *Crucifixion*, 526. Obviously, modern Orthodoxy would
express the same sense: "He is not only the sacrifice, the slaughtered Lamb,
but also the sacrificing Priest in the sense that the offering of sacrifice is His
voluntary deed. He Himself offers Himself as the sacrifice to His Father . . .
not by but according to the Father's will, to which He fully subjects His
own, filial, Divine-Human will. . . . Thus the High Priest is not only *fated* to
become a sacrifice, but He also *wills* this fate." Sergius Bulgakov, *The Lamb of
God*, trans. Boris Jakim (Grand Rapids, MI: Eerdmans, 2008), 336.

33   Magdalino, *Manuel I Komnenos*, 279. Soterichos presided as Patriarch of
Antioch in exile at the monastery *ton Hodegon* and requested the home
court advantage for the meeting but was denied. The synod took place at
the Blachernae Palace on May 12, 1157 (280).

34   The record claims that the emperor countered each of Soterichos's arguments and appealed to Paul's plea "that all of you agree, and that there be
no divisions among you" (1 Cor 1:10). Magdalino, *Manuel I Komnenos*,
280. Needless to say, historical accounts of the emperor's undefeatable
theological prowess need be taken with a grain of salt.

35   Magdalino, *Manuel I Komnenos*, 280.

36   Cited in Meyendorff, *Christ in Eastern Christian Thought*, 154.

37   Seemingly at the time of this controversy, the prayer was also modified to
drive home the resolution of the controversy with particular force. Felmy,
"Development of the Trinity," 218.

38   The original text in a modern Greek version reads, "Σὺ γὰρ εἶ ὁ προσφέρων
καὶ προσφερόμενος, καὶ προσδεχόμενος καί διαδιδόμενος." Greek Orthodox
Archdiocese of Thyateira and Great Britain, *Divine Liturgy*, 23. To suggest
its late addition is in no way to say it is without ancient precedent. As The-
odoret of Cyrus puts a similar idea, "The Lord Christ is both God and the
mercy seat, both the priest and the lamb, and he performed the work of our
salvation by his blood, demanding only faith from us." Thomas C. Oden
and Gerald Bray, eds., *Ancient Christian Commentary on Scripture*, vol. 6
(Downers Grove, IL: InterVarsity, 2005), 102.

39   The words of David Bentley Hart nicely convey this understanding: "The
donation that Christ makes of himself draws creation into God's eternal
'offering' of himself in the life of the Trinity. And simply by continuing
to be the God he is, and through the sheer 'redundancy' of the good that

flows from the infinite gesture of his love—which is generosity in excess of all calculable economy—God undoes the sacrificial logic of totality; his gift remains to the end, despite all our efforts to convert it into debt." Hart, *Beauty of the Infinite*, 372.

40 This is argued convincingly by Gordana Babić, "Les discussion christologiques et le décor des églises byzantine au XIIe siècle," *Frühmittelalterliche Studien* 2 (1968): 387–97. See also Ashton L. Townsley, "Eucharistic Doctrine and the Liturgy in Late Byzantine Painting," *Oriens Christianus* 58 (1974): 138–53; Sharon Gerstel, *Beholding the Sacred Mysteries: Programs of the Byzantine Sanctuary* (Seattle: University of Washington Press, 1999), 44–47. See also Ida Sinkević, *The Church of Saint Panteleimon at Nerezi: Architecture, Programme, Patronage* (Wiesbaden: Reichert Verlag, 2000), 35–36.

41 As Walter says,

> The written sources provide no evidence that the synods took steps to promulgate orthodox teaching on the persons of the Trinity and on Christ's oblation on Calvary by means of pictures. Nevertheless there are points of contact between the Christological issues raised and the iconography of officiating bishops. . . . The inscription of the first phrase of the prayer of the Cherubicon on Basil's roll becomes standard just at the time that Panteugenes called the orthodoxy of its last phrase in doubt. Subsequent iconographical development reiterates the orthodoxy of the prayer, by introducing the legend *Melismos*, to which there is an allusion in the prayer. Moreover the passage from preoccupation with the Trinity to preoccupation with Christ's sacrificial role is common both to the controversy and to the iconography. (Walter, *Art and Ritual*, 208–9)

42 Winfield and Winfield, *Panagia tou Arakos*, 96. "None of those who are bound with the desires," which the scroll displays, is the first part of the prayer of the Cherubic Hymn. Greek Orthodox Archdiocese of Thyateira and Great Britain, *Divine Liturgy*, 22.

43 John of Damascus's eighty-century defense of icons of Christ is premised upon reticence: "I do not depict the invisible divinity, but I depict God made visible in the flesh." John of Damascus, *Three Treatises on the Divine Images*, trans. Andrew Louth (Crestwood, NY: St. Vladimir's Seminary Press, 2003), 86. Only slowly did Byzantine visual culture move toward depictions of the Trinity beyond the Hetoimasia. Gabriel Bunge offers a fine discussion of this slow development, which culminated in Andrei Rublev's Trinity icon. Gabriel Bunge, *The Rublev Trinity: The Icon of the Trinity by the Monk-Painter Andrei Rublev* (Crestwood, NY: St. Vladimir's Seminary Press, 2007).

44 "The divine is *neither* male nor female," wrote Gregory of Nyssa, "for how could such a thing be contemplated in divinity?" Cited in Verna Harrison, "Male and Female in Cappadocian Theology," *Journal of Theological Studies* 41, no. 2 (1990): 443. Harrison explains that God's transcending gender was axiomatic for the Cappadocians, which is still the case for classic Christian thought of the past and present. This fact unfortunately does not rule out the reality that "ersatz 'orthodoxy' can simultaneously become the silent protector of an abusive sexuality." Coakley, *God, Sexuality, and the Self*, 59.

45 According to the theologian Sergius Bulgakov, "There is no such thing . . . as an absolute canon of the icon, as the Old Believers think. Such a canon would condemn the painting of icons to complete immobility and to death in so far as art is concerned. Icons are born of art and should remain in the realm of art. While founded on tradition and developing it, the icon has its own life and its place in modern art." This is not to say that for Bulgakov, theology is unimportant: "Art alone cannot create an icon, nor can theology alone." Sergius Bulgakov, *The Orthodox Church* (Crestwood, NY: St. Vladimir's Seminary Press, 1997), 143–44. Likewise, for the theologian, priest, and art historian Pavel Florensky, "It is as a mystical theologian, a *vates* or 'seer,' that the iconographer must fulfill [the artistic] task, not as a copyist." For Florensky, "to the truly creative, the presence of a canonical tradition is never a hindrance, for in every sphere of art the complexities of canonical forms act as a touchstone that, while it may break lesser talent, will serve to sharpen true creativity." Pavel Florensky, *Iconostasis*, trans. Donald Sheehan and Olga Andrejev (Crestwood, NY: Saint Vladimir's Seminary Press, 2000), 79. In the Russian novella by Leskov, *The Ensealed Angel*, an icon painter suggests a similar view: "It's an offense to us to think that we simply use set patterns as if they were stencils. In the pattern book [*podlinnik*], we're given a rule, but how it's followed is left to the freedom of the artist." N. S. Leskov, "Zapechatlennyi Angel," in *Sobranie sochinerii*, vol. 5, ed. L. Anninskii (Moscow: Ekran, 1993), 269, cited in Jefferson Gatrall and Douglas Greenfield, eds., *Alter Icons: The Russian Icon and Modernity* (University Park: Penn State University Press, 2010), 14.

46 A Marian solution to this abstract Trinitarian controversy is fitting, and causes one to wonder what other controversies she might ameliorate.

47 *Akathistos Hymn* A 12; Peltomaa, *Akathistos Hymn*, 5.

48 A similar dynamic in a different context might be at work in Jan van Eyck's "Annunciation" (ca. 1434/36) at the National Gallery in Washington, DC.

49 For Proclus of Constantinople (the great opponent of Nestorius), Christ was seated on the "richly appointed throne of the Virgin Theotokos." The phrasing deliberately subverts imperial associations. Christ, not the emperor, is the true advent, wearing the "seedless flesh" instead of a "consular toga." Maria Evangelatou, "Threads of Power: Clothing Symbolism,

Human Salvation, and Female Identity in the Illustrated Homilies by Iakobos of Kokkinobaphos," *Dumbarton Oaks Papers* 68 (2014): 282.

50 For the Italian political theorist Giorgio Agamben (insofar as I understand him), Western politics is founded on a distinction between the private realm of the household (the *oikia*) and the political realm (the *polis*). The government negotiates the line between the two realms and manages to absorb the first into its own domain through claims of sovereignty. This bipolar duality is managed by the concept of the *hetoimasia tou thronou*, the image of the empty throne, and the charade of glory that it projects: "The apparatus of glory finds its perfect cipher in the majesty of the empty throne. Its purpose is to capture within the governmental machine that unthinkable inoperativity—making it its internal motor—that constitutes the ultimate mystery of divinity." Giorgio Agamben, *The Kingdom and the Glory: For a Theological Genealogy of Economy and Government*, trans. Lorenzo Chiesa (Stanford, CA: Stanford University Press, 2011), 245. Tracing the hetoimasia to its pagan roots, Agamben follows its Christian career and then the takeover of the motif by secular political theatrics in the present. He suggests we must "profane" the hetoimasia in order to challenge this inheritance. And yet Theodore Apsevdis, effectively a stateless artist, beat Agamben to the punch. He already "profaned" the hetoimasia by reconnecting it to the God beyond political realities, even to the point of issuing a rebuke to the Crusades. Consequently, it is the Virgin of the Passion that may really offer "a life over which sovereignty and right no longer have any hold." Giorgio Agamben, *Means without End: Notes on Politics*, trans. Vincenzo Binetti and Cesare Casarino (Minneapolis: University of Minnesota Press, 2000), 114–15.

Chapter 7

1 Jaroslav Pelikan, *Credo: Historical and Theological Guide to Creeds and Confessions of Faith in the Christian Tradition* (New Haven, CT: Yale University Press, 2003), 24. The language of *begotten*, as opposed to *born*, does not necessitate temporal beginning.

2 An excellent interreligious overview of such recoveries is on offer in Thomas Schipflinger, *Sophia-Maria: A Holistic Vision of Creation*, trans. James Morgante (Yorke Beach, ME: Samuel Weiser, 1998). See also note 45 in this book's introduction.

3 The history of the interpretation of Arius is winding and instructive. Earlier figures such as John Henry Newman and Adolf von Harnack cast Arius as an Aristotelian rationalist overly influenced by Judaism. More recently, Gregg and Groh have cast Arius as offering a more attainable path of salvation. R. C. Gregg and D. E. Groh, *Early Arianism: A View of Salvation* (Philadelphia: Fortress, 1981). But one theological problem with this view

is that the ostensibly accessible Arian Jesus is nevertheless not fully human. Hanson in turn argued that Arianism is an attempt to fully accept the suffering of the Son, which in turn is undermined because the Son is not fully divine. R. P. C. Hanson, *The Search for the Christian Doctrine of God: The Arian Controversy, 318–381* (London: T&T Clark, 1988). John Behr suggests that both these recent studies may assume a unity in Arianism that may not have been present: "There was no single theological agenda shared by all those opposed to Nicaea, and their attitudes toward Arius himself varied considerably." John Behr, *Formation of Christian Theology*, vol. 2, *The Nicene Faith: Part I* (Crestwood, NY: St. Vladimir's Seminary Press, 2004), 134. Rowan Williams sees Arius's (as opposed to "Arianism's") motivation in various trends of Neoplatonism. Williams, *Arius.* Khaled Anatolios views Arianism "not as the invasion by an alien force of the pristine untroubled integrity of Christian experience but rather as one response to a conflict of interpretation within a common horizon of Christian experience," even if the refutation of Arius "became integral to the reinterpretation of Christian experience" afterward. Khaled Anatolios, *Retrieving Nicaea: The Development and Meaning of Trinitarian Doctrine* (Grand Rapids, MI: Baker Academic, 2011), 43. While Arius may have been unfairly treated, one can read him charitably today while still affirming the Nicene Creed that was designed to refute him. As Williams puts it, "The long-term credibility and sustainability of the Nicene faith may have something to do with the degree to which it succeeds—usually more or less unwittingly—in subsuming and even deepening the Christian concerns of the teachers it set out to condemn." Williams, *Arius*, 24. The provocations of Arius clearly assisted the church in inhabiting the paradox of Jesus's full humanity and full divinity: "Arianism helped to keep churchly doctrine both honest and evangelical." Pelikan, *Christian Tradition*, 201.

4 According to Pelikan, although transmissions of documents connected to this famous dispute are especially difficult to trace, it nevertheless seems clear "that the Arian controversy broke out over the exegesis of Proverbs 8:22–31." Pelikan, *Christian Tradition*, 173. It provided, according to the church father Hilary, "the greatest billow in the storm they [the Arians] raise, the big wave of the whirling tempest" (Pelikan, 193).

5 Arius as cited in Behr, *Christian Theology*, 142. Behr concludes, "Christ is finally neither fully God nor fully human, let alone both, and so human beings, consequently, are not introduced into the life of God" (145).

6 These are the words of Arius himself. God is "one and only [*monos*]," "a monad [*monas*]." "The triad is not eternal, but there was a monad first." Cited in Pelikan, *Christian Tradition*, 194.

7 Arius and the Arians enjoyed aggressive imperial support from emperors after Constantine (Constantius II and Valens).

8   The divinity of Christ had already been long established both in the Christian Scripture's earliest hymns (e.g., Col 1:15–20) as well as in its earliest sermons. The oldest surviving Christian sermon after the New Testament (2 Clement) reads, "Brethren, we ought so to think of Jesus Christ as God, as of the judge of the living and dead. And we ought not to belittle our salvation; for when we belittle him, we expect also to receive little." Likewise, the oldest surviving pagan report about Christians (from Pliny) reports them "singing a hymn to Christ as though to [a] god." Both sermons cited in Pelikan, *Christian Tradition*, 173.

9   Athanasius, *Orations against the Arians*, cited henceforth from Khaled Anatolios, trans., *Athanasius* (London: Routledge, 2004). *Orations against the Arians* is a work that represents his mature theology, composed during Athanasius's second exile in Rome, ca. 339–40. The date shows that the Council of Nicaea did not settle the matter and that those who opposed it continued to make their case, sometimes with imperial support. Athansisus's aim in this text is "to show that the Scriptures, when properly read according to their 'ecclesiastical sense,' reveal Christ to be nothing less than the eternal Word who is fully divine by nature, whose fullness of divinity is the ultimate 'security' for human redemption and deification." Anatolios, *Athanasius*, 88.

10   Compare the comments of John Behr on this passage: "Rather than reflecting on the present tense of the verb to beget in Prov 8:25, as Origen had done, to conclude that the Son is eternally, or rather timelessly, begotten by the Father, Arius seems to envision the Son's coming into existence as a specific act in some kind of 'quasi-time.' Thus, Arius insists, in various ways, that God is 'prior' to the Son, who 'was not before he was begotten.'" Behr, *Christian Theology*, 138.

11   "Since these are proverbs, and are spoken proverbially and by way of parable, one must not take the passage in question simply at face value." Anatolios, *Athanasius*, 138. For Athanasius, the term *begotten*, as opposed to *created*, was a more precise way of describing Jesus's relationship to the Father, for begetting did not necessarily entail a starting point.

12   "In saying 'he created,' she [Wisdom] is saying nothing contrary to 'he begot.'" Anatolios, 138. *Begot* was the verb that Athanasius preferred, since it included both.

13   Other orthodox interpreters such as Ambrosiaster read the passage as referring not to Christ in his divine nature but to the Christ's created humanity: "The Lord Jesus was created from the Virgin in order to redeem the works of the Father." Pelikan, *Christian Tradition*, 205. Athanasius's reading includes this sense of Christ's humanity but also the entire schema of salvation.

14   Pelikan, 170.

15   Joan Chamberlain Engelsman suggests the refusal to give Sophia a proper place results in an Arian denial of Christ's divinity, which she terms "Sophia's revenge." Joan Chamberlain Engelsman, *Feminine Dimensions of the Divine* (Asheville, NC: Chiron, 1994), 147.

16   For the complex history of the iconography of Wisdom in the East, see Donald M. Fiene, "What Is the Appearance of Divine Sophia?," *Slavic Review* 48, no. 3 (Autumn 1989): 449–76. For Wisdom in the West, see chapter 5 of Barbara Newman, *God and the Goddesses: Vision, Poetry and Belief in the Middle Ages* (Philadelphia: University of Pennsylvania Press, 2005), 190–244.

17   These are the words of art historian Keith Christiansen to describe the Stroganoff Madonna (ca. 1300) by Duccio, the Met's most expensive single acquisition. Carol Vogel, "The Met Makes Its Biggest Purchase Ever," *New York Times*, November 10, 2004, https://www.nytimes.com/2004/11/10/arts/design/the-met-makes-its-biggest-purchase-ever.html.

18   "He was born—but He had been begotten. . . . In His Human nature He had no Father, but also in His Divine Nature no Mother." Gregory of Nazianzus, Oration 29, in Phillip Schaff, ed., *Nicene and Post-Nicene Fathers*, vol. 7 (New York: Cosimo, 2007), 308. "The begetting of God must be honored in silence. It is a great thing for you to learn that he was begotten. But the manner of his generation we will not admit that even angels can conceive, much less you. Shall I tell you how it was? It was in a manner known to the Father who begot, and to the Son who was begotten. Anything more than this is hidden by a cloud, and escapes your dim sight." Gregory of Naziansus, *Theological Orations* 3.8, cited in Michael J. McClymond, *The Devil's Redemption*, vol. 2 (Grand Rapids, MI: Baker Academic), 1016. The objection could be raised that for Theodore to depict Christ in the dome with a body at all necessarily entails his having been born, but pressed up against the limits of depiction, this is a gamble the Byzantines were willing to make.

19   It one late Byzantine bilateral icon of the Virgin Mary, the Prepared Throne is depicted on one side, with a Gospel book open to the words "the kingdom prepared [ἡτοιμασμένην] for you from the foundation of the world" (Matt 25:34). Vassilaki, *Mother of God*, 410–13. Mary in this case also evokes the Wisdom referred to by Athanasius.

20   "The [H]etoimasia shows considerably more evidence of plaster working than do the roundels of the angels, and it is reasonable to assume that this is the roundel where the painter started to work." Winfield and Winfield, *Panagia tou Arakos*, 123.

21   Philip Schaff and Henry Wallace, eds., *Nicene and Post-Nicene Fathers: Second Series*, vol. 8, *Basil: Letters and Select Works* (New York: Cosimo, 2007), 54.

22   For Gregory of Nazianzus, "Things which produce time are beyond time." Gregory Nazianzen, *Faith Gives Fullness to Reasoning: The Five Theological*

Orations of Gregory Nazianzen (Leiden: Brill, 1991), 247, quoted in Clemena Antonova, *Space, Time and Presence in the Icon: Seeing the World with the Eyes of God* (Burlington, VT: Ashgate, 2010), 128.

23   For example, Daniel's scroll is from the passage that reads, "the God of heaven will set up a kingdom that will never be destroyed" (Daniel 2:44).

24   St. John of Damascus, "The Orthodox Faith," cited in Antonova, *Space, Time and Presence*, 130.

25   I thank Maria Evangelatou for this observation.

26   PG 65.713A, cited in Constas, "Weaving the Body," 183.

27   "Mary is no exception to Christ's teaching that discipleship entails 'take up [one's] cross' (Matt 16:24). Mary's faith journey post-Incarnation or journey of divine motherhood was a cross-bearing journey. . . . However, unlike her Son's crucifixion, which is saving, Mary actualizes the path of discipleship, the path of divine motherhood." Sisto, *Mother of God*, 131, 134.

28   [Pseudo-]Maximus, *Life of the Virgin*, 41.

29   "Mary realizes the relationship with the Holy Spirit in which all created hypostates are called to participate. . . . Mary is the first Spirit-bearer; however, every disciple is called to give their marian *fiat* and become Spirit-bearers; to be entirely receptive to God in his or her life." Sisto, *Mother of God*, 226.

30   John Behr, *The Mystery of Christ: Life in Death* (Crestwood, NY: St. Vladimir's Seminary Press, 2006), 119. Behr cites a similar understanding in the *Second Epistle of Clement*: "Brethren, if we do the will of our Father God, we shall belong to the first Church, the spiritual one which was created before the sun and moon" (120).

31   Behr, 131.

32   "She is the True Church of God, the True Body of Christ. The Body of Christ came out of Her, after all." Pavel Florensky, *The Pillar and Ground of the Truth*, trans. Boris Jakim (Princeton, NJ: Princeton University Press, 1997), 153. At the same time, Ephraim Radner points out the risk of such figuration. A sinless figural Mary enables the church to explain away its complicity and division. He advises, "Only a christologically figural reading of the Church can hold bodies and body together. While Christ is holy and one . . . [he] gives himself to the sinning and dividing." Ephraim Radner, *A Brutal Unity: The Spiritual Politics of the Christian Church* (Waco, TX: Baylor University Press, 2012), 153. One need not choose between a Marian or Christological figurative understanding of the church. Both may be necessary.

33   James of Kokkinobaphos, cited in Kallirroe Linardou, "Depicting the Salvation: Typological Images of Mary in the Kokkinobaphos Manuscripts," in Arentzen and Cunningham, *Reception of the Virgin*, 143. Compare the words of Isaac of Stella: "What applies universally to the Church, applies

specially to Mary, and individually to the faithful soul, by the very Wisdom of God which is the word of the Father." Isaac of Stella, *On the Assumption*, sermon 51, cited in Louis Bouyer, *The Seat of Wisdom: An Essay on the Place of the Virgin Mary in Christian Theology* (Chicago: Pantheon, 1962), 201.

34 Angus Holland, unpublished thesis, cited in F. Stuart Clarke, "Lost and Found: Athanasius' Doctrine of Predestination," *Scottish Journal of Theology* 29, no. 5 (October 1976): 440. Clarke insightfully adds, "It was, however, precisely this silence that led to the neglect of Athansius' doctrine in favour of others which seemed, superficially, to answer this question more adequately." There is much to be said for silence!

35 In his fifth-century conflict with Pelagius and later with Julian of Eclanum, Augustine, wearied by ceaseless polemics, was cornered into suggesting that if salvation is dependent upon God's grace and not human effort, then the very possibility of an individual's rescue resides entirely in God's primordial decision for or against them. Though Augustine's critique of Pelagius's rosy view of human nature hits its mark, it is later, in Augustine's disputes with Julian of Eclanum, that the debate became an "unintelligent slogging-match. . . . Seldom in the history of ideas has a man as great as Augustine or as very human, ended his life so much at the mercy of his own blind-spots." Peter Brown, *Augustine of Hippo* (Berkeley: University of California Press, 1975), 387. Alan Jacobs concludes, "And so, because a brilliant and devout old bishop could not resist the controversialists's temptation—to take even a caricature of his views and defend it to the death, rather than show dialectical weakness—the whole doctrine of original sin, in Western Christianity anyway, got inextricably tangled with revulsion toward sexuality and images of tormented infants. And there has never been a full and complete disentangling." Alan Jacobs, *Original Sin: A Cultural History* (New York: HarperOne, 2008), 66. Or simply, "Geniuses can be wrong." Edward T. Oakes, *A Theology of Grace in Six Controversies* (Grand Rapids, MI: Eerdmans, 2016), 176. Augustine never went so far as to posit the logical corollary to this doctrine that by not choosing some, God actively chose others to be damned. The sixth-century Council of Orange even forbade pursuing this line of thought, lest God seem the author of evil (Pelikan, *Christian Tradition*, 327–29). One Saxon monk who made this connection was condemned: "Gottschalk, who never recanted his view—for which he spent the rest of his life imprisoned in the monastery of Hautvillers—proposed in the late 840s that God predestines some humans to heaven and predestines others to hell." Matthew Levering, *Predestination: Biblical and Theological Paths* (Oxford: Oxford University Press, 2011), 70. Gottschalk's chief refuter was John Scottus Eriugena, whose refutation was in turn condemned (Levering, 69–75).

36 In the sixteenth century, the Reformer John Calvin's renewed emphasis on the Augustinian doctrine of grace did result in "double" predestination.

God predestined, before the world was made, some to be saved, and some to be damned, a state of affairs that circumvented the Catholic sacramental system entirely and Athanasius's holistic understanding as well. The Calvinist doctrine, as it spread to Dutch-, German-, and English-speaking Protestant communities, became the "werewolf of Reformed theology" (quoted in Peter J. Thuesen, *Predestination: The American Career of a Contentious Doctrine* [Oxford: Oxford University Press, 2009], 31). Predestination is not the entirety of Calvinism: "The sections on predestination in the final edition of Calvin's *Institutes* (1559) . . . come well into the work and occupy only around 5000 words, compared to the 14,000 words devoted to civil government" (Thuesen, *Predestination*, 29). Even so, the Calvinist system calcified in the seventeenth century with the Synod of Dort (1618–19) and Westminster Confession (1647) and migrated with fleeing Puritans into Britain's New World colonies, where it had considerable impact. Embrace or resistance of the notion of predestination largely accounts (arguably) for the foundations of modern capitalism (Max Weber's famous thesis in this respect, claims Alastair Hamilton, is as difficult to demolish as to substantiate); for why Presbyterian and Methodist churches on so many street corners are distinct; for why Utilitarian-Universalists arose in protest; and for why Transcendentalists, Mormons, Christian Scientists, and Adventists launched their institutions of protest. It is indeed "one of the most important but unacknowledged sources of discord in churches across the denominational spectrum" (Thuesen, *Predestination*, 5) and was cited as a specific reason many (Voltaire, Spinoza, Kant, Mill) criticized, or departed from, Christian faith altogether (Levering, *Predestination*, 127, 135–36). Neither did Orthodox and Catholic alternatives avoid such problems. To merely posit predestination as a matter of God's foreknowledge of virtues, a view attributed to the fourth-century theologians John Chrysostom and (in more refined form) John Cassian, still appeared to leave salvation in the hands of individuals themselves. It is no wonder, then, that the church from this point forward, whether Dominicans (taking the Augustinian approach) and Jesuits (arguing for free will) or Calvinists (Augustinians again) and Arminians (defenders of choice), would be constantly at war over these unsatisfying options. The mystical, Wisdom-centered position of Athanasius was forgotten almost entirely (Clarke, "Lost and Found," 450). It has even been argued that both Augustine's and Cassian's positions are themselves Arian (449)—that is, they do not attend to the full divinity of the Son of God. If what Calvin would call God's "secret counsel" or John Cassian's human will aided by grace is the foundation of human salvation, then Christ is only partially involved, just as he is only partially divine for Arius. The twentieth-century recovery of the older view came when Karl Barth cited Athanasius's *Orations against the Arians*: "The God of all things who created us by His Word, knew what should befall us better than we ourselves. . . . For that reason in His loving-kindness and goodness He prepared beforehand in His Word by whom He created us a provision for our salvation. . . . We were typified and represented in Him." Karl Barth, *Church Dogmatics*, vol. 2, pt. 2 (Edinburgh: T&T Clark, 1957), 109–10.

37   Richard Muller notes that this term does not technically translate as "horrible decree," and yet it became the nickname for the doctrine with that sense intended. Richard Muller, *Dictionary of Latin and Greek Theological Terms Drawn Principally from Protestant Scholastic Theology* (Grand Rapids, MI: Baker, 1985), 88. There is no question that Calvinist predestination as a doctrine has its comforts. Thomas Shepard (d. 1649) described Christ as a "bridegroom who caused the faithful to tremble even as his breasts conferred milk and comfort." This explains the stylized breasts next to the skulls and crossbones on some New England headstones (Thuesen, *Predestination*, 68). As Peter Brown noted, "Predestination, an abstract stumbling-block to the sheltered communities of Hadrumetum and Marseilles, as it would be too so many future Christians, had only one meaning for Augustine: it was a doctrine of survival, a fierce insistence that God alone could provide men with an irreducible inner core." Brown, *Augustine of Hippo*, 407. Likewise, "predestination served in [Calvin's persecuted refugee] context, much as it did for Augustine facing the disintegration of the Roman Empires, as a doctrine of consolation and survival" (Thuesen, *Predestination*, 29). Arthur Dent's popular *Plain Mans Path-Way: Wherein Every Man May Clearly See Whether He Shall Be Saved or Damned* (1601) described how "when we looke downward to ourselves, we have doubts & fears: but when we looke upward to Christ, and the truth of his promises, we feele our selves cock-sure, and cease to doubt any more" (quoted in Thuesen, *Predestination*, 67). Perhaps we see here, surfacing for a moment at least, a practical, preached version of Athanasius's Christ-centered understanding of election, even if it is born from an understanding of double-predestination. The challenge of Puritan piety was "how to maintain a healthy anxiety while simultaneously converting it into assurance" (Thuesen, 66). But this conversion too frequently failed. The Athanasian sense of predestination reduces the anxiety while maximizing the assurance.

38   "Do I make my plans according to the flesh, ready to say 'Yes, yes' and 'No, no' at the same time? As surely as God is faithful, our word to you has not been Yes and No. For the Son of God, Jesus Christ, whom we proclaimed among you, Silvanus and Timothy and I, was not Yes and No, but in him it is always Yes. For all the promises of God find their Yes in him" (2 Cor 1:17b–20a). Karl Barth comments on this passage, "It [the doctrine of election] is not a mixed message of joy and terror, salvation and damnation. . . . It does not proclaim in the same breath both good and evil, both help and

destruction, but life and death. . . . The Yes cannot be heard unless the No is also heard. But the No is said for the sake of the Yes and not for its own sake. In substance, therefore, the first and last word is Yes and not No." Barth, *Church Dogmatics*, 2:2:12–13.

39   "It is the wrath of the lamb, the wrath of redeeming love. As such the very wrath of God is a sign of hope, not of utter destruction. . . . God's wrath means that God declares in no uncertain terms that what *he has made he still affirms as his own good handiwork and will not cast it off into nothingness*." Thomas F. Torrance, *Incarnation: The Person and Life of Christ*, ed. Robert T. Walker (Downers Grove, IL: IVP Academic, 2008), 249–50.

40   Christ looks away from the viewer in the dome, eliciting one villager's comment that "he looks away from our sins, allowing time for repentance." Stylianou and Stylianou, *Churches of Cyprus*, 159. More recent theologians make the same point more severely: "My turning from God is followed by God's annihilating turning from me." Barth, *Church Dogmatics*, 4:1:253. Both mercy and judgment must be present to account for the magnitude of evil: "He was for us *before* he was against us, and for us *even as* he was against us—*pro nobis* first, last, and always." Rutledge, *Crucifixion*, 515. And so, while Theodore dutifully pronounces that the entire Trinity receives the offering of the Eucharist and the offerings of the lives of sinful parishioners like himself, gathered below, he also communicates that this is not without cost.

41   For a brilliant meditation on time and the dilemma of election, see Mark James Edwards, *Christ Is Time* (Eugene, OR: Cascade, 2022), esp. the appendix.

42   Jacob Behmen [Boehme], *The Works of Jacob Behmen: The Teutonic Theosopher*, vol. 1, ed. William Law (London: M. Richardson, 1764), 249. For elucidation of this complex passage, and of Boehme in general, see Martin, *Submerged Reality*, 44. Martin explores connections between Athanasius and Boehme, advising that "reading [Boehme] through a heresy hunting lens does him (and conversely, the reader) a great injustice" (53). Boehme is a notoriously difficult read, but if there seems to be evil in God in some of his writing (which some modern thinkers have seized upon), he also flatly declares in a late work that God "is himself the Eternal and only Good, and a beginning of every good Thing or Will; neither is it possible that any Evil at all can penetrate into him, in as much as he is in himself the one and only Good." Jacob Boehme, *The Election of Grace*, ed. William Law (1621), chap. 1, point 57, https://archive.org/details/Jacob_Boehme_Election_of_Grace-Electronic_Text.

Chapter 8

1   An earlier version of this chapter was published in Matthew J. Milliner, "Visual Cherubikon: Mary as Priest at Lagoudera in Cyprus," in Kuzmová and Znorovszky, *Mary, the Apostles*, 61–82.

2   Regarding a mosaic of Mary with the same cloth in the apse of Saint Sophia of Kyiv, Alexei Lidov cites one scholar who writes, "On [Mary's] belt there is a *lention* with which she wipes away so many tears." Lidov, "Priesthood," 17.

3   Hilda Graef, a long-standing authority on Mariology of the last century, suggests that some references to Mary can be translated as "bishop" in Byzantine culture. Hilda Graef, *Mary: A History of Doctrine and Devotion* (South Bend, IN: Ave Maria, 2009), 264.

4   Lidov, "Priesthood," 17. Lidov discusses the motif in Latin Christianity as well, where it was known as a *manipula* and appears in Roman monuments such as Santa Sabina and San Clemente (19). For a more extensive treatment of this motif, see chapter 4 of Ally Kateusz, *Mary and Early Christian Women: Hidden Leadership* (Cham, Switzerland: Palgrave Macmillan, 2019); and Kateusz, "Mary as High Priest," 23–59.

5   Kateusz, *Hidden Leadership*, 39–41. For clarity's sake, I refer to it, following Kateusz, as the eucharistic cloth. The motif is explored further in Rafca Youssef Nasr, "Priestly Ornaments and the Priesthood of the Mother of God," *Chronos* 40 (2019): 119–34. Focusing on the East, Warren Woodfin claims, "The first representations of the *encheirion* are found in the manuscript miniatures of the Menologion of Basil II (979–984), and the item thereafter appears frequently in art until the fourteenth century." Warren T. Woodfin, *The Embodied Icon: Liturgical Vestments and Sacramental Power in Byzantium* (Oxford: Oxford University Press, 2012), 17.

6   The text begins, "Birth of Mary, Revelation of James," and could be so titled, but the text has come to be named Protevangelium (Proto-Gospel) because it precedes the narratives of Matthew and Luke. Though the text claims authorship by James, traditional stepbrother of Jesus, scholarly consensus places it in the mid- to late second century. Of the 140 manuscripts, the earliest Protevangelium papyrus dates to the third or fourth century (Papyrus Bodmer 5). However, Clement and Origen (and possibly Justin Martyr) refer to it, meaning it must have been written by the end of the second century. Beverly Roberts Gaventa, *Mary: Glimpses of the Mother of Jesus* (Columbia: University of South Carolina Press, 1999), 106–7. Margaret Barker makes a compelling case that the rich symbolism of the Protevangelium is informed by diasporic Jewish communities that venerated the banished "Lady in the Temple." Margaret Barker, *Christmas: The Original Story* (London: SPCK, 2008), 136.

7   Gaventa, *Glimpses*, 122. Though censured in the West, the document was still influential through poetry and art, especially thanks to *The Golden Legend*.

8   Alexander P. Kazhdan, ed., *Oxford Dictionary of Byzantium*, vol. 3 (Oxford: Oxford University Press, 1991), 1715. For the Berlin ivory showing a procession with Mary's parents, Joachim and Anna, and seven virgins, see

Jacqueline Lafontaine-Dosogne, *Iconographie de l'enfance de la Vierge*, vol. 2 (Brussels: Académie Royale, 1964), fig. 81. The Menologion of Basil II, dating to ca. 1000 CE, has the same design. In this iconography, the Virgin is depicted twice—being received by Zechariah the priest in the temple but also seated on an elevated throne beyond him, within the sanctuary itself, as if to emphasize the fact that she resided in the temple. This long-established arrangement of the scene was inherited by Theodore Apsevdis.

9   Hennecke, *New Testament Apocrypha*, 376. Italics indicate Scriptural references, in this case Judg 8:19; 1 Sam 1:11; 2:11; 1:28.

10   Indeed, the entire scene echoes the barren Hannah's cry for a child in 1 Sam 1. Hannah also pleaded to God for a child and was rewarded with Samuel. Hannah, as in the Protevangelium, also debated the appropriate time to bring him to the temple and dropped him off just after weaning. Perhaps this makes Mary something of a second Samuel.

11   Hennecke, *New Testament Apocrypha*, 378.

12   Hennecke, 377. Scripture reference is again Judg 8:19.

13   At the same time, the other women appear to be hovering as well, so one must be cautious with this suggestion.

14   Hennecke, *New Testament Apocrypha*, 378.

15   Hennecke, 378. Cf. Gen 19:26.

16   Winfield and Winfield, *Panagia tou Arakos*, 181–82.

17   It may be too much to suggest that the eight-pointed star in the temple décor doubles as Mary's priestly *epigonation*, which "by the late twelfth-century had developed into a stiff square of material [the *epigonation*] hung by a loop from the girdle." Woodfin, *Embodied Icon*, 17.

18   Charalambos Bakirtzis and Ioannis G. Iliades, "The Illumination of the Church of Panagia tou Arakos," in Papageorghiou, Bakirtzis, and Hadjichristodoulou, *Panagia tou Arakos*, 114.

19   Hennecke, *New Testament Apocrypha*, 378.

20   The angel manifests "like the Cheshire cat," as the Winfields memorably put it. Winfield and Winfield, *Panagia tou Arakos*, 188. This was not a one-time occurrence. Derek Krueger remarks on a similar dynamic in a seventh-century chronicle of Palestinian sacred sites, where a noblewoman encounters Mary, who asks her to come to her house: "And where, Lady, is your house so I can enter it?" Mary directs her to the Monastery of Choziba, but the noblewoman objects because women are not allowed inside. "Come, go down, and I will introduce you," is the reply. Krueger concludes, "Mary thus manifests her power at and over the monastery by permitting the woman—and subsequently other women—access to male monastic space." Derek Kreuger, "Mary at the Threshold: The Mother of God as Guardian," in Brubaker and Cunningham, *Cult of the Mother*, 33.

21   PG XCVII, 803, line 32, cited in Laurentin, *Maria, ecclesia, sacerdotium*, 81.

22 Gaventa, *Glimpses*, 113.

23 Alexander P. Kazhdan, ed., *Oxford Dictionary of Byzantium*, vol. 1 (Oxford: Oxford University Press, 1991), 651.

24 Brian Daley, *On the Dormition of Mary* (Crestwood, NY: St. Vladimir's Seminary Press, 1998), 114, 32. Likewise, Modestus of Jerusalem proclaimed, "O most blessed dormition of the glorious Mother of God, through whom we have been created anew in mystery, and have become God's temple!" (Daley, 90). Iconographically, this is expressed when the icons of the repose of Saint Ephraim take the same characteristics as Dormition iconography.

25 See the ongoing research of Magdalene Breidenthal departing from her dissertation, "Leaving 'Heaven on Earth': The Visual Codes of Middle Byzantine Church Exit" (PhD dis., Yale University, 2019).

26 Theodore of Livias, "An Enconium on the Assumption of the Holy Mother of God," in Daley, *Dormition of Mary*, 73.

27 Stephen Shoemaker, *Ancient Traditions of the Virgin Mary's Dormition and Assumption* (Oxford: Oxford University Press, 2002), 379.

28 "You shall make an altar on which to burn incense; you shall make it of acacia wood. . . . Aaron shall burn fragrant incense on it. Every morning when he dresses the lamps he shall burn it" (Exod 30:1, 7); "And [Aaron] shall take a censer full of coals of fire from the altar before the Lord" (Lev 16:12). Kateusz, "Mary as High Priest," 30.

29 As a homiletic tradition emerged around this moment, suspect elements from the Dormition narrative were purged, but the trope of Mary's self-offering remained. The earlier, more heterodox tropes were even more dramatic in their priestly associations. See Kateusz's discussion of the *Gospel of Bartholomew* and the *Six Books Dormition Narrative* in Kateusz, "Mary as High Priest," 28–36. See also the helpful overview of this material in Shoemaker, *Mary in Early Christian Faith*, 121–45. John of Damascus, who offers an especially vetted rendition of the occasion, puts the following words on Mary's lips: "Into your hands, my Son, I confide my spirit! Receive the soul that is so dear to you, which you have preserved blameless. Yours is my body, too; I do not give it to the earth!" Daley, *Dormition of Mary*, 214.

30 Because most Dormition images instead depict the apostles *swinging* the censers, this seems a possible interpretation of such an unusual visual decision. I consider this interpretation a complement to Maria Evangelatou's thorough examination of the censer as a reference to the Virgin's womb and to her intercession. Maria Evangelatou, "The Symbolism of the Censer in Byzantine Representations of the Dormition of the Virgin," in *Images of the Mother of God: Perception of the Theotokos in Byzantium*, ed. Maria Vassilaki (Aldershot, UK: Ashgate, 2005), 117–31.

31 Compare the words (referenced previously) of John Climacus that contrast the natures of Christ: "Christ is frightened of dying but not terrified, thereby clearly revealing the properties of His two natures." Climacus, *Divine Ascent*, 132.

32 Aside from standard image of Christ serving his own body as officiant in the iconography of the Communion of the apostles, Ouspensky points out a bread plate from the twelfth or thirteenth century from Xeropotamou with the Christ child on the altar, flanked by the adult Christ as "the great hierarch." "This is a direct illustration of the words, 'You are the Offerer and the Offered'—words that were at the core of the discussion at the Council of 1156–57; the Christ-child is the Offering, and the Christ-Hierarch is the Offerer." Leonid Ouspensky, *Theology of the Icon*, vol. 2 (Crestwood, NY: St. Vladimir's Seminary Press, 1992), 244. In addition, John Behr once commented to me that he wonders if the Rublev Trinity, with its table whose shape seems to echo the very vessel upon it being offered, conveys a similar dynamic. The central angel (usually understood as Christ), whose garment reflects the color of the vessel's contents, almost seems to be residing in a large chalice himself as he blesses the meal. Which is to say, he is both offering and being offered at once. John Behr, personal communication with the author, March 21, 2015.

33 Because Georgian verbs do not distinguish between male and female subjects, Michel van Esbroeck appears to have mistranslated the phrase, "Elle se sacrifiait elle-même comme le prêtre et elle était sacrifiée, elle offrait et elle était offerte" (She sacrificed herself like the priest, and was sacrificed, she offered and was offered). Michel van Esbroeck, trans., *Maxime Le Confesseur: Vie de la Vierge*, Corpus Scriptorum Christianorum Orientalium (Louvain, Belgium: In Aedibus E. Peeters, 1986), 64. Simelidis, translating the original Greek text of John Geometres, renders the phrase, "He sacrificed himself as the priest and was sacrificed, he offered and was offered," which evokes the prayer of the Cherubic hymn. Simelidis, "Two Lives," 152. The edition and translation of the *Life of the Virgin* being prepared by Fr. Maximos Constas and Christos Simelidis in the Dumbarton Oaks Medieval Library will shed more light on this mysterious text. Constas, "Story of an Edition," 340. Cunningham helpfully summarizes the debate over this text in *Virgin Mary in Byzantium*, 192–94.

34 At the time of the painting of Lagoudera, the *melismos* (literally, "fracturing") of the Christ child on the altar had already been introduced in Byzantine art as a response to merely symbolic understandings of the Eucharist. A synod in 1082 condemned "those who say that the communion of the body and precious blood of our Lord and Savior Jesus Christ is a communion of ordinary bread and wine." J. Gouillard, *Le Synodikon de l'Orthodoxie* (Paris: E. de Boccard, 1967), 68–69, lines 366–67. The

depiction of a living child in the *melismos* also emphasized the leavened host to distinguish the Orthodox eucharistic practice from the unleavened bread of Latin Christians. As one eleventh-century Byzantine writer put it, "To employ bread without leaven is to deny that Christ was God as well as man." Symeon of Thessaloniki later suggested that the bread is "ensouled . . . on account of the leaven" (cited in Maria Evangelatou, "Krater of Nectar and Altar of the Bread of Life," in Arentzen and Cunningham, *Reception of the Virgin*, 110). By placing the living baby in the sanctuary of a church, the real presence of Christ in the Eucharist was communicated. Theodore, however, did not have the opportunity to make this move, as the sanctuary itself was already painted at Lagoudera. As a result, this eucharistic pressure fell upon the Virgin Mary presenting the Christ child instead. In a similar manner, "the scene of the Communion of St. Mary [of Egypt, elsewhere in the same church] substitutes for the liturgical iconographic theme of the Communion of the Apostles, which is missing in the church of Panagia tou Arakos." Konstantinidi, "Byzantine Painting," 79.

35 Baltoyianni, *Icons*, 171. In addition to her arms resembling the liturgical spoon (*labis*), Belting mentions that the reclining pose of Christ evokes the *anapeson*, a motif that shows the wakeful sleep, which also forecasts the sleep of death. Likewise, John the Baptist across the naos holds a scroll that proclaims Christ's status as the lamb of God, and Simeon forecasts the passion as well. Hans Belting, *The Image and Its Public in the Middle Ages: Form and Function of Early Paintings of the Passion* (New Rochelle, NY: Aristide D. Caratzas, 1990), 117. See also chapter 4, note 51 of this book.

36 The entire passage is worth quoting in full: "When paired with Mary, this Christ figure yields one of a number of marian images with very active, bare-limbed children that became prominent from the late eleventh century on. We link these images—I believe correctly—with the cultural and theological shift to emphasize the fleshly and eucharistic aspects of christology. But I think they exhibit a shift in the imagery of Mary, too. Mary doesn't simply present what comes from the Father; she offers what she authors, which is the flesh." Carr, "Image of Mary," 371–72.

37 Carl Jung found the same idea of the "sacrifice and sacrificed [being] one and the same" in the alchemical tradition, specifically the visions of Zosimos. C. G. Jung, *Psychology and Religion: West and East, Collected Works*, vol. 11 (Princeton, NJ: Princeton University Press, 1975), par. 353. Edward F. Edinger traces the theme to Heb 9. Edward F. Edinger, *Ego and Archetype* (Boulder, CO: Shambala, 1992), 242. The Virgin of the Passion, it seems quite likely, is the most globally pervasive instance of the motif.

38 It is precisely the matter of women serving as icons of Christ that William Witt takes up in his extended volume, *Icons of Christ*. He replicates the

arguments of the synods of 1156–57 against Pantevgenos in a modern key (though he does not mention this synod itself):

> The way in which the ordained minister acts *in persona Christi* when presiding at the church's worship is neither unique, nor is it based on male sexuality. The eucharistic minister resembles Jesus Christ in first receiving the baptismal character shared by all Christians. . . . If the church's worship is described using the language of "eucharistic sacrifice," it is necessary to affirm (as do all contemporary ecumenical agreements) that it is Jesus Christ who offers the sacrifice, not the presiding minister. It is Jesus Christ who makes himself present, not the celebrant. Moreover, as the patristic church taught, and as modern ecumenical agreements also emphasize, the Eucharist is not a new sacrifice, but simply the same sacrifice of the cross which is "re-presented." . . . The celebrant does not "offer" anything of him or herself. (Witt, 347)

Both Tina Beattie and Alison Milbank argue for female ordination on christological grounds, not those of generic modern equality. Yet they also do so while also suggesting a necessary feminine aspect of female priesthood that does not neutralize sexual difference. Tina Beattie, *God's Mother, Eve's Advocate* (London: Continuum, 2002), 194–207; Alison Milbank, "Oiling the Wheels of the Heavenly Chariot: Female Priesthood and the Divine Feminine," in *Jesus the Imagination: The Divine Feminine*, vol. 5, ed. Michael Martin (New York: Angelico, 2021), 5–13.

39 Pseudo-Epiphanius PG XLIII, 487 a., trans. John Wijingaards, in Kearns, *Virgin Mary*, 284. Kearns indicates that "Table bearer" was also a title of the priestesses of Pallas Athene (Pseudo-Epiphanius, 337).

40 Carr, "Icon at Mount Sinai," 245–47.

41 "It is likely that new emphasis on various aspects of the Virgin Mary's character, including her ascetic labours, involvement in Christ's ministry and apostolic mission, and emotional demeanour at the foot of the cross reflect a late, and highly developed, phase in her cult." Cunningham, *Virgin Mary in Byzantium*, 194. As the *Life of the Virgin* puts it, "And she was a leader and a teacher to the holy apostles, and when anything was needed, they would tell her. And they received direction and good counsel from her . . . they accomplished everything according to her direction." [Pseudo-]Maximus, *Life of the Virgin*, 126.

Chapter 9

1 Richard chose not to go himself, as he had not fully liberated Jerusalem.

2 Tyerman, *God's War*, 471.

3   Later in 1221, Al Kamil tantalized Crusaders with the relic, but he did not have it. Madden, *Concise History*, 155. Tyerman points out that had Richard kept to his earlier vow of remaining in the east until the spring of 1193, he would have been present for Saladin's death. Instead, Richard's return, prompted by his fear of losing territory to Philip, resulted in Richard's imprisonment and death. Tyerman, *God's War*, 471–72.

4   Phillips, *Fourth Crusade*, 14.

5   On this mission, it needs be remembered that "neither papal, military, nor Venetian leaders intended the crusaders to become badly indebted or to be diverted to Constantinople." David Perry, *Sacred Plunder: Venice and the Aftermath of the Fourth Crusade* (University Park: Penn State University Press, 2016), 7.

6   Phillips, *Fourth Crusade*, 112.

7   Phillips, 113.

8   Phillips, 113–14.

9   Phillips, 111.

10   Phillips, 116.

11   Phillips, 118.

12   Phillips, 118.

13   Such a move had "dampened the ardour of Richard's panegyrists not at all." Tyerman, *God's War*, 446. In addition, before Richard attacked Cyprus, there was Bohemond of Antioch's papally endorsed attack on the Greeks in 1107–8. Phillips, *Fourth Crusade*, 112.

14   Phillips, *Fourth Crusade*, 121–22. Martin's misgivings did nothing to stop the Crusade any more than the later misgivings of Bernard of Clairvaux could stop the Crusade he had helped launch. The citizens were at least spared the massacre that the Crusaders inflicted upon the inhabitants of Jerusalem in 1099. Even if there was no massacre, brawls between the knights in Zara would kill nearly one hundred people (123). Zara's capture—ironically enough—happened on the feast day of the city's patron saint, Saint Chrysogonus (November 24), whose body was kept within a city church.

15   Phillips, 125.

16   The city's population is estimated at 375,000–400,000, with Paris and Venice at approximately 60,000. Phillips, 144.

17   Phillips, 195.

18   Tyerman, *God's War*, 549.

19   This piece was presumably different from the spear discovered during the siege of Acre. Phillips, *Fourth Crusade*, 228.

20   Phillips, 229.

21   Phillips, 228–30.

22   Phillips, 231. Those who consider icons such as this no longer as the domain of the religions that created them but as the property of the secular museum and its academic edifice seem to issue a similar cry.

23 Phillips, 223.

24 "No reference to Constantinople or the early history of the icon appears until 1559, when Giovanni Battista Ramusio (1485–1557) published an account of famous voyages. He based his description of the icon's capture on an eyewitness account of the Sack of Constantinople written by Gottfried de Villehardouin (1195–1246)." Deborah Walberg, "The Cult of the Nicopeia in Seventeenth-Century Venice," in *Reflections on Renaissance Venice: A Celebration of Patricia Fortini Brown*, ed. Mary E. Frank and Blake de Maria (New York: Henry N. Abrams, 2013), 203.

25 Interestingly, this very icon appears on the reverse of the shield of Gawain questing in the film *The Green Knight* (2021). It is destroyed, forcing him to find more mature strategies than raw conquest. The only thing missing in this excellent film is a cameo of the Virgin of the Passion.

26 Manolis Chatzidakis, *Icônes de Saint-Georges des Grecs et de la Collection de l'Institut Hellénique de Venise*, no. 54 (Vicenza: Neri Pozza, 1975). This Virgin of the Passion is by Emmanuel Lambardos and dates to the early seventeenth century. The icon is viewable on the website of the Istituto Ellenico, accessed December 13, 2021, http://www.istitutoellenico.org/museum/.

27 Phillips, *Fourth Crusade*, 153.

28 Perry, *Sacred Plunder*, 183.

29 This seems to offer further evidence that the Virgin of the Passion painted by Theodore Apsevdis in Cyprus was only one instance of many similar images that have not survived.

30 Ćurčić, *Architecture in the Balkans*, 500. "Although it can be conceptually linked with the opposite scene of the Crucifixion from the 13th century, on the eastern wall of the southern choir, there is little likelihood that it belonged to the initial programme." Dragan Vojvodić, *Mediaeval Wallpaintings of Žiča* (Belgrade, Serbia: University of Belgrade, 2016), 294.

31 The fresco is very poorly preserved and survives on the east wall of the north barrel vault, near the altar. Mary's head is inclined toward the angel, but her face and Christ's expression do not survive. The fresco to the immediate left of the Virgin of the Passion is closely linked to it: Christ in the garden of Gethsemane, another indicator of Christianity gravid with suffering and loss. This Virgin of the Passion is part of the fresco layer that was added after the Byzantine recovery following the Crusader occupation, in the late thirteenth or early fourteenth century. It coincides with the first Palaiologan works in the city of Thessaloniki such as those in the Chapel of Saint Euthymios, appended to the Church of Saint Demetrios. Tsigaridas also connects this Virgin of the Passion to the late thirteenth-century icon of Saint Anna in the Vatopedi Monastery and the wall paintings in the Church of the Holy Apostles at Peć of the year 1300. Efthymios Tsigaridas, *Latomou Monastery (the Church of Hosios David)* (Munich: Wilhelm Fink Verlag, 2002), 81.

32 Zaga Gavrilović, "The Portrait of King Marko at Markov Manastir (1376–1381)," in *Studies in Byzantine and Serbian Medieval Art* (London: Pindar, 2001), 146–63.

33 Gavrilović, 146.

34 Elizabeta Dimitrova, *The Church of Saint Demetrius (King Marko's Monastery) at Sushika* (Skopje, North Macedonia: Calamus, 2020), 49.

35 Possibly painted in the early fifteenth century, this image been hailed as a "missing link" in the type's development. The clumsy hands and non-classical features of the angels and Christ's garments led one scholar to suggest its origin in a non-Constantinopolitan, possibly Sinai, workshop at the beginning of the fifteenth century. Baltoyianni, *Icons*, 171. Her reason is the triangular opening of the neck, which is characteristic of Cretan workshops. The unique feature of the Virgin's lips touching the child's hair resembles the Kykotissa, of which examples survive at Sinai. The Virgin holding the child's himation also appears in a Virgin Pelagonitissa at Sinai, and the red lettering that appears on this icon appears at Sinai as well. I have been able to inspect this icon personally, and I concur with Baltoyianni's conclusions. She argues that that the type did not proliferate because the Sinai workshop had limited influence.

36 A similar Virgin of the Passion was painted in the late fifteenth century on the wall just outside the Koumpelidiki church, since eroded—I was told by a monk—by boys playing soccer. Both images anticipate Ottoman domination, as well as the kind of faith that could outlast it.

37 The entire icon can be viewed in *Byzantine Museum of Kastoria: The Re-exhibition* (Kastoria, Greece: Ministry of Culture and Sports Ephorate of Antiquities of Kastoria, 2017), 42.

38 Athanasios Papageorghiou, Ο ΔΙΑΚΟΣΜΟΣ ΤΩΝ ΒΗΜΟΘΥΡΩΝ ΤΩΝ ΚΥΠΡΙΑΚΩΝ ΤΕΜΠΛΩΝ—ΕΙΚΟΝΟΣΤΑΣΙΩΝ ΑΠΟ ΤΟΝ 12° ΜΕΧΡΙ ΤΟΝ 19° ΑΙΩΝΑ, 103–24. These royal doors can be seen in Cyprus at the Byzantine Museum in Paphos and the Byzantine Museum of the Bishopric of Arsinoe. They were removed from small churches in Paphos and Koli, respectively. Another pair recently surfaced at the Temple Gallery in London.

39 The relief decoration, illusion of depth, and thick foliate patterns, according to Konstantia Kefala, recall Western prototypes, suggesting that the icon is a local product of a Rhodian workshop. It has been described as a "rare variant, combining the Virgin of the Passion with the seated 'Glykophilousa.'" Konstantia Kefala, catalog entry 6, in *Crusades: Myth and Realities*, ed. Yiannis Toumazis (Nicosia: Imprinta, 2005), 76. Painted during the Hospitaller period, it reflected the "aesthetic taste of the wealthy Rhodian burghers, irrespective of Creed" (Kefala, 76).

40 Andrew Stewart, "The Nike of Samothrace: Another View," *American Journal of Archaeology* 120, no. 3 (July 2016): 407.

41 Even in Northern Ireland itself there are churches dedicated to the Virgin of the Passion in her form as Our Lady of Perpetual Help, especially the Clonard Monastery, which is run by the Redemptorists. In addition to the Redemptorist centers in the city of London and throughout England, in 2014, a shrine was as dedicated to Our Lady of Perpetual Help at Westminster Cathedral. "A Shrine Dedicated to Our Lady of Perpetual Succour in the Westminster Cathedral," *Scala News*, July 8, 2014, accessed December 31, 2021, https://www.cssr.news/oldnews-en/?p=1875.

42 The 1902 estimate of shrines and churches dedicated to the image in France was twelve thousand. Clement Henze, *Il culto Mondiale della Madonna del Perpetuo Socorrso: Fuori del suo Santuario Romano* (Brooklyn: Redemptorist Headquarters, 1946), 51.

43 The Basilique Notre-Dame-du-Perpétuel-Secours near Père Lachaise Cemetery was entrusted to the Redemptorists in 1872, and was elevated to a minor basilica in 1966. On this occasion it was directly affiliated with Santa Maria Maggiore in Rome. Paroisse - Basilique Notre-Dame-du-Perpétuel-Secours, accessed April 14, 2022, https://basilique-ndps.fr/la-paroisse/ .histoire-de-la-paroisse/.

Chapter 10

1 Angelidi and Papamastorakis, "Hodegon Monastery," 373.

2 The first account we have of these Tuesday processions is from an anonymous English traveler in the late eleventh century. The processions were, therefore, old enough that Theodore Apsevdis might have witnessed this procession himself. Angelidi and Papamastorakis, "Virgin Hodegetria," 377–78.

3 This was not the first time the Hodegetria was used in victory processions. It had also been used to mark the triumph of John Tzimiskes in 971 over the Bulgars and by John II Komnenos in 1133 after Kastamonu was recaptured. Angelidi and Papamastorakis, "Hodegon Monastery," 373.

4 Angelidi and Papamastorakis, 385.

5 K. E. Fleming, "Constantinople: From Christianity to Islam," *Classical World* 97, no. 1 (Autumn 2003): 77. There was a complex series of prophecies in Islam that anticipated the Muslim triumph over Constantinople but also sowed anxiety among the conquerors due to alternate prophecies that predicted the city's recapture by Christians. Kaya Şahin, "Constantinople and the End Time: The Ottoman Conquest as a Portent of the Last Hour," *Journal of Early Modern History* 14 (2010): 317–54.

6 Speaking of the destruction of the Hodegetria icon by the Ottomans, a modern Catholic commentator writes, "It appeared to be a manifestation of divine justice, punishing the Christians of the East for their rebellion against the pope. . . . Mary, Mother of Mercy though she is, was

constrained to abandon a people who had become blinded and hardened by the constant abuses of the graces which God had bestowed on them in rich abundance." Francis J. Connell, *Our Lady of Perpetual Help* (1940; repr., Fitzwilliam, NH: Loreto, 2006), 5–6. The text boasts both an *imprimatur* and *nihil obstat!* Connell intimates that Our Lady of Perpetual Help is the bequeathal to Catholics of what the Orthodox were not worthy to keep. Ironically, a widespread opinion among the Orthodox at the Fall of Constantinople was that it was permitted by God to keep them from submitting to the papacy, hence the famous phrase of Loukas Notaras, "It is better to see ruling over this city the turban of the Turks than the Latin hat." Fleming, "Constantinople," 76.

7 Marie José Mondzain concludes her study of images in the Byzantine world by asserting, "It is up to us to be done with belief and its *holocausts.*" Marie José Mondzain, *Image, Icon, Economy: The Byzantine Origins of the Contemporary Imaginary*, trans. R. Franses (Stanford, CA: Stanford University Press, 2005), 225 (italics in original).

8 Gregory Palamas, *Mary the Mother of God: Sermons*, ed. Christopher Veniamin (Dalton, PA: Mount Thabor, 2013), 21.

9 Or perhaps the Virgin of the Passion simply enables us to see that the beloved Hodegetria icon, gravid with luminous sadness, was about far more than protection all along. Many Marian icons in the autumn of Byzantium convey an "eschatological mood . . . melancholy conclusions and worrisome foreboding." Baltoyianni, *Icons*, 11.

10 Candia was occupied in 1207, and the Venetians held the island until the Ottomans captured it in 1669. David Jacoby, "Candia between Venice, Byzantium and the Levant: The Rise of a Major Emporium to the Mid-Fifteenth Century," in Vassilaki, *Hand of Angelos*, 38.

11 Mario Cattapan, "I Pittori Andrea e Nicola Rizo da Candia," in *Thesaurismata: Bollettino Dell'Istituto Ellenico di Studi Bizantini e Postbizantini*, vol. 10 (Venezia: Instituto Ellenico Di Studi Bizzantine e Postbizantini, 1973), 249. The ship was destined for Negroponte. After the capture of Constantinople, the ship rescued several survivors, depositing them on Crete.

12 Chryssa Maltezou, "The History of Crete during the Fifteenth Century on the Basis of Archival Documents," in *The Hand of Angelos: An Icon Painter in Venetian Crete*, ed. Maria Vassilaki (Aldershot, UK: Ashgate, 2010), 33. Nevertheless, icon painters in the early fifteenth century were still in the shadow of Constantinople. Artists endured the dangerous and expensive journey because the variety and quality of supplies, not to mention artistic inspiration, were superior to those available in Crete. Robin Cormack, "The Icon in Constantinople around 1400," in Vassilaki, *Hand of Angelos*, 50.

13 Anastasia Drandaki, "Between Byzantium and Venice: Icon Painting in Venetian Crete in the Fifteenth and Sixteenth Centuries," in *The Origins*

of El Greco: Icon Painting in Venetian Crete, ed. Anastasia Drandaki (New York: Alexander S. Onassis Public Benefit Foundation, 2009). According to Drandaki, "It is no coincidence that the infrequent occurrence, indeed the almost total lack, of new wall paintings in Crete after the middle of the fifteenth century, coincides with a corresponding explosion in the production of icons by urban workshops" (14). This is not to suggest, of course, that icons were not made constantly before this. Theodore Apsevdis, in fact, produced magnificent icons himself, two of which survive and can be seen at the Byzantine Museum of the Archbishop Makarios III Culture Foundation in Nicosia.

14 The artistic ethos has been accurately described as "small-scale industrial production." Drandaki, "Between Byzantium and Venice," 16.

15 Ulrike Ritzerfeld, "In the Name of Jesus: The 'IHS'-Panel from Andreas Ritzos and the Christian Kabbalah in Renaissance Crete," *JTMS* 2, no. 2 (2015): 245–73.

16 The well-known Cretan painter Angelos Akotantos (d. 1450) might be compared to the earlier fresco painter at Lagoudera in Cyprus who preceded Theodore Apsevdis. Both the earlier painter in Cyprus and Akotantos on Crete gave us Virgin Marys that encapsulate conditions of hope before disaster, whereas Apsevdis and Ritzos paint Virgins after disaster occurred. For example, in one image attributed to Akotantos (now in the Cleveland Museum of Art), Mary's eyes are penetrated with concern. And yet there is a flutter in Christ's outer garment, an allusion to the fluttering drapery in icons of the Resurrection, inspiriting the icon with cheer. Akotantos, dying in 1450, did not live to see the disaster that would befall the Queen of Cities, though he did sell eighty of his drawings to an artist who would, the very artist whose father had been stationed outside of Constantinople with his crossbow, Andreas Ritzos. Akotantos certainly communicated impending sorrow, but Ritzos, like Theodore Apsevdis before him, shouted it. He could not afford to be less than explicit. The stream of exiles from Constantinople flowing into Crete that Akotantos witnessed would have become, for Ritzos, a torrent. The Byzantine Empire had expired, and any icon that did could not reflect that fact was certain to expire as well.

17 The classic interpretation is that the loose sandal further accentuates Christ's fear of the forthcoming passion, where his foot would be pierced (Baltoyianni, *Icons*, 133). The sandals were also a motif of late Byzantine homilies, emphasizing how the monk "may not dash his spiritual feet against stones, nor have the heel of his meditations bitten by the serpents of his mind, but that he may walk on them and step on very dragons, on the hidden beasts of wickedness and envy" (134). If so, the Virgin of the Passion indeed suggests that Christ not only is for the spiritually perfect but has become sin for us (2 Cor 5:21). Modern insight illuminates here as well: "It is through

the most earthy part of our nature that Christ is available. The medieval mind believed that the soul could enter and leave the body through the soles of the feet. It is for this reason that *soul* and *sole* bear the same significance." Robert Johnson, *Femininity Lost and Regained* (New York: Harper-Collins, 2011), 93.

18 Baltoyianni, *Icons*, 155. Compare the history of the early Galaktotrophousa in Elizabeth Bolman, "The Enigmatic Coptic Galaktotrophousa and the Cult of the Virgin Mary in Egypt," in Vassilaki, *Images of the Mother*, 13–22.

19 And yet some elements are lost in this formula as well. Gone, for example, is the bare leg that references the paschal lamb, which appears on other Cretan icons of the period. Baltoyianni, *Icons*, 17–21.

20 Lidov explains that this unique priestly garment, frequently blue in Byzantine art, is how Mary is singled out from other women in scenes such as the crucifixion: "Probably, the iconographic meaning of the golden tasseled fringe of the Virgin's maphorion is an allusion to the high priestly dignity of the Virgin, who united the Old Testament and the New Testament Churches in herself, according to the concept of Byzantine theologians." Lidov, "The Priesthood of the Virgin Mary," 16. See also Alexei Lidov, "Les motifs liturgiques dans le programme iconographiques d'Axtala," *Zograf* 20 (1989): 35–36.

21 Diana Newall, "Candia and Post-Byzantine Icons in Late Fifteenth-Century Europe," in *Byzantine Art and Renaissance Europe*, ed. Angeliki Lymberopoulou and Rembrandt Duits (London: Routledge, 2013), 125–30.

22 This loose translation is provided by Thalia Gouma-Peterson, "Crete, Venice, the 'Madonneri,' and a Creto-Venetian Icon in the Allen Art Museum," bulletin 25 (Oberlin, OH: Allen Memorial Art Museum, Winter 1968), 59. The fact that the inscription only refers to one angel, while the standardized icon contains two, has caused some to suggest that Andreas was evoking the Hodegetria icon, which is sometimes depicted with two angels. Andreas Xyngopoulos bases this observation on the survivals of single-angel Virgins of the Passion. Cretan artists like Ritzos might therefore have been influenced by the dual-angel Hodegetria icons to add a second angel but without altering the inscription, which clearly was intended for images with only one (Gouma-Peterson, 60). For Hodegetria icons with two angels, search "Virgin Hodegetria" at the Sinai Archive, accessed April 12, 2022, https://www.sinaiarchive.org.

23 Nano Chatzidakis, *Venetiae Quasi Alterum Byzantium: From Candia to Venice: Greek Icons in Italy 15th–16th Centuries*, exhibition catalog, Correr Museum, Venice (Athens: Hidryma Hellēnikou Politismou, 1993), 2n7. Robin Cormack also points out that such an order at the peak of the Renaissance shows that Europe in 1500 was interested in more than merely humanist paintings. Robin Cormack, *Painting the Soul: Icons, Death Masks and Shrouds* (London: Reaktion, 1997), 214. Data such as this reassert

Baxandall's well-known (if rather obvious) point that "money is very important in the history of art." Michael Baxandall, *Painting and Experience in Fifteenth-Century Italy: A Primer in the Social History of Pictorial Cycle*, 2nd ed. (Oxford: Oxford University Press, 1988), 1.

24 Gouma-Peterson, "Crete, Venice, the 'Madonneri,'" 66.

25 Walberg, "Cult of the Nicopeia," 201–7. Desire for Cretan icons like the Virgin of the Passion came from the Venetian upper classes but also from the monasteries extending from Mount Athos to Meteora, Patmos, Alexandria, and Sinai, as evidenced by the large monastic inventories of Cretan icons. Manolis Chatzidakis, *Études sur la peinture postbyzantine* (London: Variorum Reprints, 1976), 210–11. A consequence of this proliferation was relative monotony. In 1499, one artist was under contract to produce seven faces of the Virgin per diem over a period of two months for another artist, who presumably would paint the bodies. Anastasia Drandaki, "Greek Religious Painting after the Fall of Constantinople: Tradition and Renewal," in *From Byzantium to Modern Greece: Hellenic Art in Adversity: 1453–1830* (New York: Alexander S. Onassis Public Benefit Foundation, 2005), 16. When Ritzos's version of the Virgin of the Passion met such factorylike conditions, it was accordingly frozen in time. The image from this point forward would be dutifully copied with almost no variation at all. Artists that made Virgins of the Passion in the Ritzos formulation include Emmanuel Lambardos, Victor the Cretan, Theophanes the Cretan, and Emmanuel Tzanes, as well as works that do not bear a signature. Gouma-Peterson, "Crete, Venice, the 'Madonneri,'" 81. "In all of these," explains Gouma-Peterson, "the type is repeated with almost slavish faithfulness down to the last detail and it is difficult to detect the personal style of an artist even in those that are signed" (81, 86).

26 Drandaki, *Origins of El Greco*, catalog entry 24, pp. 76–77. There is one slight variation in this example from the Canellopoulos Museum. Christ, instead of looking at the angels, is engaging the viewer. This panel almost seems to suggest that the motif is now so familiar that an additional level of engagement is required, though without altering the essential contours. In addition, the artist seems to be flaunting that while blue sky can be included in the surrounding miniatures, the gold background of the Virgin of the Passion defiantly endures.

27 The dominance of the Ritzos paradigm is evidenced by the Virgins of the Passion that survive at the extensive collection of icons at Saint Catherine's Monastery on Mount Sinai. While they span centuries and exhibit varying levels of artistic skill, all but one (the single-angel version examined in the previous chapter, fig. 9.5) are in the Ritzos formulation. In addition, of the many Virgins of the Passion on offer in the comprehensive *Icons of the Cretan School* catalog from an international array of museums, all of them

are in the Ritzos formulation. Manolis Borboudakis, ed., *Icons of the Cretan School (from Candia to Moscow to St. Petersburg)* (Pergomos, Turkey: Adams Editions, 1993).

28 Contrary to stereotypes of a secularizing age, the icon flourished in the Renaissance period and beyond. In some cases, it was not until the Renaissance that such images "revealed themselves as miraculous, thereby becoming the focus of attention and artistic patronage." Erik Thunø, "The Miraculous Image and the Centralized Church Santa Maria Della Consalozione in Todi," in *The Miraculous Image in the Late Middle Ages and Renaissance*, ed. Erik Thunø and Gerhard Wolf (Rome: L'Erma di Bretschneider, 2003), 30; Megan Holmes, *The Miraculous Image in Renaissance Florence* (New Haven, CT: Yale University Press, 2013).

29 In Russia, a Virgin of the Passion was copied from a Cretan version in the seventeenth century and was displayed in the town of Nizhnij Novgorod. After healing a woman in the village of Palitsy, it was moved to Lykov and by 1641 was placed in Moscow on the order of Tsar Alexander Michailowitsch. It was placed near the Tverski gate, where a monastery was built in its honor, and was demolished in 1928. Ferrero, *Story of an Icon*, 90.

30 Ferrero, 108–16. This story is also outlined in detail in Clement Henze's *Mater de Perpetuo Succursu* [Mother of Perpetual Help] (n.p., anonymous English translation, Redemptorists), 50–58. The historical source for this story is a piece of parchment attached to a wooden tablet that hung in the Church of Saint Matthew. The original has been destroyed, but three copies, in relative agreement, survive in the Vatican Library.

31 Redemptorist Missionaries, *Our Lady of Perpetual Help: The Icon, Favors and Shrines* (Rome: Redemptorist Missionaries, 1998), 8. There, the image was tended by Augustinian friars, who also had a strong presence in Crete. For the Augustinians in Crete, see Maria Georgopolou, *Venice's Mediterranean Colonies: Architecture and Urbanism* (New York: Cambridge University Press, 2001). However, it seems to have been the Irish Augustinians, ejected from their homeland, who took special care of the image in the later eighteenth century. Redemptorist Missionaries, *Perpetual Help*, 10.

32 Ironically, near where the Napoleon museum is in Rome today.

33 After Napoleon destroyed the Church of Saint Matthew, the Irish Augustinians moved in 1819 to the Church of Saint Mary in Posterula near the Umberto I bridge in Rome. They brought the icon (called both the Virgin of Saint Matthew and Our Lady of Perpetual Help) with them to the new church, but so as not to compete with the image of "Our Lady of Grace" already in the church, it was placed in a private chapel. A generation later, an altar boy at Saint Mary's named Michael Marchi heard from one of the aging friars, Augustine Orsetti, about the "miraculous picture" that was kept in the church of Saint Mary's. Marchi himself later became a

Redemptorist priest and resided in the newly constructed Church of Saint Alphonsus, which was constructed atop the ruins of the former Church of Saint Matthew (destroyed by Napoleon). When a visiting Jesuit asked these new Redemptorists about the original icon, Marchi recalled the story told to him by the aging Augustinian friar, Augustine Orsetti. Redemptorist Missionaries, *Perpetual Help*, 11–13.

34 Redemptorist Missionaries, 14.

35 This image, clearly the most famous example of the Virgin of the Passion, was given a more westernized appearance when it was repainted in the eighteenth century. In a recent restoration, the wood has been carbon-dated to the fourteenth–fifteenth centuries, hence, leading Ferrero to conclude that this most famous image is "a unique copy, made in the 18th century, of a venerated icon of the 14th century." Ferrero, *Story of an Icon*, 102. See also Ferrero, *Santa Maria del Perpetuo Socorro*; and Fabriciano Ferrero, "Nuestra Señora del Perpetuo Socorro: Informacion Bibliografica y Cronologia General," *Spicilegium Historicum Congregationis SSmi Redemptoris* 38, no. 2 (1990): 456–502.

36 There is an irony here, which is the exact reverse of the way that art history is normally understood. Popular perception still imagines the copyists of the Middle Ages, who labored under the tyranny of dogma before the secular Renaissance enabled artists at last to express themselves. For example, Adolphe Napoléon Didron, who brought the painter's manual of Dionysios of Fourna to Western readers in 1845, complains that Greek artists are "enslaved to traditions as the animal to its instinct" precisely *because* "the invention and the idea belong to the fathers, the theologians of the catholic church." Cited in Robert Nelson, *Hagia Sophia, 1850–1950: Holy Wisdom, Modern Monument* (Chicago: University of Chicago Press, 2004), 46. The truth, however, when it comes to the Virgin of the Passion at least, is that individual expression, variety of form, and named artists come down to us in the Middle Ages (Theodore Apsevdis) and among Orthodox painters on Crete (Andreas Ritzos), while the mass copying of this icon, with little to no variation, is what marks this image in the Italian Renaissance and into the present.

37 Henze, *Mother of Perpetual Help*, 106.

38 E. E. Y. Hales, *Pio Nono* (Garden City, NY: Image, 1954), 79. This strategy, it should be noted, immediately backfired.

39 Hales, 98.

40 Pius IX continued to dispute his losses, insisting that "justice be rendered Me, that there be restored to the Holy See what was unjustly take from it, and which I feel it my bounden duty, in conscience, energetically to bestir myself to reclaim." Hales, 208. But there are also glimmers that he saw things more in accord with the spirit of the icon to which he was so

attracted. In an 1859 letter to Queen Isabella II of Spain, he wrote, "It is a real comfort for Me to be able to share, though in the smallest degree, in His glorious Passion" (Hales, 206).

41 Hales, 329.

42 The crown was given to the icon in 1867. Ferrero explains, "Such a coronation was reserved only for religious images that had been venerated over a long period of time and which had been instrument so extraordinary grace for the faithful." Ferrero, *Story of an Icon*, 112. Ferrero claims that "members of the eastern Church saw this coronation as an ecumenical gesture" (113). Although the superior general of the Redemptorists then "solemnly swore that these crowns would never be removed from the image," the icon was restored in 1994 to its original, crownless condition, which is how it appears today (113).

43 For Clement Henze, the icon is "the heir of that singular blessing, which the Blessed Virgin is related to have given herself to the Hodegetria, so wretchedly destroyed in 1453." Henze, *Mother of Perpetual Help*, 11. Interpreting the dangling sandal on Christ's foot, Henze places these words on the lips of the Virgin, addressed to Orthodox Christians: "Why, therefore, ought not all, who are united in the veneration of this same Image, be also associated in the same faith and the same obedience toward the Holy Roman Apostolic See? You behold in this Picture a sandal that is on the point of falling from the Divine Infant's right foot. This is a warning to you of the present miserable condition, in which your Church, once so flourishing and so bound to Christ in art, is now existing. Hence return as quickly as possible to that rock upon which my Son built His universal Church" (158). At the same time, Henze's work illustrates a sincere and sustained ecumenical effort, anticipating the ethos of the Second Vatican Council. The icon, for Henze, is a means by which "those most ancient and grand traditions of Byzantine art" have been passed to the entire world (162). Henze would have encountered the image not only at Saint Alphonsus but also at the Oriental College in Rome (160). He saw it to be "symbolical of the perfect ecclesiastical union between the East and the West" (158). Of all the images of Mary, "Does any one of them seem more fitted to be the happy link between the Latin and the Greek churches, than this glorious Image of Perpetual Help?" (157).

Conclusion

1 Théophile Gautier, *Constantinople of Today*, trans. Robert Howe Gould (London: David Bogue, 86 Fleet Street, 1854), 229–30.

2 Tom Holland, *Dominion* (New York: Basic Books, 2019), 10.

3 "The faith is at once the most enduring legacy of classical antiquity, and the index of its utter transformation." Holland, 10.

4 Rebecca West, *Black Lamb and Grey Falcon: A Journey through Yugoslavia* (New York: Penguin, 1940), 913. Alan Jacobs argues that West indeed found her way, without quite realizing it, to the Christian doctrine of original sin—but only to that: "West comes, at last . . . to one of the worst positions a person can occupy in thinking of her fellow human beings: an Augustinian anthropology without its accompanying theology. She sees with absolute clarity our innate dividedness, the immovable and constant presence of an ever vigilant ugly head, always determined to expel nourishment and thereby to reject life and to choose death instead. But the Christian idea that the death of Christ somehow redeems our death wish, transforms it . . . makes the entry point to a heavenly kingdom—this idea she cannot accept." Jacobs, *Original Sin*, 226.

5 West, *Black Lamb*, 913.

6 West, 796–97.

7 Christianity does not endorse the "infinitely disgusting . . . belief that by shedding the blood of an animal one will be granted increase; that by making a gift to death one will receive a gift of life" (West, *Black Lamb and Grey Falcon*, 914). Instead, it exposes and overturns the logic of sacrifice from within. It may be that the theology of Soterichos Pantevgenos, where the Father was appeased by the atoning sacrifice of Christ, betrays an intrusion of the kind of sacrificial logic West deplored into Christianity, a theology that indeed (in West's words) "pollutes the works of love" (914). West is therefore perfectly right to repudiate a "doctrine of the Atonement too absurd to be set down in writing, [in which] it is pretended that Christ came to earth to cook up a senseless and ugly magic rite, to buy with his pain an unrelated good" (914). The Virgin of the Passion, as shown in chapter 6, instead illustrates the unified love of the Godhead, freely offered and freely received, a love that required no transaction to procure.

8 For a detailed approach to goddess figurines embraced by goddess feminism today in their original Cretan context, and why connecting them to "the Goddess" is risky, see Goodison and Morris, "Beyond the 'Great Mother,'" 113–32. The authors explain, "While some [such figures] might be seen as divine, we are far from a static unitarian picture of a 'Goddess.' The evidence about life in these early [Cretan] communities is too sparse to give further clues about the meanings the figures may have had for the people who used them" (Goodison and Morris, 115). See also note 19 in this book's introduction. The myth of a lost matriarchal age, embraced by many goddess enthusiasts, has long been employed by men to prove that society had advanced beyond it, making such a view fodder for "fascists, male supremacists, and misogynists championing the evolutionary fitness of male dominance." Cynthia Eller, *Gentlemen and Amazons: The Myth of Matriarchal Prehistory, 1861–1900* (Berkeley: University of California Press, 2011),

191. Hutton claims the goddess movement's foundational facts are wrong in the same way that it is wrong, for example, to say that Manchester is the political capital of the United Kingdom. Ronald Hutton, *The Triumph of the Moon* (Oxford: Oxford University Press, 1999), 366. A single-volume assessment that summarizes an enormity of scholarship is by the feminist theologian Rosemary Radford Ruether, *Goddesses and the Divine Feminine: A Western Religious History* (Berkeley: University of California Press, 2005). Even a sympathetic overview of goddess feminism concludes that if new liberating figures are imagined in the future, "these would have to be checked against new findings from the fields of archaeology and history so that they do not stray too far into the realm of utopian fantasy as some believe the Goddess has." Sarah Marie Gallant, "Imagination, Empowerment, and Imaginary Figures," in *Feminist Spirituality: The Next Generation*, ed. Chris Klassen (Washington, DC: Lexington, 2009), 28. The Virgin Mary, I suggest, is one such figure who can endure this scrutiny.

9 As Giuseppe Fornari states,

> [Ancient society] always follows the same pattern of salvation for all through individual sacrifice (*at-one-ment*), a pattern interpreted by the archaic communities, according to the only view available to them, as the omnipotent victim against whom there is an imperative need to defend themselves but who, once killed, becomes beneficent. . . . The myth always presents the hero as committing undifferentiating crimes to which society has to respond by expelling him, followed by his transfiguration into a beneficent divine being. . . . Where the Bible has influenced cultures, it has acted as an antimythic force; for the first time in history it stood up for victims against their persecutors and taught a view diametrically opposed to the view of all mythologies worldwide. . . . Jesus appears as the vanquisher of sacrifice and its controlling, persecutory logic. (Giuseppe Fornari, *Dionysus, Christ, and the Death of God*, 2 vols. [East Lansing: Michigan State University Press, 2021], 1:58–60)

Likewise, Hart asserts, "the gods themselves are bound by certain evil necessities . . . the tragic is older than the gods. . . . It is just this mythos—this pagan metanarrative of ontological violence—that the Christian narrative has from its beginning rejected and against which it must pose itself as an alternative wisdom." Hart, *Beauty of the Infinite*, 383.

10 Puzzlingly enough, the very same book that hails goddess images as liberating for us today also indicates in passing that "[at Tophet] thousands and thousands of burial urns have been unearthed containing the burned

bones of infants, a vow fulfilled to Tanit [the Phoenician form of Astarte] or Ba'al Hamon." William G. Dever, *Did God Have a Wife? Archaeology and Folk Religion in Ancient Israel* (Grand Rapids, MI: Eerdmans, 2005), 218. The fact that Dever connects Tanit to Asherah as well might give an indication as to why biblical authors did not give Asherah an enthusiastic embrace either. For an insightful view as to how Mary overcame a culture of sacrifice, see Fornari, *Death of God*, 2:322–23. Even so, Dever posits that Asherah, often depicted as a nursing mother, is more "chaste" than the lascivious Canaanite goddesses like Astarte: "The more blatant sexuality of Canaanite religion is [in Asherah] now restrained and redirected" (187). He notes the possibility that Asherah reverence continued in the tradition of the Virgin Mary, especially in Eastern Christianity (190–92). Here, his work dovetails with Margaret Barker's daring theories about the "Lady in the Temple." Margaret Barker, *The Mother of the Lord*, vol. 1, *The Lady in the Temple* (London: T&T Clark, 2012).

11 As Solmsen concludes his study of Isis, Christianity, in comparison to Isis, offered "love of a more outgoing kind and broader in scope, love between man and his neighbor, love for the poor and the downtrodden, even, in principle at least, for one's enemy." Friedrich Solmsen, *Isis among the Greeks and Romans* (Cambridge, MA: Harvard University Press, 1979), 113.

12 Tom Hare, *ReMembering Osiris: Number, Gender, and the Word in Ancient Egyptian Representational Systems* (Stanford, CA: Stanford University Press, 1999), 111. Atum "acts in complete autonomy of desire, without the need of a partner, and his progeny are accidental, a supplement to the interiority of his autoerotic intent" (113). But "monotheistic pathologies" (to use Hare's words) such as Judaism are much different. Ruether points out that "Yahweh is never depicted as having a penis or as actively sexual, unlike other male gods such as Enki or Baal" (*Goddesses*, 76). Beattie explains that in Trinitarian theology, "in creation and in the new creation by way of the Virgin Birth, God creates ex nihilo, not through phallic insemination but through the spontaneous fecundity of maternal being." Beattie, *After Postmodernity*, 360. Hare, therefore, may be right to suggest that the vast difference between monotheism and polytheism is the latter's phallic, even masturbatory focus resulting in the man's "sovereignty, paternity, dominion" (*ReMembering Osiris*, 154, 236). On the cross, however, "the death of the Just One achieves the metamorphosis of the paternal image in the direction of a figure of kindness and compassion." Paul Ricoeur, "Fatherhood: From Phantasm to Symbol," in *The Conflict of Interpretations*, trans. Robert Sweeney (Evanston, IL: Northwestern University Press, 1974), 493. In contrast to Egyptian phallocentrism, "For Ambrose, the virginity of Mary had consisted principally in the fact that her body had not been entered by a male penis, and her womb had received no alien seed." Brown, *Body and Society*, 407.

13   See note 39 in chapter 1 of this book.

14   From the ruins of Artemis's temple at Ephesus, the "poor loving" Christians who had won over the population constructed ten churches, culminating in the episcopal Church of the Virgin Mary. Rogers, *Artemis of Ephesos*, 282. See also note 14 in chapter 1 of this book.

15   Marina Warner, *Alone of All Her Sex: The Myth and the Cult of the Virgin Mary* (New York: Knopf, 1976). Warner made the case that Mary's exaltation left regular women behind, which has no doubt often been the case. But it was no different in the world that preceded Mary. Preston asserts, "The presence of powerful goddesses in a religious pantheon rarely reflects anything about the role of females in that particular society." James J. Preston, "Conclusion: New Perspectives on Mother Worship," in *Mother Worship: Themes and Variations*, ed. James J. Preston (Chapel Hill: University of North Carolina Press, 1982), 327–28. Ruether concludes her extended study of goddesses by suggesting that, with the exception of the cult of Demeter, "concepts of goddesses bear the clear marks of classist and, indeed, royal ideology. Creating these goddesses was the work of men and women of the royal and priestly classes, reflecting their interests and validating their roles. Once cannot ascertain a decisive difference between the imagining of men and women in these classes." Ruether, *Goddesses*, 301. What changed in the shift from paganism to Christianity is the possibility of appealing this patriarchal norm. Namely, by appealing to the fact that God (who is beyond gender) saved the world without the assistance of men (in the Annunciation), even if men have been reticent to accept the full scope of this mystery.

16   "To its pagan critics, Christianity was a religion notorious for close association with women." Brown, *Body and Society*, 140. Stark's well-founded sociological conclusion is that "the Christian woman enjoyed far greater marital security and equality than did her pagan neighbor." Rodney Stark, *The Rise of Christianity* (San Francisco: HarperCollins, 1997), 105. For in-depth examinations of this complicated topic, see Lynn Cohick, *Women in the World of the Earliest Christians* (Grand Rapids, MI: Baker Academic, 2009); and Lynn Cohick and Amy Brown Hughes, *Christian Women in the Patristic World: Their Influence, Authority, and Legacy in the Second through Fifth Centuries* (Grand Rapids, MI: Baker Academic, 2017). [Pseudo-]Maximus articulates the aspiration remarkably well: "There was no end to the servitude and pain and affliction of women, but when the archangel said to the holy Virgin, 'the Lord is with you,' all the debts of affliction were erased . . . there is no longer the lordship of man over you." [Pseudo-]Maximus, *Life of the Virgin*, 51.

17   Epiphanius of Salamis, *The Panarion of Epiphanius of Salamis, Books II and III. De Fide*, 2nd ed., trans. Frank Williams (Leiden: Brill, 2013), 637.

Witt argues that this is, in fact, the "traditional" position against women's ordination. Catholic and Orthodox churches have rightly abandoned the argument based on female inferiority, which leaves them needing new arguments against it. Witt, *Icons of Christ*, 190–91. Interestingly, both Epiphanius's recent biographers come away with hard-earned negative impressions of this divisive figure who evinced "a genuine mean streak, a meanness of spirit, a nastiness even." Jon F. Dechow, review of *Epiphanius of Cyprus: A Culture Biography of Late Antiquity*, by Andrew S. Jacobs and *Epiphanius of Cyprus: Imagining an Orthodox World*, by Richard Kim, *Catholic Historical Review* 104, no. 3 (Summer 2018): 533–34. Which is to say, Ephraim Radner may be right to see in "Epiphanian exclusionism" a negative turning point in Christian history. Radner, *Brutal Unity*, 140.

18   Epiphanius of Salamis, *Panarion of Epiphanius of Salamis*, 638–39. Shoemaker does not feel that there is enough evidence to conclude that Mary functioned as a priest among the Kollyridians, who Epiphanius was railing against. Yet he concludes that "behind Epiphanius's harangue there seems to be an actual group of relatively 'orthodox' Christians who allowed women to participate in some forms of liturgical leadership and were pioneers in the veneration—not worship—of the Virgin Mary." Shoemaker, *Mary in Early Christian Faith*, 163.

19   Neophytos, sermon on the meeting of Mary and Simeon, cited in Carr, "Icon at Mount Sinai," 246.

20   In a sermon on the presentation of Mary in the temple, Neophytos writes, "We know that the entry of the all-pure [Virgin] into the holy of holies has symbolically called our nature [he was addressing male monks] to sanctification." Cited in Henry Maguire, "*Abaton* and *Oikonomia*: St. Neophytos and the Iconograpny of the Presentation of the Virgin," in *Medieval Cyprus: Studies in Art, Architecture, and History in Memory of Doula Mouriki*, ed. Nancy Patterson Ševčenko and Christopher Moss (Princeton, NJ: Princeton University Press, 1999), 96. When the Russian monk Basil Barski visited the Virgin of the Vetches church in Cyprus in 1735, it had become a monastery limited to men. He insisted, "When some shameless and obstinate women tried repeatedly to . . . enter the church, they were repeatedly repelled from the entrance to the church by some unseen power of the Holy Virgin" (Maguire, "*Abaton* and *Oikonomia*," 104). On the contrary, some unseen power may be using the image that arose from the same church to welcome them in. See Sarah Hinlicky Wilson, *Woman, Women and the Priesthood in the Trinitarian Theology of Elisabeth Behr-Sigel* (London: T&T Clark, 2015).

21   Epiphanius's rhetoric, "Never at any time has a woman offered sacrifice to God" (*Panarion of Epiphanius*, 638), made in the face of evidence of precisely that, is a fine illustration of Gary Macy's observation of the

methodology of many who pursue this question: "If women were (and are) incapable of being ordained, then they cannot have been ordained in the past. References to the ordination of women must either be not truly Christian (i.e. heretical) or they must really mean something other than what they seem to mean." Gary Macy, *The Hidden History of Women's Ordination: Female Clergy in the Medieval West* (New York: Oxford University Press, 2008), 5.

22 C. S. Lewis, in an influential article arguing against the priesthood of women, suggests that "never, in so far as I know, in all [the Middle Ages] was anything remotely resembling a sacerdotal office attributed to [Mary]." C. S. Lewis, "Priestesses in the Church?," in *God in the Dock* (Grand Rapids, MI: Eerdmanns, 1970), 234. Lewis, brilliant as he was, would surely have revised his position had he been aware of René Laurentin's massive volume on the subject (see notes 29 and 46 of this book's introduction). Likewise, Thomas Hopko's assumption that "we find no women bishops or priests" in church history (Thomas Hopko, "Presbyter/Bishop: A Masculine Ministry," in *Women and the Priesthood*, new ed., ed. Thomas Hopko [Crestwood, NY: St. Vladimir's Seminary Press, 1999], 152) overlooks the evidence that Mary at least functioned in precisely this way. The most widely recognized name in the Anglosphere Orthodox world, Metropolitan Kallistos Ware, shifted his earlier opinion on the issue, stating that he finds the "iconic" argument against women's ordination—that only a male priest can signify Christ—to no longer be convincing: "What I would plead is that we Orthodox should regard the matter as essentially an open question." Elisabeth Behr-Sigel and Kallistos Ware, *The Ordination of Women in the Orthodox Church* (Geneva: World Council of Churches, 2000), 50. Metropolitan Anthony Bloom has expressed similar opinions, based in part on Mary's role in priesthood. See Bloom's preface to Elisabeth Behr-Sigel, *The Ministry of Women in the Church* (Redondo Beach, CA: Oakwood, 1991), xiii–xiv. See also Witt, *Icons of Christ*, discussed in note 38 of chapter 8 of this book. Still, whatever one's stand on such contemporary issues, Mary's priestly function can be celebrated by those of more traditional persuasion as well when her sacerdotal function is understood as personifying the church. See Fr. S. M. Emile Neubert, *Mary and the Priestly Ministry* (New Bedford, MA: Academy of the Immaculate, 2009). Neubert (d. 1967), a devout traditionalist, insists, "Mary gave substantial existence to Christ-Priest when she have Him a physical body. The priest gives Him a new, accidental existence in giving Him a Eucharistic body. Mary offers up the Holy Victim in union with Jesus. The priest offers Him up in repeating the words of Jesus" (35–36).

23 "Mary does not act, even in the imaginary, as . . . agent or celebrant, nor is she depicted as elevating, blessing, or breaking the elements of bread and

wine as a priest might do." Kearns, *Virgin Mary*, 275. Mary can be "prominent and close to the altar (though not on it)" (266). Similarly, for Nancy Jay, sacrifice is a male "remedy for having been born of a woman," and male priesthood is an attempt to rival the female womb. According to Jay, the taboo against women—especially mothers and menstruating women—from male rituals of sacrifice is because such rituals are intended to rival them, making strong female priesthood impossible. Jay unambiguously asserts that the creation of ritual space is "always political action involving struggles for power, including power over women's reproductive capacities." Jay, *Throughout Your Generations*, xxvi–xxvii.

24 Meghan DiLuzio concludes that while women could not perform divination in Roman society, "priestesses performed many of the same religious rituals as male priests, as well as others unique to their specific priestly roles, and they did so in an official capacity . . . operating in the public sphere from the very beginning." Meghan DiLuzio, *A Place at the Altar: Priestesses in Republican Rome* (Princeton, NJ: Princeton University Press, 2016), 241. The tradition of Marian priesthood shows that this is the case for the Christian tradition as well.

25 "The sacrifice that Christian theology upholds is inseparable from the gift: it underwrites not the stabilizing regime of prudential violence, but the destabilizing extravagance of giving and giving again, of declaring love and delight in the exchange of signs of peace, outside of every calculation of debt or power." Hart, *Beauty of the Infinite*, 350. The late Sergius Bulgakov arrived at this understanding of peaceful inter-Trinitarian sacrifice (correcting his earlier view) in his posthumously published *Eucharistic Sacrifice*:

> The Son receives this very Word not as His own, but as the Revelation of the Father, and gives Himself to the Father, and filially offers sacrifice. His very existence as the Son is already a sacrifice, and the Son, as Son, is the High Priest forever ("according to the order of Melchizedek"). . . . Now, this assumes the acceptance of the Son's sacrifice by the Father, and thus the sacrificial offering itself is a dyadic, mutual act of Divine love, which is the Holy Spirit. He is Hypostatic love itself, as the bond of love between the Father and the Son, its in-spiration, joy and exultation, the Gift of God, the Gift of the Holy Trinity within itself—the Glory of God. (Sergius Bulgakov, *Eucharistic Sacrifice*, trans. Mark Roosien [South Bend, IN: University of Notre Dame Press, 2021], 19–20)

26 Fornari's explanation for Christian violence should not be taken as an excuse: "There has ever thrived a persecutory Christianity in perpetual contradiction with the gospel message." Fornari, *Death of God*, 2:350.

27   Although William Cavanaugh defends Christianity on this score in *The Myth of Religious Violence: Secular Ideology and the Roots of Modern Conflict* (Oxford: Oxford University Press, 2009), the extended response from Ephraim Radner in *Brutal Unity* lays the blame on the exclusionary violence of Christianity nonetheless.

28   Dan Jones, *The Templars* (New York: Viking, 2017).

29   Barth, *Church Dogmatics*, 2:2:110. For a helpful encapsulation and commentary on Barth's doctrine of election, see Adam Neder, *Participation in Christ: An Entry into Karl Barth's Church Dogmatics* (Louisville, KY: Westminster John Knox, 2009), 15–28. Oakes helpfully points out that the proof texts used to counter this position ("Jacob I have loved, but Esau I have hated" [Rom 9:13 NASB]) employ "hatred" as a Semitism for "loved less." Furthermore, "since Paul's readers, especially his Jewish-Christian ones, would have identified not just themselves but also their former co-religionists (the non-Christian Jews) *with Jacob*, the 'hate' that God 'feels' toward Esau *must* be merely provisional, otherwise the whole point of the entire letter to the Romans would be lost ('first Jews, then Greeks')." Oakes, *Theology of Grace*, 171–72. Likewise, Rutledge explains, "As Paul's train of thought unfolds to its climax, the term 'ungodly' comes to embrace all humanity. The Jacob-Esau dichotomy therefore becomes no dichotomy at all, but a summation of God's dealings with the entire human race in its twinned identity simultaneously *both* reprobate *and* elect." Rutledge, *Crucifixion*, 607.

30   For Karl Barth, the Pauline/Athanasian understanding of election did not entail universalism: "It is His concern what is to be the final extent of the circle. If we are to respect the freedom of divine grace, we cannot venture the statement that it must and will finally be coincident with the world of man as such." Barth, *Church Dogmatics*, 2:2:417. Barth insists, "Not all hear this word. Not all are obedient to him. But it comes to all, it is relevant to all, it is said for all and to all, it is said clearly and acceptably enough for all." Barth, *Church Dogmatics*, 4:1:317. Sergius Bulgakov's similar understanding does adopt what could fairly be called a universalist view: "Heaven does not exist in its fullness as long as and insofar as hell exists. . . . Hell dissolves into nothing, which is its genuine foundation." Sergius Bulgakov, *Bride of the Lamb*, trans. Boris Jakim (Grand Rapids, MI: Eerdmann's, 2001), 489, 491. But not before Bulgakov takes extreme measures to emphasize the seriousness of sin: "One must indisputably admit the full validity of the axiom that every evil of which a human being is guilty must be fully and totally expiated by him, even if he is forgiven. Sin cannot be remitted *for free*, without suffering, for that would not be mercy but a denial of justice. God's justice does not tolerate sin . . . the idea that one can avoid with impunity the consequences of sin is insane, craven,

and false" (484). This often misunderstood "wise fire" of purgation is not *so that* humans can be saved but *because* they have been. While insisting God's primordial choice includes all humanity, I leave the question as to whether all humanity will accept this choice open.

31   Not far from the very Boston salons where these tortured questions were addressed (Theusen, *Predestination*, 44–72), a massive basilica to the Virgin of the Passion, in the form of Our Lady of Perpetual Help, has been raised. In the very city where Lutherans raged over the issue, the famous Saint Alphonsus "Rock" Liguori Church has been erected that contains a resolution (Theusen, *Predestination*, 148–68). Princeton, that school established by firm predestinarians, did not have to wait for Barthian theologians for relief (welcome as such relief may be). Assistance also came via the Cretan Virgin of the Passion icon purchased in 1911 by Allan Marquand, himself suspect of abandoning Calvinist orthodoxy.

32   See note 45 in this book's introduction. The fact that Wisdom is not a fourth member of the Trinity does not signify that she is necessarily less than God. Sergius Bulgakov's theology in particular offers both created and uncreated Wisdom:

> The Divine Sophia exists in a dual mode: in her own mode, which belongs to her in eternity; and in the creaturely mode, as the world. Only such an identification of the two modes of Sophia, with their simultaneous differentiation, can explain why, although God is the Creator, this does not change his divinely sophianic being or introduce in the latter a non-divine or extra-divine principle. . . . God *has* Divine Sophia. She belongs to God, and she herself in this sense *is* God, His eternal power and divinity, the *uncreated* divine essence. In contrast, the creaturely Sophia, or the world, belongs not to God, but to herself. She is created (or more precisely, is eternally being created) by God, is God's creation. (Bulgakov, *Bride of the Lamb*, 46, 61–62)

Sophia as a figure is necessarily "reflective, living, adaptative, simultaneously literal and figurative . . . both person and principle." Martin, *Submerged Reality*, 42.

33   Georg Wilhelm Friedrich Hegel, *Vorlesungen über die Philosophie der Religion: Teil 3: Die vollendete Religion*, ed. Walter Jaschke (Hamburg: Felix Menier Verlag, 1984), 249–50. This translation is from Bruce Marshall, "The Absolute and the Trinity," *Pro Ecclesia* 23, no. 2 (May 2014): 152.

34   Marshall efficiently encapsulates the classic theological position: "We may come to know that the one God is a Trinity of Persons from the revealed economy of salvation, and perhaps even from creation itself, but nothing in

the contingent history of creation or salvation realizes, perfects, intensifies, or otherwise alters the divine Persons in either their distinction or their unity." Marshall, "Absolute and the Trinity," 163.

35 "By marking this distinction of [Christ's divine and human] natures, the tradition affirmed that God truly suffers and dies on the cross, but not in a way that disturbs or alters his divinity." Marshall, "Absolute and the Trinity," 163.

36 Another way of putting the same point would be to say that when God descends into the depths of creation to rescue humanity, he does not—as would an incompetent liberator—take the entire rope with him but instead keeps one end of it firmly suspended in his infinite peace, where he intends to elevate humanity (by grace, not nature) as well.

37 Hart, *Beauty of the Infinite*, 375.

38 See note 43 in chapter 10 of this book.

39 The Third Ecumenical council in 431 offered no addition to the Nicene Creed. Its proceedings instead read, "It is not permitted to produce or write or compose any other creed than the one which was defined by the holy fathers who were gathered together by the Holy Spirit at Nicaea." Pelikan and Hotchkiss, *Creeds and Confessions*, 167. Theotokos ("Mother of God") remains a theologically legitimate declaration, but there is no need to continue to dismiss the global witness of the Assyrian Church of the East as unacceptably "Nestorian." Rittgers, a Protestant, sees in the choice between East and West an "impossible choice between two mothers. . . . All Christians must be considered schismatics; no Christian church is immune from this accusation, including Catholics and the Orthodox." Ronald Rittgers, epilogue to *Protestantism after 500 Years*, ed. Mark Noll and Thomas Albert Howard (Oxford: Oxford University Press, 2016), 336, 338.

40 P. P. D'Orazio e Buschi, *La Madonna del Perpetuo Soccorso: Storia della Sacra Immagine e del Suo Culto Nel Mondo* (Verona: Ghindini e Fiorini, 1953). The cloud of incense in the image might be understood as the need to accept "the clouded vision that unity brings upon churches defined by division." R. R. Reno, "The Debilitation of the Churches," in *The Ecumenical Future*, ed. Carl E. Braaten and Robert W. Jenson (Grand Rapids, MI: Eerdmans, 2004), 69. Reno concedes that "any progress toward Christian unity will undermine and diminish the sophisticated theological systems born in the polemical centuries that followed the Reformation." In the same volume, Brian Daley explains that the chief way the Patristic era spoke of the church is through images, because the mystery of the church "cannot be exhaustively plumbed by a single idea or expressed in a single term, but that it must be teased out in an almost inexhaustible stream of images and analogies, which release to us new aspects of the one mystery." "The fathers," he continues, "think and write about the church almost exclusively in the language of *symbol*." Brian E. Daley, "Rebuilding the Structure of Love,"

in Braaten and Jenson, *Ecumenical Future*, 95–97. This is not to argue for a dismantling of essential Christian convictions. Instead, Daley points to the Nicene Creed, which, for Basil the Great, was sufficient to restore those who had departed from the faith (90). It is this Nicene inheritance that the Virgin of the Passion represents. Radner, inspired by Pavel Florensky, argues for "pneumatic incoherence," including a "deliberate dismantling of logical articulation[s]." Ephraim Radner, *Spirit and Nature: The Saint Médard Miracles in 18th-Century Jansenism* (New York: Crossroad, 2002), 371–72. Radner is elaborating on Pavel Florensky's essay, "On the Holy Spirit," in *Ultimate Questions: An Anthology of Modern Russian Thought*, ed. Alexander Schmemann (Chicago: Holt, Rinehart, Winston, 1965).

41 For the "Age of Mary" reference, see Carrie Gress, *The Marian Option* (Charlotte, NC: Tan Books, 2017). Charlene Spretnak counsels,

> Rather than positioning Mary as the deal-breaker of the ecumenical project, it would be far wiser to reframe the issue with a both/and response: Ecumenical gatherings of the three branches of Christianity in various locations around the world could honor Mary's biblical presence—while still allowing the Catholics and the Orthodox [and Anglicans!] on their own respective turf to honor Mary's mystical, cosmological dimensions as well. . . . The wisest course for ecumenism would be for the Western branches of Christianity—that is, Protestantism and Roman Catholicism—to lean in the direction of the Eastern Orthodoxy, who have cultivated both a rich sense of Mary's mystical, cosmological presence *and* a well-developed tradition of regarding the Creation as sacred. (Charlene Spretnak, *Missing Mary: The Queen of Heaven and Her Re-emergence in the Modern Church* [New York: Palgrave Macmillan, 2004], 148–49)

42 The icon has a large following among Coptic Orthodox and Ethiopian Orthodox Christians especially. Raymond A. Silverman, "Ethiopian Orthodox Visual Culture in the Age of Mechanical Reproduction: A Research Note," *Material Religion* 5, no. 1 (May 2015): 88–103. Even if these communities do not assent to the Council of Chalcedon, the fact that its original theological milieu at the Virgin of the Vetches church appeals to the *unity* of Christ (against Pantevgenos's theology of partition) makes it fitting for such communities.

43 In Ritzos's classic version of the image, only the cross touches the halo of Mary. If the spear to Mary's right could signifies her own contribution ("a sword will pierce your heart too"), and the cross to her left as Christ's work, then it is profoundly instructive that only one of these makes contact with the Virgin, signifying salvation by Christ's work, not our own: "Only when we give no place to our works in justification are our works

themselves 'justified.'" Michael Horton, *Justification*, vol. 1 (Grand Rapids, MI: Zondervan, 2018), 216. In addition, if Martin Luther pitted the theology of glory (understood as the gold background of the icon perhaps) against the theology of the cross, then the Virgin of the Passion, which foregrounds the cross, is even more paradigmatically Lutheran. The icon's original biblical attribution to Mary "full of grace" (Luke 1:28 RSVCE) at Lagoudera also makes it an especially biblical image fit for Protestants. For additional Protestant convergences with Orthodoxy, see Bradley Nassif, "*Concerning Those Who Imagine That They Are Justified by Works*: The Gospel According to St. Mark—the Monk," in *The Philokalia: A Classic Text of Orthodox Spirituality*, ed. Brock Bingaman and Bradley Nassif (Oxford: Oxford University Press, 2012), 89, 134. Finally, Protestants who protest the doctrine of Mary's Immaculate Conception as formulated by Catholicism might be especially drawn to the Virgin of the Passion because of its iconographical roots in the meeting of Mary and Simeon in the temple (*Hypapante*). Early church teachers such as Origen and Cyril of Alexandria used Mary's purification on this occasion as a reminder that she too needed to be saved. Pauline Allen, "Portrayals of Mary in Greek Homiletic Literature," 74–77, 82–84.

44 The Clonard monastery, itself a haven even for those alienated from Christianity, soon became "a space or sanctuary where politicians could come under the invitation of the Church in order to find some way of making peace." Kevin Rafter, "Priests and Peace: The Role of the Redemptorist Order in the Northern Ireland Peace Process," *Etudes Irlandaises* 28, no. 1 (2003): 164. The Redemptorist Peace Ministry's express aim was to "intervene directly and to do all she [the Church] can to bring its violent dimensions and their tragic consequences to an end" (Rafter, 166).

45 "Christians outside of the Roman Empire were [therefore] soon seen not only as followers of Jesus, but also of the Roman emperor." Vince Bantu, *A Multitude of Peoples: Engaging Ancient Christianity's Global Identity* (Downers Grove, IL: InterVarsity, 2020), 18.

46 For an initial foray in this direction that explores how images thwart the divisions of the Reformation, see Matthew J. Milliner, "Visual Ecumenism: The Coy Communion of Art," in *Come, Let Us Eat Together: The Sacraments and Christian Unity* (Downers Grove, IL: IVP Academic, 2018). It seems to follow that the long-standing visual embrace of the Virgin and Child among miaphysite Christians in particular thwarts attempts to deem them theologically suspect.

47 Even a critic of Sophiology like Georges Florovsky admitted, "There are two images of Sophia: the true and real one and the false one. The holy temples in Byzantium and Russia were built in the name of the first image of Sophia." Paul Gavrilyuk, *Georges Florovsky and the Russian Religious*

Renaissance (Oxford: Oxford University Press, 2014), 103, citing Florovsky, letter to Bulgakov, 22 July (New Style, August 4, 1926).

48 The icon was so named by the Redemptorists to celebrate the 150th anniversary of its promulgation by Pius IX in 2016. Though there is an Orthodox way to approach the same understanding. The cross (the angel on the right) and the sword that pierced Mary's heart (the angel on the left) perfectly encapsulate Saint Maria Skobtsova's counsel, derived from Simeon's prophecy, of the dual commandment, love of God and neighbor: "For Mother Maria, the spiritual exercise of *imitatio Christi* (imitation of Christ) must be supplemented by *imitatio Matris* (imitation of the Mother) . . . the unity of the sword and cross represents the indivisibility of the first and second Gospel commandments, and the necessary integration of personal and collective spiritual pursuits." Natalia Ermolaev, "Our Mother of Paris," in *Framing Mary: The Mother of God in Modern, Revolutionary, and Post-Soviet Russian Culture*, ed. Amy Singleton Adams and Vera Shevzov (DeKalb: Northern Illinois University Press, 2018), 200. Mother Maria lived this vision through to her death at the Ravensbrück concentration camp.

49 Thomas Aquinas, "Commentary on Boethius's *De Trinitate*," trans. Rose Emmanuella Brennan, in *The Trinity and the Unicity of the Intellect* (Eugene, OR: Wipf & Stock, 2009), 10.

50 Ann Blackman, "Moscow's Big Mak Attack," *Time*, February 5, 1990, http://content.time.com/time/subscriber/article/0,33009,969321,00.html.

51 Nadezda Rychkova, "Constructing a Religioscape: The Case of Pushkinskaya Square in Moscow," in *Urban Religious Events: Public Spirituality in Contested Spaces*, ed. Paul Bramadat et al. (London: Bloomsbury Academic, 2021), 45–61. Pushkinskaya Square is the "unofficial center of Moscow, as opposed to the Red Square." The Community of the Strastnoy Monastery began in 2006 as an effort to prevent the construction of an underground parking garage that would have disturbed the burials of nuns once buried beneath the destroyed monastery. They have since met every Saturday to pray and process around this popular Moscow square. A granite monument was erected in 2012, which reads "The Strastnoy Monastery by the name of the Most Holy Theotokos Strastnaya ['of the Passion'] Icon stood here. It was founded in 1654 and destroyed in 1937" (49). Other encroachments on Pushkinskaya Square include icons and a cross under the stairs leading to the 1961 "Rossiya" cinema. The history of the icon covered in this book points to a possible affinity between the Community of the Strastnoy Monastery, marked by deliberate humility (59), and the anti-Putin activists who also seek to elucidate the square's connection to the events of perestroika (49).

52 Adams and Shevzov suggest, "Mary often confounds the secular/religious divide, belonging to no one and everyone . . . [She] challenges Soviet

ethnographer Nikolai Matorin's observation in 1931 that devotion to the Mother of God distracted women from the kind of social activism that gave women a voice and a place in the social sphere." Adams and Shevzov, *Framing Mary*, 26–28.

53 Remensnyder, *Conquistadora*.

54 Christopher Pool, *Olmec Archaeology and Early Mesoamerica* (Cambridge: Cambridge University Press, 2007), 116, 138, 237. "Infant sacrifice [among the Olmec] foreshadows the Aztecs' offerings of children to Tlaloc and Chalchiutlicue, gods associated with rain and water" (97). Mary offers a sacrifice as well, albeit the bloodless sacrifice of the Eucharist. As if to illustrate this fact, a variety of churches dedicated to Our Lady of Perpetual Help ring the municipality of Veracruz where *La Virgen* (also *Señor*) *de las Limas* was found (in Jesús Carranza), including *Capilla de la Virgen del Perpetuo Socorro* in Coatzacoalcos and *Parroquia Nuestra Señora del Perpetuo Socorro y San Francisco de Asís* in Veracruzana.

55 I pursue this further in chapter 3 of Matthew J. Milliner, *The Everlasting People, G. K. Chesterton and the First Nations* (Downers Grove, IL: InterVarsity, 2021).

56 Milliner, 117.

57 Milliner, 118.

58 Nor are those of European descent left out. The image depicts Blessed Stanley Rother (1935–81), who was murdered in Guatemala, where he insisted on returning despite warnings that he was on a death list for his work among the Tz'utujil people. "The shepherd," he insisted, "cannot run at the first sign of danger." Matthew Bunson, "Father Stanley Rother," National Catholic Register, September 18, 2017, https://www.ncregister .com/interview/father-stanley-rother-the-shepherd-cannot-run-at-the-first -sign-of-danger.

59 This church was instrumental in the spread of devotion to the icon around the world. T. L. Skinner, *The Redemptorists in the West* (St. Louis, MO: Redemptorists Fathers, 1933), 122–50. Ferrero, *Story of an Icon*, 113.

60 Not surprisingly, this famous church is a focal point of racial justice in St. Louis. Jennifer Brinker, "Catholic Racial Justice Collaborative Calls for Prayer, Action to End Racism at Prayer Vigil at Rock Church," *St. Louis Review*, July 9, 2020, https://www.archstl.org/catholic-racial-justice -collaborative-calls-for-prayer-action-to-end-racism-at-prayer-vigil-at-rock -church-5480. The church's worship can be viewed at its YouTube channel. St. Alphonsus Ligouri "Rock" Catholic Church, "First Sunday of Lent, 2022," YouTube video, accessed March 14, 2022 https://www.youtube .com/watch?v=wni1BwxtL_8.

61 "[Haiti] experienced world history's only successful slave revolt [and] most Haitian Catholics attribute the independence and the care of their homeland

nation to the Blessed Mother, but especially to Our Lady of Perpetual Help." Terry Rey and Alex Stepick, *Crossing the Water and Keeping the Faith: Haitian Religion in Miami* (New York: New York University Press, 2013), 36.

62 Courtney Hall Lee, *The Black Madonna* (Eugene, OR: Wipf & Stock, 2017), 89.

63 The Our Lady of Perpetual Help church in the Velachery neighborhood is a fifteen-minute drive from the Shri Ashtalakshmi temple on the coastline devoted to Lakshmi. For a sympathetic treatment of Lakshmi devotion, see Constantina Rhodes, *Invoking Lakshmi: The Goddess of Wealth in Song and Ceremony* (Albany: SUNY Press, 2010). This is not to suggest the two traditions cannot be in fruitful conversation: "The [Christian] response [to Hinduism's goddess tradition] may be to venerate Mary more intensely, even while insisting she is not God—and now more precisely and interestingly, not a goddess . . . this may be the nearest approximation to an affirmative response [to Hinduism] available to Christians. Is veneration of Mary the same as worshiping these goddesses? No, but it is a measured, consequent way of honoring the invitation to worship a female person possessed of body and spirit, powerful and intensely present in a world where divine males seem to recede into the background." Francis X. Clooney, *Divine Mother, Blessed Mother: Hindu Goddesses and the Virgin Mary* (Oxford: Oxford University Press, 2005), 237.

64 Our Lady of Perpetual Help Chapel is in Tai O within Hong Kong, and just across the Zhujiang River estuary is the large statue of Guanyin in Macau. For the influence of the Virgin Mary on Guanyin, see Yü Chün-fang, *Kuan-Yin: The Chinese Transformation of Avalokitesvara* (New York: Columbia University Press, 2001). The Lotus Sutra (composed before 200 CE) lists seven of the thirty-three manifestations of Avalokitesvara to be female, while the complete feminization of Guanyin was in place by the Ming dynasty (1368–1644 CE). Yü Chün-fang argues, however, that the artistic appearance of Guanyin with a child in this period is the possible result of Christian influence. "The rise in the production of Madonna images [in the later Ming] heavily influenced the manner in which *songzi* Guanyin images were produced," as is apparent in the ivory statues from Zhangzhou. Jeremy Clarke, *The Virgin Mary and Catholic Identities in Chinese History* (Hong Kong: Hong Kong University Press, 2013), 27.

65 Mitsui modeled his version of Our Lady of Perpetual Help on the nineteenth-century Japanese print *Chujo-hime and the Spirit of Her Wicked Stepmother*, which relates the story of a noble-born girl's becoming a Buddhist nun. The original print's Marian overtones inspired the fusion.

66 Jaroslav Folda, "The Use of Çintamani as Ornament: A Case Study in the Afterlife of Forms," in *Byzantine Images and Their Afterlives*, ed. Lynn Jones (London: Routledge, 2016). In Buddhism, the same symbol is a gem

comparable to the philosopher's stone or Holy Grail. It is "a metaphor for various stages of the path, including initial aspiration to achieve buddhahood, the rarity of rebirth as a human being with access to the dharma, and the merit arising from the teachings of the Buddha." Robert E. Buswell Jr. and Donald Lopez Jr., *The Princeton Dictionary of Buddhism* (Princeton, NJ: Princeton University Press, 2013), 193.

67   For a brilliant exposition of Symeon the New Theologian's heart-centered practice and its revival with Thomas Keating and the Centering Prayer movement, see Cynthia Bourgeault, *The Heart of Centering Prayer: Nondual Christianity in Theory and Practice* (Boulder, CO: Shambala, 2016), 66–76. The Jesuit priest William Johnston is among the most responsible navigators of terrain shared by Buddhists and Christians. In addition to his many books, see especially his autobiography, *Mystical Journey* (Maryknoll, NY: Orbis, 2006).

68   "The intellectual faculty in man's soul, though spiritual, dwells in the brain, that is to say in the head: in the same way, the spiritual faculty which we term the spirit of man, though spiritual, dwells in the upper part of the heart, close to the left nipple of the chest and a little above it." E. Kadloubovsky and E. M. Palmer, eds., *The Art of Prayer: An Orthodox Anthology* (London: Faber & Faber, 1966), 194. For Symeon the New Theologian, "true and unerring attentiveness and prayer means that the intellect keeps watch over the heart while it prays; it should always be on patrol within the heart, and from within—from the depths of the heart—it should offer up its prayers to God. . . . It will keep watch always within the heart, repulsing and expelling all thoughts sown there by the enemy." Symeon the New Theologian, "The Three Methods of Prayer," in *The Philokalia: The Complete Text*, vol. 4, ed. and trans. G. E. H. Palmer, Philip Sherrard, and Kallistos Ware (London: Faber & Faber, 1995), 71.

69   The passage from Gregory of Sinai continues: "To eat the lamb of God upon the soul's noetic altar is not simply to apprehend Him spiritually or to participate in Him; it is also to become an image of the Lamb as He is in the age to come." Palmer, Sherrard, and Ware, *Philokalia*, 237.

70   Thomas Keating, Basil Pennington, and others freshly formulated instruction in Centering Prayer based on the fourteenth-century classic *The Cloud of Unknowing* partly in response to the challenge of Buddhism. Their aim was specifically to reach the young people who were seeking a Buddhist retreat center, but stumbled upon Saint Joseph's Abbey in Spenser, Massachusetts instead.

71   Perhaps especially because the cross in the Virgin of the Passion reminds us of the differences between Buddhist and Christian contemplation: "Emptiness in St. John of the Cross can never be separated from the cross of Jesus, who 'emptied himself taking the form of a slave' to be raised and to have a name above all names. The nothingness of St. John of the Cross is always

rooted in the crucified Jesus of Nazareth." William Johnston, *"Arise, My Love . . .": Mysticism for a New Era* (Maryknoll, NY: Orbis, 2002), 140–41.

72 This triangular table of ceramic, yonic place settings of history's famous women amalgamated into uniformity gains inspiration from the island of Crete, where once (presumably) "the male consort/son was always subordinate to the goddess, never developing an independent god status." Judy Chicago, *The Dinner Party* (London: Merrell, 2007), 50. In fact, Minoan Crete shows a record of "gods as well as goddesses, and they are many not one." Goodison and Morris, "Beyond the 'Great Mother,'" 132. The Brooklyn Museum was founded in 1895, and the parish was founded in 1893. "Our Parish History," Basilica of Our Lady of Perpetual Help, accessed August 9, 2021, https://olphbkny.org/parish-history.

73 A copy of the icon of Our Lady of Perpetual Help arrived at the church from Rome on December 4, 1881, the same year that the Redemptorists took charge of the parish. "The History of St. Patrick's, Toronto," St. Patrick's Parish, Toronto, accessed August 9, 2021, https://stpatricksto.archtoronto.org/en/our-community/about-us/.

74 Fifteen minutes away from Google headquarters in Mountain View, California, and Apple headquarters in Cupertino stands one of her shrines. She is the patroness of the Saint Aloysius Gonzaga Retreat House in Los Gatos, California. "Our Patrons," SSPX Retreats, accessed August 9, 2021, https://sarh.ca.sspx.org/en/our-patrons.

75 For a digital novena to the image, see "Novena to Our Lady of Perpetual Help," Our Lady of Perpetual Help Retreat and Spirituality Center, accessed March 14, 2022, https://olph-retreat.org/novenatoolph. Pasay, "Our Lady of Perpetual Help Tattoo," YouTube video, November 23, 2020, 1:48, https://www.youtube.com/watch?v=qS4uodhCJaA.

76 Examples of films and television series include *The Avengers* (2012), *Don Jon* (2013), or the concluding episode of the series *Justified* (2015). Based on the 1998 Alan Warner novel *The Sopranos*, the *Our Ladies of Perpetual Succour* play was written for the stage by Lee Hall, which premiered in 2015, in turn becoming the film *Our Ladies* in 2019. The brewery, inspired by the Our Lady of Perpetual Help church and school in New Albany, opened in New Albany, Indiana, in 2019. Brooke McAfee, "Our Lady of Perpetual Hops Opens in New Albany," *News and Tribune*, October 26, 2019, https://www.newsandtribune.com/news/our-lady-of-perpetual-hops-opens-in-new-albany/article_52f480f8-f77a-11e9-8119-631f41f9b362.html.

77 Nick Mafi, "Santiago Calatrava Explains the Transformation of Lower Manhattan 20 Years after 9/11," *Architectural Digest*, September 9, 2021, https://www.architecturaldigest.com/story/santiago-calatrava-explains-transformation-lower-manhattan-20-years-after-911. I thank John Landsdowne for this reference.

78   The event confirms the postsecular feminist insight that agency "can actually be conveyed through and supported by religious piety." Rosi Braidotti, "In Spite of the Times: The Postsecular Turn in Feminism," *Theory, Culture & Society* 25, no. 6 (2008): 2. It also happily complicates the claim that in this icon, "Mary's chief traits are the passive abilities to console and nurture." Kelly and Kelly, "Our Lady of Perpetual Help," 14.

79   Over 214 million people watched part of the London Olympics, while one estimate of Europe's population near 1192 is around 50 million. Scott Collins, "London Olympics: NBC Coverage Most-Watched TV Event in U.S. History," *Los Angeles Times*, August 13, 2012, https://www.latimes.com/entertainment/tv/la-xpm-2012-aug-13-la-et-st-london-olympics-dubbed-mostwatched-event-in-us-history-by-nbc-20120813-story.html; Paul Halsall, "Medieval Sourcebook: Tables on Population in Medieval Europe," Fordham University, accessed January 19, 2022, http://www.fordham.edu/halsall/source/pop-in-eur.asp.

80   "In the age of . . . fast-circulating visualization technologies, the mystical overtones of global icons and the semi-religious cult and following they evoke have become permanent features of our culture." Braidotti, "Postsecular Turn," 12.

81   *Akathistos Hymn* H 5, cited in Peltomaa, *Akathistos Hymn*, 9. "Hail" is an inadequate translation of the Greek χαῖρε, which is still used as a formal greeting in modern Greek. The original, and continuing, sense is "honor," not "worship."

Appendix

1   Ephraim and Basil at Bethlehem preceded him, who signed their work in the mosaics of 1169 at Bethlehem. Lucy-Anne Hunt, "Art and Colonialism: The Mosaics of the Church of the Nativity in Bethlehem (1169) and the Problem of 'Crusader' Art," *Dumbarton Oaks Papers* 45 (1991): 73–74. There is also Theodore the Scribe, who made the eleventh-century Theodore Psalter. Charles Barber, ed., *Theodore Psalter: Electronic Facsimile* (Urbana: University of Illinois Press, 2000). There are also names in the Menologion of Basil II (ca. 1000) who could refer to artists and miniaturists. But as far as monumental painting goes, Theodore Apsevdis is the first on record that I am aware of in the Byzantine world.

2   The French scholar Adolphe Napoléon Didron (1806–67) obtained Dionysios's "Painter's Manual" and translated it into French. Didron, *Manuel d'Iconographie Chrétienne, Greque et Latine, avec une introduction et des notes* (Paris: Imprimerie Royale, 1845). Didron wasted no time in declaring Manuel Panselinos to be "le Raphael ou plutôt le Giotto de l'école byzantine" (7). For a recent study of Dionysios's manual, see G. Kakavas, *Dionysios of Fourna: Artistic Creation and Literary Description* (Leiden: Alexandros, 2008).

3 Mango and Hawkins, "Hermitage of St. Neophytos," 183.

4 For an overview of the opinions, see Ćurčić, "Architecture of Panagia Araki-otissa," 38n66.

5 Winfield and Winfield, *Panagia tou Arakos*, 319, 320.

6 Winfield and Winfield, 320.

7 Nicolaïdès considers the handwriting comparisons inconclusive. Andréas Nicolaïdès, "L'église de la Panagia Arakiotissa à Lagoudéra, Chypre: Etude iconographique des fresques de 1192," *Dumbarton Oaks Papers* 50 (1996): 136–37. Having compared the handwriting of both monuments, I find the similarities overwhelming. The kappa is the same; the lambda is the same (with a lower left leg). The encircled alphas are exactly the same. The upsilon arms share an upper terminal line. Nicolaïdès claims that the crosspiece of the chi is very high at the Enkleistra, while the chi crosspiece is low at Lagoudera, but the example he refers to seems to be because a finger of a saint holding the scroll at the Enkleistra is threatening to obscure the letter, so the artist pushed the crosspiece down, rendering this particular discrepancy less significant. Nicolaïdès claims, "The left leg of [the Enkleis-tra painter's] delta starts high enough, thus forming an isosceles triangle, and differs significantly from that of the delta or lambda by the artist from 1192 from the Panagia Arakiotissa" (8–9). Yet there are other deltas and lambdas in both monuments that, in my view, appear to match quite well. Panayotidi, unlike Nicolaïdès, claims that the lettering shows no substantial difference. Maria Panayotidi, "The Question of the Role of the Donor and of the Painter: A Rudimentary Approach," *Deltion* 17 (1994): 148, 371.

8 Konstantinidi, "Byzantine Painting," 49–88.

9 Konstantinidi, 84.

10 Konstantinidi, 65.

11 Konstantinidi, 65, 84.

12 The possibility that the inscription would be placed later, after Authentes died, is made less likely by the fact that the burial inscription, bearing the "same form and quality as those of the church's frescoes," was most likely made in 1192 along with the completion of the frescoes. Konstantinidi, 65.

13 Ćurčić suggests the inscription "may have addressed his appeal to his friend Lord Leon, to intercede on his behalf." Ćurčić, "Architecture of Panagia Arakiotissa," 44. This seems more fitting with the humble place of the inscription.

14 "The first *iguman* (*hegumenos*) of Studenica, Dionisije, who was appointed to the post by Stefan Nemanja in 1197, was buried against the outside wall of the church at the time of his death (date unknown), side-by-side with the interior tomb of the monastic founder, Stefan Nemanja. The position of his tomb is marked by an inscription incised into the marble façade just above the foundation of the church." Ćurčić, 44. Konstantinidi rightly

indicates that this same arrangement might apply to Leon and his father, (the) Authentes, as well. Konstantinidi, "Byzantine Painting," 65. But especially if the artist Theodore Apsevdis had become a monk, this arrangement would not be impossible for Leon (the inner tomb) and Apsevdis (the outer tomb). Nonetheless, who lies in the tombs is of less of concern to me than the name of the artist himself, which I believe to be Theodore Apsevdis.

15 Konstantinidi, "Byzantine Painting," 84.

16 Mango and Hawkins, "Hermitage of St. Neophytos," 206.

17 The Byzantine painter Michael Astrapas developed and adapted his style as well, conforming to a classicizing style when required. Konstantinos M. Vapheiades, "The Wall-Paintings of the Protaton Church Revisited," *Zograf* 43 (2019): 125. According to Vapheiades, his early style does not include the Church of the Peribleptos at Ohrid, with which the artist is often identified. This belongs, rather, to his father, Euthymios.

18 Ćurčić, "Architecture of Panagia Arakiotissa," 38. Interestingly enough, these positions can inhabit the same volume. The new position represented by Konstantinidi (3) is bookended in the same volume by Ćurčić and Papageorghiou, who both represent the traditional position (1). Papageorghiou, Bakirtzis, and Hadjichristodoulou, *Panagia tou Arakos*.

19 Hadjichristodoulou, while citing both the traditional and newer positions regarding Theodore Apsevdis, nevertheless claims that "Apseudes seems also to have painted the icons at Enkleistra and the church of the Panagia tou Arakos, as shared stylistic details between the murals and these icons demonstrate." Christodoulos A. Hadjichristodoulou, "The Iconostasis, the Portable Icons and the Wall Paintings of the 17th Century," in Papageorghiou, Bakirtzis, and Hadjichristodoulou, *Panagia tou Arakos*, 106.

20 Maria Panayotidi also finds the evidence sufficient to claim Apsevdis painted both churches, Lagoudera representing "a more mature phase" of his artistic development. Panayotidi, "Question of the Role," 371. Castiñeiras even points to Master Alexander, a Catalan painter who was likely "from Cyprus, and quite possibly raised in . . . the orbit of the workship of Theodore Apseudes." Manuel Castiñeiras, "Catalan Panel Painting around 1200: The Eastern Mediterranean and Byzantium," in *Romanesque and the Mediterranean*, ed. Rosa Bacile and John McNeill (Leeds: Routledge, 2016), 314.

21 Mango and Hawkins, "Hermitage of St. Neophytos," 206.

22 Winfield and Winfield, *Panagia tou Arakos*, 319–20.

23 Konstantinidi, "Byzantine Painting," 49–88.

24 Konstantinidi, 65.

25 Konstantinidi, 81; Winfield and Winfield, *Panagia tou Arakos*, 317.

26 Winfield and Winfield, *Panagia tou Arakos*, 322; 325. Konstantinidi, "Byzantine Painting," 85.

27 See Matthew J. Milliner, "Man or Metaphor? Manuel Panselinos and the Protaton Frescoes," in *Approaches to Byzantine Architecture and Its Decoration: Studies in Honor of Slobodan Ćurčić*, ed. Mark J. Johnson, Robert Ousterhout, and Amy Papalexandrou (Burlington, VT: Ashgate, 2011), 221–38.

28 Milliner, 226. This naming has been instructive and can be understood allegorically, Manuel being "God with us" and Panselinos "full moon," meaning the artist who—like the moon reflecting the sun—fully reflects the light of the heavenly saints. The name Theodore Apsevdis, *Apsevdis* meaning "truthful" or "he who does not lie," achieves the same instructive effect that Dionysios of Fourna achieved in using the name Manuel Panselinos, albeit on much firmer footing.

29 Vapheiades, "Wall-Paintings," 113–28. Letters were found during the restoration that can make the name of "Eutychios," one of the two painters who painted the Peribleptos Church in Ohrid, corresponding to Michael signing his name "Michael son of Eutychios" (Vapheiades, 115). According to Vapheiades, Astrapas worked on the Protaton along with the unnamed painter of the chapel of Saint Euthymios in Thessaloniki between 1309 and 1311. For the complex issue of Michael Astrapas's signature on other churches, see Miodrag Marković, "Michael's and Eutychios's Artistic Work: Present Knowledge, Dubious Issues and Direction of Future Research," *Zbornik Narodnog Muzeja* 17, no. 2 (2004): 95–117 (in Serbian with an English summary). I thank Jelena Bogdanovic for this reference.

30 "How shall we get beyond the 'circle of hermeneutics'? By transforming it into a *wager*." Paul Ricouer, *The Symbolism of Evil*, trans. Emerson Buchanan (Boston: Beacon, 1967), 355. See also Cynthia Bourgeault, *Love Is Stronger Than Death* (Rhinebeck, NY: Monkfish, 1997), 149.

BIBLIOGRAPHY

Acheimastou-Potamianou, Myrtali. *Greek Art: Byzantine Wall Paintings.* Athens: Ekdotike Athenon, 1994.

Agamben, Giorgio. *The Kingdom and the Glory: For a Theological Genealogy of Economy and Government.* Translated by Lorenzo Chiesa. Stanford, CA: Stanford University Press, 2011.

———. *Means without End: Notes on Politics.* Translated by Vincenzo Binetti and Cesare Casarino. Minneapolis: University of Minnesota Press, 2000.

Alexiou, Margaret. *The Ritual Lament in Greek Tradition.* 2nd ed. Revised by Dimitrios Yatromanolakis and Panagiotis Roilos. Lanham, MD: Rowman & Littlefield, 2002.

Allen, Pauline. "Portrayals of Mary in Greek Homiletic Literature (6th–7th Centuries)." In *The Cult of the Mother of God in Byzantium: Texts and Images,* edited by Leslie Brubaker and Mary B. Cunningham. Burlington, VT: Ashgate, 2011.

Amadi, Francesco. *Chroniques d'Amadi et de Strambaldi.* Paris: Imprimerie Nationale, 1891.

Amis, Robin. *A Different Christianity.* Chicago: Praxis Institute Press, 2016.

Anatolios, Khaled. *Retrieving Nicaea: The Development and Meaning of Trinitarian Doctrine.* Grand Rapids, MI: Baker Academic, 2011.

Angelou, Athanasios. "Nicholas of Methone: The Life and Works of a Twelfth-Century Bishop." In *Byzantium and the Classical Tradition,* edited by Margaret Mullett and Roger Scott. Birmingham, UK: Centre for Byzantine Studies, 1981.

Aquinas, Thomas. "Commentary on Boethius's *De Trinitate.*" In *The Trinity and the Unicity of the Intellect,* translated by Rose Emmanuella Brennan. Eugene, OR: Wipf & Stock, 2009.

Arentzen, Thomas. *Virginity Recast: Romanos and the Mother of God.* Lund, Sweden: Lund University Press, 2014.

Asbridge, Thomas. *The Crusades: The Authoritative History of the War for the Holy Land.* New York: HarperCollins, 2011.

Athanasius. *Orations against the Arians.* Translated by Khaled Anatolios. London: Routledge, 2004.

Bakirtzis, Nikolas. "Locating Byzantine Spatial Considerations and Strategies in Rural Landscape." In *Experiencing Byzantium*, edited by Claire Nesbitt and Mark Jackson. London: Routledge, 2020.

———. "Revising the Monastic Legacy of Saint Sozomenos near Potamia." In *The Art and Archaeology of Lusignan and Venetian Cyprus (1192–1571)*, edited by Michalis Olympios and Maria Parani. Turnhout: Brepols, 2019.

Baltoyianni, Chrysanthe. *Icons: The Mother of God in the Incarnation and the Passion*. Athens: Adams Editions, 1994.

Bantu, Vince. *A Multitude of Peoples: Engaging Ancient Christianity's Global Identity*. Downers Grove, IL: InterVarsity, 2020.

Barber, Charles, ed. *Theodore Psalter: Electronic Facsimile*. Urbana: University of Illinois Press, 2000.

Barber, Malcolm. *The New Knighthood: A History of the Order of the Temple*. Cambridge: Cambridge University Press, 1994.

Barker, Margaret. *The Mother of the Lord*. Vol. 1, *The Lady in the Temple*. London: T&T Clark, 2012.

Barth, Karl. *Church Dogmatics*. Vol. 2, pt. 2. Edinburgh: T&T Clark, 1957.

———. *Church Dogmatics*. Vol. 4, pt. 1. Edinburgh: T&T Clark, 1956.

Baun, Jane. "Apocalyptic Panagia: Some Byways of Marian Revelation in Byzantium." In *The Cult of the Mother of God in Byzantium: Texts and Images*, edited by Leslie Brubaker and Mary B. Cunningham. Burlington, VT: Ashgate, 2011.

———. "Discussing Mary's Humanity in Medieval Byzantium." In *The Church and Mary*, edited by R. N. Swanson. Woodbridge, UK: Boydell, 2004.

Baxandall, Michael. *Painting and Experience in Fifteenth-Century Italy: A Primer in the Social History of Pictorial Cycle*. 2nd ed. Oxford: Oxford University Press, 1988.

Beattie, Tina. *God's Mother, Eve's Advocate: A Gynocentric Refiguration of Marian Symbolism in Engagement with Luce Irigaray*. London: Continuum, 2002.

———. *The New Catholic Feminism*. London: Routledge, 2006.

———. *Theology after Postmodernity*. Oxford: Oxford University Press, 2013.

Beck, Hans-Georg. *Kirche und Theologische Literatur im Byzantinishcen Reich*. Munich: C. H. Beck, 1959.

Becker, Kenneth. *Unlikely Companions: Carl Gustav Jung and Ignatius Loyola*. Leominster, UK: Gracewing, 2002.

Behmen [Boehme], Jacob. *The Works of Jacob Behmen: The Teutonic Theosopher*. Vol. 1. Edited by William Law. London: M. Richardson, 1764.

Behr-Sigel, Elisabeth, and Kallistos Ware. *The Ordination of Women in the Orthodox Church*. Geneva: World Council of Churches, 2000.

Behr, John. *Formation of Christian Theology*. Vol. 2, *The Nicene Faith: Part I*. Crestwood, NY: St. Vladimir's Seminary Press, 2004.

———. *The Mystery of Christ: Life in Death*. Crestwood, NY: St. Vladimir's Seminary Press, 2006.

Belting, Hans. *The Image and Its Public in the Middle Ages: Form and Function of Early Paintings of the Passion*. New Rochelle, NY: Aristide D. Caratzas, 1990.

———. *Likeness and Presence: A History of the Image before the Era of Art*. Translated by Edmund Jephcott. Chicago: University of Chicago Press, 1994.

———. Review of "Byzantine Art and the West" by Otto Demus. *Art Bulletin* 54, no. 4 (December 1, 1972).

Bernard of Clairvaux. *In Praise of the New Knighthood: A Treatise on the Knights Templar and the Holy Places of Jerusalem*. Translated by M. Conrad Greenia OCSO. Trappist, KY: Cistercian, 2000.

Bird, Jessalynn, Edward Peters, and James M. Powell, eds. *Crusade and Christendom: Annotated Documents in Translation from Innocent III to the Fall of Acre, 1187–1291*. Philadelphia: University of Pennsylvania Press, 2013.

Blackman, Ann. "Moscow's Big Mak Attack." *Time*, February 5, 1990. http://content.time.com/time/subscriber/article/0,33009,969321,00.html.

Bloom, Anthony. Preface to *The Ministry of Women in the Church*. Redondo Beach, CA: Oakwood, 1991.

Boehme, Jacob. *The Election of Grace*. Edited by William Law, 1621. https://archive.org/details/Jacob_Boehme_Election_of_Grace-Electronic_Text.

The Book of Common Prayer. New York: Church Hymnal Corporation, 1979.

Booth, Phil. *Crisis of Empire: Doctrine and Dissent at the End of Late Antiquity*. Berkeley: University of California Press, 2013.

Borboudakis, Manolis, ed. *Icons of the Cretan School (from Candia to Moscow to St. Petersburg)*. Pergomos, Turkey: Adams Editions, 1993.

Boss, Sarah Jane, ed. *Mary: The Complete Resource.* Oxford: Oxford University Press, 2007.

———. *Virgin in Mary: New Century Theology.* New York: Continuum, 2004.

Bourgeault, Cynthia. *The Heart of Centering Prayer: Nondual Christianity in Theory and Practice.* Boulder, CO: Shambala, 2016.

———. "Why Feminizing the Trinity Won't Work." In *The Holy Trinity and the Law of Three.* Boulder, CO: Shambala, 2014.

———. *Love Is Stronger Than Death.* Rhinebeck, NY: Monkfish, 1997.

Bouyer, Louis. *The Seat of Wisdom: An Essay on the Place of the Virgin Mary in Christian Theology.* Chicago: Pantheon, 1962.

Braaten, Carl E., and Robert W. Jenson, eds. *Jews and Christians: People of God.* Grand Rapids, MI: Eerdmans, 2003.

Braidotti, Rosi. "In Spite of the Times: The Postsecular Turn in Feminism." *Theory, Culture & Society* 25, no. 6 (2008).

Breidenthal, Magdalene. "Leaving 'Heaven on Earth': The Visual Codes of Middle Byzantine Church Exit." PhD diss., Yale University, 2019.

Brinker, Jennifer. "Catholic Racial Justice Collaborative Calls for Prayer, Action to End Racism at Prayer Vigil at Rock Church." *St. Louis Review,* July 9, 2020. https://www.archstl.org/catholic -racial-justice-collaborative-calls-for-prayer-action-to-end-racism -at-prayer-vigil-at-rock-church-5480.

Brock, Sebastian. *Fire from Heaven: Studies in Syriac Theology and Liturgy.* Aldershot, UK: Ashgate, 2006.

Brown, Peter. *Augustine of Hippo.* Berkeley: University of California Press, 1975.

———. *The Body and Society.* New York: Columbia University Press, 1988.

Brubaker, Leslie, and John Haldon. *Byzantium in the Iconoclast Era, c. 680–850: A History.* Cambridge: Cambridge University Press, 2011.

Brundage, James A. *The Crusades: A Documentary Survey.* Milwaukee: Marquette University Press, 1962.

Bulgakov, Sergius. *Bride of the Lamb.* Translated by Boris Jakim. Grand Rapids, MI: Eerdmann's, 2001.

———. *Eucharistic Sacrifice.* Translated by Mark Roosien. South Bend, IN: University of Notre Dame Press, 2021.

———. *The Lamb of God.* Translated by Boris Jakim. Grand Rapids, MI: Eerdmans, 2008.

———. *The Orthodox Church*. Crestwood, NY: St. Vladimir's Seminary Press, 1997.

———. *Sophia: The Wisdom of God; An Outline of Sophiology*. Hudson, NY: Lindisfarne, 1993.

Bunge, Gabriel. *The Rublev Trinity: The Icon of the Trinity by the Monk-Painter Andrei Rublev*. Crestwood, NY: St. Vladimir's Seminary Press, 2007.

Bunson, Matthew. "Father Stanley Rother." National Catholic Register, September 18, 2017. https://www.ncregister.com/interview/father-stanley-rother-the-shepherd-cannot-run-at-the-first-sign-of-danger.

Buschi, P. P. D'Orazio e. *La Madonna del Perpetuo Soccorso: Storia della Sacra Immagine e del Suo Culto Nel Mondo*. Verona: Ghindini e Fiorini, 1953.

Buswell, Robert E., Jr., and Donald Lopez Jr. *The Princeton Dictionary of Buddhism*. Princeton, NJ: Princeton University Press, 2013.

Byzantine Museum of Kastoria: The Re-exhibition. Kastoria, Greece: Ministry of Culture and Sports Ephorate of Antiquities of Kastoria, 2017.

Cameron, Averil. "Enforcing Orthodoxy in Byzantium." *Studies in Church History* 43 (2007).

———. "Introduction: The Mother of God in Byzantium: Relics, Icons, Texts." In *The Cult of the Mother of God in Byzantium: Texts and Images*, edited by Leslie Brubaker and Mary B. Cunningham. Burlington, VT: Ashgate, 2011.

Camille, Michael. *Image on the Edge: The Margins of Medieval Art*. London: Reaktion, 1992.

Carr, Annemarie Weyl. *Asinou across Time: Studies in the Architecture and Murals of the Panagia Phorbiotissa, Cyprus*. Dumbarton Oaks Studies 43. Washington, DC: Dumbarton Oaks, 2013.

———. "Iconography and Identity: Syrian Elements in the Art of Crusader Cyprus." In *Religious Origins of Nations? The Christian Communities of the Middle East*, edited by Bas Ter Haar Romeny. Leiden: Brill, 2010.

———. "The Presentation of an Icon at Mount Sinai." *Deltion* 17 (1994).

———. "Thoughts on the Economy of the Image of Mary." *Theology Today* 56, no. 3 (October 1999).

———. "Threads of Authority: The Virgin Mary's Veil in the Middle Ages." In *Robes and Honor: The Medieval World of Investiture*, edited by Stewart Gordon. New York: Palgrave, 2001.

———. "The 'Virgin Veiled by God': The Presentation of an Icon on Cyprus." In *Reading Medieval Images: The Art Historian and the Object*, edited by Elizabeth Sears and Thelma K. Thomas. Ann Arbor: University of Michigan Press, 2002.

Castiñeiras, Manuel. "Catalan Panel Painting around 1200: The Eastern Mediterranean and Byzantium." In *Romanesque and the Mediterranean*, edited by Rosa Bacile and John McNeill. Leeds: Routledge, 2016.

Cattapan, Mario. "I Pittori Andrea e Nicola Rizo da Candia." In *Thesaurismata: Bollettino Dell'Istituto Ellenico di Studi Bizantini e Postbizantini*. Vol. 10. Venice: Instituto Ellenico Di Studi Bizzantine e Postbizantini, 1973.

Cavanaugh, William. *The Myth of Religious Violence: Secular Ideology and the Roots of Modern Conflict.* Oxford: Oxford University Press, 2009.

Chatzidakis, Manolis. *Études sur la peinture postbyzantine.* London: Variorum Reprints, 1976.

———. *Icônes de Saint-Georges des Grecs et de la Collection de l'Institut Hellénique de Venise.* Rev. ed. Vicenza: Neri Pozza, 1975.

Chatzidakis, Nano. *Venetiae Quasi Alterum Byzantium: From Candia to Venice: Greek Icons in Italy 15th–16th Centuries.* Exhibition catalog. Correr Museum, Venice. Athens: Hidryma Hellēnikou Politismou, 1993.

Chesterton, G. K. *Orthodoxy.* New York: Doubleday, 1959.

Chicago, Judy. *The Dinner Party.* London: Merrell, 2007.

Christ, Carol. *Odyssey with the Goddess: A Spiritual Quest in Crete.* New York: Continuum, 1995.

———. *A Serpentine Path: Mysteries of the Goddess.* Cleveland, OH: FAR Press, 2016.

———. "Why Women, Men and Other Living Things Still Need the Goddess: Remembering and Reflecting 35 Years Later." *Feminist Theology* 20, no. 3 (2012).

Chün-fang, Yü. *Kuan-Yin: The Chinese Transformation of Avalokitesvara.* New York: Columbia University Press, 2001.

Churchill, Winston. *A History of the English-Speaking Peoples.* Vol. 1. New York: Dorset, 1956.

Clark, Anne L. "The Priesthood of the Virgin Mary: Gender Trouble in the Twelfth Century." *Journal of Feminist Studies in Religion* 18, no. 1 (Spring 2002).

Clarke, F. Stuart. "Lost and Found: Athanasius' Doctrine of Predestination." *Scottish Journal of Theology* 29, no. 5 (October 1976).

Clarke, Jeremy. *The Virgin Mary and Catholic Identities in Chinese History*. Hong Kong: Hong Kong University Press, 2013.

Climacus, John. *The Ladder of Divine Ascent*. Translated by Colm Luibheid and Norman Russell. Mahwah, NJ: Paulist, 1982.

Clooney, Francis X. *Divine Mother, Blessed Mother: Hindu Goddesses and the Virgin Mary*. Oxford: Oxford University Press, 2005.

Coakley, Sarah. "'Femininity' and the Holy Spirit?" In *Mirror to the Church: Reflections on Sexism*, edited by Monica Furlong. London: SPCK, 1988.

———. *God, Sexuality, and the Self: An Essay "On the Trinity."* Cambridge: Cambridge University Press, 2013.

———. *The New Asceticism*. London: Bloomsbury Continuum, 2015.

———. *Power and Submissions*. Oxford: Blackwell, 2002.

Cohick, Lynn. *Women in the World of the Earliest Christians*. Grand Rapids, MI: Baker Academic, 2009.

Cohick, Lynn, and Amy Brown Hughes. *Christian Women in the Patristic World: Their Influence, Authority, and Legacy in the Second through Fifth Centuries*. Grand Rapids, MI: Baker Academic, 2017.

Collingwood, R. G. *The Idea of History*. Oxford: Clarendon, 1993.

Collins, Scott. "London Olympics: NBC Coverage Most-Watched TV Event in U.S. History." *Los Angeles Times*, August 13, 2012. https://www.latimes.com/entertainment/tv/la-xpm-2012-aug-13-la-et-st-london-olympics-dubbed-mostwatched-event-in-us-history-by-nbc-20120813-story.html.

Connell, Francis J. *Our Lady of Perpetual Help*. 1940. Reprint, Fitzwilliam, NH: Loreto, 2006.

Constas, Nicholas P. "Weaving the Body of God: Proclus of Constantinople, the Theotokos, and the Loom of the Flesh." *Journal of Early Christian Studies* 3, no. 2 (Summer 1995).

Cormack, Robin. *Painting the Soul: Icons, Death Masks and Shrouds*. London: Reaktion, 1997.

———. *Writing in Gold: Byzantine Society and Its Icons*. London: George Philip, 1985.

Cselényi, István. *The Maternal Face of God? Explorations in Catholic Sophiology*. Kettering, OH: Angelico, 2017.

Cunningham, Mary B. *The Virgin Mary in Byzantium, c.400–1000*. Cambridge: Cambridge University Press, 2021.

Ćurčić, Slobodan. "Architecture of Panagia Arakiotissa, Lagoudera." In *The Church of Panagia tou Arakos*, edited by Athanasios Papageorghiou, Charalambos Bakirtzis, and Christodoulos Hadjichristodoulou. Nicosia: Leventis Foundation and Bank of Cyprus Cultural Foundation, 2018.

Daley, Brian. *On the Dormition of Mary*. Crestwood, NY: St. Vladimir's Seminary Press, 1998.

Dante. *Paradiso*. Translated by Robert Hollander and Jean Hollander. New York: Anchor, 2008.

Dawkins, R. M. *The Monks of Athos*. London: George Allen & Unwin, 1936.

Dechow, Jon F. Review of *Epiphanius of Cyprus: A Culture Biography of Late Antiquity*, by Andrew S. Jacobs and *Epiphanius of Cyprus: Imagining an Orthodox World*, by Richard Kim, *Catholic Historical Review* 104, no. 3 (Summer 2018).

Demacopoulos, George E. *Colonizing Christianity: Greek and Latin Religious Identity in the Era of the Fourth Crusade*. New York: Fordham University Press, 2019.

de Troyes, Chrétien. *Perceval; or, The Story of the Grail*. Translated by Ruth Harwood Cline. Athens: University of Georgia Press, 1985.

Dever, William G. *Did God Have a Wife? Archaeology and Folk Religion in Ancient Israel*. Grand Rapids, MI: Eerdmans, 2005.

DeYoung, Rebecca Konydyk. *Vainglory: The Forgotten Vice*. Grand Rapids, MI: Eerdmans, 2014.

Didron, Adolphe Napoléon. *Manuel d'Iconographie Chrétienne, Greque et Latine, avec une introduction et des notes*. Paris: Imprimerie Royale, 1845.

DiLuzio, Meghan. *A Place at the Altar: Priestesses in Republican Rome*. Princeton, NJ: Princeton University Press, 2016.

Dimitrova, Elizabeta. *The Church of Saint Demetrius (King Marko's Monastery) at Sushika*. Skopje, North Macedonia: Calamus, 2020.

Douthat, Ross. *The Decadent Society: How We Became the Victims of Our Own Success*. New York: Simon & Schuster, 2020.

Drandaki, Anastasia. "Between Byzantium and Venice: Icon Painting in Venetian Crete in the Fifteenth and Sixteenth Centuries." In *The Origins of El Greco: Icon Painting in Venetian Crete*, edited by Anastasia Drandaki. New York: Alexander S. Onassis Public Benefit Foundation, 2009.

———. "Greek Religious Painting after the Fall of Constantinople: Tradition and Renewal." In *From Byzantium to Modern Greece: Hellenic Art in Adversity: 1453–1830*. New York: Alexander S. Onassis Public Benefit Foundation, 2005.

Edbury, Peter W. *The Kingdom of Cyprus and the Crusades, 1191–1374*. Cambridge: Cambridge University Press, 1991.

Edinger, Edward F. *Ego and Archetype*. Boulder, CO: Shambala, 1992.

Edwards, Mark James. *Christ Is Time*. Eugene, OR: Cascade, 2022.

Eller, Cynthia. *Gentlemen and Amazons: The Myth of Matriarchal Prehistory, 1861–1900*. Berkeley: University of California Press, 2011.

Elsner, Jaś. "Iconoclasm as Discourse: From Antiquity to Byzantium." *Art Bulletin* 94, no. 3 (2012).

Elytis, Odysseus. *Axion Esti*. Translated by Edmund Keely and George Savidis. Pittsburgh, PA: University of Pittsburgh Press, 1974.

Engelsman, Joan Chamberlain. *Feminine Dimensions of the Divine*. Asheville, NC: Chiron, 1994.

Ephraim the Athenian. *A Narrative of the Founding of the Holy Monastery of Kykkos and the History of the Miraculous Icon of the Mother of God*. Translated by Andreas Jakovljevic. Nicosia: Research Centre of Kykkos Monastery, 1996.

Epiphanius of Salamis. *The Panarion of Epiphanius of Salamis, Books II and III. De Fide*. 2nd ed. Translated by Frank Williams. Leiden: Brill, 2013.

Erasmus. *Collected Works of Erasmus*. Vol. 27. Translated by A. H. T. Levi. Toronto: University of Toronto Press, 1974.

Erbele-Küster, Dorothea. *Body, Gender and Purity in Leviticus 12 and 15*. London: Bloomsbury T&T Clark, 2017.

Esbroeck, Michel van, trans. *Maxime Le Confesseur: Vie de la Vierge*. Corpus Scriptorum Christianorum Orientalium. Louvain, Belgium: In Aedibus E. Peeters, 1986.

Euripides. *Hippolytus*. Translated by Gilbert Murray. Harvard Classics 8. New York: P. F. Collier & Son, 1909.

Evagrius of Pontus. "Dreams of Vainglory and Sadness." In *The Greek Ascetic Corpus*, translated by Robert E. Sinkewicz. Oxford: Oxford University Press, 2003.

———. *The Praktikos & Chapters on Prayer*. Translated by John Bamberger. Kalamazoo, MI: Cistercian, 1981.

Evangelatou, Maria. "Krater of Nectar and Altar of the Bread of Life." In *The Reception of the Virgin in Byzantium: Marian Narratives in*

Texts and Images, edited by Thomas Arentzen and Mary B. Cunningham. Cambridge: Cambridge University Press, 2019.

———. "The Symbolism of the Censer in Byzantine Representations of the Dormition of the Virgin." In *Images of the Mother of God: Perception of the Theotokos in Byzantium*, edited by Maria Vassilaki. Aldershot, UK: Ashgate, 2005.

Evans, Helen C. *Byzantium: Faith and Power*. New Haven, CT: Yale University Press, 2004.

Felmy, Karl Christian. "The Development of the Trinity Doctrine in Byzantium (Ninth to Fifteenth Centuries)." In *The Oxford Handbook of the Trinity*, edited by Gilles Emery and Matthew Levering. Oxford: Oxford University Press, 2011.

Fenwick, Kenneth, ed. *The Third Crusade: An Eye-Witness Account of the Campaigns of Richard Coeur-de-Lion in Cyprus and the Holy Land*. London: Folio Society, 1958.

Ferrero, Fabriciano. "Nuestra Señora del Perpetuo Socorro: Informacion Bibliografica y Cronologia General." *Spicilegium Historicum Congregationis SSmi Redemptoris* 38, no. 2 (1990).

———. *Nuestra señora del Perpetuo Socorro: Proceso histórico de una devoción Mariana*. Madrid: Editorial el Perpetuo Socorro, 1966.

———. *Santa Maria del Perpetuo Socorro: Un icono de la Santa Madre de Dios "Virgen de La Passion" con el Presagio gloriosa Cristo*. Madrid: Editorial el Perpetuo Socorro, 1994.

———. *The Story of an Icon*. Translated by Michael McGreevy. Cambridge: Redemptorist, 2001.

Fiene, Donald M. "What Is the Appearance of Divine Sophia?" *Slavic Review* 48, no. 3 (Autumn 1989).

Fiorenza, Elizabeth Schüssler. *Jesus: Miriam's Child, Sophia's Prophet*. 2nd ed. London: Bloomsbury T&T Clark, 2015.

Fleming, K. E. "Constantinople: From Christianity to Islam." *Classical World* 97, no. 1 (Autumn 2003).

Florensky, Pavel. *Iconostasis*. Translated by Donald Sheehan and Olga Andrejev. Crestwood, NY: Saint Vladimir's Seminary Press, 2000.

———. *The Pillar and Ground of the Truth*. Translated by Boris Jakim. Princeton, NJ: Princeton University Press, 1997.

Folda, Jaroslav. "The Use of Çintamani as Ornament: A Case Study in the Afterlife of Forms." In *Byzantine Images and Their Afterlives*, edited by Lynn Jones. London: Routledge, 2016.

Fornari, Giuseppe. *Dionysus, Christ, and the Death of God*. 2 vols. East Lansing: Michigan State University Press, 2021.

Foucault, Michel. *The History of Sexuality: An Introduction*. Vol. 1. Translated by Robert Hurley. London: Penguin, 1990.

Freedberg, David. *The Power of Images: Studies in the History and Theory of Response*. Chicago: University of Chicago Press, 1991.

Friedman, John Block. *The Monstrous Races in Medieval Art and Thought*. Syracuse, NY: Syracuse University Press, 2000.

Frymer-Kensky, Tikva. *In the Wake of the Goddesses: Women, Culture, and the Biblical Transformation of Pagan Myth*. New York: Free Press, 1992.

Galatariotou, Catia. *The Making of a Saint: The Life, Times and Sanctification of Neophytos the Recluse*. Cambridge: Cambridge University Press, 1991.

Gallant, Sarah Marie. "Imagination, Empowerment, and Imaginary Figures." In *Feminist Spirituality: The Next Generation*, edited by Chris Klassen. Washington, DC: Lexington, 2009.

Gautier, Théophile. *Constantinople of Today*. Translated by Robert Howe Gould. London: David Bogue, 86 Fleet Street, 1854.

Gaventa, Beverly Roberts. *Mary: Glimpses of the Mother of Jesus*. Columbia: University of South Carolina Press, 1999.

Gavrilović, Zaga. "The Portrait of King Marko at Markov Manastir (1376–1381)." In *Studies in Byzantine and Serbian Medieval Art*. London: Pindar, 2001.

Gavrilyuk, Paul. *Georges Florovsky and the Russian Religious Renaissance*. Oxford: Oxford University Press, 2014.

Constas, Maximos. *And a Sword Shall Pierce Your Own Soul (Lk 2:35): The Kenosis of Christ and the Mother of God in Orthodox Iconography*. Allston, MA: Holy Resurrection Orthodox Church, 2013.

George-Tvrtković, Rita. *Christians, Muslims and Mary: A History*. Mahwah, NJ: Paulist, 2018.

Georgopolou, Maria. *Venice's Mediterranean Colonies: Architecture and Urbanism*. New York: Cambridge University Press, 2001.

Gerhold, Victoria. "Defeating Solomon: Intertextuality and Symbolism in the Legend of Hagia Sophia." *Scripta Mediaevalia* 11, no. 1 (2018).

Gerstel, Sharon. *Beholding the Sacred Mysteries: Programs of the Byzantine Sanctuary*. Seattle: University of Washington Press, 1999.

Gilmour-Bryson, A. *The Trial of the Templars in Cyprus*. Leiden: Brill, 1998.

Goodison, Lucy, and Christine Morris. "Beyond the 'Great Mother': The Sacred World of the Minoans." In *Ancient Goddesses: The Myths and the Evidence*. London: British Museum Press, 1998.

Gouma-Peterson, Thalia. "Crete, Venice, the 'Madonneri,' and a Creto-Venetian Icon in the Allen Art Museum." Bulletin 25. Oberlin, OH: Allen Memorial Art Museum, Winter 1968.

Graef, Hilda. *Mary: A History of Doctrine and Devotion*. South Bend, IN: Ave Maria, 2009.

Greek Orthodox Archdiocese of Thyateira and Great Britain. *The Divine Liturgy of Our Father among the Saints John Chrysostom*. Oxford: Oxford University Press, 1995.

Greenfield, Douglas, ed. *Alter Icons: The Russian Icon and Modernity*. University Park: Penn State University Press, 2010.

Gregg, R. C., and D. E. Groh. *Early Arianism: A View of Salvation*. Philadelphia: Fortress, 1981.

Gregory of Nazianzus. "Oration 29." In *Nicene and Post-Nicene Fathers*, vol. 7, edited by Phillip Schaff. New York: Cosimo, 2007.

Gress, Carrie. *The Marian Option*. Charlotte, NC: Tan Books, 2017.

Haldon, John. *Byzantium in the Seventh Century: The Transformation of a Culture*. Cambridge: Cambridge University Press, 1997.

————. *The Empire That Would Not Die: The Paradox of Eastern Roman Survival, 640–74*. Cambridge, MA: Harvard University Press, 2016.

Hales, E. E. Y. *Pio Nono*. Garden City, NY: Image, 1954.

Halsall, Paul. "Medieval Sourcebook: Tables on Population in Medieval Europe." Fordham University. Accessed January 19, 2022. http://www.fordham.edu/halsall/source/pop-in-eur.asp.

Hanson, R. P. C. *The Search for the Christian Doctrine of God: The Arian Controversy, 318–381*. London: T&T Clark, 1988.

Harbison, Craig. "Visions and Meditations in Early Flemish Painting." *Simiolus: Netherlands Quarterly for the History of Art* 15, no. 2 (1985).

Hare, Tom. *ReMembering Osiris: Number, Gender, and the Word in Ancient Egyptian Representational Systems*. Stanford, CA: Stanford University Press, 1999.

Harper, Kyle. *From Shame to Sin: The Christian Transformation of Sexual Morality in Late Antiquity*. Cambridge, MA: Harvard University Press, 2016.

Hart, David Bentley. *The Beauty of the Infinite: The Aesthetics of Christian Truth*. Grand Rapids, MI: Eerdmans, 2003.

Hegel, Georg Wilhelm Friedrich. *Vorlesungen über die Philosophie der Religion.* Vol. 3, *Die vollendete Religion.* Edited by Walter Jaschke. Hamburg: Felix Menier Verlag, 1984.

Heller, Joseph. *Catch-22.* New York: Simon & Schuster, 1996.

Hennecke, Edgar. *New Testament Apocrypha.* Vol. 1. Edited by Wilhelm Schneemelcher. Translated by R. McL. Wilson. Philadelphia: Westminster, 1963.

Henze, Clement. *Il culto Mondiale della Madonna del Perpetuo Socorrso: Fuori del suo Santuario Romano.* Brooklyn: Redemptorist Headquarters, 1946.

———. *Mater de Perpetuo Succursu: Prodigiosae Iconis Marialis ita nuncupatae monographia.* Bonn, Germany: Collegium Josephinum, 1926.

Herrin, Judith. *Byzantium: The Surprising Life of a Medieval Empire.* Princeton, NJ: Princeton University Press, 2007.

———. "The Imperial Feminine in Byzantium." *Past and Present* 169, no. 1 (November 2000).

Hetherington, Paul, trans. *The "Painter's Manual" of Dionysios of Foura.* London: Sagittarius, 1981.

"The History of St. Patrick's, Toronto." St. Patrick's Parish, Toronto. Accessed August 9, 2021. https://stpatricksto.archtoronto.org/en/our-community/about-us/.

Holland, Tom. *Dominion.* New York: Basic Books, 2019.

Holmes, Megan. *The Miraculous Image in Renaissance Florence.* New Haven, CT: Yale University Press, 2013.

"Homily 1:1." In *Proclus of Constantinople and the Cult of the Virgin in Late Antiquity: Homilies 1–5, Texts and Translations.* Translated by Nicholas Constas. Leiden: Brill, 2003.

Hopko, Thomas. "Presbyter/Bishop: A Masculine Ministry." In *Women and the Priesthood,* new ed., edited by Thomas Hopko. Crestwood, NY: St. Vladimir's Seminary Press, 1999.

Horton, Michael. *Justification.* Vol. 1, Grand Rapids, MI: Zondervan, 2018.

Hugh of St. Victor. *The Didascalicon of Hugh of St. Victor: A Medieval Guide to the Arts.* Translated by Jerome Taylor. New York: Columbia University Press, 1991.

Hughes, Bettany. *Venus and Aphrodite: A Biography of Desire.* New York: Basic Books, 2020.

Hughes, Dennis. *Human Sacrifice in Ancient Greece,* London: Routledge, 1991.

Hunt, David, and J. N. Coldstream. *Footprints in Cyprus: An Illustrated History*. Revised ed. London: Trigraph, 1990.

Hunt, Lucy-Anne. "Art and Colonialism: The Mosaics of the Church of the Nativity in Bethlehem (1169) and the Problem of 'Crusader' Art." *Dumbarton Oaks Papers* 45 (1991).

Hunt, Sir David, ed. *Footprints in Cyprus: An Illustrated History*. London: Trigraph, 1982.

Hurbanič, Martin. *The Avar Siege of Constantinople in 625: History and Legend*. Cham, Switzerland: Palgrave Macmillan, 2019.

Hutton, Ronald. *The Triumph of the Moon*. Oxford: Oxford University Press, 1999.

Ihnat, Kati. *Mother of Mercy, Bane of the Jews: Devotion to the Virgin Mary in Anglo-Norman England*. Princeton, NJ: Princeton University Press, 2016.

Jacobs, Alan. *Original Sin: A Cultural History*. New York: HarperOne, 2008.

Janin, R. *La Géographie Ecclésiastique de L'Empire Byzantin*. Vol. 3. Paris: Centre National de la Recharche Scientifique, 1969.

Jay, Nancy. *Throughout Your Generations Forever: Sacrifice, Religion, and Paternity*. Chicago: University of Chicago Press, 1992.

Jenkins, Philip. *The Lost History of Christianity*. New York: HarperOne, 2009.

John of Damascus. *Three Treatises on the Divine Images*. Translated by Andrew Louth. Crestwood, NY: St. Vladimir's Seminary Press, 2003.

Johnson, Elizabeth. *She Who Is: The Mystery of God in Feminist Theological Discourse*. New York: Crossroad, 1994.

———. *Truly Our Sister: A Theology of Mary in the Communion of Saints*. New York: Continuum, 2006.

Johnson, Robert. *Femininity Lost and Regained*. New York: HarperCollins, 2011.

———. *Inner Work: Using Dreams and Active Imagination for Personal Growth*. San Francisco: HarperSanFrancisco, 1986.

Johnston, William. *"Arise, My Love . . .": Mysticism for a New Era*. Maryknoll, NY: Orbis, 2002.

———. *Mystical Journey*. Maryknoll, NY: Orbis, 2006.

"Joint Catholic-Orthodox Declaration of His Holiness Pope Paul VI and the Ecumenical Patriarch Athenagoras I." Libreria Editrice Vaticana, December 7, 1965. https://www.vatican.va/content/paul-vi/

en/speeches/1965/documents/hf_p-vi_spe_19651207_common
-declaration.html.

Jones, Dan. *The Templars*. New York: Viking, 2017.

Jones, Serene. *Feminist Theory and Christian Theology*. Minneapolis:
Fortress, 2000.

Joselit, David, Carrie Lambert-Beatty, and Hal Foster, eds. "A Questionnaire on Materialisms." *October* 155, no. 155 (Winter 2016).

Jung, C. G. *Psychology and Religion: West and East, Collected Works*.
Vol. 11. Princeton, NJ: Princeton University Press, 1975.

Kadloubovsky, E., and E. M. Palmer, eds. *The Art of Prayer: An Orthodox Anthology*. London: Faber & Faber, 1966.

Kakavas, G. *Dionysios of Fourna: Artistic Creation and Literary Description*. Leiden: Alexandros, 2008.

Kalavrezou, Ioli. "Images of the Mother." *Dumbarton Oaks Papers* 44
(1990).

Kaldellis, Anthony. *The Christian Parthenon: Classicism and Pilgrimage
in Byzantine Athens*. New York: Cambridge University Press,
2009.

———. *Romanland*. Cambridge, MA: Harvard University Press, 2019.

———. "'A Union of Opposites': The Moral Logic and Corporeal
Presence of the Theotokos on the Field of Battle." In *Pour l'amour
de Byzance: Hommage à Paolo Odorico*, edited by Christian Gastgeber, Charis Messis, Dan Ioan Mureşan, and Filippo Ronconi.
Frankfurt: Peter Lang, 2010.

Kalopissi-Verti, Sophia. "Painters in Late Byzantine Society: The Evidence of Church Inscriptions." *CahArch* 42 (1994).

Kateusz, Ally. "Introduction to Mary as High Priest in Early Christian
Narratives and Iconography." In *Mary, the Apostles, and the Last
Judgment*, edited by Stanislava Kuzmová and Andrea-Bianka
Znorovszky. Trivent Medieval Series. Budapest: Trivent, 2020.

———. *Mary and Early Christian Women: Hidden Leadership*. Cham,
Switzerland: Palgrave Macmillan, 2019.

Kazhdan, Alexander P., ed. *Oxford Dictionary of Byzantium*. Vols. 1, 3.
Oxford: Oxford University Press, 1991.

Kazhdan, Alexander P., and Ann Wharton Epstein. *Change in Byzantine Culture in the Eleventh and Twelfth Centuries*. Berkeley:
University of California Press, 1985.

Kazhdan, Alexander P., and Giles Constable. *People and Power in Byzantium*. Washington, DC: Dumbarton Oaks, 1982.

Kearns, Cleo McNelly. *The Virgin Mary, Monotheism, and Sacrifice.* Cambridge: Cambridge University Press, 2008.

Keating, Thomas. *Foundations for Centering Prayer and the Christian Contemplative Life.* New York: Continuum, 2006.

Kelly, Amy. *Eleanor of Aquitaine and the Four Kings.* Cambridge, MA: Harvard University Press, 1950.

Kelly, Timothy, and Joseph Kelly. "Our Lady of Perpetual Help, Gender Roles, and the Decline of Devotional Catholicism." *Journal of Social History* 32, no. 1 (Autumn 1998).

Keuls, Eva C. *The Reign of the Phallus: Sexual Politics in Ancient Athens.* Berkeley: University of California Press, 1993.

Kinnamos, John. *Deeds of John and Manuel Comnenus.* Translated by Charles Brand. New York: Columbia University Press, 1976.

Kolovou, Loulia. *Anna Komnene and the Alexiad: The Byzantine Princess and the First Crusade.* Philadelphia: Pen & Sword History, 2020.

Komnene, Anna. *The Alexiad.* Translated by Elizabeth A. S. Dawes. Independently published, 2021.

Konstantinidi, Chara. "Byzantine Painting in the Church of the Panagia tou Arakos." In *The Church of Panagia tou Arakos*, edited by Athanasios Papageorghiou, Charalambos Bakirtzis, and Christodoulos Hadjichristodoulou. Nicosia: Leventis Foundation and Bank of Cyprus Cultural Foundation, 2018.

Kurke, Leslie. "Inventing the *Hetaira*: Sex, Politics, and Discursive Conflict in Archaic Greece." *Classical Antiquity* 16, no. 1 (April 1997).

Kurtén, Björn. *How to Deep-Freeze a Mammoth.* New York: Columbia University Press, 1986.

Ladner, Gerhard. "Origin and Significance of the Byzantine Iconoclastic Controversy." *Medieval Studies* 2 (1940).

Lafontaine-Dosogne, Jacqueline. *Iconographie de l'enfance de la Vierge.* Vol. 2. Brussels: Académie Royale, 1964.

Larchet, Jean-Claude. *Therapy of Spiritual Illnesses: An Introduction to the Ascetic Tradition of the Orthodox Church.* Vol. 1. Montreal: Alexander, 2012.

Laurentin, René. *Maria, ecclesia, sacerdotium: Essai sur le développement d'une idée religieuse.* Paris: Nouvelles Éditions Latines, 1952.

———. *Marie, l'eglise et le sacerdoce: Etude théologique.* Paris: Nouvelles Éditions Latines, 1953.

Lazaridou, Anastasia. *Transition to Christianity: Art of Late Antiquity, 3rd–7th Century AD*. New York: Alexander S. Onassis Public Benefit Foundation, 2011.

Lee, Courtney Hall. *The Black Madonna*. Eugene, OR: Wipf & Stock, 2017.

Leithart, Peter. *Defending Constantine*. Downers Grove, IL: IVP Academic, 2010.

Leskov, N. S. "Zapechatlennyi Angel." In *Sobranie sochinerii*, vol. 5, edited by L. Anninskii. Moscow: Ekran, 1993.

Levering, Matthew. *Predestination: Biblical and Theological Paths*. Oxford: Oxford University Press, 2011.

Lewis, C. S. "Priestesses in the Church?" In *God in the Dock*. Grand Rapids, MI: Eerdmans, 1970.

Lidov, Alexei. "The Aerial Icon of Heavens: Kaavod-Doxa-Slava Bozhia and the Luminous Clouds in the Domes of Byzantine Churches." In *Air and Heavens in the Hierotopy and Iconography of the Christian World*. Moscow: Russian Academy of Arts, 2019.

———. "Les motifs liturgiques dans le programme iconographiques d'Axtala." *Zograf* 20 (1989).

———. "The Priesthood of the Virgin Mary as an Image-Paradigm of Christian Culture." *IKON* 10 (2017).

Limberis, Vasiliki. *Divine Heiress: The Virgin Mary and the Creation of Christian Constantinople*. London: Routledge, 1994.

Lossky, Vladimir. *The Mystical Theology of the Eastern Church*. Crestwood, NY: St. Vladimir's Seminary Press, 2002.

Louth, Andrew. "The Place of *Theosis* in Orthodox Theology." In *Partakers of the Divine Nature: The History and Development of Deification in the Christian Tradition*, edited by Michael J. Christensen and Jeffery A. Wittung. Madison, NJ: Fairleigh Dickinson University Press, 2007.

Lukes, Steven. *Power*. Oxford: Blackwell, 1986.

Macy, Gary. *The Hidden History of Women's Ordination: Female Clergy in the Medieval West*. New York: Oxford University Press, 2008.

Madden, Thomas F. *The New Concise History of the Crusades*. Updated ed. Lanham, MD: Rowman & Littlefield, 2005.

Mafi, Nick. "Santiago Calatrava Explains the Transformation of Lower Manhattan 20 Years after 9/11." *Architectural Digest*, September 9, 2021. https://www.architecturaldigest.com/story/santiago-calatrava-explains-transformation-lower-manhattan-20-years-after-911.

Magdalino, Paul. *The Empire of Manuel I Komnenos: 1143–1180.* Cambridge: Cambridge University Press, 2002.

Magoulias, H. J. *O City of Byzantium: Annals of Niketas Choniates.* Detroit: Wayne State University Press, 1984.

Maguire, Eunice Dauterman, and Henry Maguire. *Other Icons: Art and Power in Byzantine Secular Culture.* Princeton, NJ: Princeton University Press, 2007.

Maguire, Henry. "Abaton and Oikonomia: St. Neophytos and the Iconograpny of the Presentation of the Virgin." In *Medieval Cyprus: Studies in Art, Architecture, and History in Memory of Doula Mouriki,* edited by Nancy Patterson Ševčenko and Christopher Moss. Princeton, NJ: Princeton University Press, 1999.

———. *Art and Eloquence in Byzantium.* Princeton, NJ: Princeton University Press, 1081.

———. "The Heavenly Court." In *Byzantine Court Culture 829–1204,* edited by Henry Maguire. Washington, DC: Dumbarton Oaks, 1997.

———. "The Iconography of Symeon with the Christ Child in Byzantine Art." *Dumbarton Oaks Papers* 34/35 (1980/1981).

Maltezou, Chryssa. "The History of Crete during the Fifteenth Century on the Basis of Archival Documents." In *The Hand of Angelos: An Icon Painter in Venetian Crete,* edited by Maria Vassilaki. Aldershot, UK: Ashgate, 2010.

Mango, Cyril A., ed. *The Art of the Byzantine Empire 312–1453: Sources and Documents.* Toronto: University of Toronto Press, 1985.

Mango, Cyril, and Ernest J. W. Hawkins. "The Hermitage of St. Neophytos and Its Wall Paintings." *Dumbarton Oaks Papers* 20 (1966).

Mango, Cyril, Michael Vickers, and E. D. Francis. "The Palace of Lausus at Constantinople and Its Collection of Ancient Statues." *Journal of the History of Collections* 4, no. 1 (1992).

Marković, Miodrag. "Michael's and Eutychios's Artistic Work: Present Knowledge, Dubious Issues and Direction of Future Research." *Zbornik Narodnog Muzeja* 17, no. 2 (2004).

Marshall, Bruce. "The Absolute and the Trinity." *Pro Ecclesia* 23, no. 2 (May 2014).

Martin, Michael, ed. *The Heavenly Country.* Kettering, OH: Angelico, 2016.

———. *The Submerged Reality: Sophiology and the Turn to a Poetic Metaphysics*. Kettering, OH: Angelico, 2015.

Maximus the Confessor. *The Life of the Virgin*. Translated by Stephen Shoemaker. New Haven, CT: Yale University Press, 2012.

———. *On the Cosmic Mystery of Jesus Christ: Selected Writings from Maximus the Confessor*. Translated by Paul M. Blowers and Robert Louis Wilken. Crestwood, NY: St. Vladimir's Seminary Press, 2003.

Mays, James L., ed. *Harper's Bible Commentary*. San Francisco: Harper & Row, 1988.

McAfee, Brooke. "Our Lady of Perpetual Hops Opens in New Albany." *News and Tribune*, October 26, 2019. https://www .newsandtribune.com/news/our-lady-of-perpetual-hops-opens-in -new-albany/article_52f480f8-f77a-11e9-8119-631f41f9b362 .html.

McBrien, Richard P., ed. *The Catholic Encyclopedia*. San Francisco: Harper-Collins, 1995.

McCall, Thomas H. *Forsaken: The Trinity and the Cross, and Why It Matters*. Downers Grove, IL: IVP Academic, 2012.

McClure, Laura K. *Women in Classical Antiquity: From Birth to Death*. Hoboken, NJ: Wiley-Blackwell, 2020.

McClymond, Michael J. *The Devil's Redemption*. Vol. 2. Grand Rapids, MI: Baker Academic, 2018.

Merton, Thomas. *New Seeds of Contemplation*. New York: New Directions, 2007.

Metropolitan Museum of Art. *The Vatican: Spirit and Art of Christian Rome*. New York: Harry N. Abrams, 1982.

Meyendorff, John. *Christ in Eastern Christian Thought*. Washington, DC: Corpus, 1969.

Milbank, Alison. "Oiling the Wheels of the Heavenly Chariot: Female Priesthood and the Divine Feminine." In *Jesus the Imagination: The Divine Feminine*, vol. 5, edited by Michael Martin. New York: Angelico, 2021.

Milliner, Matthew J. *The Everlasting People, G. K. Chesterton and the First Nations*. Downers Grove, IL: InterVarsity, 2021.

———. "Man or Metaphor? Manuel Panselinos and the Protaton Frescoes." In *Approaches to Byzantine Architecture and Its Decoration: Studies in Honor of Slobodan Ćurčić*, edited by Mark J. Johnson, Robert Ousterhout, and Amy Papalexandrou. Burlington, VT: Ashgate, 2011.

———. "Visual Cherubikon: Mary as Priest at Lagoudera in Cyprus." In *Mary, the Apostles, and the Last Judgment*, edited by Stanislava Kuzmová and Andrea-Bianka Znorovszky. *Trivent Medieval Series*. Budapest: Trivent, 2020.

———. "Visual Ecumenism: The Coy Communion of Art." In *Come, Let Us Eat Together: The Sacraments and Christian Unity*. Downers Grove, IL: IVP Academic, 2018.

Mondzain, Marie José. *Image, Icon, Economy: The Byzantine Origins of the Contemporary Imaginary*. Translated by R. Franses. Stanford, CA: Stanford University Press, 2005.

Muller, Richard. *Dictionary of Latin and Greek Theological Terms Drawn Principally from Protestant Scholastic Theology*. Grand Rapids, MI: Baker, 1985.

Nasr, Rafca Youssef. "Priestly Ornaments and the Priesthood of the Mother of God." *Chronos* 40 (2019).

Nasrallah, Laura Salah. *Christian Responses to Roman Art & Architecture*. Cambridge: Cambridge University Press, 2010.

Nassif, Bradley. "Concerning Those Who Imagine That They Are Justified by Works: The Gospel According to St. Mark—the Monk." In *The Philokalia: A Classic Text of Orthodox Spirituality*, edited by Brock Bingaman and Bradley Nassif. Oxford: Oxford University Press, 2012.

Nazianzen, Gregory. *Faith Gives Fullness to Reasoning: The Five Theological Orations of Gregory Nazianzen*. Leiden: Brill, 1991.

———. *Nicene and Post-Nicene Fathers: Second Series*. Vol. 7. Edited by Philip Schaff and Rev. Henry Wallace. 1893. Reprint, New York: Cosimo Classics, 2007.

Neder, Adam. *Participation in Christ: An Entry into Karl Barth's Church Dogmatics*. Louisville, KY: Westminster John Knox, 2009.

Needleman, Jacob. *Lost Christianity*. New York: Jeremy P. Tarcher, 1980.

———. "The Used Religions." In *Sacred Tradition & Present Need*, edited by Jacob Needleman and Dennis Lewis. New York: Viking, 1975.

Nelson, Robert. "Image and Inscription: Pleas for Salvation in Spaces of Devotion." In *Art and Text in Byzantine Culture*, edited by Liz James. New York: Cambridge University Press, 2007.

Neubert, Fr. S. M. Emile. *Mary and the Priestly Ministry*. New Bedford, MA: Academy of the Immaculate, 2009.

Neville, Leonora. *Anna Komnene: The Life and Work of a Medieval Historian*. Oxford: Oxford University Press, 2016.

Newall, Diana. "Candia and Post-Byzantine Icons in Late Fifteenth-Century Europe." In *Byzantine Art and Renaissance Europe*, edited by Angeliki Lymberopoulou and Rembrandt Duits. London: Routledge, 2013.

Newman, Barbara. *God and the Goddesses: Vision, Poetry and Belief in the Middle Ages*. Philadelphia: University of Pennsylvania Press, 2005.

Nicolaïdès, Andréas. "L'église de la Panagia Arakiotissa à Lagoudéra, Chypre: Etude iconographique des fresques de 1192." *Dumbarton Oaks Papers* 50 (1996).

Nietzsche, Friedrich. *Twilight of the Idols*. Translated by Richard Polt. Indianapolis: Hackett, 1997.

"Novena to Our Lady of Perpetual Help." Our Lady of Perpetual Help Retreat and Spirituality Center. Accessed March 14, 2022. https://olph-retreat.org/novenatoolph.

O'Carroll, Michael. *Theotokos: A Theological Encyclopedia of the Blessed Virgin Mary*. Wilmington: Michael Glazier, 1983.

Oakes, Edward T. *A Theology of Grace in Six Controversies*. Grand Rapids, MI: Eerdmans, 2016.

Oden, Thomas C., and Gerald Bray, eds. *Ancient Christian Commentary on Scripture*. Vol. 6. Downers Grove, IL: InterVarsity, 2005.

"Our Parish History." Basilica of Our Lady of Perpetual Help. Accessed August 9, 2021. https://olphbkny.org/parish-history.

"Our Patrons." SSPX Retreats. Accessed August 9, 2021. https://sarh.ca.sspx.org/en/our-patrons.

Ouspensky, Leonid. *Theology of the Icon*. Vol. 2. Crestwood, NY: St. Vladimir's Seminary Press, 1992.

Ouspensky, Leonid, and Vladimir Lossky. *The Meaning of Icons*. Crestwood, NY: St. Vladimir's Seminary Press, 1983.

Palamas, Gregory. *Mary the Mother of God: Sermons*. Edited by Christopher Veniamin. Dalton, PA: Mount Thabor, 2013.

———. *The Triads*. Mahwah, NJ: Paulist, 1983.

Pallas, Methodius D. I. *Die Passion und Bestattung Christi in Byzanz: Der Ritus—das Bild*. Munich: W. & I. M. Salzer, 1965.

Palmer, Matushka Constantina. "Axion Esti Icon Arrives in Thessaloniki from Mount Athos." YouTube video. Accessed November 17, 2021. https://www.youtube.com/watch?v=OInVuA3pBXY&t=216s.

Panayotidi, Maria. "The Question of the Role of the Donor and of the Painter: A Rudimentary Approach." *Deltion* 17 (1994).

Papadakis, Aristeides, with John Meyendorff. *The Christian East and the Rise of the Papacy: The Church 1071–1453 A.D.* Crestwood, NY: St. Vladimir's Seminary Press, 1994.

Papageorghiou, Athanasios. "The Monastery of the Panagia tou Arakos." In *The Church of Panagia tou Arakos.* Edited by Athanasios Papageorghiou, Charalambos Bakirtzis, and Christodoulos Hadjichristodoulou. Nicosia: Leventis Foundation and Bank of Cyprus Cultural Foundation, 2018.

Papanikola-Bakirtzis, Demetra, and Maria Iacovou, eds. *Byzantine Medieval Cyprus.* Nicosia: Bank of Cyprus, 1998.

Parpulov, Georgi R. "Psalters and Personal Piety in Byzantium." In *The Old Testament in Byzantium*, edited by Paul Magdalino and Robert Nelson. Washington, DC: Dumbarton Oaks Research Library and Collection, 2010.

Pasay. "Our Lady of Perpetual Help Tattoo." YouTube video. November 23, 2020. 1:48. https://www.youtube.com/watch?v=qS4uodhCJaA.

Pelikan, Jaroslav. *Credo: Historical and Theological Guide to Creeds and Confessions of Faith in the Christian Tradition.* New Haven, CT: Yale University Press, 2003.

———. *The Christian Tradition: A History of the Development of Doctrine.* Vol. 1, *The Emergence of the Catholic Tradition (100–600).* Chicago: University of Chicago Press, 1971.

———. *Imago Dei: The Byzantine Apologia for Icons.* Princeton, NJ: Princeton University Press, 1990.

———. *The Spirit of Eastern Christendom (600–1700).* Chicago: University of Chicago Press, 1977.

Pelikan, Jaroslav, and Valerie Hotchkiss. *Creeds and Confessions of Faith in the Christian Tradition: Early, Eastern and Medieval.* Vol. 1. New Haven, CT: Yale University Press, 2003.

Peltomaa, Leena Mari. *The Image of the Virgin Mary in the Akathistos Hymn.* Leiden: Brill, 2004.

———. "Role of the Virign Mary at the Siege of Constantinople in 626." *Scrinium* 5, no. 1 (2009).

Pentcheva, Bissera. *Hagia Sophia: Sound, Space and Spirit in Byzantium.* University Park: Penn State University Press, 2017.

———. *Icons and Power.* University Park: Penn State University Press, 2005.

———. *The Sensual Icon: Space, Ritual and the Senses in Byzantium.* University Park: Penn State University Press, 2013.

Perry, David. *Sacred Plunder: Venice and the Aftermath of the Fourth Crusade.* University Park: Penn State University Press, 2016.

Peterson, Jeanette Favrot. *Visualizing Guadalupe: From Black Madonna to Queen of the Americas.* Austin: University of Texas Press, 2014.

Phillips, Jonathan. *The Fourth Crusade and the Sack of Constantinople.* New York: Penguin, 2004.

Pierre Le Gentil. "The Work of Robert de Boron and the *Didot Perceval.*" In *Arthurian Literature in the Middle Ages: A Collaborative History*, edited by R. S. Loomis. Oxford: Clarendon, 1959.

Pius IX. Preface to *Marie et le Sacerdoce.* 2nd ed. By Mgr. Van den Berghe. Paris: Louis Vivès, 1875.

Pool, Christopher. *Olmec Archaeology and Early Mesoamerica.* Cambridge: Cambridge University Press, 2007.

Pope Innocent II. "Omne Datum Optimum (March 29, 1139)." In *The Templars: Selected Sources*, edited by Malcolm Barber and Keith Bate. Manchester: Manchester University Press, 2002.

Preston, James J. "Conclusion: New Perspectives on Mother Worship." In *Mother Worship: Themes and Variations*, edited by James J. Preston. Chapel Hill: University of North Carolina Press, 1982.

Radner, Ephraim. *A Brutal Unity: The Spiritual Politics of the Christian Church.* Waco, TX: Baylor University Press, 2012.

———. *Spirit and Nature: The Saint Médard Miracles in 18th-Century Jansenism.* New York: Crossroad, 2002.

Rafter, Kevin. "Priests and Peace: The Role of the Redemptorist Order in the Northern Ireland Peace Process." *Etudes Irlandaises* 28, no. 1 (2003).

Redemptorist Missionaries. *Our Lady of Perpetual Help: The Icon, Favors and Shrines.* Rome: Redemptorist Missionaries, 1998.

Reilly, Diane J. "Bernard of Clairvaux and Christian Art." In *A Companion to Bernard Clairvaux*, edited by Brian Patrick McGuire. Danvers, MA: Brill, 2011.

Remensnyder, Amy G. *La Conquistadora: The Virgin Mary at War and Peace in the Old and New Worlds.* Oxford: Oxford University Press, 2014.

Reno, R. R. "The Debilitation of the Churches." In *The Ecumenical Future*, edited by Carl E. Braaten and Robert W. Jenson. Grand Rapids, MI: Eerdmans, 2004.

Rey, Terry, and Alex Stepick. *Crossing the Water and Keeping the Faith: Haitian Religion in Miami*. New York: New York University Press, 2013.

Rhodes, Constantina. *Invoking Lakshmi: The Goddess of Wealth in Song and Ceremony*. Albany: State University of New York Press, 2010.

Ricoeur, Paul. "Fatherhood: From Phantasm to Symbol." In *The Conflict of Interpretations*, translated by Robert Sweeney. Evanston, IL: Northwestern University Press, 1974.

———. *The Symbolism of Evil*. Translated by Emerson Buchanan. Boston: Beacon, 1967.

Riley-Smith, Jonathan. *The Oxford Illustrated History of the Crusades*. Oxford: Oxford University Press, 2001.

Rilke, Rainer Maria. *Selected Poems of Rainer Maria Rilke*. Translated by Robert Bly. New York: Harper & Row, 1981.

Rittgers, Ronald. Epilogue to *Protestantism after 500 Years*, edited by Mark Noll and Thomas Albert Howard. Oxford: Oxford University Press, 2016.

Roberts, Robert C. *Spiritual Emotions: A Psychology of Christian Virtues*. Grand Rapids, MI: Eerdmans, 2007.

Rogers, Guy Maclean. *The Mysteries of Artemis of Ephesos: Cult, Polis, and Change in the Graeco-Roman World*. New Haven, CT: Yale University Press, 2012.

Ruether, Rosemary Radford. *Goddesses and the Divine Feminine: A Western Religious History*. Berkeley: University of California Press, 2005.

Rumore, Kori, and Laura Rodríguez Presa. "Why 200,000 People Travel Each December on Foot, by Horse, and Even Semitruck to Visit the Shrine of Our Lady of Guadalupe in Des Plains." *Chicago Tribune*, December 11, 2019.

Russell, Norman. *Fellow Workers with God: Orthodox Thinking on Theosis*. Crestwood, NY: St. Vladimir's Seminary Press, 2009.

Rutledge, Fleming. *The Crucifixion: Understanding the Death of Jesus Christ*. Grand Rapids, MI: Eerdmans, 2015.

Rychkova, Nadezda. "Constructing a Religioscape: The Case of Pushkinskaya Square in Moscow." In *Urban Religious Events: Public Spirituality in Contested Spaces*, edited by Paul Bramadat, Mar Griera, Marian Burchardt, and Julia Martinez-Ariño. London: Bloomsbury Academic, 2021.

Şahin, Kaya. "Constantinople and the End Time: The Ottoman Conquest as a Portent of the Last Hour." *Journal of Early Modern History* 14 (2010).

Schaff, Philip, and Henry Wallace, eds. *Nicene and Post-Nicene Fathers: Second Series.* Vol. 8, *Basil: Letters and Select Works.* New York: Cosimo, 2007.

Schearing, Linda S. "Double Time . . . Double Trouble? Gender, Sin, and Leviticus 12." In *Leviticus: Composition and Reception*, edited by Rolf Rendtorff, Robert A. Kugler, and Sarah Smith Bartel. Leiden: Brill, 2003.

Schibille, Nadine. *Hagia Sophia and the Byzantine Aesthetic Experience.* Farnham, UK: Ashgate, 2014.

Schipflinger, Thomas. *Sophia-Maria: A Holistic Vision of Creation.* Translated by James Morgante. Yorke Beach, ME: Samuel Weiser, 1998.

Schmemann, Alexander, ed. *Ultimate Questions: An Anthology of Modern Russian Thought.* Chicago: Holt, Rinehart, Winston, 1965.

Schorr, Dorothy C. "The Iconographic Development of the Presentation in the Temple." *Art Bulletin* 28, no. 1 (March 1946).

Scully, Vincent. *The Earth, the Temple and the Gods.* Rev. ed. New Haven, CT: Yale University Press, 1979.

Sewter, E. R. A., trans. *The Alexiad of Anna Comnena.* Harmondsworth, UK: Penguin, 1969.

Shichtman, Martin B. "Politicizing the Ineffable: The *Queste del Saint Graal* and Malory's 'Tale of the Sankgreal.'" *Culture and the King: The Social Implications of the Arthurian Legend,* edited by Martin B. Shichtman and James P. Carley. Albany: State University of New York Press, 1994.

Shoemaker, Stephen J. *Ancient Traditions of the Virgin Mary's Dormition and Assumption.* Oxford: Oxford University Press, 2002.

———. *Mary in Early Christian Faith and Devotion.* New Haven, CT: Yale University Press, 2016.

———. "The (Pseudo?-)Maximus *Life of the Virgin.*" *Journal of Theological Studies* 67, no. 1 (April 2016).

"A Shrine Dedicated to Our Lady of Perpetual Succour in the Westminster Cathedral." *Scala News,* July 8, 2014. https://www.cssr .news/oldnews-en/?p=1875.

Silverman, Raymond A. "Ethiopian Orthodox Visual Culture in the Age of Mechanical Reproduction: A Research Note." *Material Religion* 5, no. 1 (May 2015).

Simelidis, Christos. "Two Lives of the Virgin: John Geometres, Euthymios the Athonite, and Maximos the Confessor." *Dumbarton Oaks Papers* 74 (2020).

Simms, Ronda R. "Mourning and Community at the Athenian Adonia." *Classical Journal* 93, no. 2 (December 1997–January 1998).

Sinkević, Ida. *The Church of Saint Panteleimon at Nerezi: Architecture, Programme, Patronage.* Wiesbaden: Reichert Verlag, 2000.

Sisto, Walter Nunzio. *The Mother of God in the Theology of Sergius Bulgakov: The Soul of the World.* Oxfordshire: Routledge, 2018.

Skinner, T. L. *The Redemptorists in the West.* St. Louis, MO: Redemptorists Fathers, 1933.

Solmsen, Friedrich. *Isis among the Greeks and Romans.* Cambridge, MA: Harvard University Press, 1979.

Solomon, Nanette. "Making a World of Difference: Gender, Asymmetry, and the Greek Nude." In *Naked Truths: Women, Sexuality, and Gender in Classical Art and Archaeology,* edited by Ann Olga Koloski-Ostrow and Claire L. Lyons. New York: Routledge, 1997.

Soskice, Janet Martin. *The Kindness of God: Metaphor, Gender, and Religious Language.* Oxford: Oxford University Press, 2008.

Spretnak, Charlene. *Missing Mary: The Queen of Heaven and Her Re-emergence in the Modern Church.* New York: Palgrave Macmillan, 2004.

St. Alphonsus Ligouri "Rock" Catholic Church. "First Sunday of Lent, 2022." YouTube video. Accessed March 14, 2022. https://www.youtube.com/watch?v=wni1BwxtL_8.

St. John of the Cross. *The Poems of St. John of the Cross.* Translated by Willis Barnstone. New York: New Directions, 1972.

Stark, Rodney. *God's Batallions: The Case for the Crusades.* New York: HarperOne, 2010.

———. *The Rise of Christianity,* San Francisco: HarperCollins, 1997.

Stewart, Andrew. "The Nike of Samothrace: Another View." *American Journal of Archaeology* 120, no. 3 (July 2016).

Strickland, Debra Higgs. "Monstrosity and Race in the Late Middle Ages." In *The Ashgate Research Companion to Monsters and the Monstrous,* edited by Asa Simon Mittman and Peter Dendle. Burlington, VT: Ashgate, 2012.

Symeon the New Theologian. *Divine Eros: Hymns of Saint Symeon the New Theologian.* Translated by Daniel K. Griggs. Crestwood, NY: St. Vladimir's Seminary Press, 2010.

———. "The Three Methods of Prayer." In *The Philokalia: The Complete Text*, vol. 4, edited and translated by G. E. H. Palmer, Philip Sherrard, and Kallistos Ware. London: Faber & Faber, 1995.

Taft, Robert F. *The Byzantine Rite: A Short History*. Collegeville, MN: Liturgical, 1992.

———. *The Great Entrance: A History of the Transfer of the Gifts and Other Pre-anaphoral Rites of the Liturgy of St. John Chrysostom.* Rome: Pont. Institutum Studiorum Orientalium, 1975.

Tatian. "Address of Tatian to the Greeks." In *Ante-Nicene Fathers*, vol. 2, translated by J. E. Ryland, edited by A. Cleveland Coxe. Peabody, MA: Hendrickson, 2004.

Tatić-Djurić, Mirjana. "Iconographie de la Vierge de Passion: Genese du Dogme et des Symboles." In *De Culto Mariano: Saeculis XII–XV, Acta Congressus Mariologici Mariani Internationalis Romae Anno 1975 Celebrati*, vol. 6. Rome: Pontificia Academia Mariana Internationalis, 1981.

Taylor, Michael D. "The Pentecost at Vézelay." *Gesta* 19, no. 1 (1980).

Theodore the Studite. *Writings on Iconoclasm*. Translated by Thomas Cattoi. Mahwah, NJ: Paulist, 2015.

Thuesen, Peter J. *Predestination: The American Career of a Contentious Doctrine*. Oxford: Oxford University Press, 2009.

Thunø, Erik. "The Miraculous Image and the Centralized Church Santa Maria Della Consalozione in Todi." In *The Miraculous Image in the Late Middle Ages and Renaissance*, edited by Erik Thunø and Gerhard Wolf. Rome: L'Erma di Bretschneider, 2003.

Thykoottam, Samuel. *The Mother of God in the Syriac Tradition*. Kerala, India: St. Ephrem Ecumenical Research Institute, 1989.

Tomberg, Valentin [published anonymously]. *Meditations on the Tarot*. New York: Penguin, 1985.

Torrance, Thomas F. *Incarnation: The Person and Life of Christ*. Edited by Robert T. Walker. Downers Grove, IL: IVP Academic, 2008.

Tsakiridou, C. A. *Icons in Time, Persons in Eternity: Orthodox Theology and the Aesthetics of the Christian Image*. Farnham, UK: Ashgate, 2013.

Tsigaridas, Efthymios. *Latomou Monastery (the Church of Hosios David)*. Munich: Wilhelm Fink Verlag, 2002.

Tyerman, Christopher. *God's War: A New History of the Crusades*. Cambridge, MA: Belknap of Harvard University Press, 2006.

Tympas, G. C. Carl. *Jung and Maximus the Confessor on Psychic Development: The Dynamics between the "Psychological" and the "Spiritual."* London: Routledge, 2014.

Vapheiades, Konstantinos M. "The Wall-Paintings of the Protaton Church Revisited." *Zograf* 43 (2019).

Vassilaki, Maria, ed. *Mother of God: Representations of the Virgin in Byzantine Art.* Milan: Skira, 2000.

Versluis, Arthur, ed. *Wisdom's Book: The Sophia Anthology.* St. Paul, MN: Paragon, 2000.

———. *Wisdom's Children: A Christian Esoteric Tradition.* Albany: State University of New York Press, 1999.

"Virgin Hodegetria." Sinai Icon Collection. Accessed April 12, 2022. https://www.sinaiarchive.org.

Vogel, Carol. "The Met Makes Its Biggest Purchase Ever." *New York Times,* November 10, 2004. https://www.nytimes.com/2004/11/10/arts/design/the-met-makes-its-biggest-purchase-ever.html.

Vojvodić, Dragan. *Mediaeval Wallpaintings of Žiča.* Belgrade, Serbia: University of Belgrade, 2016.

Walberg, Deborah. "The Cult of the Nicopeia in Seventeenth-Century Venice." In *Reflections on Renaissance Venice: A Celebration of Patricia Fortini Brown,* edited by Mary E. Frank and Blake de Maria. New York: Henry N. Abrams, 2013.

Walsh, M. J. K., N. Coureas, and Peter W. Edbury. *Medieval and Renaissance Famagusta: Studies in Architecture, Art and History.* Burlington, VT: Ashgate, 2012.

Walter, Christopher. *Art and Ritual of the Byzantine Church.* London: Variorum, 1982.

Warner, Marina. *Alone of All Her Sex: The Myth and the Cult of the Virgin Mary.* New York: Knopf, 1976.

Weil, Simone. *Simone Weil Reader.* Edited by George A. Panichas. New York: David McKay, 1977.

West, Rebecca. *Black Lamb and Grey Falcon: A Journey through Yugoslavia.* New York: Penguin, 1940.

Wilken, Robert Louis. *The First Thousand Years.* New Haven, CT: Yale University Press, 2013.

Williams, Rowan. *Arius: Heresy & Tradition.* Rev. ed. Grand Rapids, MI: Eerdmans, 2001.

Wilson, Sarah Hinlicky. *Woman, Women and the Priesthood in the Trinitarian Theology of Elisabeth Behr-Sigel.* London: T&T Clark, 2015.

Winfield, David, and June Winfield. *The Church of the Panaghia tou Arakhos at Lagoudera, Cyprus: The Paintings and Their Painterly Significance*. Washington, DC: Dumbarton Oaks, 2003.

Witt, William. *Icons of Christ: A Biblical and Systematic Theology for Women's Ordination*. Waco, TX: Baylor University Press, 2020.

Wolf, Gerhard. *Salus Populi Romani: Die Geschichte römischer Kultbilder im Mittelalter*. Weinheim, Germany: VCH Acta Humaniora, 1990.

Woodfin, Warren T. *The Embodied Icon: Liturgical Vestments and Sacramental Power in Byzantium*. Oxford: Oxford University Press, 2012.

INDEX

Page numbers followed by *n* refer to notes.

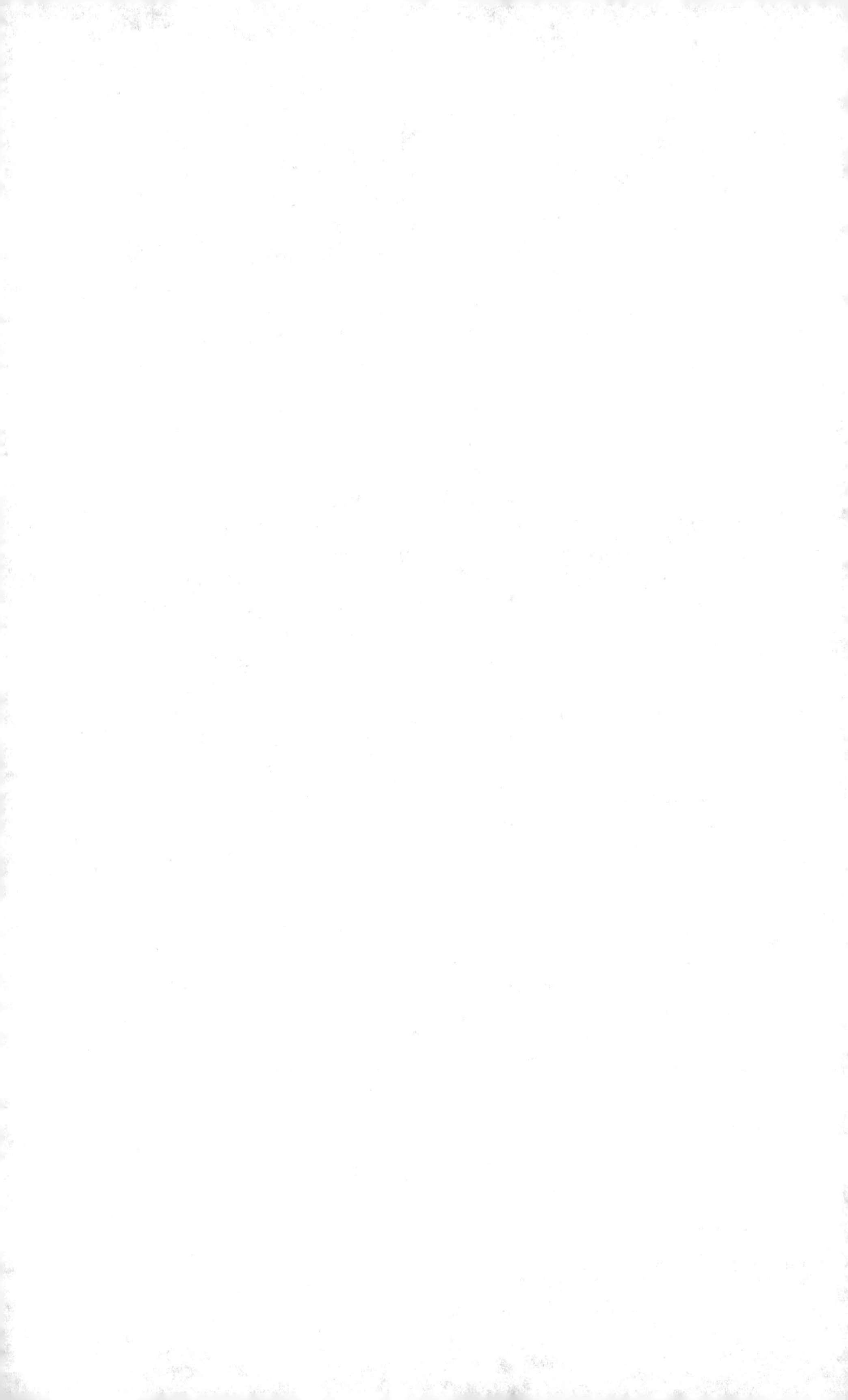

IMAGE PERMISSIONS

Fieldwork Archives, Dumbarton Oaks, Trustees for Harvard University, Washington, DC

Fig. 4.1. Sharon Dunbar

Fig. 4.2. Slobodan Ćurčić

Fig. 4.3. The Byzantine Institute and Dumbarton Oaks Fieldwork Records and Papers, ca. late 1920s–2000s, MS.BZ.004, Image Collections and Fieldwork Archives, Dumbarton Oaks, Trustees for Harvard University, Washington, DC

Fig. 4.4. Kritzolina, CC BY-SA 3.0

Fig. 4.5. The Byzantine Institute and Dumbarton Oaks Fieldwork Records and Papers, ca. late 1920s–2000s, MS.BZ.004, Image Collections and Fieldwork Archives, Dumbarton Oaks, Trustees for Harvard University, Washington, DC

Fig. 4.6. Rabe! CC BY-SA 3.0

Fig. 4.7. Author

Fig. 5.1. Sharon Dunbar (after Richard Anderson)

Fig. 5.2. The Byzantine Institute and Dumbarton Oaks Fieldwork Records and Papers, ca. late 1920s–2000s, MS.BZ.004, Image Collections and Fieldwork Archives, Dumbarton Oaks, Trustees for Harvard University, Washington, DC

Fig. 5.3.1 Svetlana Tomeković

Fig. 5.3.2. Shakko, Pubic Domain

Fig. 5.4.1. The Byzantine Institute and Dumbarton Oaks Fieldwork Records and Papers, ca. late 1920s–2000s, MS.BZ.004, Image Collections and Fieldwork Archives, Dumbarton Oaks, Trustees for Harvard University, Washington, DC

Fig. 5.4.2. The Byzantine Institute and Dumbarton Oaks Fieldwork Records and Papers, ca. late 1920s–2000s, MS.BZ.004, Image Collections and Fieldwork Archives, Dumbarton Oaks, Trustees for Harvard University, Washington, DC

Fig. 6.1. Slobodan Ćurčić

Fig. 6.2.1. James Kokkinobaphos, Homilies (Vat.gr. 1162, 130v). Vatican Apostolic Library, used with permission

Fig. 6.2.2. The Byzantine Institute and Dumbarton Oaks Fieldwork Records and Papers, ca. late 1920s–2000s, MS.BZ.004, Image Collections and Fieldwork Archives, Dumbarton Oaks, Trustees for Harvard University, Washington, DC

Fig. 6.2.3. The Byzantine Institute and Dumbarton Oaks Fieldwork Records and Papers, ca. late 1920s–2000s, MS.BZ.004, Image Collections and Fieldwork Archives, Dumbarton Oaks, Trustees for Harvard University, Washington, DC

Fig. 7. 1. The Byzantine Institute and Dumbarton Oaks Fieldwork Records and Papers, ca. late 1920s–2000s, MS.BZ.004, Image Collections and Fieldwork Archives, Dumbarton Oaks, Trustees for Harvard University, Washington, DC

Fig. 7.2.1. Slobodan Ćurčić

Fig. 7.2.2. The Metropolitan Museum of Art, Public Domain

Fig. 7.3. Slobodan Ćurčić

Fig. 7.4.1. Slobodan Ćurčić

Fig. 7.4.2. The Byzantine Institute and Dumbarton Oaks Fieldwork Records and Papers, ca. late 1920s–2000s, MS.BZ.004, Image Collections and Fieldwork Archives, Dumbarton Oaks, Trustees for Harvard University, Washington, DC

Fig. 8.1. The Byzantine Institute and Dumbarton Oaks Fieldwork Records and Papers, ca. late 1920s–2000s, MS.BZ.004, Image Collections and Fieldwork Archives, Dumbarton Oaks, Trustees for Harvard University, Washington, DC

Fig. 8.2. The Byzantine Institute and Dumbarton Oaks Fieldwork Records and Papers, ca. late 1920s–2000s, MS.BZ.004, Image Collections and Fieldwork Archives, Dumbarton Oaks, Trustees for Harvard University, Washington, DC

Fig. 8.3. The Byzantine Institute and Dumbarton Oaks Fieldwork Records and Papers, ca. late 1920s–2000s, MS.BZ.004, Image Collections and Fieldwork Archives, Dumbarton Oaks, Trustees for Harvard University, Washington, DC

Fig. 8.4. Svetlana Tomeković

Fig. 8.5.1. Author

Fig. 8.5.2. The Byzantine Institute and Dumbarton Oaks Fieldwork Records and Papers, ca. late 1920s–2000s, MS.BZ.004, Image Collections and Fieldwork Archives, Dumbarton Oaks, Trustees for Harvard University, Washington, DC

Fig. 8.5.3. The Byzantine Institute and Dumbarton Oaks Fieldwork Records and Papers, ca. late 1920s–2000s, MS.BZ.004, Image Collections and Fieldwork Archives, Dumbarton Oaks, Trustees for Harvard University, Washington, DC

Fig. 8.5.4. The Byzantine Institute and Dumbarton Oaks Fieldwork Records and Papers, ca. late 1920s–2000s, MS.BZ.004, Image Collections and Fieldwork Archives, Dumbarton Oaks, Trustees for Harvard University, Washington, DC

Part III. Gallerie degli Uffizi (Inv. no. 3886), used with permission

Fig. 9.1. Dino Stanin via Google Maps

Fig. 9.2.1. Public Domain

Fig. 9.2.2. The icon is under the rights of the Hellenic Institute of Venice
    and it was granted by the Hellenic Institute of Byzantine and Post-
    Byzantine Studies in Venice in the year 2021.
Fig. 9.3. Dragan Vojvodić
Fig. 9.4. Raso, Public Domain
Fig. 9.5.1. Author
Fig. 9.5.2. Author
Fig. 9.6.1. Author
Fig. 9.6.2. Lykokoï, CC BY-SA 4.0
Fig. 9.7.1. Google Earth
Fig. 9.7.2. Author
Fig. 9.7.3. Author
Fig. 9.7.4. Author
Fig. 10.1. Dimitry Ivanov, Public Domain
Fig. 10.2. MapMaster, CC BY-SA 4.0
Fig. 10.3. Gallerie degli Uffizi (Inv. no. 3886), used with permission
Fig. 10.4. LimosaCorel, CC BY-SA 3.0
Fig. 10.5.1. National Shrine of Our Mother of Perpetual Help, Phillippines
Fig. 10.5.2. Marian Library, University of Dayton
Fig. 10.6.1. National Shrine of Our Mother of Perpetual Help, Phillippines
Fig. 10.6.2. Marian Library, University of Dayton
Fig. 10.6.3. Marian Library, University of Dayton
Fig. 10.6.4. Marian Library, University of Dayton
Fig. 10.6.5. Marian Library, University of Dayton
Fig. 10.6.6. Marian Library, University of Dayton
Fig. 10.6.7. Marian Library, University of Dayton
Fig. C.1. Author
Fig. C.2.1. George Kalantzis
Fig. C.2.2. Author
Fig. C.3. Marian Library, University of Dayton
Fig. C.4.1. George Kalantizis
Fig. C.4.2. Author
Fig. C.5. Author, courtesy of Our Lady of Perpetual Help Cathedral, Okla-
    homa City, OK
Fig. C.6.1. Author, courtesy of St. Alphonsus Ligouri "Rock" Catholic
    Church in St. Louis, MO
Fig. C.6.2. Author, courtesy of St. Alphonsus Ligouri "Rock" Catholic
    Church in St. Louis, MO
Fig. C.6.3. Author
Fig. C.7. Daniel Mitsui
Fig. C.8. Reuters/Alamy Stock Photo. Photographer: David Gray,
    August 10, 2012, used with permission